THE HISTORY OF ANTI-SEMITISM

THE HISTORY OF ANTI-SEMITISM
Volume I: From the Time of Christ to the Court Jews
Volume II: From Mohammed to the Marranos
Volume III: From Voltaire to Wagner
Volume IV: Suicidal Europe, 1870–1933

LÉON POLIAKOV

THE HISTORY OF ANTI-SEMITISM

VOLUME TWO
From Mohammed to the Marranos

Translated by Natalie Gerardi

UNIVERSITY OF PENNSYLVANIA PRESS

Philadelphia

10 9 8 7 6 5 4 3 2 1

Published 2003 by
University of Pennsylvania Press
Philadelphia, Pennsylvania 19104-4011

Library of Congress Cataloging-in-Publication Data

Poliakov, Léon, 1910–
    [Histoire d l'antisémitisme. English]
    The history of anti-semitism / Léon Poliakov
        p.   cm.
    Vol. 1 translated by Richard Howard, vol. 2 translated by Natalie Gerardi,
vol. 3 translated by Miriam Kochan, vol. 4 translated by George Klin
    Includes bibliographical references and index
    Contents: v. 1. From the time of Christ to the court Jews—v. 2. From
Mohammed to the Marranos—v. 3. From Voltaire to Wagner—v. 4. Suicidal
Europe, 1870–1933.
    ISBN 0-8122-3766-8 (v. 1: cloth : alk. paper)—ISBN 0-8122-1863-9 (v. 1 :
paper : alk. paper)—ISBN 0-8122-3767-6 (v. 2. : cloth : alk. paper)—ISBN
0-8122-1864-7 (v. 2. : paper : alk. paper)—ISBN 0-8122-3768-4 (v. 3. : cloth :
alk. paper)—0-8122-1865-5 (v. 3. : paper : alk. paper)—ISBN 0-8122-3769-2
(v. 4. : cloth : alk. paper)—ISBN 0-8122-1866-3 (v. 4. : paper : alk. paper)
    1. Antisemitism—History. I. Title
DS 145.P4613   2003
305.892'4'009—dc22   2003057081

"And were it only for the faith I have in God and in the tenets and beliefs of the holy Roman Catholic Church, and besides that I am a mortal enemy of the Jews . . ."

Sancho Panza in Don Quixote

That the hatred of the nations tends to assure the survival of the Jews has moreover been demonstrated by experience. When a king of Spain compelled the Jews either to embrace the State religion or to go into exile, a very large number became Roman Catholics, and as they then shared all the privileges of ethnic Spaniards and were considered eligible for equal honors, they fused so well with the Spaniards that, soon after, nothing remained of them, not even a memory. Those whom the king of Portugal obliged to convert traveled a different road. They continued to lead a separate life because they were excluded from all respected occupations. I also give credit in this matter to the mark of circumcision, which I believe is uniquely capable of guaranteeing the Jewish nation eternal existence. I could believe without qualification, knowing the mutability of human affairs, that if the principles of their religion do not subdue their hearts, the time will come when the Jews will re-establish their kingdom, and that God will choose them once again.

Spinoza, Tractatus Theologico—Politicus,
"OF THE VOCATION OF THE HEBREWS"

Contents

Foreword   ix

BOOK ONE | ISLAM

1   *Before Islam*   3
    Babylonia—North Africa—Spain
2   *The Prophet*   19
3   *The Caliphs*   29
    The Umayyads—The Abbasids and the Caliphate of
    Baghdad
4   *Islam and the Infidels*   46
    The Christians—The Jews

BOOK TWO | SPAIN

Part One: Spain of the Three Religions   87
    5   *Moslem Spain*   87
    6   *La Reconquista*   106
    7   *The Golden Age*   116
        Spain of the Three Religions—The Jewish Nation of Spain
        —The Subreconquista

Part Two: Toward Unity of the Faith   147
    8   *The Decline*   147
        The Mounting Danger—Vox Populi, Vox Dei—The Rout
        of the *Aljamos*
    9   *The Impasse—Marranism*   170

10   *The Inquisition* 183
11   *Spain's Fateful Hour*   204
     The Citadel of Faith—The Cult of Purity of the Blood, or
     Iberian Racism

Part Three: The Marrano Epic   233
     12   *The Marranos of Portugal*   233
     13   *The Marrano Dispersion*   245
          The Duke of Naxos—The Sabbatians—Spinoza

Conclusion   Modern Spain   279
          Limpieza, Anti-Semitism, and the Inquisition

Appendices
     a: *The Jews of the Holy See*   303
     b: *The Moors and Their Expulsion*   328

Notes   358
Index   391

Foreword

The preparation of this volume has required five years of work; to measure up to its subject, fifteen or twenty years would have been needed to make possible a broader study of the diverse cultures involved, their social, religious, and literary lives. The two comparative essays at the end of the book would alone have been worthy of development into independent studies. But five years are time enough to permit a revision of points of view, a maturation of judgment. May the author be permitted to say that since the completion of the previous volume, his views have altered in respect to an essential aspect of his work? He had thought that by yoking himself to the task of writing a detailed history of anti-Semitism, he would make a useful contribution to the struggle against this unhealthy passion. Today he is not so sure. May he in this foreword step out of the role of historian and, taking a philosophical stance in viewing the object of his study, briefly explain why?

To write the history of anti-Semitism is to write the history of a persecution that, in the bosom of Western society, was linked with the highest values of this society, for it was pursued in their name; to put the persecutors in the wrong—repeating the phrase of François Mauriac, "to require an accounting from Christianity"—is to place this society and its values in question. (This placing in question also applies to the persecuted, to the extent that they constitute a part of this society, without being entirely part of it. Such is the marginal situation of the Jews, whence their faculty for seeing things at the same time from the inside and from the outside, with all kinds of resulting consequences. But that is another story.) The Jewish historian thus becomes a denouncer, and neither the precautions he takes in the name of the rules of his art, nor the affection he comes to experience for the subject of his study, nor the justice he forces himself to render to all the protagonists discussed, can make any change in this fundamental posture. This is why an enterprise that often takes on the appearance of a prosecution may not run the risk, while recalling ancient events, of reanimating hidden animosities; whether even the recollection of wrongs done to the Jews may not serve to keep alive a climate in which one day, God forbid, new menaces may arise.

The study of the passionate and dedicated literature of two thousand years on this subject—the stream of ink that preceded or followed the stream of blood—has often led the author to wonder whether the writings and actions in favor of the Jews did not lead in the long run to the same results as the writings that attacked them, as instruments in a vast accord that assured the continuance of anti-Semitism. From this point of view, the effects of the apologias of Judaism often turned out to be in fact the very opposite of their authors' expectations. But to the extent that their pleadings and discourses turned against them, the hatred of the nations thus stimulated became a factor in the preservation of Judaism. This is not the least among the fascinating aspects of the problem.

The author is not a practicing Jew. Today, most of the apologists of Judaism are not; nor is this a recent development, as the history of medieval Spain discloses. But the chapters of this book that deal with the tragedy of the Spanish Jews also describe how the unbelieving fathers helped hasten the catastrophes that drew their sons back to the ancient God of Israel. At times the spiral seems endless; so it was in Biblical times, to judge by the Prophets, and so it is in our day, when the worst eruption of hatred Judaism has ever had to face has contributed to its remarkable resurgence, both within Israel and without.

In the judgment of the rabbis, these dramatically repeated cycles are but the reverse side of election, and the interpretation of Christian theology is not very different. It can be concluded with equal validity that "faith in the divine destiny of the Jews has been an important influence on their truly strange fate," as I wrote in the foreword to the first volume of this history.

Basically it is not important to determine whether the question is one of a superior Will or of the idea men have of this Will; it is enough that from either Divine Will or myth a multiform process has unfolded, involving all levels of religious, cultural, social, and economic life, the description of which is the purpose of the present volume, the one that has preceded it, and the one that will follow. By the power of Jewish faith in the Christian world, prophecies have come to pass, and the Jews have sustained their faith in a role the world has assigned them for two thousand years. Into this complex tissue the present study weaves a special thread, one that originally powerfully commanded the author's attention.

More precisely, the persecutions, which sharpen the Jews' sense of justice, also incite them to dwell upon them, sometimes even to adapt to the role of victim; this adaptation, in fact, has been their role historically. It has served to increase the temptation of the executioners. It manifests itself in various ways and at various levels, with the result that one may speak of a veritable sacrificial-lamb complex on the part of the scapegoats. In the unconscious depths of the soul, adaptation doubtlessly corresponds to a wish to identify with the dominant society, that of the executioner. At the conscious level, the soul may wish to be redeemed by the summary dichotomy: "We are the Just and they are the Unjust." It is of little importance that this is to a large extent true; on the contrary, the more correct the Jew, the more in error he seems in the eyes of the world. Another facet of this pride is extreme humility, which derives from the same source, but which leads to a more open identification with the hangman; the Jew in this case participates in anti-Semitism, bears witness against himself, and annihilates himself in thought—at times, even in action. For more than a century the type of Jew who is ashamed of or conceals his Jewishness has been widely recognized, but it will be seen that in the Spain of the Middle Ages a similar phenomenon was already known.

Let us observe in passing the close psychological relationship between the elitist Jew, for whom status reflects superiority, and the apologetic Jew, who is rebuffed and afflicted by status: both are fascinated by it. But the question of status is of no great importance: in extreme cases it becomes a kind of function, a consequence of the Jews' awesome burden in Western society. In this respect there is no difference between the practicing Jew, faithful to the ancient God of Israel and to the idea of the Chosen People, and the Jew of circumstance, the unbeliever whose ties with Judaism are irrational and sentimental, who is attracted to it only so far as he unconsciously aspires to free himself from it, but whose Jewish sensibilities are no less keen. Both are part of the living body of Judaism, whose ungrateful social role seems to be—in the eyes of the world surrounding it and even in the eyes of the Jews themselves—to symbolize the great ethical values, to personify the forces of moral conflict (the dictates of conscience or Evil incarnate, as the case may be), and, as a scapegoat, to serve as a barometer of the tensions of Christian society.

In the preceding volume the effort was to show—for instance, through the Jews in China and in India, two small historical groups without a history—that this role is played effectively only in the midst of Western culture, and that it is linked to the relationship between Judaism and her daughter religions: anti-Semitism is only the social projection of the particular tension resulting from this relationship. The present volume brings several other elements to the

support of this thesis. We see that the Jews found themselves identified by a special insignia only in those regions of
the globe where their faith in a transcendent Creator was
taken over in one way or another by the peoples in the midst
of whom they dwelt. The sufferings of the Jews, as well as
their survival, must be due in the final analysis to the fact
that Judaism and its message was taken seriously. This
thesis, a "natural" explanation of the history of the Jews
founded upon religious psychology, seems to satisfy the first
requirement of the science of history. It permits one to question all orders of eschatological interpretation, which,
through the ages, seems to demand supernatural explanation. Even if the "natural" explanation does not conform to
the great "socio-economic" interpretative schemes that so
predominate modern historiography; even if, on the contrary, it postulates the inadequacy of these schemes, that is
because of the uniqueness of Jewish history: not only its
point of departure, but its whole "antinatural" unfolding,
seem to be both a crisis of conscience and a choice preceding
and determining a way of life.

Further, one may wonder what will happen in a society
that is de-Christianized, or heading that way; the case of
Jews in Communist countries immediately comes to mind.
In our time, all the efforts of Communism to "solve the
Jewish problem" seem once again to have led to the opposite
result: new tensions, a new coil in the spiral. Particularly in
the Soviet Union, there is a new grip on Jewish conscience in
direct proportion to the ambiguity of the Jew: he is urged to
"assimilate" while at the same time he is subjected to discrimination for being Jewish.[1] The consequences have been,
under our very eyes, a new resurgence of Judaism, especially
among the rising generation, and the courageous struggle we
see for the right to emigrate to Israel. It is tempting to see

---

[1] Among the various works dealing with the condition of the Jews in the
U.S.S.R., one of the best and most scrupulous of recent books is that of
François Fejto, *Les Juifs et l'Antisémitisme dans les pays communistes*
(Paris, 1960).

here a new manifestation of the survival of the "Eternal People," with all their troubled destiny. To do this would be to forget that up to the present, forty years of "antireligious campaigns" have not had much power to overcome a tradition of twenty or thirty centuries: for everything goes on in the U.S.S.R. as though the mental structures—Jewish as well as Christian—rooted in this tradition, transcending class cultures or ideologies, had not been touched by the revolutionary mutation of 1917. The "Great Schism of the West" seems to have been, at least in respect to this question, a schism only in the literal sense of the word. The collective traditions and beliefs that made for Judeo-Christian antagonism in the Holy Russia of the czars has been allowed to survive in essence under the Communists.

One might also look at the present situation in its relation to World War II and the Nazi occupations, which isolated the first targets of Hitlerian fury, the memory of which has served to reinforce Jewish identity. Likewise, it is permissible to foresee that the ancient structures may wear down in the more or less distant future, making possible total de-Judaization and de-Christianization, in accordance with the will of the leaders and the precepts of official doctrine. But whatever it may become in the future, for the present the status of Jews in the Communist countries has little bearing upon our subject. At most it makes an opportune appearance to remind the historian of the rules of his craft, which prescribe that he beware of premature and pseudo-prophetic judgments.

In a subject such as this one, many other rules risk being breached at every step. The spatial and temporal limits of Jewish history are more or less identical with those of universal history, and it is of relevance to all the areas of classic historical scholarship (with the sole exception of military history). To these is added a rich internal history, which is, above all, that of an idea and a faith lived with unparalleled intensity. Thus, a work such as this reveals not only the insufficiencies of the author, of which he himself is only too aware, but also the inevitable weaknesses inherent in all attempts at panoramic history. In order to remedy this to whatever extent possible, I have solicited on numerous occasions the assistance of my colleagues and friends, to whom I here wish to express thanks. My gratitude goes in particular to Gaston Wiet of the Collège de France, who has guided me with great kindness through the history of Islam, and who has also been so good as to read the proof of the parts of this book that cover it; to Israel Revah, of the École Pratique des Hautes Études, who has done the same for that part which concerns the Portuguese Inquisition and the marranos; to R. P. Paul Démann and to Rabbi Charles Touati, who have taken the trouble to read the manuscript in its entirety and to whom I owe countless precious suggestions; to Emmanuel Levinas, who, in the course of friendly conversations, opened up dazzling vistas of Talmudic science of which I was largely ignorant; to Louis Schoffman of the College of Modern Languages, of Brooklyn, New York, who put at my disposal with extreme generosity his unpublished text on the Spanish Jews in the Middle Ages. My indebtedness is no less great to three scholars whose works are cited in the notes with exceptional frequency: Professor I. Baer of the University of Jerusalem, the prestigious specialist in the history of the Spanish Jews, and A. Dominguez Ortiz of Madrid and Albert A. Sicroff of Princeton, New Jersey, who devoted themselves to pioneering research in the previously virgin field of the status of "New Christians" and of the *limpieza de sangre.*

BOOK ONE

ISLAM

one

Before Islam

In this introductory chapter I shall limit myself to a brief examination of the origins of three Jewish colonies that were destined, each in their own way, to play leading roles over the centuries.

During the first millennium of the Christian era, Mesopotamia, the ancient land of Abraham, became what could be considered a capital of Judaism. It was here that the normative rules for life in Dispersion were definitively codified (the Babylonian Talmud). Closer to home, in Spain, after centuries of intermixed Judaism, Islam, and Christianity, there were born the glorious Sephardim, whose incalculable civilizing contribution to the rise of Europe reached its peak during the Renaissance. Even today, the Sephardim are second in importance only to the Ashkenazim. Finally, there are the Jews of North Africa, whose history is little known and most unusual. Until recently they seemed destined for a unique future, for they represented the last foothold of traditional Judaism on the ancient continent.

This review does not include Palestine, except to recall that even after the fierce Roman repressions of A.D. 70 and 135 it still had a sizable Jewish population governed by a patriarch, *nasi*, officially recognized by Rome. Talmudic studies flourished there for many more years, and on at least two occasions, in A.D. 352 and 614, the Jews made desperate attempts to regain control of the country. But they were merely a minority, and, with the Dispersion, their prestige and influence declined more and more from generation to

generation. Their contacts with the non-Jewish population—
the principal subject of this study—are of no particular
interest.

Babylonia

Of all the Jewish colonies of the ancient Dispersion, none
was older, more stable, nor probably larger than that of
Babylonia. As far as we can determine now, at the distance
of a thousand years, it was twice called upon to play a leading role in Jewish history. Its origins go back to time immemorial, and in any case to the first organized deportation of
the children of Israel, when the Ten Tribes were forced into
exile by the Assyrian King Sargon II around 720 B.C. In an
inscription on the walls of the palace of Khorsabad, this
prince put their number at exactly 27,290 people. Traces of
the Ten Tribes were quickly lost, but they were joined, a few
generations later, by the two tribes of Judea, protagonists of
that amazing spiritual adventure, the Babylonian exile. It
has been said that the history of Judaism began in 586 B.C.
across the Babylonian border, and that Judaism needed this
forced separation from the homeland and the Temple to
achieve universality and spirituality. The role of the first
exile was certainly crucial in the development of basic
Jewish traditions. It was here that the indestructible fidelity
to Zion was born and the last vestiges of idolatry extirpated.
Here, too, the Pentateuch reached its final form. And most
important, it was here that the exiles learned a lesson from
their history and succeeded both in finding a meaning in
their trials and in transmitting that meaning to their heirs—
in other words, that they developed their peculiar historical
memory as Jews.

This is all the more remarkable in that, however heart-
rending Lamentations and the strains of Psalm 137 may be,
the material conditions of exile were not at all unhappy—
quite the contrary. Deportation of conquered tribes was a

common political practice in the ancient Orient, and once it was accomplished, the Assyrian, Babylonian, or Persian monarchs allowed the exiles to live and work in peace according to their ancestral customs and governed by their traditional chiefs. The Jews were no exception to the rule, and the Book of Kings tells us that Jehoiachin, king of Judah, ate at the table of the king of Babylonia "continually all the days of his life" (II Kings 25: 29). Likewise, Babylonian seals and tablets designate him as "King of Judah." According to legend, this descendant of David gave birth to the line of exilarchs, the "chiefs of the exile," who would dominate the Jewish colony of Babylonia for many centuries to come.

These were the conditions under which the exiles, who were skilled and hard-working farmers, quickly settled down on the fertile plains of Mesopotamia, "building houses and planting gardens" as the prophet recommended. The books of Ezra and Nehemiah show clearly that only a minority decided to participate in the great adventure of the Return that the Persian conquest made possible a half century later. The majority remained in Babylonia and endured there. Little is known about their history in succeeding centuries, but their presence is corroborated by the discovery (in Nippur, in particular) of cuneiform tablets and commercial documents bearing Jewish names. Also, intellectual contact continued unbroken between the colony and the mother country; many young Babylonians went to Palestine to study, among them, in the first century B.C., Hillel, who became the most illustrious of the Jewish scholars. But it was not until the second century of the Christian era, after the Roman campaigns of 70 and 135 had sown desolation in Judea, that the Babylonian Jewish community emerged from the shadows. It then remained the principal center of Judaism for many centuries.

At this time Mesopotamia formed the western boundary of the Parthian Empire, the traditional bitter enemy of Rome. The Jewish colony grew larger and larger as fugitives arrived from Palestine. "It is almost unbelievable how they multiplied there," Josephus tells us(1).

Some cities, such as Nehardea, Pumbedita, Sura, and Mahuza, were populated almost exclusively by Jews. According to the best recent estimates, there were at least a million Babylonian Jews in the third century A.D. (2). Subject to political upheavals and religious conversions, self-governing Jewish communities sometimes appeared fleetingly: Adiabene, whose King Izates converted in the beginning of the first century; the brigand kingdom founded in the same era by the brothers Asinaeus and Anilaeus, which "controlled all the business of Mesopotamia" for fifteen years (3), and, three centuries later, a Jewish principality around the city of Mahuza that lasted seven years, according to the medieval chronology *Seder 'Olam*. But these were unusual instances. As numerous as they were, the Jews remained a minority, with no foreign allies and little political power. Thus, except for a few instances of intermittent and localized clashes, the Parthian kings let them live in peace, and the life of the Jews compared favorably with that of the Christians, who were persecuted as agents of enemy Rome from the fourth century onward.

By a remarkable coincidence the state religion of the Parthian (or Persian) Empire was Zoroastrianism, the only religion besides Judaism that had gradually evolved the concept of monotheism—the perception of a single moral principle dictating the destiny of the world and man. Certain passages of the Zend-Avesta, the sacred book of Zarathustra, are remarkable for their economy of style and purity, and it is not surprising that, read from afar, they were able to capture the imagination of a Nietzsche. The question that naturally comes to mind is whether there was intermixture and borrowing between the two monotheistic traditions, and if so, what.

While there are certain aspects of Zoroastrianism that are disturbing to our Judeo-Christian sensibilities, such as the cult of incest—marriage between son and mother or between brother and sister was considered particularly pious—or the abandonment of bodies, which could not be buried or cremated but instead were left to the vultures of the desert, there are also remarkable similarities to Judaism, especially regarding formal ritual and the passionate quest for purity.

". . . Religion intervened in the minutiae of daily life, and day and night the individual ran the risk of falling into sin or impurity for the slightest inattention. . . . It was obligatory to pray to the sun four times a day; it was obligatory to pray to the moon, fire, and water; it was obligatory to pray on going to bed, getting up, washing oneself, putting on one's belt, eating, relieving oneself, sneezing, cutting one's hair and fingernails, lighting the lamps, etc. The fire in the hearth must not go out, sunlight must not fall on the fire, fire and water must not meet. The formalities necessary to cleanse the impurity from one who had touched a corpse or to cleanse a menstruating woman, or a woman who had just given birth—especially if the child was stillborn—were extremely wearing and onerous" (4).

These regulations are strikingly reminiscent of certain passages of the Talmud—precisely that Talmud which was codified into its definitive form at that time in Babylonia. However, the best scholars on the subject (5) believe that Jewish borrowings from the ideas around them were limited to a few superstitions—fruits of the luxuriant Oriental imagination—and some baroque descriptions of demons or angels that can be found in the Haggadah, but that Zoroastrianism had no influence at all on the religious and ethical concepts of Judaism itself. This conclusion seems indisputable considering that the Babylonian Talmud is nothing more than the definitive compilation of a system of interpretation developed essentially under Palestinian skies. At best, the similarities and hidden analogies between the teaching of Moses and that of Zoroaster contributed—in the absence of any direct relationship, which would have resulted in rivalry—to a reciprocal understanding that made the fate of the Babylonian Jews so mild and so exceptionally enviable.

Therefore, right from the outset we shall avoid seeking signs of "anti-Semitism," of special discrimination, and instead shall see what life was like at a time that was crucial for the future development of Judaism in the Dispersion.

Within the Parthian Empire, whose population was stratified into closed castes—clergy, soldiers, officials, populace—the Jews constituted a separate caste with their own territories where they pursued the whole gamut of occupations known at the time, especially agriculture. It was truly a closed society, enjoying nearly complete autonomy. It was administered by a hereditary chief, the exilarch, who had a sumptuous court at Nehardea and who was responsible only to the king. His ancestry, as we have seen, could be traced to King David. The exilarch had the right to dispense complete justice to his subjects, but in relation to the king he was a loyal and obedient satrap. It was in Babylonia that the traditional Jewish maxim was coined: "The law of the state is the final law."[1] His power was tempered only by the authority traditionally accorded the judgments of the sages, the "Amoraim," guardians and disseminators of the sacred teaching and codifiers of the Talmud. It is the Talmud that is our principal source of information on the history of the Babylonian Jews. Through the subtleties of its juridical discussions and the capricious meanderings of its legends and parables we come to learn innumerable details about daily life and customs. We come to know the high regard the sages of Israel had for manual labor, the dominant occupation of the time and much more highly valued than commerce. We can see their victorious struggle for the purity of family customs, all the while showing a fairly pronounced Oriental contempt for women. True, on the majority of these points we can extract fairly contradictory opinions from the ocean of the Talmud (which the scholars took delight in

[1] *Dina de malkhuta dina.* This principle was first formulated at the beginning of the third century by the head of the Academy of Nehardea, Mar Samuel.

contrasting one with another), but if there is one on which there is unanimity it is the absolute primacy accorded to study. A text says it most expressively: "The whole world lives from the breath of the scholars." Moreover, it was avowed that each day only the sight of the scholars and students caused divine anger to turn away from the world. From then on, Jewish instruction was obligatory, free, and universal; needless to say, this applied only to sacred studies. Nevertheless, certain Talmudists did not disdain "Greek science" so long as it dealt with the exact sciences, and they employed astronomy and mathematics.

But on the whole, the Jewish population, which was dense and compact, had little contact with the surrounding world, and for several centuries, until the Arab conquest, it retained the traditional Aramaic as its everyday language. The extraordinary degree to which the Jews were established in Mesopotamia can be seen in some maxims from the Talmud, which contrast strikingly with the classical accents of the Dispersion and the permanent longing for Zion. Certain scholars resolutely prohibited leaving the country, even for Palestine: "Whosoever emigrates from Babylonia to Palestine breaks a positive Biblical commandment," R. Judah ben Ezekiel maintained, referring to a verse of Jeremiah.[2] This sage even forbade his students to receive instruction from Palestinian scholars. His celebrated masters Rab and Samuel called the regions of Sura and Pumbedita where they taught "the land of Israel" (6). One might say that the Babylonian Jews had a real superiority complex rooted in the antiquity of their colony as well as the superiority of their status. It was expressed in adages such as these:

"All countries are as dough in comparison with Palestine, and Palestine is as dough relative to Babylonia."

"Babylonia stands in presumption of being pure, until you

---

[2] Jeremiah, 27: 22: "They shall be taken to Babylon and stay there until I recall them, says the Lord."

know wherewith it became impure; other countries are presumed to be impure, until you know wherewith they are pure."

"R. Ismael bar Joseph asked the Rabbi: 'For what good deed does God let the Babylonians live?' 'For the study of the law,' the Rabbi replied. 'And the Palestinians?' 'For their tithes.' 'And the people of other countries?' 'Because they observe the Sabbaths and the holidays'" (7).

The Babylonian Jews were fond of glorifying what they considered to be the purity of their line, which they claimed went back exclusively to the first Exile and consequently to Abraham. The felicity of their condition also explains certain remarks along the line of *ubi bene, ibi patria.*

There were even some authors who saw the first Exile not as divine punishment, but as a species of blessing, as the following commentary shows:

"Our Talmudic academies were not persecuted and the Jews were not hunted down; we were conquered neither by Yavan [Greece] nor by Edom [Rome]. God accorded a blessing to Israel when, twelve years before the destruction of Jerusalem, He exiled King Jehoiachin, accompanied by illustrious men, to Babylonia where the Torah was able to develop uninterruptedly to our generation" (8).

The Palestinian sage Johanan ben Zakkai spoke otherwise, and he was subtler and more profound:

"Why were the Jews exiled to Babylonia? Because their ancestor Abraham had come from there. It is like a woman misbehaving toward her husband. To whom does he send her? He sends her back to her father's house" (9).

Such was the oasis that for nearly a thousand years harbored the principal center of Judaism, the place where the Talmud was codified in its definitive form, the place whose influence and prestige were recognized throughout the Dispersion. The Arab conquest, as we shall see, helped to intensify that predominance, and although the Seljuk invasions put an end to it three or four centuries later, an important Jewish colony still survived in Mesopotamia until our time—until 1950, to be exact. That year the entire community was transplanted to Israel, thus bringing to an end 2,500 years of uninterrupted Jewish presence in the "land of Abraham."

North Africa

Until recently, North Africa was the only place in the world where Judaism survived in its traditional forms, leading an almost medieval existence behind the walls of the *mellahs*. There have been picturesque descriptions of these subtropical ghettos, with their narrow streets seething with crowds of poor people and lined with shops where squatting artisans and merchants make and sell everything imaginable. In southern Tunisia there were even tribes of Jewish troglodytes who lived in caves cut into the limestone. All observers have been struck by the poverty of the North African Jews, and the Arabs regard them with that traditional disdain which goes back to the era of conquering Islam, when the special laws were enacted for the *dhimmis*, or "protected" Jews and Christians, meaning that they were entitled to the protection of the Believers but were required to live in abasement.

Still, the Jews of North Africa had their hour of glory. And their history, so little known and so unlike the history of the Jews everywhere else, is worth recalling.

It goes way back to the protohistoric times when the Phoenicians colonized "Ifriqiya" and founded the city of Carthage. This gave rise to numerous legends. If we are to believe Ibn Khaldun, the famous Arab historian, the whole Berber people is of Palestinian stock and Goliath was their first king (10). According to the Byzantine historian Procopius, the Berbers descended from Amorite and other tribes put to flight by Joshua, son of Nun (11). These may be legends, but they indicate that several centuries before Christ, Semitic colonizers, the same ones who founded

Carthage, had imposed on North Africa their culture and also their language—a language that was much closer to Hebrew than to Aramaic or Arabic (12).

As to religion, we know that the Carthaginians worshipped the god Baal. It has been noted that this cult, with its emphasis on human submission to the will of the divine, corresponds to a feeling which was hardly known among the Greeks and the Romans and which presaged Jewish monotheism (13). Bold as this may seem, it deserves some consideration. Moreover, certain local cults of ancient North Africa were literally impregnated with actual Jewish influences. Thus, remarkable magic tablets have been discovered on the site of the port of Hadrumetum, bearing the name of Jehovah, sometimes invoked alone, sometimes along with other divinities. For example: "I adjure thee, demon spirit who art here, by the sacred name Aoth, Alaoth, the God of Abraham, the Jao of Isaac, Jao, Aoth, Abaoth, the God of Israel . . ." (14). It is thus most likely that from earliest times the Jews came and settled in North Africa in the wake of the Phoenicians, preparing the terrain for the spread of Judaism. And, consequently, for Christianity. Thus it is easier to understand why, in the first centuries after Christ, and before Islam, "in the period which extends from Tertullian and Cyprian to Augustine, North Africa instructed all the Christiandom of the West" (15).

. Under these conditions, when large numbers of Jews began to scatter throughout the world—and despite the indestructible legend, it must be recalled that that Dispersion took place well before the war of Judea and the destruction of the Temple—it was in North Africa that they found the friendliest welcome. Moreover, according to a Talmudic tradition, the Ten Tribes had been carried to Africa and Rabbi Akiba had later paid an extended visit to that region (16). For their part, the Fathers of the Church, such as Saint Jerome, Tertullian, and Saint Augustine, often mention how ancient and prosperous were the Jewish colonies of Mauretania, Numidia, and Libya. Just as in other parts of the world, Judaism spread in these regions at least as much through proselytism as through immigration—perhaps more. Taking into account the influences and the syncretisms we have mentioned, to be able to trace one's ancestry back to Abraham, the common ancestor, conferred considerable nobility on a person. The gradual and silent disappearance of the old Phoenician colonizers can probably be explained precisely by their conversion to Judaism (17).

But while these Jewish colonies, which were particularly numerous in the cities along the coast, were scarcely distinguishable from the colonies of Asia Minor, Syria, or Alexandria, at the beginning of the Christian era North Africa received a completely different type of Jewish immigration, and this one is much more interesting as regards the subject at hand. It is known that the Zealots, who put up stubborn resistance to Vespasian and Titus in 69–70, were not entirely annihilated during the Judean war. Groups of them migrated to Cyrenaica, where in 112 the Jews fomented a new rebellion ("the last corner of the world where we see the Jew with sword in hand," observed E. F. Gautier) and penetrated even farther west. They succeeded in imposing their religion on the Berber nomads who lived along the edge of the desert, fighting their own war against Rome. It seems they carried their religion even farther, beyond Timbuktu, to the Fulani, the black people of the Niger. For more than a century this theory, supported by the most varied archaeological and linguistic arguments, has been debated among anthropologists (18). Today there is new corroboration, drawn from the confused ancestral reminiscences that resurface as these peoples achieve greater self-awareness. The case of the Falashas, those black tribes of Ethiopia that have retained their Judaism intact, can be cited as another indication of this.

But regardless of what once took place south of the Sahara and the legendary Jewish kingdoms that are supposed to have prospered there, we know for sure that in the north numerous Berber tribes eventually adopted Judaism.

The cult of Jehovah was a powerful cohesive and unifying factor for them at the time of the battles that pitted them against the Roman Empire. When Christianity became the official religion of the state, the significance of this factor became even greater, for at that time the ancient Jewish coastal colonies, harassed and persecuted, eventually faded and disappeared, as did the various heretical Christian sects. The result was that Judaism finally survived in North Africa not in the peaceful settlements of the Dispersion but rather among the fierce warriors of the interior.

When the waves of conquering Islam began to break over these regions, the Christian coastal area was quickly submerged while the Judaized Berber tribes put up a long and stubborn resistance to the Arabs. Their principal stronghold was the Aures Mountains, which had always been hospitable to rebels, and they were led by an inspired woman, a queen and prophetess named Kahina. According to the historian Ibn Adhari, after destroying Carthage the Arab general Hassan inquired who was the most powerful chief in Africa. He was told: "It is a woman named El-Kahina, who lives in the Aures; all the people of Ifriqiya fear her and all the Berbers obey her; were she to be killed, the whole Maghreb would submit to you and you would encounter no more rivalry or resistance" (19).

In the year 66 of the Hegira (A.D. 688) Hassan tried to seize the Aures but was repulsed with heavy losses. The Arabs retreated to Tripolitania and for nearly five years Kahina was the uncontested queen of the whole Maghreb. She governed, it seems, with an iron fist, but little is known about her ephemeral reign. The Arab historians furnish more details about her death. In 693 Hassan's troops launched a second offensive. The queen was warned in a prophetic dream that she would fall in the final battle. She nevertheless went to war, "for to abandon her country to the invader would be a disgrace for her people," and she was killed after recommending to her two sons to surrender to the enemy and convert to Islam. Thus, according to Arab historians, Jewish domination in North Africa came to an end.

⌐ The whole area was quickly Islamized. What Jewish outposts survived and under what conditions it is impossible to ascertain. According to E. F. Gautier, one of the most authoritative sources on the subject, "That whole period in the history of North Africa is a black hole, a bottle of ink." A good many Jews of Syrian or Yemenite origin came to settle in the wake of the invaders. The city of Kairouan, in particular, which at that time was one of the centers of Mediterranean commerce, contained a prosperous Jewish community and was the site of a philosophical school (the medical treatises of Isaac Israeli, who lived there at the beginning of the tenth century, were considered authoritative in medieval Europe) (20). Later, other Jewish elements from Egypt and especially from Spain after the 1492 expulsion arrived in those areas. These *forasteros* (foreigners) imposed on the local Pelethite (meaning autochthon, literally Philistine) communities their superior culture and their particular religious rites. But essentially, the Jews of Tunisia, Algeria, and Morocco are of entirely indigenous origin, descendants of the ancient tribes with sonorous names: Jerawa, Fendelawa, Medyna, Botr, Beranese. It has even been said that "that amalgamized population which reached its peak with Kahina (who epitomizes the African epic) is the most indigenous, the most African of all" (21). Moreover, certain of these Jewish tribes retained their independence until fairly recently; those of Ulad Aziz in the Aures, for instance (22). And according to a local legend, as late as the seventeenth century the Jews of Tilatou exacted tribute from the surrounding Moslem peoples (23). Within the Sahara itself the independent Jewish state of Gourara survived until the end of the fifteenth century (24). Such a past doubtless explains the fiery and often quarrelsome temperament of the Jews of North Africa.

Spain

Are there any speculations that have not been indulged in regarding the origin of the Spanish Jews? These people had a legitimate claim to a glorious antiquity, but at a very early date they expanded on these claims and made their origin go back to the beginning of time. Doubtless the principal reason for this was to prove that their ancestors had nothing to do with the Crucifixion, to which should be added their piercing need to demonstrate that they were living in a land which belonged to them. A gravestone in Sagunto was reputed to cover the tomb of Adoniram, the legendary servant of King Solomon who was sent on a mission to this distant land. The names of cities seemed to speak an eloquent language. Was not Escalona the Biblical Escalon? Maqueda, Makeda? Jopes, Joppe (Jaffa)? And was not the name of the former capital itself, Toledo, derived from *Toledoth* (generations)? According to an even more fantastic etymology, which is of recent date (these games never end), Andalusia would be a contraction of (*G*)*an-Eden* and thus would mean paradise (25). These legends, and a hundred similar ones, were diligently collected in 1799 by a scholar of most Catholic Spain and published by the Royal Academy of Madrid (26), for the Jews were not the only ones interested. As to the facts, here is what they seem to be:

It is most likely that some Jews came to Spain, just as to North Africa, in the wake of the Phoenicians and Carthaginians and settled there at a very early date, several centuries before Christ. But there is no certain proof of this. The allusions that some have believed the Talmud to contain are imprecise and open to debate. The New Testament seems clearer when it tells us that Saint Paul visited or wished to visit Spain (Romans 15:24, 28), for we know that the apostle carried the gospel generally to places where there were Jews or people under Jewish influence. It is likely that the ghettos of Spain prospered and multiplied in the course of the following centuries because, around the year 300, the Council of Elvira, according to the Dictionary of Catholic Theology "the oldest council of the Church of which disciplinary canons survive," published numerous and varied stipulations cautioning the Christians against the Jews. It was forbidden, under pain of excommunication, to eat with them (Canon 50), to intermarry, or to have them bless the crops (Canon 49). These precepts were to be repeated by all of Christian Europe in succeeding centuries.

Neither the elevation of Christianity to the rank of official state church nor the upheavals attendant upon the disintegration of the Roman Empire and the Germanic invasions were able to prevent the spread of Judaism in Spain, for three centuries later it became the object of far more severe and exacting legislation—legislation that again created a precedent to be repeated in other lands in the course of the centuries to come.

The Visigoth kings who governed Spain from the beginning of the sixth century were at first followers of the "Arian heresy" and generally rather tepid on matters of religion. But in 589 one of them, Reccared, was converted to Catholicism and undertook to issue numerous laws against the Jews—as well as against his former coreligionists—which were later expanded by his successors. Concerning these laws, Montesquieu, in *The Spirit of Laws,* offered this peremptory judgment: "All the maxims, principles and views of the present inquisition, are derived from the code of the Visigoths and the monks have only copied against the Jews, the laws formerly enacted by bishops. . . . The laws of the Visigoths are puerile, clumsy and foolish; they attain not their end; they are stuffed with rhetoric, and void of sense, frivolous in substance and bombastic in style" (27). Whatever the validity of this condemnation as a whole, it is true that several centuries later the Inquisition, far from doing any original work, merely dug out of an arsenal of texts that had been written by theologians and jurists of the seventh century laws which were both extraordinarily meticulous

and absurdly inventive. The second part of this work will
deal with them, but for the moment they interest us only to
the extent that a thousand years or so before Torquemada
they led to *marranismo* before there were marranos—that
is, pretending to be converted while secretly professing
Judaism—and even more violent anti-Christian feeling.

, As regards these feigned conversions, it is apparent from
examination of the laws enacted to track down these false
Christians that such conversions were frequent. Specifically,
the ex-Jews were required to report to their bishop each
Saturday and Jewish holiday to show that they no longer
observed these days. But what if they were traveling? In this
case the convert had to present himself to a churchman at
each stage of the voyage and obtain a certificate of nonobservance of the Sabbath. The priest was supposed to
communicate this to the priests of neighboring parishes, and
upon his return home the traveler had to deliver to his
bishop a complete collection of these certificates (28).

In case of transgression, the designated penalty was
decalvatio. Scholars today are seeking in vain to determine
the exact nature of this punishment. Also, it is impossible to
ascertain whether under King Erwig, the author of this law,
seventh-century Spain had enough learned churchmen to
keep the necessary paper work up to date. Probably Montesquieu was right when he spoke of laws that were "void of
sense."

, It was not long before the effects of resentment began to
appear. This question, too, is the subject of scholarly debate,
but it is very likely that the old chronicles of Roderic of
Toledo and Lucas of Tuy are telling the truth when they say
that the Jews took the initiative in "betrayal"—that is, that
they advised the Arabs of the best ways and means to
accomplish the invasion of the Iberian Peninsula, which
took place in 711, and that at the time of the conquest the
Jews rendered substantial aid to the conquerors (29).

two

The Prophet

There are as many theories about Mohammed as there are biographies, someone has said. And, I might add, these biographies do not even agree on where he received his knowledge of sacred history—whether his teachers were Jews or Christians—a detail that immediately brings home to us how extraordinarily sparse and inaccurate our knowledge of the origins of Islam is. And yet, Mohammed is the only great founder of a religion to stand before us as a complete human being. We can follow his religious experience step by step. But unfortunately, the book he bequeathed to us—the Koran—was not set down in writing until well after his death. Why did he allow this to happen? Why did this man, whose genius was above all to understand how much power lay in the possession of a revealed Book and who, it now seems certain, knew how to read and write (30)—why did he not record the revelations he received during his lifetime? Was it because, following the example of the first Christians, he expected the Final Judgment imminently and thus thought it unnecessary to transmit his message to a highly unlikely posterity (31)? Or was it simply because he was so intuitive, often making his instructions fit the circumstances, that he kept postponing setting them down definitively up to the end? Whatever the reason, the written version of the Koran as it has come down to us dates from the time of Caliph Othman, Mohammed's third successor, some twenty years after his death, which considerably diminishes its value as a historical source, since there could have been additions or omissions in the interim. Nevertheless, the Koran is still our principal guide to everything concerning the birth of Islam.

But if, because of this, the Orientalist's task is somewhat arduous, archaeology and ethnography have come along at the right time to lend him a hand. Today we are quite well informed about conditions in Arabia at the beginning of the seventh century. This desert bordering the great Byzantine and Persian empires was dotted with a few scattered oases and peopled by Bedouin tribes leading nomadic and patriarchal lives quite similar to those of the first Biblical tribes and, like them, practicing circumcision. They worshipped stone idols, the best known of which was the black stone shrine, the Kaaba, at Mecca.

Great trade routes crossed the region, linking Syria and Yemen, the Indian Ocean and the Mediterranean. At the junctions of these camel trails, cities had sprung up— Medina and especially Mecca, where many a clan chieftan had settled down to become a prosperous merchant dealing with both Byzantine and Persian officials and travelers. In this way, too, the ideas and conceptions of the more advanced countries were disseminated. Thus, from time immemorial, aided by the relatedness of the languages, the Arabs were quite familiar with Biblical legend and willingly saw themselves as descendants of Abraham through Ishmael, who had been driven into the desert. In later times, appreciable numbers of Jews and then Nestorian Christians, both fleeing the persecutions of Rome and Byzantium, settled among them. Both began to proselytize actively (32). Certain tribes—the Taghlib and the Najran—converted to Christianity; others—the Kainuka, the Nadir, the Kuraiza—converted to Judaism. In both instances the religions were certainly adapted to the needs of the nomads, simplified greatly, and often reduced to a few summary rituals. (This simplification is doubtless the reason for the fantastic travesties of certain concepts essential to the two faiths that appeared in the Koran.) Doubtless, too, the first apostles of monotheism in Arabia—Jews or Christians—each propagated the hatred and suspicion of the rival that had already crystallized in secular competitions, especially insofar as the Christian doctrine of a rejected Israel was concerned.

This was the situation in Arabia around 570 when the child destined to change the world was born in Mecca. Orphaned at an early age, the future prophet was raised by his uncle, a rich merchant, and from childhood on he probably had the opportunity to accompany his uncle on his voyages and to visit the more advanced countries, particularly Christian Syria. But in Mecca, too, which was a lively commercial center, he could have had many occasions to meet Christians and Jews. How or from whom he acquired his knowledge of the holy Jewish and Christian scriptures is a question that will probably never be resolved satisfactorily. This knowledge, moreover, as we shall see, was singularly inaccurate and riddled with extraordinary gaps.

At twenty-five the young Mohammed married a rich widow, Khadijah, fifteen years his senior, and from then on he traveled with his wife's caravans. Thus, during his youth he had ample occasion to broaden his horizons and become familiar with other lands and other customs. He was already in his forties when, amid terrible anguish, he had the visions and revelations in which the Archangel Gabriel ordered him, in the name of God, to bring his fellow citizens the message of the one Allah—visions and revelations that are described in the Koran in enough detail so that one can see how many traits they have in common with the religious experiences other great mystics have described.

According to Moslem tradition, Mohammed first preached in Mecca for ten years, from 612 to 622, with little success. He recruited only a few dozen followers and was mocked and even persecuted by the people of Mecca. He then decided to move with his flock to Medina (Yathrib), a city located a few hundred miles to the north and populated mostly by Jewish or Jewish-influenced tribes. There he met with success and his converts grew rapidly in number on a ground already prepared by the teachings of monotheism. (Although these questions may be most obscure, a comparison with the early success of the Christians among the *metuentes*, the "proselytes of the porch," would perhaps be appropriate here.[1])

But the rigorist Jews, the local doctors of the Law whose backing and moral approval were so essential to Mohammed, as we can see from the ardent appeals of the Koran, were skeptical and contemptuous. This resulted in quarrels and skirmishes, but by this time the disappointed Prophet was powerful enough to resort to force. He expelled some of the Jews and, with the blessing of Allah, massacred the rest. This explains the contrasts in how the Koran treats the Jews, glorifying them in some passages (where they are the "children of Israel") and denouncing them in later ones (then they are the *Yahud*). This is also why Mecca was substituted for Jerusalem as the place where prayers should be directed (*qibla*) and Yom Kippur was replaced by Ramadan as the great fast (33).

Once he was in control of Medina and the surrounding area, the Prophet went on to reach a compromise with Mecca, his native city, and to become the theocratic leader of Arabia. (Moreover, from many things in the Koran we can conclude that he was scarcely conscious of a universal mission and that he intended the Arab community alone to benefit from his message (34).) In this undertaking, which lasted from 622 until his death in 632, he showed amazing ability as a leader and a strategist, striking Mecca's lines of communication with the outside and reducing the city to his mercy in 630. In the course of his campaigns he dealt with the Christian Arab tribes and succeeded in subduing them; here again, he met with incomprehension, if not

[1] On the *metuentes*, see Volume 1 of our *History of Anti-Semitism: From the Time of Christ to the Court Jews*, p. 10.

scorn, and here, too, the Koran shows his disappointment and reflects a gradual change of attitude.[2]

The last years of the Prophet's life seem to have been calm and peaceful. Khadijah had died many years before and for political reasons he entered into several other marriages. He governed his community paternally, a simple, humane, and wise man who remained accessible to the least of his followers. He was mounting an expedition against Syria when he died suddenly in 632.

These are the factual elements of the Prophet's biography that can be ascertained from reading the Koran, that book which is so baffling to the Western mind. It is certainly tedious reading for us, and Carlyle's judgment—"A wearisome confused jumble, crude, incondite. . . . Nothing but a sense of duty could carry any European through the Koran"—still remains true for us. But also true is the second part of the proposition: ". . . there is a merit quite other than the literary one. If a book come from the heart, it will contrive to reach other hearts; all art and authorcraft are of small amount to that." A book of genuine religious inspiration, the Koran recalls the Old Testament in its function as a universal guide, reaching into all domains of existence. True, its composition is much more confusing and its repetitions interminable. (But as its commentators have observed, "God never tires of repeating himself.") And just as the Old Testament was supplemented by the initially oral transmission of the Mishnah and the Talmud, the Koran was also added to by the Islamic transmission of the *hadith,* which was not fixed in writing until much later (in the ninth century).

If the genius of Mohammed was to fuse and transpose the teachings of the two rival religions to make them accessible to the Arabs (Jesus, whom he accorded an eminent place,

---

[2] Cf. particularly Sura V, 76, seq. "Thus the relationship with the Christians ended as that with the Jews had ended—in war," Richard Bell wrote in this regard (*The Origin of Islam in Its Christian Environment,* London, 1926, p. 159).

was for him the latest of the great prophets), he often, as we have already mentioned, displayed ignorance of their exact meaning. Thus, he thought that the Jews, sharing in the Christian error in their own way, believed Ezra was the son of God, and that the Christian Trinity was composed of God the Father, Christ, and Mary (to him, the Christians were polytheistic). Moreover, he confused Mary with Miriam, the sister of Aaron (Sura XIX, 29). Also, he sometimes confused Jewish and Christian teaching and thus exhorted the Jews of Medina to follow him in the name of the Gospels.[3] Perhaps this ignorance was his strength; perhaps old Renan was right when he said: "Knowing too much is an obstacle to creating. . . . If Mohammed had studied Judaism and Christianity closely, he would not have drawn a new religion from them. He would have become either Jewish or Christian, and it would have been impossible for him to fuse these two religions in a way that suited the needs of Arabia . . ." (35).

As to what part Judaism and Christianity each played in the teachings of Mohammed, one is easily convinced of the preponderant influence of Judaism. From the transcendental point of view the rigid monotheism of the Old Testament was maintained and, if possible, affirmed with even greater vigor. "There is no God but one God." "Assuredly they have disbelieved who say: 'Allah is one of three.'" "Say: 'He is Allah, One, Allah the Eternal; He brought not forth, nor hath he been brought forth; Co-equal with Him there hath never been any one.'" The Koran hammers this theme ceaselessly. As to the rites of Mohammedanism, the Law of Moses, which had long since fallen into disuse among the Christians, was maintained in a somewhat milder form by Mohammed in most areas, especially those that dealt with

---

[3] Particularly in Sura VII, 156 (". . . Who follow the messenger the native prophet, whom they find mentioned in the Torah, and the Evangel in their possession . . .") and Sura II, 81 (". . . We gave Moses the Book and followed him up by the messengers after him, and we gave Jesus, son of Mary, the Evidences . . .").

dietary prescriptions and the prohibition of pork,[4] the ablutions and purifications and the rules for sex life (just as in the Old Testament, considered good and necessary), or the rhythm of the daily prayers and the fasts. From the Christians he borrowed only the cult of Jesus and faith in the Immaculate Conception. But he resolutely denied the Crucifixion.[5] Moreover, why would Jesus have allowed himself to be sacrificed? In fact, the notion of original sin, on which the Gospels put so much stress, is barely suggested in the Old Testament and is ignored completely by the Koran. Thus one can see that Islam has much more in common with Judaism than with Christianity. True, on many points it is possible to perceive the influence of very ancient traditions common to both the Arabs and the Jews, such as circumcision (which the Koran does not mention explicitly anywhere!).

But Islam is close to Christianity in one respect. Just as the Fathers of the Church searched the Old Testament prophecies for the announcement of the coming of Christ, Mohammed attributed to those same prophets—but more especially to Abraham and Jesus—the announcement of his own coming.[6] The Moslem theologians perfected this

---

[4] On the other hand, camel meat, so essential to the diet of the nomads, was allowed. The prohibition of pork is reiterated by the Koran in several places; in one context, the reason given seems to suggest that pork was a tribal divinity in Arabia. (Sura V, 4: ". . . the flesh of swine, that over which any other [name] than Allah has been invoked. . . .") Deuteronomy gives no reason for the prohibition of pork.

[5] The Crucifixion was a Jewish fable, and the Jews were censured precisely "for having said, 'We killed the Messiah, Jesus, son of Mary, the messenger of Allah,' though they did not kill him and did not crucify him, but he was counterfeited for them . . ." (Sura IV, 156). This interpretation shows the influence of Nestorianism, which taught that there were two natures of Jesus Christ. It may also have been influenced by some of the other old Oriental heresies (Docetist, Corinthian, Saturnian, etc.) which taught different variations on the same subject.

[6] Abraham: Sura II, 120–123 ("When Abraham said: . . . our Lord, raise up also amongst them a messenger . . ."). Jesus: Sura LXI, 6 ("And when Jesus, son of Mary, said: 'O children of Israel, I am Allah's messen-

method, sometimes referring to the same texts as the Christians and reading them in a new way.[7] And if the "people of the Book" (the Christians and Jews) did not find anything of the sort in these texts, it was because they were both unfaithful witnesses, believers in a half-truth; for they had "forgotten part of the word" or, even worse, "they desire to extinguish Allah's light with their breath." They were then forgers "concealing of the Book and dispensing with much." From this point of view there was no difference between Jews and Christians, even if Mohammed often underscored his preference for the latter; they were placed on the same level as the Jews, and Allah, who until then had supported the Christians against the Jews, now punished them in the same way for their unbelief.

"The Jews and the Christians say: 'We are the sons and the beloved of Allah'; say: 'Why then does he punish you for your sins?'"

"The Jews say: 'The Christians have no ground to stand on,' and the Christians say: 'The Jews have no ground to stand on'; (this) though they both recite the Book. So also those who have no knowledge [i.e., the pagan Arabs who have no knowledge of revealed religion] say much the same. Allah will judge between them on the Day of Resurrection in regard to that in which they have been differing."

But if Mohammed disputed the two religions' true descent from Abraham ("Abraham was not a Jew, nor was he a Christian, but he was a Hanif, a Moslem, and he was not one of the Polytheists"; Sura III, 60), the degree to which he showed his respect for each is remarkable. Was this the politician, coming to terms with reality? Or was it the mystic bearing witness with his particular genius? The fact is that many verses of the Koran pathetically proclaim both free-

---

ger to you . . . announcing the good tidings of a messenger who will come after me, bearing the name Ahmad.'")

[7] Thus Habakkuk 3: 3–7; Daniel 2: 37–45; Isaiah 5: 26–30 *et passim* and even Song of Songs 5: 10–16. The Gospels are made to contribute in the same way.

dom of conscience ("There is no compulsion in religion!" "If the Lord so willed, all those in the land would believe in a body; wilt thou then put constraint upon the people that they may be believers?") and the inalienable right of the "people of the Book"—the Jews and the Christians—to worship the Eternal in their very imperfect fashion. The essential injunction is issued in the same terms three different times in three different suras: "Those who have believed, those who have followed the Jews [i.e., "judaized," a pun on the name Yahud], the Nasara [the Christians], and the Sabi'in [literally "baptizers"; who they were has not been satisfactorily explained], whoever has believed in Allah and the Last Day, and has acted uprightly, have their reward with their Lord; fear rests not upon them nor do they grieve" (II, 99; V, 73; XXII, 17). At times the Prophet finds even more moving ways to express this idea: "And do not drive away those who call upon their Lord in the morning and in the evening desiring his countenance; no part of their reckoning falls upon thee, nor any of thine upon them, that thou shouldst drive them away, and be one of the wrongdoers" (VI, 52). Moreover, he notes that among the infidels one finds good and bad: "Among the people of the Book are those who, if one entrusts them with a talent, will pay it back; but among them are others who, if one entrusts them with a dinar, will not pay it back except so long as one remains standing over them" (III, 68). Later we shall examine how theologians and legislators have applied these fundamental precepts.

But, one may ask, what about "kill the infidels, wherever you find them; take them, lay siege to them"—in a word, the Holy War, the jihad. Certainly that too is in the Koran, but these imprecations and this violence were expressly reserved to the polytheists, to the Arab idolaters who refused to accept the theocratic order instituted by the Prophet for his people. (It was only with the Crusades that the notion of Holy War was extended to the fight against the Christians.) Mohammed was merciless toward these wrongdoers whose opposition endangered his work; for the rest, Islam is a religion of tolerance above all. Nothing could be farther from the truth than the traditional conventions that depict it as shattering all resistance by fire and steel. On the whole, it is a religion to the measure of man, taking his limits and weaknesses into account. "This religion is comfort" says the Moslem tradition. "Allah wants ease for you and not dismay," the Koran says again. It is a religion that demands neither the sublime nor the impossible, less intent than Christianity on raising humanity toward inaccessible heights but also less inclined to plunge it into blood baths.

These, then, are the fundamental precepts that constitute the starting point for our study. But religious commandments, whatever their tenor may be, collide with the realities of life in society—with the mores of men, their techniques, habits, and needs. These commandments can be applied in many contradictory—and often unexpected—ways. Step by step we are now going to retrace the fate of the Jews in the Moslem countries and, where useful, compare it with that of the Christians.

three

The Caliphs

The Umayyads

The twelfth-century French chronicler Guibert of Nogent,
in commenting on certain aspects of the Moslem religion,
explained them by the circumstances in which the Prophet is
supposed to have died: One day, it seems, the Prophet got
drunk, fell asleep on the main road, and was eaten by pigs;
as a result, his successors strictly prohibited both drinking
wine and eating pork. According to other medieval authors,
Mohammed is supposed to have been an Oriental bishop
who aspired to the throne of Saint Peter. In his disappointment at not being elected pope, he founded a heretical sect
of his own. Though today people are generally somewhat
better informed about the history and character of Islam and
its founder, it still seems worthwhile to sketch briefly the
history of this great civilization.

In the decade after the death of Mohammed in 632, his
successors, the caliphs Abu Bakr and Umar, conquered a
great part of the ancient world, destroying the powerful
Persian Empire and dislodging the Byzantines from Syria
and Egypt. Eventually, as is known, Islam dominated an
area extending from the Pyrenees to Hindustan. That some
obscure tribes could expand at such vertiginous speed
stupefied their contemporaries and continues to astound
historians today (36): "Conquering Islam" has become a
proverbial phrase. To orthodox Moslems these swift triumphs were evidently merely an example of the aid that

Allah accords true believers. In the fourteenth century, however, the wise Ibn Khaldun, that veritable precursor of modern sociology, offered another explanation. "When two parties are equal in number and strength," he wrote, "the one more accustomed to nomadic life wins victory." To this day, the nomads' military superiority over sedentary people has remained the great traditional explanation.

However, there is another point of view that has generally been somewhat neglected. Christianity, Islam, Judaism—today the differences are clear and distinct. But this was far from true in those days. Precisely in these classical centers of religious ferment of the Middle East, innumerable Christian sects had sprung up: Nestorians, Monophysites, Jacobites, Arians, Docetists, Jewish sympathizers of various persuasions, and others of which nothing has remained but the name. These sects were sometimes tolerated by Byzantium; more often they were severely persecuted. Each had its own interpretation of the sober recital of the Gospels, the differences generally centering on the dogma of the Trinity and the true nature of Jesus: man-god in one person? or in two? or only the Messiah?

This is why at its inception Islam was considered by the Christians—and also by the pagans—simply as a new Christian sect. Many writings bear witness to this, such as *De Haeresibus Liber* of Saint John of Damascus, in which "the superstition of the Ismaelites" is listed along with 102 other Christian heresies (and the wise theologian states that "the false prophet Mamed, having immersed himself in the Old and New Testaments, and having had conversations with a certain Arian monk, created his own sect") (37). This conception persisted in Europe throughout the Middle Ages. There are echoes of it in Dante's *Divine Comedy*, where Mohammed is described as a "fomenter of discord and of schism" (38), as well as in various legends where he is presented as a heretical cardinal, disappointed at not having been elected pope (39). In these circumstances it is easier to understand why the Monophysites of Syria, persecuted by

Byzantium, and the Nestorians of Mesopotamia, oppressed in Persia, should have given the conquerors—who were also their blood brothers or cousins—an enthusiastic welcome.

"All of Syria lay down docilely like a camel," the Arab general Khalid is supposed to have said after the conquest of the province (40). The cities capitulated one after the other, for the new masters were generous and tolerant and their arrival was tantamount to liberation. After taking Damascus, for example, Khalid demanded ink and parchment and wrote:

"In the name of Allah, the compassionate, the Merciful! This is what Khalid will accord the people of Damascus when he enters: he promises to guarantee the safety of their lives, property and churches. The wall of the city will not be demolished; no Moslem will be lodged in their houses. We give them the pact of Allah and the protection of His Prophet, the caliphs and the believers. Nothing but good shall befall them if they pay tribute" (41).

Even more significantly, Khalid made an agreement with the Christians of Hira that they would serve the Moslems as "eyes, i.e., as guides and helpers," in that Persian city (42).

As to the Jews, it seems that they too came over to the camp of the conquerors willingly, but in Syria, at least, they were few in number and they had little influence at that time. We shall speak of Mesopotamia below, for during the first century of Islam (until 750) the first dynasty of the caliphs, the Umayyads, chose to live in Damascus. They looked to the West, and Islam's budding culture, its customs and traditions, took shape under Grecian and Syro-Christian influences.

Doubtless the already deeply rooted Christian aversion to the Jews also became part of that heritage. The terms for the capitulation of Jerusalem offer an illustration. Over the years, Palestine had been the site of bloody battles: the Persians had attacked it in 614, the local Jews had allied themselves with the Persians, and then, after the Byzantine reconquest in 629, the Christians had taken cruel revenge.

Emperor Heraclius—the same one who is supposed to have
asked King Dagobert to expel the Jews from France—authorized the Christian population to exercise summary justice toward the Jews, and even banned them from the city of
Jerusalem.[1] This same ban is supposed to have been renewed by Caliph Umar, when he in turn seized the Holy
City in 638. Among other "guarantees" given to the Christians: "They shall not be persecuted in matters of religion
and no one among them shall be harassed in the slightest to
make him believe"; also: "The Jews shall not inhabit the city
jointly with them" (43). Even if the episode is apocryphal
(which some specialists currently consider it) (44), the
legend is nonetheless typical.

While making these political concessions, the Moslems
also borrowed many traditions and legends from the conquered peoples, especially from the Christians, which they
appropriated and added to their own store—as often happens in such cases. We shall return to that heritage, but for
now we shall simply recall a classical Moslem tradition that
is really just a travesty of one of the stories with which the
Christians liked to embellish the biography of Jesus.

According to Ibn Ishaq (the first biographer of Mohammed) the future Prophet was accompanying his uncle on a
trip to Syria when the caravan stopped near a hermitage
where a pious and wise Christian monk named Bahaira
lived. The monk invited the travelers to eat. Young Mohammed had remained outside to guard the camels, but the

[1] According to Byzantine chroniclers the Jews had slaughtered the
Christians after the arrival of the Persians, and the Christians were getting
ready to take their revenge when the Byzantines arrived. Heraclius, who was
unaware of the atrocities the Jews had committed a short time before, had
at first sworn to protect them. However, on the insistence of the Christians
of Jerusalem, he obtained release from his oath in return for a week's fast:
"Pro juramenti transgressione per unam hebdomadam esse jejunandam."
(Georgius Monachus, *Chronicon breve*, Migne, *Patrologie grecque*, Vol.
110, p. 830.) The story is unlikely (how could the emperor have been
unaware of the Jewish atrocities at that point?) but typical of the way
the Oriental ecclesiastical chroniclers took anti-Semitism for granted.

hermit insisted that the young boy join them. Then he asked the uncle many questions about the child, for he had seen between his shoulders the seal of the gift of prophecy. And in conclusion, he said to the uncle: "Return to your country with your nephew and look out for the Jews, for if they see him and recognize what I have recognized in him, they will seek to do him harm."

The same legend, with the child Jesus as its hero, is part of the fund of legends of Oriental Christianity. It appears in a "Gospel of Childhood" and also in an apocryphal Apocalypse, called the "Apocalypse of Bahaira" (45).

It is interesting to note that later on the Christians joined the Jews as future enemies of the Prophet. This is how the story was told in the tenth century by the celebrated Arab historian Masudi:

"Bahaira the monk . . . revealed to Abu Bakr and to Belal what would happen to Mohammed, and he begged them to give up the voyage, and to warn his parents against the attempts of the Jews and the Christians . . ." (46).

Thus, many versions evolved according to the humor of the narrator and the disposition of the listeners. There is one in which the Christian monk implored the future prophet: "Be merciful to the Christians when you have gained power . . . do not permit anyone to impose any tribute or any tax on them." In another variation it was perfidious Jews who had Mohammed make such a promise. This one was a Christian legend, and it told of how the Jews had him assassinated when he did not keep his promise. The legend also circulated in a Moslem version, and its origin has been lost in the darkness of time (47), but it can be linked to the well-known tradition that Mohammed died poisoned by a Jewish woman.

So once more in history the conquerors absorbed the customs and the way of thinking and feeling of the conquered. For what was Islam at that time, and who were the Moslems? A tiny stratum of rulers, experienced military men endowed with uncontested political genius, who preferred to leave the technical and administrative matters to the vanquished Persians and especially the Syrians. This state of affairs is reflected in certain *hadiths,* which tell how once the Arab conquest was achieved, the lieutenants of Umar the Implacable immediately requested him to leave the Christian specialists in office. "Money has increased to such an extent that they alone are capable of counting it," Abu Musa is supposed to have written him. "In my district there is a Christian scribe without whom I cannot complete the taking of the poll-tax," Moawia is supposed to have reported (48). It is typical that, until 693, the official administrative language of the Umayyad caliphate was Greek and that coins bearing Greek inscriptions continued to be minted in Damascus.

Greco-Syrians too were the top officials and administrators, such as those who came from the rich Mansur family, the next to the last descendant of which, Sahlan Mansur, was finance minister to several caliphs. The Mansur line ended with a young scientific prodigy who was to shed luster on the Eastern Church as Saint John of Damascus. The word "Chrysorrhoas" remains attached to his name not, as is commonly supposed, because his word was a golden stream, but because his family was in charge, among other things, of the irrigation system (Chrysorrhoas is the Greek name for the Barada River that flows near Damascus) (49). It was men such as these who transmitted to Islam both Greek science and philosophy, the study of which was to flourish in Baghdad a few generations later, and the technology inherited from the Roman Empire.

The Umayyads also borrowed from the solid Persian administrative traditions, as can be seen in the etymology of terms relating to the postal system and, especially, to fiscal organization. Even the word *kharaj,* a land tax levied on non-Moslems, is of Persian origin; the *karaga* was already mentioned in the Babylonian Talmud. Also of Persian origin was the custom of having the *dhimmis,* the protected people, wear distinctive clothing or a mark of some kind. It originated as a seal stamped on the neck of the tribute payers who had paid their tax and thus it began as a sort of good-conduct certificate rather than as a humiliation.

But as long as the seat of the caliphs remained in Damascus, Christian influences predominated. The bulk of the population, which belonged to a variety of sects, continued to be administered by their bishops or their patriarchs who were at the same time their secular leaders. This was the origin of the *milla* system, "confessional nations" which are typical of the East even to this day. (The Moroccan Jews in their *mellah* are an example of this.) Out of necessity, but also in accordance with the teachings of Mohammed, the first caliphs showed a remarkable degree of religious tolerance. In many towns they conquered they were content to take over a portion—perhaps a quarter or a half, as the case might be—of the principal church for their devotions; the rest of the building remained at the disposal of the Christians, so that they were practically worshipping together (50).

But perhaps tolerance is not the right word. This was not so much a demonstration of the understanding or even the skepticism that Islam, once it evolved—the refined Islam of the great period—was to evince; rather, it was a matter of summary compromises at a level understandable to minds still hardly bent to the teachings of monotheism. The early Umayyads were first and foremost men who appreciated the good life, eager to enjoy the riches that were available, men who delighted in good food and good fellowship, no matter what the religion. Not content to surround himself with such Christian ministers as Sahlan Mansur, Caliph Abd al-Malik had as court poet the Christian Akhtal, known for his love of Bacchus. When the caliph suggested that he embrace Islam, he retorted sharply: "Never will I go around braying like an ass!" (51)

Is it true that the statute of the *dhimmis*, protecting Christians and Jews, dated from the time of the Umayyads, as the Moslem jurists were to claim one or two centuries later?

These jurists liked to base themselves on ancient and venerable precedents, and they thus attributed this statute to Caliph Umar, second successor to Mohammed. Actually, it was enacted much later. Be that as it may, here are the terms and conditions—a dozen of them—of the famous "Umar pact."

There were six essential conditions:

The *dhimmis* shall not make any use of the Koran in jest and shall not falsify its text.

They shall not speak of the Prophet falsely or contemptuously.

They shall not speak of the cult of Islam irreverently or derisively.

They shall not touch a Moslem woman nor seek to marry her.

They shall not attempt to lead a Moslem from his faith nor make any attempt against his property or his life.

They shall not give succor to the enemy nor harbor spies.

Breaking any of these six conditions would nullify the treaty and deprive the *dhimmis* of Moslem protection.

There were six more conditions that were regarded as desirable; violation of these was punishable by fines or other penalties, but did not nullify the treaty of protection:

The *dhimmis* shall wear the *ghiyar*, a distinctive sign, which was ordinarily yellow for Jews, blue for Christians.[2]

They shall not build any house higher than those of the Moslems.

They shall not ring their bells nor read their books aloud, nor what they tell of Ezra and the Messiah Jesus.

They shall not drink wine in public nor display their crosses or their swine.

They shall bury their dead in silence and not allow their lamentations or sounds of mourning to be heard.

[2] Note that for the Arabs the color yellow did not have that pejorative sense that it later acquired in Europe. On the contrary, it was looked upon with favor.

They shall not ride horses, neither thoroughbred nor common; they may, however, ride mules or asses (52).

To these twelve conditions, so revealing of the mixture of scorn and benevolence which characterized the Moslems' attitude toward the unbelievers, must be added a thirteenth, which was absolutely basic: the *dhimmis* must pay tribute in two different forms, the *kharaj*, which was the land tax mentioned above, and the *jizya*, a poll tax to be paid by adult men "wearing the beard." The famous jurist Mawerdi commented: "It was demanded with a degree of contempt, for it was a payment demanded of the *dhimmis* for their infidelity; but it was also a gentle demand, for it was remuneration paid for the shelter we gave them" (53).

Thus, a sort of organic symbiosis developed between conqueror and conquered that, with a few passing exceptions, made it possible for Jewish and Christian districts to exist peacefully and prosperously in all parts of the Islamic Empire until our time.

The Abbasids and the Caliphate of Baghdad

Arab domination aroused much resentment in the conquered lands, which became all the more virulent as, from generation to generation, Islam spread and the new converts—particularly those who were officials or technicians—did not relish being looked down on as second-class Moslems. The assassination of the Prophet's son-in-law Ali on the eve of the accession of the Umayyads gave birth to the Shi'ite schism, and here the discontent found a rallying point. According to their ideology, the caliphs of Damascus were usurpers. The Abbasid family, which supported the Ali partisans, started a rebellion in Iran that ended in 750 when Caliph Merwan was defeated and killed in upper Egypt and a new dynasty ascended the throne. This new dynasty immediately proceeded to get rid of the Shi'ites. It then moved the capital of the empire to Baghdad, which had been newly founded, and for two centuries its power was firmly entrenched.

These two centuries are remembered for such men as the prestigious Harun al-Rashid (786–809) and al-Mamun, the friend of science (813–33), but beginning around 900, the Abbasid Empire began to disintegrate. It was too vast to withstand the incessant provincial uprisings and the ambitions of the Turkish mercenaries. There were far-reaching consequences of the transfer of the capital from Damascus— a city steeped in Byzantine influences—to Baghdad—in the center of the richest province of the Empire—where Persian and even Hindu influences were more pronounced and where the court of the caliphs came under the influence of Asiatic rites and festivals. Moreover, this transfer coincided with the era when Islam became the numerically preponderant religion, so that there was no longer a warrior minority ruling over a majority: Baghdad was the seat of a universal ecumenical empire, united by the Arabic language and by the Koran. No matter that the majority of converts to Islam were profit seekers whose religion was superficial; no matter that an al-Mamun could exclaim of the new converts:

" . . . their convictions, I am well aware, are just the opposite of that which they profess. They belong to a class who embrace Islam not from any love of this our religion, but thinking thereby to gain access to my Court and share in the honor, wealth and power of the Realm; they have no inward persuasion of that which they outwardly profess. . . . And indeed, I know of one and another . . . who were Christians, and embraced Islam unwillingly. They are neither Moslems nor Christians but imposters" (54).

Even if the fathers only gave lip service to their faith in Islam, the sons often became the principal Moslem theologians and interpreters. And in the course of the two centuries of the Abbasid caliphate, Moslem civilization achieved its definitive form, thanks to a remarkable amalgam of their ancient technical and intellectual legacy and the monotheistic inspiration of the Koran.

These centuries are perhaps as meaningful for world history as the age of Pericles or the Renaissance. But they still hold many riddles for the historian, for while the political and religious history of the Abbasids is well known, the social and economic history of their time is still almost completely unknown.[3] And yet, how many gaps in the history of our own civilization could be bridged by the answers to these questions, giving us a better understanding of how our world became what it is. For this era seems to have witnessed tremendous changes, which a pioneer in the field, Professor S. D. Goitein, recently termed the first "bourgeois revolution" (55). The origins of capitalist institutions and techniques were once traced to the sixteenth century and later moved back to Italy or Flanders of the Middle Ages; perhaps it is in fabled Baghdad where they will one day be situated definitively. We shall adduce below the few facts— at the moment disparate and fragmentary—which allow us to suggest these views. What we do know for certain is that the incessant military expeditions and the administration of an immense empire—much larger than the Roman Empire— led to the formation of an opulent caste of financiers and the

[3] The Moslem world would seem to have been composed almost exclusively of rulers, wise men, and artists! Far be it from me to minimize their role, which would be going to the opposite extreme, but without trying to revive the eternal debate between those who believe in historical materialism and those who do not, I would say that today few historians of the western Middle Ages would not consider the economic and social structures as an essential part of their discipline.

. . . What do we know of rural life, of the changes, if any, that the Arab conquest produced in the lives of the peasants, and subsequent developments? Do we know anything about how the ancient city turned into the medieval city, anything about urban society? Even in the domain of commerce, which one might think better explored, how many shadowy areas there still are, and how many delusions of knowledge! (Cf. Cahen, *l'Histoire économique et sociale de l'Orient musulman médiéval*, Islamica, 1955, IV, pp. 96 ff.

development of new commercial techniques, and that simultaneously people were leaving the countryside and sprawling cities were springing up. First among them was Baghdad, which the "postmaster" Yakubi described as follows:

"It is the largest city, unequaled in East or West. . . . All the countries of the world have their own section there with a commercial and business center; that is why one finds gathered there something which does not exist in any other city of the world . . . merchandise imported from India, Sind, China, Tibet, the lands of the Turks, the Dailamites, the Khazars and the Abyssinians—from everywhere, in a word—to the point where in Baghdad things are more abundant than in their country of origin. . . . All the goods of the world are shipped there, all the treasures of the world gathered together, all the blessings of the universe concentrated. . . " (56).

From India to the Pyrenees dozens of other cities sprang up, bustling and populous, each with its *suq al Sagha*, money market—wasn't it necessary to exchange the dirhems, the silver coins used in the eastern part of the empire, for the dinars, the golden coins of the West?—and their *qaysaria*, market of fabrics and precious merchandise, for which intrepid merchants and navigators had traveled all the way to China and deep into the heart of Africa. Each city also had its slave market and its artisans' workshops—usually founded and maintained by the state—and each harbored countless hierarchies of officials and soldiers.

At the heart of these human ant hills, which certain tales from the *Thousand and One Nights* describe so colorfully, there was very lively intellectual activity. Just as the Fathers of the Church had once accomplished the prodigious task of reconciling the dogmas of the Christian revelation with the exigencies of Aristotelian reason, now it was necessary to accommodate that reason to a new revelation, studded with Gnostic, Zoroastrian, and even Hindu influences. Certain aspects of this work show the imprint of the Grecian subtlety, which sometimes seems so sterile to us: the heated debates on the nature of the Koran—created or uncreated—inevitably bring to mind the debates over the sex of angels. . . . Their most lasting result was the elaboration of exegetical commentaries on the Koran, the *hadith,* which elucidated the obscurities and contradictions in the sacred text. These commentaries were a series of rules and dictums transmitted, it was assured, from mouth to mouth by the companions of Mohammed and their successors thanks to an oral "chain" going back directly to the Prophet. Which is not unlike the transmission of the Mishna and the Talmud, as we have already pointed out. As to the contents of the *hadith,* often they were no more than a transcription of either Midrashic or New Testament texts (57). The *hadiths* also contained the various rules—often variously interpreted—developing the principles laid down by Mohammed regarding the treatment of the *dhimmis,* those people of the Book. Generally speaking, a great tolerance toward them characterized theory as well as practice, and the *hadiths* even went so far as to quote the Prophet: "To do evil to a *dhimmi* is to do evil to me" (58). This peaceful coexistence of rival religions resulted in respect for the opinions of others and sometimes led all the way to open skepticism.

A remarkable broadmindedness is typical of the great era of Islam. Let us follow, for example, the famous historian and geographer Masudi through his *Meadows of Gold.* In the first volume he tells, in his flowery language, the history of the Biblical patriarchs. But, in fact, who was the son Abraham consented to sacrifice to God, he wonders. "Some think that Isaac was to be the victim, whilst others maintain it was Ishmael . . ." and he gives the pros and cons of the two theses to show that the question is not of such importance after all. However, Masudi was far from being an unbeliever. Further on, in Volume 2, he delights in relating a religious discussion that is supposed to have taken place in Egypt (we shall reprint the amusing text of the anecdote in a footnote; in Europe it was known from one of Boccaccio's

tales, but it actually goes back to the Greeks of Alexandria[4])
and thus concludes on the subject of his hero: "This Copt,
after what we know of his history and opinions, destroyed
exegesis and tradition by putting all religions on the same
level." In another work, "The Warning," Masudi speaks with
great respect of wise men, both Christians and Jews (particularly Abu Kathir, teacher of the famous Gaon Saadia),
with whom he discussed theological matters, apparently one
of his favorite pastimes.

Such discussions, which were inevitable from the moment
Islam granted tolerance and even protection to those who
differed in belief and worship, contributed to the development of a spirit of free thought, if not simply a spirit of
skepticism. For example, the first attempts at Biblical criticism were well before the Enlightenment, for they came
from the pen of certain Islamic polemicists. Thus, in the
eleventh century, the learned poet Ibn Hazm cast doubt
upon the age of the patriarchs ("If Methuselah had lived as
long as Genesis says, he would have died on Noah's ark," he
observed), picking out many other contradictions in the Old
Testament, and, just as Voltaire would do centuries later, he
compiled a catalogue of its blasphemies.

To attack the Koran itself as openly as this would have
been tantamount to profaning the Prophet. But if the Arab

---

[4] Ahmed, son of Touloun, Masudi recounts, was informed that there
was in the Said, in the confines of Egypt, a Copt 130 years old, whose
wisdom was vaunted. The old man belonged to the Jacobite Christian sect.
One day Ahmed ordered the Copt to be questioned about the proofs of the
Christian religion. To the questions that were put to him, the old man
made the following response: "The proof of the truth of Christianity, I find in
its errors and its contradictions, which are repugnant to reason and rouse
the spirit, so inadmissible and confused are they. Analysis cannot strengthen
them nor discussion demonstrate them. If reason and common sense were
to submit them to a rigorous examination, no proof would establish their
truth. Well, since so many peoples, so many powerful kings distinguished
by their knowledge and wisdom have accepted and embraced the Christian
faith, I must conclude that if they have adopted it despite all the contradictions of which I speak, it is because proofs evident to them, signs and
dazzling miracles, have led their conviction toward that belief." (*Meadows
of Gold*, t. II, p. 386.)

thinkers did not dare to do so, or if no traces of such writings remain, there were writers—talented writers—who took pleasure in composing iconoclastic imitations of the Koran, much to the delight of the initiate. This was done by Mutanabbi, often considered as the greatest Arab stylist, and also by the blind poet Abu'l-Ala al-Maarri, prince of the skeptics of the Orient. The latter was objected to, it seems, because his work was well written but did not produce the impression of the true Koran. "Let it be read in the mosques for four hundred years" he replied, "and you will be delighted with it" (59). Elsewhere, Abu'l-Ala attacked religion in general in very strong terms: "O fools awake! The rites ye sacred hold / Are but a cheat contrived by men of old" (60). So "religion, opiate of the people" has antecedents both ancient and of high quality.

Let us also recall the colorful figure of the celebrated Al-Jahiz, perhaps the greatest of the Arab prose writers of the classical era, "quick to throw weak minds into doubt . . . the last of the theologians, the mocker of the ancients, the ablest in finding proofs, the most dependable in inflating what is small and in deflating what is large" (61). Here is an example of his way of treating matters of religion:

"In the Koran, it is said: 'Your Lord *inspired* the bees'; then Ibn Habit and his Ignorantine *sufis*[5] claimed that there are prophets among the bees, for Allah used the same expression 'inspire' for them as for the apostles of Jesus. And actually why not? Not only can there be prophets among the bees, but all bees are prophets, for the Koran has said that Allah has inspired all of them: it did not specify that it was the mothers, or the queens or the males only" (62).

But this banterer was also a remarkable psychologist. In an epistle in defense of the Jews to which we shall return later, he observed that "man indeed hates the one whom he knows, turns against the one whom he sees, opposes the one whom he resembles, and becomes observant of the faults of

---

[5] Hermits or monks, preachers of Islam.

those with whom he mingles; the greater the love and intimacy, the greater the hatred and contention."

As another example of the perceptive spirit of the authors
of that time, let us mention again that amazing observation
of Doctor Ibn Butlan, author of a treatise comparing the
qualities of slaves from different places: "They say: were the
Negro to fall from heaven to the earth he would beat a
rhythm while falling" (63).

In such an atmosphere, it was not surprising that the
dhimmis—Jews or Christians—also sharply criticized the
customs and the religion of their masters. Abu'l-Aswad, the
creator of Arabic grammar, tells that one day the exilarch of
Babylon approached him in these terms: "Seventy generations have passed between me and King David, yet the Jews
still recognize the prerogatives of my royal descent, and
regard it as their duty to protect me; but you have slain the
son [actually grandson] Husain of your Prophet after one
single generation" (64). The Christian apologist Al-Kindy
challenged the Moslems even more aggressively: "Judge for
yourselves, if your master was a prophet as you claim. For is
it the business of prophets to arm patrols and gangs to seize
the goods of other men? Why did your master not leave this
profession to thieves and highwaymen?" (65)

Let us point out again that the intimate intermingling of
men who practice different religions gave rise to inevitable
interpenetrations among these religions themselves, which today are called "syncretic phenomena." We will speak of
these later, as far as contacts between Judaism and Islam are
concerned. For now let us simply point out that it was traditional for the Moslems to take part in the holidays and
pilgrimages of the Christians and to visit their convents and
that certain borrowings have persisted throughout the centuries, notably in the practices of the various Moslem orders
and confraternities. It was also usual that in case of drought
or any other threatened disaster the caliphs themselves
ordered the Christians and the Jews to join their prayers
with those of the Moslems (66).

At the same time, the first great mystics, founders, and moving forces behind those orders of sufism that played such an important role in the propagation of Islam and in its implantation among the masses, often showed their understanding of the other religions. Certain of them came to the Christian convents to study theology and listen to the sermons of the hermits. "Sermons of monks, reports of their actions, veracious news emanating from condemned souls. Sermons which heal us, for we receive them . . ." wrote Ibrahim ibn al Jonayd around 900 (67). There is the story, too, that a certain mystic of the tenth century, passing by a Jewish cemetery with his disciples, exclaimed: "Here are the souls which have been received in Paradise better than ours will be. . . ."

Just as the great Orientalist Snouck Hurgronje has written: "There is in Islam something interreligious. . . ."

It would be easy to find commonplace explanations for this deep-seated originality of Islam and point to the pressing reasons that impelled the Arab conquerors to protect the lives and religions of the *dhimmis,* who were diligent farmers or artisans and pillars of the economic life of the caliphate—a state of affairs that resulted in their receiving an "ideological blessing." But I prefer to stress another aspect of the question, one that perhaps rests on a more profound truth: the gentle precepts of Christ presided at the birth of the most combative, the most intransigent civilization that human history has ever known, while the warlike teachings of Mohammed gave rise to a more open and more conciliatory society. For it is true, once again, that where too much is demanded of man, he is subjected to astonishing temptations, and that he who tries too hard to play the angel plays the beast.

But enough of these speculations. Let us now examine the actual fate of the two religious minorities—Christians and Jews—called upon henceforth to perpetuate themselves in the protective shadow of Islam.

four

Islam and the Infidels

The Christians

We have seen how at the beginning of the Arab expansion the conquerors placed no value on converting the subjugated peoples. Quite the contrary, in fact, for the laws they passed went so far as to penalize the new converts to Islam. A *dhimmi* who became a Moslem had to turn over his real estate—the only thing of any value in the countryside—to his *milla,* his community of origin. (The corresponding *hadith* attributed this rule to a decision of Caliph Umar, who is supposed to have forbidden his faithful Al Ash'ath to accept an inheritance from his aunt because she had married a Jew (68).) Thus it seems that one's patrimony was supposed to remain with the cult of one's ancestors. Actually, the rule corresponded to the time-honored procedures of nomadic conquerors, who found it more convenient to exploit and exert pressure on the sedentary people they had subjugated through taxes and extortion rather than by appropriating their lands. Thus, for the *dhimmis* to provide good revenue, it was necessary to keep them bound to their soil and their religion. They were even (and this has remained true almost to this day) exempt from all military service, a glory that was reserved for believers. The various *millas* or confessional nations often administered their own laws and constituted, in effect, "nations without country" or "uprooted religions" (J. Weulersse), and this is a first analogy with the case of the Jews.

Under these conditions, as we have already mentioned, Christianity did not suffer any losses at the beginning of the Arab conquest; in fact, according to one learned observer, it even continued to attract new converts.[1] Why, then, did it finally disappear almost completely from the vast Islamic Empire?

To get a clear answer to this question, we must look at the cities and the countryside separately.

In the cities, which were the strongholds of Islam, the Christians continued to furnish the administrators, the technicians, and also the intellectual leaders for several generations. At first the conquerors showed a marked preference for them over the people of other sects. They ranked immediately below the True Believers, constituting a veritable aristocracy. The shrewd Jahiz noted this in Baghdad in the ninth century and examined the reasons:

"I shall begin to enumerate the causes which made the Christians more liked by the masses than the Magians, and made men consider them more sincere than the Jews, more endeared, less treacherous, less unbelieving and less deserving of punishment. For all this there are manifold and evident causes. They are patent to one who searches for them . . ." (69).

The first reason Jahiz perceived was the prestige of the Christians, who had founded or conquered numerous kingdoms and who had given the world numerous scholars and sages:

"Our masses began to realize that the Christian dynasties were enduring in power, and that a great number of Arabs was adhering to their faith: that the daughters of Byzantium bore children to the Moslem rulers, and that among the Christians were men versed in speculative theology, medi-

---

[1] "Another cause for the growth and expansion of Christianity," wrote Jahiz in his *Reply to the Christians,* "is the fact that the Christians draw converts from other religions and give none in return (while the reverse should be true) for it is the younger religion that is expected to profit from conversion."

cine, and astronomy. Consequently they became in their estimation philosophers and men of learning, whereas they observed none of these sciences among the Jews. The cause for the lack of science among the Jews lies in the fact that the Jews consider philosophic speculation to be unbelief. . . ."

Jahiz continued:

"Another cause for the admiration accorded by the masses to the Christians is the fact that they are secretaries and servants to kings, physicians to nobles, perfumers, and money changers, whereas the Jews are found to be but dyers, tanners, cuppers, butchers, and cobblers. Our people observing thus the occupations of the Jews and the Christians concluded that the religion of the Jews must compare as unfavorably as do their professions, and that their unbelief must be the foulest of all. . . ."

The third reason for the Christians' popularity, according to Jahiz, was social mimetism:

"We know that they ride highly bred horses and dromedary camels, play polo . . . wear fashionable silk garments, and have attendants to serve them. They call themselves Hasan, Husayan, Abbas, Fadl and Ali. There remains but that they call themselves Mohammed, and employ the forename 'Abul-Kasim.' For this very fact they are liked by the Moslems!"

This shrewd analysis gives us a hint of why Christianity suffered such losses in the cities, at least among the elite. A sort of social snobbery made it easy for the Christians to renounce their faith, and their faith was not strong enough to resist the enormous intellectual ferment of the great cities. At the same time as Jahiz was writing in Baghdad, at the other pole of the Moslem civilization, in far-off Cordova, Bishop Alvaro was complaining as follows:

"My fellow-Christians delight in the poems and romances of the Arabs; they study the works of Mohammedan theologians and philosophers, not in order to refute them, but to acquire a correct and elegant Arabic style. Where today can a layman be found who reads the Latin commentaries on Holy Scriptures? Who is there that studies the Gospels, the Prophets, the Apostles? Alas! the young Christians who are most conspicuous for their talents have no knowledge of any literature or language save Arabic; they read and study with avidity Arabic books; they amass whole libraries of them at vast cost, and they everywhere sing the praises of Arabian lore. On the other hand, at the mention of Christian books they disdainfully protest that such works are unworthy of their notice. The pity of it! Christians have forgotten their own tongue and scarcely one in a thousand can be found able to compose in fair Latin a letter to a friend!" (70)

For their part, the Moslem authors stigmatized the new converts. "The Christian turns to Islam out of greed and not out of love," sang the poet Abu'l-Ala. "He is seeking glory, or he fears the judge, or he wants to marry" (71). Even high dignitaries of the Church were converted; the Christian annals of Syria and elsewhere record the names of numerous metropolites or bishops who became Moslem because they had committed the sin of the flesh or for some other reason (72).

Violent persecutions, unleashed by intolerant caliphs such as Mutawakkil, "the Christian-hater" (847–61), and especially, a century and a half later, by the foolish Caliph Hakim of Egypt (996–1021), resulted in mass conversions. But Oriental Christianity was not dealt its final blow until the Crusades. Until then, the loss was very slow and marked principally by a progressive decline in the social status of the Christians. From the tenth century on, it seems, Jahiz's observations on the occupations of the Christians and the Jews are no longer valid, for the traveler Moqadassi observed while visiting Syria: "Most of the bankers, the money changers, the dyers and the tanners are Jews; most of the doctors and officials are Christians" (73). Thus the Jews and the Christians were more or less equal on the social scale. In fact, at the beginning of the tenth century the Jewish "firm" of ben Phineas and ben Amram was entrusted with the financial operations of the caliphs (see Chapter 5). As to the Christians' preponderance in government, this was to continue for centuries. Their opponents claimed that some of them even set themselves up openly as "masters of the country" and that in robbing the public treasury they were trying to exercise a sort of right of reparation.[2] The *ulamas* complained bitterly about this "Christian invasion"; as late as the fifteenth century one of them recalled that "the exercise by these Christians of functions in the governmental bureaus is one of the worst evils, which results in the exaltation of their religion, in that the majority of the Moslems, to conduct their affairs, must present themselves to these officials . . . it is necessary to humiliate oneself and appear meek with them, be they Christians, Jews or Samaritans" (74). At the time of the struggle against the Crusaders, moreover, these officials were commonly accused of espionage. "If only the Moslem princes had known of the treason committed by the Christian scribes," an *ulama* railed; "if they had been aware of the correspondence they carried on with the Franks, the enemies of the princes; the vows they took for the ruin of Islam and its people; and if they had seen the efforts they made to attain this end, certainly that would have convinced the princes to make it their duty to prohibit them from holding public office and to remove them . . ." (75).

[2] An anti-Christian polemic attributed to the scribe Rahib, known as the Monk (beginning of the twelfth century), the following remarks: "We are the masters of this country [Egypt] in respect to population as well as land taxes; the Moslems have taken it from us, they have seized it by force and violence, and it is from our hands that they have torn the Empire. All that we have been able to do to the Moslems is merely compensation for what we have suffered at their hands; and moreover, there could never be a comparison between what is happening today and the massacre of our kings and our great families at the time of the conquest. I will say, also, that all the money that we steal from their kings or caliphs is legitimately acquired, for it is only a small portion of what belongs to us; and when we make them any payment, it is a favor on our part for which they should be grateful." ("'Fetwa' relatif à la condition des 'dhimmis'," translated by M. Belin, *Journal asiatique*, 1851, p. 458.)

In the long run this hope was fulfilled. Against the background of the hatred and anti-Christian uprisings of the thirteenth and fourteenth centuries, systematic purges took place, particularly in Egypt. In the words of a contemporary, "The Christians, who were not able to regain their jobs . . . began to pretend to practice Islam and to pronounce the two formulas of Moslem law" (76). This was the time of mass conversions.

On the other hand, all throughout the first centuries of the Hegira, the doctors of Islam continued to maintain relations with Christian thinkers and to study theology with the monks or the ascetics. And the Moslem masses continued to participate in the Christian holidays and many of the rites, processions, and days of rejoicing instituted by their common ancestors, who had been Christians or pagans. Because of this common background, as we have already mentioned, many an anti-Jewish Christologic theme was circulated.

For example, there is a defense of Islam, *The Book of Religion and Empire*, written in the ninth century by the Christian apostate Ali Tabari (77). One of the chapters was entitled "The prophecy of the Christ about the Prophet— may God bless and save both of them." In it Ali Tabari wrote: "It is indeed evident to the Christians especially, and to the Jews generally, that God has intensified his Wrath against the Children of Israel, has cursed them, forsaken them and their religion, and told them that he will burn the stem from which they multiplied, destroy the mass of them, and plant others in the desert and in the waste and dry land. On this subject, how great is my amazement at the Jews, who avow all these things and do not go beyond contemplating them, and burden themselves with claims through which they become full of illusion and deception. To this the Christians bear witness by their evidence against the Jews, morning and evening, that God has completely destroyed them, erased their traces from the register of the earth, and annihilated the image of their nation." That such an appeal to the witness of Christians against Jews was not an isolated one is confirmed by Jahiz, among others, who concluded his work (cited above) as follows: "The Christians also believe that the Magians, the Sabians, and Manichaeans, who oppose Christianity, are to be pardoned as long as they do not aim at falsehood, and do not contend stubbornly against the true belief, but when they come to speak of the Jews they brand them as obstinate rebels, not merely as people walking in error and confusion." (While in the Islamic world Christian influences contributed to turning the Moslems against the Jews, in Europe the anti-Christian persecutions of the East were attributed to the Children of Israel—which means those started by Caliph Hakim, who persecuted all the *dhimmis* with equal fervor. See Vol. 1, p. 36.) This Christian-inspired anti-Jewish vein still has unexpected ramifications today among some apologists of Islam. Thus, a Pakistani Moslem, arguing with a Protestant missionary on the subject of Jesus, wrote at the beginning of his tract: "The Jews see Jesus on the cross, and it is a death which, according to the Old Testament, is an accursed death . . ." (78).

Was the converse of this true: did the Jews, for their part, set their Moslem masters against the Christians? Some Christian or Moslem chronicles contain descriptions of riots that are supposed to have been provoked by the Jews; but on the level of thought, whatever the reason, there is no trace of anti-Christian propaganda of Jewish inspiration in Moslem writing.

While the status of the Christians in the cities declined very slowly, in the countryside it deteriorated rapidly from the very beginning of the conquest. Particularly those old granaries, the Nile Valley and the fertile crescent, became the object of heavy exploitation by Moslem masters. The first "bourgeois revolution" in history resulted from the clash and confrontation between nomadic conquerors and an old settled civilization and was marked by a mass exodus from the countryside and the ruin of centuries-old cultures. The peasants, who were at the end of their tether, deserted their lands and became vagrants. To combat this, the Umayyads resorted to Draconian measures. They forbade moving from place to place, instituted procedures to mark the bodies of the Christian fellahs—generally a mark on the hand—to facilitate supervision, and made passports obligatory for travelers. Violators were punished by having a hand cut off, and collective fines were imposed on the depopulated villages (79).

Later, particularly during the period of anarchy that marked the decline of the Abbasids, as well as at the time of the Mongol invasions, civil wars and banditry intensified the suffering of these miserable serfs. The few Christian chronicles that describe their tribulations sound in spots strangely like the Jewish chronicles of the Christian Middle Ages.

In one of the best known, the Syriac scholar Bar Hebraeus described, among other things, a massacre that took place in Iraq in 1285. A band of Kurds and Arabs several thousand men strong planned to kill all the Christians of the Mawsil region. These then "took their wives and their sons, and their daughters, together with all their cattle, and they went and took refuge in the mansion of the uncle of the Prophet, who was called Nakib Al-Alawhin, that peradventure the marauders might pay respect to that building, and that there they might be saved from the slaughter and spoliation of the city. Then the remainder of the Christians who had no place whereto to flee and could not take refuge in the mansion of the Nakiba, remained terrified, and trembling, and weeping and wailing over themselves, and over their evil fate, though in reality it was through those who had gone there [i.e., to the mansion of the Nakiba] that the evil fate came."

The chronicle continued:

"And they placed ladders in position and went up them and captured the mansion, and they looted and robbed the whole of the people who were therein. . . . And they put to the torture not only the Christians but the Arabs also. . . .

And when they had made an end there they went to the quarter of the Jews, and they looted their houses and plundered all their community" (80).

This tale of Bar Hebraeus, with its indictments and its imprecations, resembles in many respects the chronicle of Solomon bar Simeon, relating how in 1096 bands of crusaders slaughtered the Jews of Worms, who had sought shelter in the palace of the bishop Adalbert.[3]

But aside from a few isolated incidents of this sort, little is known about the silent sufferings of these eastern Christian communities that can be authenticated. An earlier chronicler, the "pseudo"-Denys of Tell-Mahre, in compiling the recitals of his predecessors, stated:

"As to the hard and bitter times which we ourselves and our fathers have endured, we have not found any chronicle on this subject, nor on the persecutions and suffering that have befallen us for our sins. . . . We have not found anyone who has described or commemorated that cruel era, that oppression which continues to weigh on our land even to this day . . ." (81).

On the whole, even if we know something about the progressive Islamization of the cities, we still know nothing about the conditions under which the Islamization of the countryside took place. Sometimes all we have is a point of departure and a point of arrival. Thus, in what is now North Africa, where Tertullian, Cyprian, and Saint Augustine once flourished, where there were two hundred dioceses in the seventh century, there were only five in 1053. It is believed that Abd al-Mumin destroyed the last traces of native Christianity there around 1160 (82). In Egypt the de-Christianization was slower, and it accelerated only in response to the advance of the Crusaders. There, great Christian persecutions followed by mass conversions marked the period of the government of the Mamelukes, which began in 1250 (83). Today, the Monophysite Copts make up a tenth of the

[3] See Volume 1 (*From the Time of Christ to the Court Jews*), pp. 43–4.

population. A similar slow decline took place in Syria, where the number of Christians of various sects is at about the same level today. (In Iraq, on the other hand, Nestorian Christianity was almost wiped out during the first century of Arab domination (84).)

Not that the actual life of the fellahs in the Islamic countries was at all changed by their turning from one religion to another. Just as one of the most enlightened specialists on this subject wrote recently: "Doubtless history has been hard on the peasant classes everywhere, but we believe that in no other civilization does one find as fixed or as conscious or as sustained a resolve to keep them outside both the terrestrial city and the city of God" (85).

Anyone who has occasion to work on these questions is struck by the extent to which their study has been neglected. A few encyclopedia articles will be his meager ration. The study of the ancient Christian heresies such as Nestorianism remains the preserve of specialists. What does the word "Nestorianism" signify for the educated man? At most, that vicious satire by Evelyn Waugh or a few paradoxical treatments by Toynbee.

There was a time, however, when Nestorianism was the form in which the message of the Gospels was carried to the four corners of the globe. Inspired by the virtuous example of Saint Thomas (who, according to legend, went out to preach the Gospel in the Far East), between the sixth and eleventh centuries Nestorian missionaries scored great success in the Indies, in the Malay Archipelago, in China, and above all in central Asia and Mongolia, where many warlike tribes were converted en masse. For a time the spread of Christianity in these regions coincided with that of Judaism, but while at the outset the former had more impressive results than the latter, it later died out much more rapidly. Why? An English author, L. Browne, attributes the final defeat of the Nestorians to a theological defect, to the erroneous concept they developed about the divine nature of

Jesus (86). A French scholar, Cardinal Tisserant, explains it more simply by the lack of trained priests. He also stresses the success of Islam, with its "easy morality," among the nomadic Mongols, in a sense going back to the widely held thesis that Islam is the religion par excellence for nomads (87).

But we know for certain that from the time of the first encounters at the beginning of our millennium the Mongols' sympathies were with Christianity rather than with Islam. In particular, the armies of Genghis Khan, who had conquered Asia all the way to the Euphrates but were unable to overcome the bitter resistance of the Mamelukes, tried to form an alliance with Christian Europe for the purpose of putting down Islam once and for all. At the end of the thirteenth century, Khan Arghun sent Nestorian ambassadors to Europe for this purpose, and he also offered to convert to Christianity himself. But at the Holy See as well as at the courts of France and England, these emissaries were received indifferently, if not scornfully. Shortly after that humiliation, Khan Arghun's successor, Hulagu, finally opted for Islam (88). His conversion was a milestone; afterward, in both Asia and Africa, Islam was always to make greater inroads than Christianity, especially after the latter allowed itself to be carried along on the wave of colonial expansion and consequently became feared and hated.

And here is some more food for thought. Until approximately the end of the first millennium, Christianity was a religion in continuous expansion. In a few short centuries the Christian flame had spread peacefully throughout the ancient world; after the fall of the Roman Empire, and even after the Islamic invasions, that flame continued to burn with its ancient ardor while obscure and peaceful missionaries carried it all the way to the North Pole and to the shores of the Pacific.

Charlemagne, however, who had had himself crowned emperor at Rome, evangelized the Saxons not by word but by fire and iron. After such resort to the "secular arm" had become a custom of the Church, and particularly after the triumph at Canossa, when the papacy preached the Crusades and threw Christian troops into battle against the Holy Land and the East, the progress of evangelization stopped completely. Could it be that the Crusades were actually the clergy's great treason? What they did was not only to harden the hearts of the Jews—massacred by the thousands by bands of Crusaders—but also the hearts of the Moslems, pious worshippers of Jesus who were set upon by the fierce contemners of Mohammed.[4] The result was that the Crusades led to the almost complete disappearance of Christianity in the lands of Islam. They marked the high point after which Christian expansion was not only halted but reversed. This process, which like the expansion has also continued for almost a millennium, seems irrevocable, particularly considering not only the losses experienced on foreign fronts but also the internal loss that has been going on for more than a century in face of what it is agreed is a "paganization" of the Europeans, both intellectuals and workers. Viewed against the background of this course of events, the religious revivals that spring up from one generation to the next are mere flashes in the pan. While the Communist offensive is tearing down whole walls of the Christian edifice in Europe and in Asia, Islam is making steady progress in Africa. It looks as though the ebb of Christianity has coincided with the preponderance of Western civilization, as though in the long run the paradox of an evangelical message sustained by force revealed itself for what it was: an indefensible contradiction.

[4] We have seen that the Moslem "Holy War" was extended to the Christians at the time of the Crusades. As for the distortion of the figure of Mohammed, the great Italian orientalist F. Gabrieli suggests this in a few lines: *La deformazione odiosa, per quarto ingenua, che la leggenda medievale d'Occidente compì sulla persona di Maometto, con tratti che qui e superfluo rievocare, e che contastono per un musulmano dolorosamente con l'aureola di rispetto e venerazione che ha recinto sempre, sulle orme del Corano, la pur alterata figura del Redentore cristiano. . . .* (F. Gabrieli, *Storia e civiltà musulmana*, Naples, 1947, p. 252.)

The Jews

As we have already said, the oppressed and humble Jewish communities of Syria, Palestine, and Egypt under the Christian empire, and the flourishing center of Mesopotamia under Persian domination, joyously welcomed the Moslem invaders. The rest of the population did the same, but in the case of the Jews there seems to have been an extra attraction, which has often been noted and referred to as the close "relationship" of "Semitic cousins."

Relationship: the notion merits closer examination, for it carries a powerful emotional charge and thus constitutes an active historical factor. Looking at the era we are discussing—the first centuries of the Hegira—there is no reason for saying that the Jews were more closely "related" to the Arabs than to their neighbors, the Christian fellahs, or to the Byzantine or Persian population as a whole. Moreover, such a biological ("racial") relationship, even if it existed, could never be proved. In the opinion of the experts the peoples of this area today show indefinable mixtures, and very probably this was also true in ancient times. In sum, looked at in this way, the question does not make sense and consequently is of no interest. Linguistically, however, the Arabic language comes from the same root as Hebrew and Aramaic, the lingua franca of the time. (They are all "Semitic" languages, whose particular structure gives a similar inflection to the way of thinking.[5])

[5] Lately Louis Massignon has shown the significance of this relationship for the development of religious thought: "The general grammatical conditions (lexicon, morphology, syntax) of our Indo-European languages determine a presentation of an idea quite different from the form it would take in the Semitic languages. The Arian presentation of an idea . . . is periphrastic. It is achieved by means of words with unstable and nuanced outlines, and endings capable of being modified by appositions and groupings. The verbal tenses soon became relative to the agent, "egocentric," "polytheistic." Finally, the word order is didactic, hierarchical in ample sentences thanks to graduated conjunctions. The Semitic presentation of

The tradition of a common origin of the Jews and the Arabs goes back, as we know, to the Book of Genesis: Ishmael, first-born of Abraham, who was driven into the desert with his mother Hagar, became the ancestor of the Arabs (the patriarch is also supposed to have sent "eastward" the six sons he had afterward by Keturah, another concubine; see Genesis 16: 10–12 and 25: 6). In Isaiah 21: 13 the Arab caravans are called "caravans of Dedanites": to the commentators, another proof of the relationship, for *Dedan* means "cousin." Moreover, in Jewish texts the Moslems are generally termed Ishmaelites. The Koran, for its part, makes this version integrally its own: not only is Abraham the common ancestor, but he, together with his son Ishmael, built the temple of Mecca (Sura II, 121). We have already spoken of the veneration the Prophet showed for those he considered as his best respondents; in any case, numerous verses of the Koran are dedicated to the glorification of the patriarchs and the prophets:

"Among the descendants of Abraham, we favor with our light David, Solomon, Job, Moses and Aaron. It is thus we reward virtue.

"And Zechariah and John and Jesus and Elias—each one of the righteous. And Ismael and al-Yasa [probably Elisha] and Jonah and Lot—each one We gave preference above the worlds."

---

an idea is gnomic. It resorts to rigid words with immutable and always perceptible roots. Only slight modalization is permitted, all internal and abstract—consonants interpolated by sense—vocal nuances by acceptance. . . . The verbal tenses, even today, are "absolute." They concern only the action; they are "theocentric," affirming the transcendence and the imminence of the single agent. Finally, the order of the words is "lyrical," parceled in halting phrases, condensed, autonomous. Hence the misunderstanding of those who, not knowing how to enjoy the powerful and explosive concision of the Semitic languages, consider them unsuited for mysticism, even though they are the languages of the revelation of transcendent God, of the prophets and the psalms." (L. Massignon, *Essai sur les origines du lexique technique de la mystique musulmane*, p. 48.)

This is but one example (Koran, VI, 85–86) among many (89).

Later, the theology of Islam was developed chiefly in Baghdad, that is, in that Mesopotamia which for centuries was the fortress of Jewish tradition. Jews who had converted to Islam, such as Abdallah ibn Salam and Kaab l'Ahbar, helped determine the form and methods of Islam (90): we have already pointed out the similarities in construction between the Talmud and the *hadiths*. And the religious folklore of the first centuries of Islam was abundantly fed by Jewish sources, from the marvelous stories of the patriarchs and the prophets from the Haggadah; those legends, known under the significant title of "Israiliyah," have remained popular to this day.

Thus, in various areas and in different ways, an awareness of the relationship between the Arabs and the Jews solidified. Let us also recall that the barrier of jealousy that exists between circumcised and uncircumcised could not exert its indefinable but definite influence in this instance, and that the observances relative to the pure and the impure were similar among the Jews and the Moslems.[6] All of these various factors doubtless contributed to the rise in the prestige and social standing of the Jews, which is reflected in many Jewish maxims and legends of the time.

Thus the legend tells how Bostanai, the first exilarch of the Moslem era, was solemnly enthroned by Caliph Umar, who wanted this descendant of King David to marry a captive Persian princess. Or the prophecy attributed to Rab, the founder (in the third century) of the Academy of Sura: "Rather under Ishmael than under a stranger!" (91) Or,

[6] Here is Louis Massignon's view on this matter: "For the Moslem, the Jew is canonically pure, his meat is licit, thus it is better to leave the silver trade (and its contact) to him, for the ordinary Christian, who eats blood and pork and drinks wine and beer, touches dead bodies and dogs, is the worst of the ten impurities. . . ." (*"La Futuwwa ou 'pacte d'honneur' artisanal entre les travailleurs musulmans au moyen âge,"* la *Nouvelle Clio*, May–October, 1952, p. 175, No. 1.)

around 750, an apocalypse, "the secret visions of Rabbi Simon ben Yochaï" according to which the "kingdom of Ishmael was destined by God to restore the house of David to its throne after having overthrown 'the domination of Edom'" (that is, the Christians) (92). Or again, that proliferation of Judeo-Moslem sects that will be discussed below.

The quasi-royal powers of the exilarch and the prestige he enjoyed at the court of the caliphs offer further evidence of the respect of the Moslems for the house of David. A Talmudist of the tenth century, Nathan ha-Babli, has left the following description:

"When the exilarch leaves his house, he does so only in a carriage of state, accompanied by a large retinue. If the exilarch desires to pay his respects to the King, he first asks permission to do so. As he enters the palace the King's servants hasten to meet him, among whom he liberally distributes gold coin, for which provision has been made beforehand. When led before the King his seat is assigned to him. The King then asks what he desires. He begins with carefully prepared words of praise and blessing, reminds the King of the customs of his fathers, gains the favor of the King with appropriate words, and receives written consent to his demands; thereupon, rejoiced, he takes leave of the King" (93).

Benjamin of Tudela, the famous twelfth-century voyager, in his pride as a Jew was no less amazed at such glory: "For thus Mohammed commanded . . . and ordered that every one, whether Mohammedan or Jew or belonging to any other nation in his dominion, should rise before him (the Exilarch Daniel) and salute him, and that any one who should refuse to rise up should receive 100 stripes. And every fifth day when he goes to pay a visit to the great Caliph, horsemen, Gentiles as well as Jews, escort him, and heralds proclaim in advance 'Make way before our Lord, the son of David, as is due unto him.'" (94).

Having visited all the countries of the East and the West,

Benjamin of Tudela often mentions the good relations between Jews and Moslems. Of the Caliph Al Abbasi, he says: "This great king . . . is kind unto Israel . . . is well versed in the law of Israel. He reads and writes the holy language (Hebrew)." Describing the grave of Ezekiel (who according to tradition died in Persia), he told how the Jews built a great synagogue there. "Distinguished Mohammedans also come hither to pray, so great is their love for Ezekiel the Prophet." Both also prayed at the grave of the prophet Daniel, and thus we can see the practical meaning of common devotions, which we have already mentioned and which have persisted until modern times (95).

Documents discovered in Cairo and recently deciphered show that in the eleventh century the Egyptian caliphs of the famous Fatimid dynasty paid a regular subsidy for the upkeep of the rabbinical academy of Jerusalem (96). The caliphs, who surrounded themselves with Jewish ministers and counselors, were known as Judeophiles to the point where their enemies, in a practice that did not begin yesterday, accused them (quite wrongly) of themselves being of Jewish stock (97).

There is every indication that the favorable conditions of a common cultural background helped make Jewish scholars and theologians receptive to Arab thought. In fact, on this level the closeness of the Judeo-Arabic interpretation can be seen in influences that worked both ways: the Jews helped mold the doctrine of Islam, and the preoccupation of Arab thinkers with profane studies, with the "Greek sciences," produced profound echoes among the Jews of that time. While efforts at Hellenization a thousand years before had not produced lasting results and, on the contrary, had caused uprisings such as that of the Maccabees, under Islam Jewish thought opened wide to Greek rationalism. At the most extreme, there were some Jewish freethinkers who openly propagated very heretical concepts. At the beginning of the ninth century, a certain Hayawaith of Balkh did not hesitate to doubt the Biblical miracles and even revolted against the idea of a chosen people: "How could God divide the people into his own and strangers, and state that his heritage was destined only for the people of Israel?" (98) Jewish skepticism has always been the child of the environment. That Hayawaith was not alone can be seen from another manuscript dating from the same time, in which Biblical analysis goes even further, in the name of the morality of the Decalogue itself: "How," the anonymous author of this work wonders, "could the Eternal order His prophet Hosea to take a prostitute as wife?"—and so on (99). But this was only the undertaking of a few isolated scholars, perhaps influenced more by Manichaeism or Zoroastrianism than by Hellenism (100), for the prevailing current of that time led to a harmonious conciliation between Biblical revelation, interpreted allegorically, and Greek science and philosophy. That effort, which was begun by the famous Gaon Saadia and other Talmudists, reached what was to be its definitive expression for several centuries in the monumental work of Moses Maimonides, whose memory to this day is revered by Jewish, Christian, and Moslem theologians alike.

This open-mindedness, this new receptiveness of Judaism to external influences, has impressed historians for many years. They have given many different explanations, each of which, doubtless, contains a bit of the truth. The essence can be summarized in a few words: because of the very high level of Arab civilization, it had something to offer the Jews, and what it offered was developed and presented in a manner and a language that were accessible and familiar to them. Arabic, according to Maimonides and numerous other authors, was nothing more than an inferior form of Hebrew (101). Moreover, it is known that the grammar and syntax of Hebrew as well as the punctuation of the vowels date from that time, the creation of anonymous Masorites who doubtless worked under the influence and in imitation of learned Arab philology. Moreover, as Arabic had become the daily language of the Jews, even works of a strictly religious nature were often written in that language. In their content, too, certain Islamic accents are sometimes revealed. Thus, in a letter of consolation to his persecuted brothers, the father of Maimonides, himself a famous Talmudist, spoke of God and his Apostle (Moses) in terms partially borrowed from the Koran, referring to Abraham by the paraphrase the "Mahdi of God" (102). There is nothing heterodox in this; just as the great culture and the broadmindedness of his illustrious son did not cause him to deviate by one iota from the traditional commandments of Judaism. One has only to read his *Iggeret Teman* (epistle to the persecuted Jews of Yemen) and the ingenious and eloquent way he explained the past and present persecutions to which the Jews were exposed on the part of "nations instigated by envy and impiety."[7]

[7] "Remember, ours is the true and authentic Divine religion, revealed to us through Moses, the master of the former as well as the later prophets, by means of which God has distinguished us from the rest of mankind, as Scripture says, 'Only the Lord had a delight in thy fathers to love them and He chose their seed after them, even you above all peoples' (Deuteronomy 10:15). This did not happen because of our merits, but rather as an act of Divine grace, and on account of our forefathers who knew God. . . . Therefore all the nations instigated by envy and impiety rose up against us, and all the kings of the earth motivated by injustice and enmity applied themselves to persecute us. They wanted to thwart God, but he cannot be thwarted. Ever since the time of Revelation, every despot or slave that has attained to power, be he violent or ignoble, has made it his first aim and his final purpose to destroy our law, and to vitiate our religion, by means of the sword, by violence, or by brute force, such as Amalik, Sisera, Sennacherib, Nebuchadnezzar, Titus, Hadrian, may their bones be ground to dust and others like them. This is one of the two classes which attempt to foil the Divine will.

"The second class consists of the most intelligent and educated among the nations, such as the Syrians, Persians and Greeks. These also endeavor to demolish our law and to vitiate it by means of arguments which they invent, and by means of controversies which they institute. They seek to render the Law ineffectual and to wipe out every trace thereof by means of their polemical writings, just as the despots plan to do it with the sword. But neither the one nor the other shall succeed. We possess the divine assurance given to Isaiah concerning any tyrant who will wish to undermine our Law and to annihilate it by weapons of war, that the Lord will demolish them so that they will have no effect. This is only a meta-

Nevertheless, in another famous epistle, *Iggeret ha-Chemad* (Letter to the Apostates), that same Maimonides absolved the Jews who, threatened with death, pretended to embrace Islam. It is meritorious, he said in substance, to forfeit one's life in such a case; but it is not in any case an obligation. In support of this thesis, he stated specifically that the persecutors were often content with a brief profession of faith, "Allah is one, and Mohammed is his prophet" and for the rest let the Jews live according to their customs and practice the commandments of the Torah.

Later, one of his epigones of the fourteenth century, Moses of Narbonne, went so far as to state that the prayer of the Moslems was irreproachable, because they professed the oneness of God and they were circumcised (103).

Given such laxity among the teachers, it is not surprising that many of the simple faithful attempted to follow the Law of Moses and that of Mohammed at the same time. A Spanish cabalist, Joseph ben Schalom, has left a most characteristic description of this. After stating that "the Chris-

---

phorical way of saying that his efforts will be of no avail, and that he will not accomplish his purpose. In like manner whenever a disputant shall attempt to demonstrate the falsity of our Law, the Lord will shatter his arguments and prove them absurd, untenable, and ineffective. The Divine promise is contained in the following verse, 'No weapon that is formed against thee shall prosper; and every tongue that shall rise against thee in judgment thou shalt condemn' (Isaiah 54:17). . . .

"After that there arose a new sect which combined the two methods, namely, conquest and controversy, into one, because it believed that this procedure would be more effective in wiping out every trace of the Jewish nation and religion. It, therefore, resolved to lay claim to prophecy and to found a new faith, contrary to our Divine religion, and to contend that it was equally God-given. Thereby it hoped to raise doubts and to create confusion, since one is opposed to the other and both supposedly emanate from a Divine source, which would lead to the destruction of both religions. For such is the remarkable plan contrived by a man who is envious and querulous. He will strive to kill his enemy to save his own life, but when he finds it impossible to attain his objective, he will devise a scheme whereby they both will be slain." (Translated by B. Cohen, *Moses Maimonides, Epistle to Yemen,* American Academy for Jewish Research, 1952, pp. ii–iii.)

tians are integrally idolaters" and that "the Moslems . . . also follow an idolatrous cult" this enemy of philosophy continued thus:

"Consider carefully the foolishness of those of our co-religionists who praise and exalt the religion of the Moslems, thus transgressing the precept of the Law: 'Do not find any grace in them.' Not content with that, when the Moslems profess their faith at the hour when they gather in the mosques, these Jews who are poor in spirit, who have nothing to do with religion, go with them, reciting by their side the *Hear, O Israel.* Then they give the highest praise to the nation of that despicable individual [Mohammed]. As a result of this attitude, they and their children cling to the Moslems, they vilify the holy religion of Israel, deny the Law of the Lord and follow emptiness and vanity. I am not surprised to see the simple people of our nation praise the Moslems; what distresses me is that even those who pretend to be in fact of the religion of Israel, I mean certain notables of our community, proclaim praise of the Moslems and bear witness to their unitarian faith" (104).

From such views and such practices we can get a better idea of the relations between Judaism and Islam and see how they differed from the relations between the Jews and the Christians in the same era. In addition to affinities of language and culture, the religious teaching itself of Islam made cohabitation with the Jews easy to the point where it was hard to avoid the conclusion that there was nothing incompatible between the two religions and that one could belong to both at the same time. At the time Islam began, there was a veritable proliferation of schismatic Jewish sects (Isawites, Yudghanites, Mushkhanites, etc.) that professed that Mohammed was a prophet sent by God to the Arabs or even to the whole human race, with the exception of the Jews alone. The Arab theologians made no mistake about these subtleties. One of them wrote (around 800):

"Today, in parts of Iraq, the Jews recognize that there is

no God except Allah and that Mohammed was sent by God, but they pretend that he was sent only as prophet to the Arabs and not to the Israelites. . . . If, then, any Jew recognizes that Mohammed was sent by God, he still cannot be regarded as a Moslem until he states that he has broken with his old religion and clearly sworn that he has embraced Islam . . . for as far as they are concerned, this epithet that they use (the name of *mouslim*) does not prove that they have the true faith. They must still declare that they have repudiated their old religion. Moreover, if a Jew says: 'I have left Judaism' and he does not add: 'I have embraced Islam' he cannot pass for a Moslem, for after leaving Judaism he could have embraced Christianity. If on the other hand, he declares that he has accepted Islam, only then is there no ambiguity" (105).

The above shows how the tradition of Judaism practiced in secret and, where necessary, under the guise of adherence to Islam, was a constant factor in the lives of the Jews whose history unfolded in the shadow of the crescent, to the point where later, in a land that had again become Christian, it led to the extraordinary phenomenon of marranism, a method of adaptation completely unknown in the purely European Jewish communities of northern and eastern Europe.

Under the heading of Jewish sectarian movements, the Karaites must certainly be mentioned. They rejected the Talmud completely, believing that its traditional interpretation of the Old Testament was no longer valid in the era of Islam, and maintained that henceforth the sacred texts should be interpreted differently according to a new and careful reading (whence the name of the sect; *Karo* means "to read"). The influence of Moslem theology and its great effort to interpret the Koran certainly played a role in this. The position of the Karaites has been compared to that of the Protestant reformers. This doctrine was so successful that it led to a real schism—the only one in Jewish history. For centuries it flourished in Persia, Palestine, and Egypt,

then spread to Spain and Poland. Even today it still has
some followers.

All of this ferment was not isolated from the changes that
were taking place at this time among the mass of the Jews—
changes of a vital importance to their history. At the outset,
on the eve of the Arab conquest, they had devoted themselves to agriculture, to the point where the majority of the
rules of the Talmud related to a nation of farmers. Three or
four centuries later they had become a nation of merchants
and artisans, townspeople. This was a real socio-economic
mutation, of which there are a number of examples in history, such as the Armenians, who were still farmers and
artisans at the end of the Middle Ages and became the chief
businessmen of the Ottoman Empire with the beginning of
the Renaissance. In the final analysis it is difficult to determine the reason for such phenomena. As far as the Jews are
concerned, we must take into account the economic upheavals created by the Arab conquest, the prosperity of the
cities and the poverty of the countryside, and the "bourgeois
revolution" of Islam. In the ninth century, for example, a
farm worker earned on the average six pieces of gold
(dinars) a year and had to pay an annual tax of one piece of
gold (106); strong measures were taken to keep him from
deserting the land. On the other hand, at that time commerce was enjoying the impressive expansion that we have
already mentioned. From Scandinavia all the way to China,
enterprising Arab travelers plowed the seas, sailed up the
rivers, and set up their counters. Under Islam, commerce
was considered as one of the most honorable pursuits, even
pleasing to God. Had not the Prophet himself, as well as
many of his companions, pursued it? The hub of these international activities was Baghdad, located right in the center
of an area densely populated by Jews. And there was no
legislation and no social barrier to prevent the Jews from
dedicating themselves to commerce.
Consequently, one could say that the structure of Judaism

at the time of this revolution was not unlike, for example, the Judaism of tolerant nineteenth-century Europe. Thriving communities throughout the Moslem Empire were composed of artisans and small shopkeepers on the one hand, and financiers and businessmen with international connections on the other. Sometimes two or more Jewish communities, one composed of local Jews and another of Jews who had come from other provinces, coexisted in the same city. Thus, as we can learn from the study of names, that period saw an east-to-west Jewish migration; many Jews in Egypt or Barbary bore the names of Persian or Mesopotamian cities. These communities were ruled oligarchically. Rich men—the great financiers—exercised the function of Nagid, or prince of the Jews, in charge of relations with the authorities, and that of Pekid-ha-Soharim, the "representative of the merchants," a sort of consul charged with protecting local and foreign Jewish commercial interests; they often handed these posts down from father to son. (Frequently the two functions were exercised by the same person.)

Despite the scarcity of documents, it is sometimes possible to reconstruct a profile of certain personalities. This is what Arab sources tell us about Joseph ben Phineas and Aaron ben Amram, two bankers who flourished in Baghdad under Caliph Muktadir (908–39) (107).

Ben Phineas and ben Amram headed a banking firm and were greatly trusted by both the rich Jews and non-Jews, who deposited their capital with them. In addition, the vizier deposited with them the proceeds of fines imposed on dishonest officials who had got rich too quickly. Therefore, at the beginning of each month they would advance the treasury the thirty thousand dinars of gold necessary to pay the salary of the troops. They were not always accurately reimbursed, but their position made it possible for them to engage in numerous other profitable operations and speculations. They instituted a regular caravan service between the great cities, across the desert; they organized maritime expeditions bound for the Indies and China; they mounted raids for black slaves on the eastern coast of Africa. They were not ignorant of the art of financial arbitrage, based on the fact that the caliphate of the Abbasids was on both the silver and the gold standard, the former Byzantine provinces having remained on the gold standard (gold dinars), while the Persian provinces retained the silver standard (silver dirhems). The relationship between the two moneys, which fluctuated between 1:14 and 1:20 from year to year, opened vast possibilities for speculation. Financial techniques of that era included not only the use of bills of exchange (*suftaja*) but also that of sight drafts (*sakk*, from which the word "check" was derived), which an Arab chronicler describes as follows:

"The vizier Ibn al-Furat took his pen and wrote an order to his banker, Aaron ben Amram, asking that he pay for his account and without other notice 2,000 dinars to Ali ben-Isa, in payment of a fine which had been imposed on him. Muhassin al-Furat also ordered the banker to pay this Ali ben-Isa 1,000 dinars to be deducted from his account in the bank of Aaron ben Amram" (108).

Giants of finance in Baghdad and bankers to the caliphs for a quarter of a century, ben Phineas and ben Amram may have been the first, but they were not alone. Another chronicle (109) tells us that the majority of the merchants of Tustar, in Persia, were Jews. In Isfahan, known as the second Baghdad because of its flourishing trade, the Yahud section was the business center. The governor of the province of Ahwaz also used the services of several Jewish bankers (the source mentions Yakub, Israel ben Salih, Sahl ben Nazir). Siraf, the principal port of the caliphate in the tenth century, even had a Jewish governor, named Ruzbah (the Persian equivalent of Yomtov).

Farther to the west, in Egypt, let us mention the meteoric career of the sons of Sahl, Abu Sa'ad and Abu Nasr, the favorites of the Fatimid caliphs az-Zahir and al-Mustansir (110). Their prosperity has served as the basis of many an Arab legend. The palace that Abu Sa'ad had built in Cairo is said to have been so large that three hundred trees could be planted, in silver vases, on the terrace. The widow of az-Zahir is supposed to have received a gift of a ship made of fine silver from the brothers. . . . In fact, that widow was a former Sudanese slave girl whom the brothers had sold to az-Zahir. She became his favorite wife and after his death exercised the functions of regent in the name of her son al-Mustansir. Abu Sa'ad became her confidant and her vizier. This permitted the brothers to increase their fortunes tremendously. But it also led to their downfall. The regent asked Abu Sa'ad to recruit a personal guard composed of black warriors for her, and soon the Negro faction and the Turkish faction had a confrontation in the court. The latter succeeded in winning, and the Banu Sahl were assassinated in 1047.

From all of this it should not be concluded that finance and commerce were at any time a Jewish monopoly. Christians as well as Moslems continued to excel in it, and it is impossible, given the scarcity and inaccuracy of the sources, to furnish the slightest indication of the role of one group in relation to the others. In addition, Arab sources mention only the leaders and tell us next to nothing about the activities of the small or medium-sized merchants. For an idea of this, we shall have recourse to a Jewish source that is extraordinarily rich in one example (but an example that unfortunately is unique), that is, the *Geniza* (secret chamber) of the synagogue of Old Cairo.

According to an old Jewish custom a document bearing the holy name of God—which means practically any document of any kind—may not be destroyed. No matter how insignificant its contents, it was carefully preserved in a *Geniza* such as most synagogues contained. But the vicissitudes of fate, wars, and persecutions, together with the destructive effects of time, have caused these precious archives to disappear, for they would be some ten centuries old, with the exception of those of Cairo, which were preserved thanks to the dry climate of the Nile Valley. For two or three generations scholars have been deciphering this inexhaustible mine of information on the intellectual, social, and economic life of the Jews—and the non-Jews—of the time (111).

Thus we learn that the large and small Jewish merchants circulated money and merchandise among all the cities of the huge Islamic Empire and that their activities even extended well beyond its borders. Great numbers of them could be found in all the ports of East Africa, India, and Ceylon. They came not only from the great cities of North Africa, such as Tangiers, Qairawan, Tripoli, and Alexandria, but also from humble villages whose names have been forgotten. What did they trade in? Let us leave the answer to a specialist in the *Geniza* of Old Cairo, Professor S. D. Goitein of Jerusalem:

> "Even more instructive is a study of the goods which, according to the *Geniza,* were shipped to and from India. I have made a provisional list which comprises seventy-four commodities going west and 103 going east. Those coming from the East can be classified as follows:
>
> A Spices, aromatics, dyeing and varnishing plants and medical herbs—36 items
> B Iron and steel (a chief commodity)—6 varieties
> C Brass vessels—12 items
>
> This group may be a special case. I have the impression that North African Jews, especially one, of whom we have many documents, developed this industry in an Indian town with the help of Yemenite Jewish craftsmen referred to in a letter, because the raw material, as well as the ingredients, of this industry were shipped to India from the West.
>
> D Silk and other textiles and clothes, only 8 items
> E Pearls, beads, cowryshells and ambergris—4 items
> F Chinese porcelain, Yemenite stone pots and African ivory—3 items

G Tropical fruits, such as mangoes and coco-nuts—5 items

TOTAL—74 items

It goes without saying that this list does not cover all the exports from India and other Eastern countries known to us from literary sources. Thus timber was a very important item of export from India, but never occurs in my texts, which obviously can only mean that at that time Jews did not specialize in this commodity, although, in later centuries, the timber trade became one of their favorite occupations. Likewise, there is in the whole of the *Geniza*, as far as I have read it, not a single reference to slave trade by Jews, either in Indian and African or Mediterranean waters, while, in earlier centuries, Jews were heavily engaged in the export of slaves to the realm of Islam.

As eastbound (sent from Egypt and other Mediterranean countries) the following commodities appear in the *Geniza* papers:

A Textiles (including silk which, at certain periods, was a means of payment in the same way as gold)—36 items

B Vessels and ornaments of silver, brass, glass and other materials—23 items

C Household goods, such as carpets, mats, frying pans, tables, etc.—7 items

D Chemicals, medicaments, soap, paper, books—19 items

E Metal and ingredients for the brass industry (see above)—7 items

F Corals (a staple article of first-rate importance)—1 item

G Food-stuffs, such as cheese, sugar, olive oil and raisins, linen, oil for lamps, etc.—10 items

TOTAL—103 items

India and Africa exported mostly raw materials and metals, while the Middle East sent mostly industrial products and consumer goods which, it appears from the documents, were needed largely by the Westerners living out in India or Aden or East Africa. This situation has some similarity to the relations of Europe with her spheres of colonial expansion in modern times" (112).

This being the case, there is every reason to believe that the old Jewish colonies of Mesopotamia had become the center of an international commerce and that they were as flourishing as those of North Africa. Unfortunately, there is no source comparable to the Geniza of Cairo for this. The *Geniza* has furnished us with many other precious clues about the lives and customs of the Jews of those times. For example, we learn that contrary to the widely held opinion, they practiced monogamy as a rule, and it was even expressly stipulated in marriage contracts. An indication of the high status of Jewish women of the time is that many marriage contracts contained a clause stipulating that the husband could not leave on business trips without the consent of the wife. Naturally, in those days such trips were long and risky. Perhaps we should also consider this clause in the light of another bit of evidence, that the young Jewish women of Yemen who were renowned for their beauty were an added attraction for many a voyager. In any case, we are left with the conclusion that there existed a feeling of romantic love among these Oriental Jews that was completely unknown in the austere ghettos of Europe. Other documents tell us that they tended to look down on their unfortunate European brothers and to consider them of inferior origin.

It would be wrong to conclude from all of this that the status of the Jews under Islam was always flourishing. In the eastern part of the empire there were sporadic persecutions, directed at both the Jewish and Christian *dhimmis*. The best known, and perhaps the cruelest, was that of the Fatimid caliph Hakim, who in 1012 had all the churches and synagogues in Egypt and Palestine destroyed and prohibited the practice of all religions other than Islam. It is significant that the only way the Moslem historians could explain this decision was to attribute it to a sudden madness of the caliph. In the western part of the empire, Christianity disappeared in the twelfth century, while Judaism prospered (the disparity in their history recalls to us how much better equipped Judaism was than Christianity to survive under a foreign domination). In the twelfth century, first under the Almoravides dynasty and then under the Almohades, there were fierce persecutions from which, as we shall see, the Jews often escaped by taking refuge in Christian territory. (Judah Halevi and the family of Moses Maimonides were among them.) It has been pointed out in this regard that these were not Arab dynasties, for both were of Berber origin, and their intolerance was merely the fervent expression of zeal by new converts. Be that as it may, to me interpretations of this sort seem more valid in the case of princes who belonged to the Shi'ite sect, which had always been intolerant and was so by doctrine. It has been established, in fact, that Shi'ites were responsible for many of the persecutions we know about, such as those of Yemen (one of which, around 1172, inspired Maimonides to write his epistle, quoted above) and those that were endemic to Persia in a more recent past, as we shall see below. But, above all, what we know is doubtless much more meager than what we do not know. The Spanish Jewish chronicler Ibn Verga's terse phrase sums it up: "A great persecution took place in the great city of Fez; but as I have not found anything precise about it, I have not described it more fully" (113).

It appears that the Jews were included in the anti-Christian persecutions of Egypt mentioned above (according to a Moslem chronicle dating from that time, they are even supposed to have implored the sultan: "I beg of you, in the name of God, do not burn us in company with these dogs of

Christians—your enemies as well as ours. Burn us by ourselves and away from them") (114).

But in any case, no matter how many and how intense
these tribulations may have been, a spotty catalogue of
them, compiled by chance from chronicles, will not tell us
what the attitude of the Moslem masses was toward the
Jewish infidel. We have an eloquent indication of this from
the way of life of the Jews, as we have reconstructed it, and
from the broad range of professions they practiced, as opposed to a situation where they were relegated to a single
and humiliating trade. The study of Islamic tradition, its
literature and its fables, legends, and tales is even more
revealing from this point of view. So in conclusion, we shall
embark on this enchanting voyage.

The Sabians and the idolaters soon disappeared from the
Islamic Empire. Besides the True Believers, there remained
only Christians and Jews. Is it possible to detect any nuance
of difference in the Moslems' feelings toward the one or the
other, and if so, what was it?

Few Orientalists have asked this question, and the ones
who have, have not come up with the same answer. Thus,
according to Francesco Gabrieli, "On Moslem lips *Yahudi*
acquired the same shade of scorn and hostility that the term
"Jew" had in the Western world—more hostile and more
scornful than the term *Nasrani*, for although Christianity
was on the same level as Judaism as far as official treatment
of the two rival religions was concerned, it was subject to
less animosity. This was due not to greater doctrinal affinity,
but to the more conciliatory attitude Mohammed had displayed toward the Christians who were his contemporaries,
for they had given him less trouble than the Jews of
Medina. . . ." Von Grunebaum, on the other hand, says,
"Tension . . . between Christians and Moslems was much
more marked than that between Jews and Moslems, probably on account of the backing the Christians were likely to
receive from the West. The *Thousand and One Nights* elo-

quently describes the hatred created by the Crusades. . . . In the beginning, relations between Moslems and Christians were satisfactory enough, much better than those between Moslems and Jews. But little by little, the situation was reversed . . ." (115).

Bearing in mind the maxim "In every literature a society contemplates its own image," let us take a look at the sources. We shall begin with the *Thousand and One Nights*. In this vast cycle, with themes borrowed from all the folklores of the Orient, there are a certain number of Jewish tales. The characters of these tales practice their religion in the Moslem manner, doubtless for the greater edification of the audience, but they are called Children of Israel, and the plots seem to have been borrowed from old forgotten *midrashim*. We cannot resist reproducing one of these tales in a footnote.[8]

---

[8] The following tale, entitled "The Pious Couple," was translated [into French] by Raymond Schwab; cf. "Cinq contes inédits des Mille et une Nuits," *Évidences*, Paris, No. 57, May, 1956.

THERE was among the Children of Israel a man who was very pious and shy. He and his wife earned their living by making fans and mats. When he was finished, the holy man carried them to the streets and squares to look for a buyer; then he returned home and, along with his wife, devoted himself to prayer and fasting.

One day as the pious husband, who was still young and comely, passed the house of a rich and important man, the lady of the house looked out and fell desperately in love with him. Then one day, when her husband was away on a trip, the lady went out, called the pious husband on the pretext of buying some of his merchandise, lured him into her house, closed the door, and declared her love.

The man reacted coolly, but the lady became more and more insistent.

"I would like to ask you for something," he finally said.

"You have but to ask."

"I would like a little clean water and permission to go upstairs to wash."

The lady showed him the way and left him alone with a jar of water. The man performed his ablutions and then prayed.

Afterward he looked around and saw that the room he was in was very far from the ground. However, so great was his fear of defying the teachings of Allah and of disobeying his rules that he gained courage. So he threw himself from the balcony, but Allah sent him an angel who carried him

There are several others in the same vein, which show Judaism as an exemplary pinnacle of faith, Israel being destined by this virtue to remain an example among nations. Apart from this role, which appears to be assigned exclusively to the Jews, many Jews and many Christians appear in the tales meant for pure entertainment, with no didactic aim. Treatment of them varies, and these characters are sometimes good, sometimes bad, with no apparent preference. There are Jews who are usurers, or dishonest magicians, as well as Jews who are *bons vivants,* or helpful neighbors. There are valiant Christian gentlemen and charming Christian ladies, just as among them there are traitors and cowards and frightful witches. (Cf. the Mother of Calamities who appears during more than a hundred

---

on outstretched wings and deposited him on earth, safe and sound, without the slightest discomfort.

He then returned empty-handed to his wife who was awaiting him and told her all that had happened.

The couple performed their ablutions and prayed.

They had hardly finished when the roof of the house suddenly parted and a large ruby came down, filling the whole house with light. "Praise be to Allah, praise be to Allah!" they cried loudly, and they were overcome with joy.

As it was already very late at night, they went to bed. The wife dreamed that she was in paradise, where she saw a number of seats, all in a row.

"But whom do they belong to?" she asked.

"These are the chairs of the prophets and the seats of the companions and the devout men," was the reply.

"I wonder which one of these seats is my husband's?"

She was shown a chair with a hole in it.

"But why does it have a hole?" she asked sadly.

"The hole was left by the ruby that came down through the roof of your house."

With this, the woman awoke with tears in her eyes, sad that her husband's seat was imperfect beside the seats of the other companions. She told him of her distress and urged him to pray to God to put the ruby back in its place, "For," she said, "it would be better to struggle against hunger and poverty for the rest of our days than to have an imperfect seat in paradise."

The pious couple lifted their arms to Allah, the ruby rose to the sky again right before their eyes, and they lived in poverty and piety until the day when the Almighty called them to his side.

consecutive nights.) Many of the tales are set against the background of the wars between Islam and Byzantium or the battles against the Crusaders, and they depict the Christian armies with their kings and their brave knights, while there are no Jewish armies; that is the principal difference, one which is quite natural. In another cycle, the romance of Antar, the warlike "Jews of Kheybar" are depicted (in memory of the battles Mohammed had to fight at Medina). While they are treacherous, they do not lack courage. Moreover, they are allied to the Byzantine Christians (116).

This was exceptional and the judgment of Jahiz Hayawan is not without psychological subtlety: "In weak peoples, pride is stronger and more general, but their state of abasement and weakness prevents it being shown (only wise men know this) like our subjects in Sind and the Jews protected by us" (117).

There is also the *Al-Mostatraf,* a vast popular encyclopedia, a sort of catchall, corresponding to a combination of practical reminders, rules of etiquette, and an almanac in our times. In various places the Infidels and their ruses are mentioned, but without excessive malice. Thus, we learn that to play a trick on the Moslems, a Christian "King of Roum" decided to demolish the famous lighthouse of Alexandria, which was a thousand cubits high. This is how he did it: he sent some priests to Egypt who made believe they wanted to embrace Islam. One night these priests buried some treasure near the lighthouse, and the next day they dug it up. All the people of Alexandria came running to dig in the ground all around the lighthouse, with the result that it finally toppled over. Then there is the story of a Jew who wanted to destroy a vizier. He forged the vizier's handwriting and carried on an imaginary correspondence with Infidel princes that was prejudicial to the interests of Islam. When he was apprehended, he was beheaded.

The chapter "On Fidelity to the Sworn Faith" uses as example the Jewish king-poet Samawal, who had already

symbolized that virtue in pre-Islamic Arab poetry. Adages
warn against the *dhimmis:* "Do not entrust any office either
to the Jews or to the Christians; for, by their religion, these
are people who take bribes . . ." (from the chapter "On the
Collection of Taxes"), or stigmatize them: "In general, it is
permitted to curse those who possess despicable qualities, as
for example when one says: 'God damn the wicked. God
damn the infidels. God damn the Jews and the Christians . . .'" (from the chapter "On Knowing When to Keep
Silent"). The chapter on epigrams contains the following:
". . . it often happens that a piece of wood is split in two:
half to be used in a mosque and the remainder to be used in
the latrines of a Jew." As you can see, there is a little bit of
everything in our encyclopedia. In conclusion, here is a
supremely impartial story, from the chapter "On the Prohibition of Wine":

"A Christian and a doctor of the Koran found themselves
on board a boat. The Christian poured some wine into a
bowl from a wineskin he had with him and drank it. Then he
filled the bowl again and offered it to the doctor, who took it
without thinking. 'May my life serve as ransom for yours,'
the Christian told him. 'Watch out, it's wine. . . .'

'And how do you know it's wine?'

'My servant bought it from a Jew who swore that it was
wine.'

Upon that, the doctor emptied the bowl and said to the
Christian: 'Fool that you are. We traditionalists consider the
testimony of [the names of some of the Prophet's compan-
ions] as unreliable, and you expect us to put faith in the
testimony of a Christian who reports a fact on the authority
of a Jew! By God, the only reason I emptied the bowl was to
show how little faith one must have in such testimony'"
(118).

This shows what a great variety of attitudes and situations
there are in Moslem folklore. As we have already mentioned,
the Jewish adherence to the Law of Moses did not pass
unnoticed. The authors judged it according to their inclina-

tions and their temperament. Thus, a poet made this comparison: "The rising of the sun enchants us as the arrival of the Sabbath delights the Jews."

The theologian Ghazali praised the piety of the Jews: "Consider the Jew and his steadfastness in his faith, which neither threats, intimidation, insults nor admonition, neither demonstrations nor proofs can shake." The poet and freethinker Abu'l-Ala, mentioned above, was less favorable to them: "All that ye tell of God is vamped-up news / Old fables artfully set out by Jews." The theologian Ibn Hazm, in a passage that shows an excellent gift of observation, makes fun of the itinerant Jewish rabbis:

"The Jews are scattered from east to west, and from north to south. When one of their communities is visited by a coreligionist from afar, it makes a show of strict observance and displays an excess of ceremonious precaution; if the visitor is a doctor of the Law, he begins to lay down his precepts and to prohibit this and that. The more he complicates their existence, the more they cry: 'In truth, here is a real wise man' for it is the one who imposes the strictest abstentions on them who passes among them for the wisest" (119).

Let us also point out that, faithful to the teaching of the Koran on charity, its doctors prescribed that it be extended to the Infidels. Witness this apology that adorns a juridical treatise of the ninth century, the *Kitab al-Kharadj* (Book of the Land Tax):

"Caliph Umar, passing a house where an old blind man was begging, came up behind him, touched his arm and said: 'Who are you?'

'I am a follower of the revealed religion.'

'Which one?'

'I am a Jew.'

'And who forces you to do what I see you doing?'

'I beg to pay the tribute and for something to meet my needs and my food.'

Then Umar, taking him by the hand, led him to his own

house, where he gave him a few small things; after which he sent this message to the keeper of the public treasury: 'See to this man and his like, for we have not done right as regards him. After profiting from his youth we humiliate him in his old age. Have him be given something of the alms tithes of the Moslems, for he is of those whom Allah qualifies as indigent when he says: "The alms tithes are only for the poor and needy." (Koran I, X, 60) . . . The poor are the Moslems, but this man is one of the needy of the people of the book.' And he freed this old man and his like from the tribute" (120).

Western Christian tradition contains many an unforgettable lesson of exemplary charity, but one looks in vain for the figure of a poor Jew worthy of commiseration.

BOOK TWO

SPAIN

Part One

Spain of the
Three Religions

five

Moslem Spain

There are, in the old Arab histories, certain allusions to the help that the Spanish Jews are supposed to have given the Moslem conquerors at the time of the invasion in 711. According to a version cited by Christian chroniclers such as Lucas of Tuy—and not without a certain self-righteousness—at the end of the seventh century the Jews are supposed to have hatched a conspiracy to overthrow the Visigoth kings with the aid of conquering Islam. Considering the way they were persecuted after the reigning dynasty was converted to Catholicism, this hardly seems unlikely. The historian Ibn Haiyan states that the Jews let General Tarik into the gates of Toledo, the Visigoth capital, which had been abandoned by its inhabitants. What we know for certain is that as the Arab conquerors advanced, they entrusted the Jews with guarding the cities that fell to them.

Just as in the Orient a century before, the conquest was quick and disconcertingly easy (Tarik's troops probably numbered a mere seven thousand men). And just as in the Orient, historians have called it a "historical miracle." Actu-

strong an imprint as their presence. "At one and the same time they were part of Spain and they were not," Americo Castro observed. "They left Spain very Jewish; they went away very Spanish," Salvador de Madariaga exclaimed, thus putting his finger on the extraordinary epic of the exiles. And, in fact, they have shown a loyalty toward the land from which they were expelled that is unlike anything else in human history. The best proof of this is their spoken language, that Ladino which is really just Renaissance Castilian, handed down for twenty generations from father to son in Salonica or in Marrakesh and revered almost as much as the Torah and the prophets. This is the extraordinary human phenomenon that the next chapters will attempt to describe, as we dig through the dense Christian compost of Spain to its Jewish and Moslem subsoils.

In 1941, at the height of the European turmoil, a center of Jewish history, the Arias Montano Institute, was solemnly inaugurated in Madrid. This new institute was strictly apolitical: neither a gesture of sympathy toward persecuted Judaism nor a copy of those "Research Institutes on Jewish questions" that their friends, the Germans, were then establishing in all the conquered countries of Europe. For Franco's Spain, it was a matter of turning back toward its distant past. Nearly five hundred years after their expulsion, the Sephardim—*Nuestros judios,* as the Spanish historians call them—had become one of the principal subjects for historical research on that side of the Pyrenees. They were also, in effect, a touchstone: was the 1492 expulsion just or unjust? That question continues to plague Spanish honor, and the answer given to it varies with ideologies and orientations. "It was an infamy which has stained our national history," President Alcala Zamora exclaimed in 1935, and numerous Spanish freethinkers followed suit. "It was a necessity, neither good nor bad, but simply unavoidable," defenders of Catholic orthodoxy reply. What is important about this debate is that the Jewish question is at the center of all interpretations of Spanish history, for the rabbis and the sages of Israel were the first artisans of the culture and the language of the land of Cervantes. One could even say that the void the Jews left behind marked Spain with as

ally, the Arian heresy had not been uprooted without some turmoil and Catholicism had not yet had time to put down strong roots in Visigoth Spain. The same factors that had come into play in the Orient, then, probably facilitated the Arab conquest of Spain, which was made all the easier because the reigning dynasty was torn by internal strife—a conflict between two pretenders to the throne. But it was particularly Islam's traditional policies—the time-honored practices of tolerant domination and of a slightly disdainful benevolence toward the *dhimmis*—that enabled it to win over large sectors of the population so quickly. The Visigoth monarchy crumbled like a house of cards. Only in the mountains of the north did a few Christian principalities survive: Navarre, León, and Galicia. These pockets of resistance, bases of the future *Reconquista,* were neglected by the invaders, who, once they reached the Pyrenees, were in a hurry to press forward. In Gaul they were repulsed by the last Merovingians. In Spain, however, they became firmly entrenched and settled there for several centuries, leaving an indelible imprint on the country.

Only recently has the full significance of this Islamization of Spain begun to be appreciated. Today we know what a decisive role the Hispano-Morisco culture played in the development of the philosophy, the science, the poetry—the whole culture—of Christian Europe. Its influence penetrated the highest reaches of medieval thought, all the way to the *Summa* of Saint Thomas Aquinas and Dante's *Divine Comedy.* "Several centuries before the Renaissance made half-dried-up springs flow freely again, the river of civilization which streamed out of Cordova preserved and transmitted to the world the essence of ancient thought" (121). (We shall see the role the Spanish Jews played in this.) As to Spain itself, Spanish historians and thinkers have not yet reckoned the balance of how much the country's national character and spirit owe to the Moslem past. This legacy still lives on: merely consider the architecture, the traditional effacement of women, or recall that the exclamation which is so evocative, so typically Spanish, *Ole!*, is really a transliteration of Allah. Just as *Cid,* "glorious lord," comes from *Sidi.*[1] (Words have their history. The international fortunes of "admiral," that other borrowing from the Arabic, are well-known; it is less well-known that *cordonnier* (shoemaker) is a testimony to the prestige the leathers of Cordova once enjoyed.)

By a curious reversion, at the very time the Syrian Umayyad dynasty was disappearing in the Orient (where the Byzantine influences were giving way to Persian in the caliphate), one of its offshoots came to power in Spain. Fleeing the persecutions of the Abbasids, Abd-ar-Rahman, a grandson of Caliph Hisham, succeeded in seizing Cordova in 756. Other refugees followed him, and the former Syrian clans became the new ruling class of Arab Spain, which then declared its political independence of Baghdad. Baghdad's cultural supremacy continued longer and did not fade until the following century. It is said that in 822, Abd-ar-Rahman II succeeded in attracting the singer Ziriyab, social arbiter of Baghdad, to his court. Ziriyab created a musical conservatory and also taught the Moslem nobility of Spain the proper way to serve food and the subtleties of gourmandise, good taste in furniture, dress, and even make-up (122). A refined, worldly way of life started to develop in Cordova. Intellectually, too, this city began to rival Baghdad. Abd-ar-Rahman II founded a library that a century later contained nearly four hundred thousand volumes. Starting in the tenth century, brilliant work was done in philology, law, poetry, and theology, and at the end of that century the illustrious Ibn Hazm, prince of the Islamic poets and a great theologian, was born in Cordova. Finally, in 929, Abd-ar-Rahman III assumed the supreme title of Caliph and Commander of Believers that until then had devolved exclusively on the caliph of Baghdad. At that time, Byzantium sought an alli-

---

[1] Corneille knew this: ". . . and in their language 'Cid' means 'lord'. . . ." (*Le Cid,* Act IV, Verse 1,223.)

ance with powerful Cordova, and the emperor of Germany
sent his ambassadors. Johannes of Göritz's account of his
years as ambassador must be read for its description of the
pomp of Cordova—how the caliph granted an audience
enthroned "like a divinity, or almost" (123). In the far-off
convent in Saxony the poetess Hrosvitha spoke of Cordova
as the "ornament of the world" (124).

⸴ In those days Cordova was a crossroads of civilizations, a
mosaic of races, religions, and languages. Arabic may have
been the language of scholarship and administration, but the
Roman dialects were still the everyday speech of most
people. There were even some pious Moslem ascetics who to
the end of their days never knew the language of Mohammed (125). Generally speaking, the Christians under
Moslem domination—the *mozarabes*—participated fully in
all aspects of civilization. Some converted to Islam; others
absorbed Oriental culture while remaining Christian. A
large proportion—perhaps the majority—of the population
was *mozarabe*. They retained their old social classes—servants, clergy, and nobility—which were of Gothic origin. In
each province they were represented and ruled by an elected
chief, the *kumis* (otherwise called *comes*, "count"), who was
in some cases a descendant of the Visigoth kings. They do
not seem to have had to wear any special insignia, and
except for a series of tragic incidents in the middle of the
ninth century when clerics eager for martyrdom insisted on
publicly profaning the name of Allah (126), the *mozarabes*
were rarely persecuted.

- It was the same with the Jews. True, information on this
subject is scarce until the tenth century. Arab voyagers tell
us that there were Jewish quarters in the principal cities
such as Cordova, Granada, and Toledo; that the number of
Jews increased due to the influx of Jews from North Africa;
that they were enterprising voyagers and businessmen; and
that they served as scribes to the Moslem chiefs. From the
mention of Jews of Saragossa in ancient French chronicles
we can conclude that there were important Jewish commu-

nities along the banks of the Ebro at that time. The geographer al-Makdisi mentions—and this is corroborated by the Christian bishop Liutprand—that the Jews were engaged in the slave trade, and that the city of Lucena, populated mostly by Jews, specialized in the castration of future eunuchs (but for purposes of Christian edification, this aspect of the activities of the Spanish Jews was later highly exaggerated) (127). The poet Sa'id ibn Sina sang of Andalusia as the "land where children and Jews are polite and honest instinctively" (128). Arab manuscripts mention that it was a Jewish musician, Abu Nasr Mansur, who had interceded to have Ziriyab, the social arbiter, come to Cordova. Another manuscript tells us that there were many conversions to Islam among these Jews. Essentially, this is about all that is known of them, for it was not until the middle of the tenth century that they emerged from the shadows, thanks to the minister and doctor Hasdai ben Isaac ibn Shaprut, a highly colorful character who was to become the organizer of the Spanish Jews and to remain their symbol.

Born into a rich family in Cordova, Hasdai ben Isaac ibn Shaprut, the Abu Yusuf of the Arab chroniclers, assimilated the principal secular sciences of his time at a very young age. First he distinguished himself as a doctor—the inventor of al-Faruk, a panacea that brought him great fame. Abd-ar-Rahman III, the prince who assumed the title of caliph and who, during his long and glorious reign, turned Cordova into a metropolis of the West, made him part of his retinue and, according to the custom of the time, availed himself of the ability and prestige of his doctor for confidential diplomatic missions. In this capacity Hasdai ibn Shaprut became involved in the disputes of the Christian kingdoms of the north of the peninsula. Ibn Khaldun's account of the differences between Fernán Gonzales, count of Castile, and his nephew, Sancho I the Obese, king of León, tells how the Jewish diplomat first cured Sancho I of his obesity, then helped him to overcome his sworn enemy, and finally convinced him to swear homage to the caliph, his master (129). Hasdai was also in charge of receiving foreign missions, and he performed this task skillfully. "I have never seen a man of such subtle intellect as the Jew Hasdai," Johannes of Göritz, the envoy of the emperor Otto, is supposed to have exclaimed after dealing with him (130).

Such high position in the court gave Hasdai the leadership over the Jewish community and the honorary title of *nasi*. Just as his master had freed himself from the supremacy of Baghdad, Hasdai tried to free Spanish Judaism from the traditional pre-eminence of the *geonim* of Babylonia. He encouraged Talmudic studies and surrounded himself with grammarians and writers (Moses ben Enoch, Menahem ben Saruk, Dunash ben Labrat), the very men whose works would henceforth cast some light on the history of the Jews of Spain. Doubtless, this patronage was not displeasing to the caliph, and there is reason to believe that Hasdai, in imitating him, was merely acting as a zealous minister. But his initiatives came at the right time, and a new era began (131). Spanish Judaism flourished and in turn assumed supremacy for several centuries over the other Jewish communities in the Islamic lands and the budding Western Jewish communities.

The name of Hasdai ibn Shaprut is also remembered for his famous correspondence with Joseph, the Jewish king of the Khazars. On learning that somewhere in the Orient there was a mysterious Jewish kingdom, Hasdai sent one of his friends in search of it. He gave his messenger a letter for King Joseph in which he described the country he administered and its history. He did not fail to make a point of his eminent position in the court: all the revenues of the country and all diplomatic matters passed through his hands, he wrote. But as a Jew he would rejoice in knowing that there was an independent Jewish state in the world, and he asked of its origins, its importance, and its glory. "I will then disregard my honors, I will leave my position and my family, I will travel over hills and valleys, land and water, to come and bow before my king."

The reply which King or Khagan Joseph sent him—a document which was at one time disputed but which today is generally regarded as authentic—described the people and the history of the legendary Jewish kingdom on the shores of the Caspian. "I, too," the king said in conclusion, "would like to know you—you and your wisdom. If that were possible, if I could speak to you face to face, you would be my father and I would be your son. . . ."

Even more fascinating than Hasdai ibn Shaprut was Samuel ibn Nagrela, minister of King Habbus of Granada, for the golden age of the Spanish Jews began with him. We know a great deal about this man who had so many gifts, thanks particularly to the autobiographical poems he left (132). The portrait that emerges makes one think of a prince of the Renaissance, just as Arab Spain, with its wars, its intrigues, its small states, and its intellectual ferment, recalls in so many respects the Italy of the cinquecento.

Abu-Ibrahim Samuel ben Yosef Halevi ibn Nagrela, to call him by his full Arabic name, was born in Cordova in 993 to a rich Jewish family. He received an excellent education, both Jewish and Arabic, as was customary. From the time he was very young he was deeply religious, and he was convinced that the hand of God had marked him for a great destiny. "I shall rely on Thy message as on a sword; in the face of my enemies I shall rely on Thee . . ." he exclaimed in one of his poems. After an adventurous youth, about which little is known, he gained the confidence of King Habbus (according to legend, he gained it thanks to skill in caligraphy; in fact he was a past master of the prestigious and flourishing art of Arabic diplomatic formulae). Remarkably, he was appointed to command troops during several campaigns. But this Jewish warrior distinguished himself just as much in religious debates. He wrote a dissertation in Arabic enumerating the various internal contradictions in the Koran, thus arousing the ire of his old friend Ibn Hazm, the famous Andalusian theologian, who attacked him furiously.

"A man who was filled with hatred toward our Prophet

. . . and being conceited in his vile soul as a result of his wealth. His riches, his gold and silver, robbed him of his wretched senses; so he compiled a book in which he set out to demonstrate the alleged contradictions in the Word of God, the Koran. . . . Let the king stay far away from these evil-smelling, unclean people, upon whom God has inflicted curse and malediction, contempt and abasement, infamy, ire, degradation and vileness as upon no other people. Know that the garments with which God clothes them are more dangerous than war and more contagious than leprosy" (133).

Such incitement may have contributed to the anti-Jewish riots that broke out in Granada a generation later. But the climate of Moslem tolerance, marked by heterodoxy in Andalusia even more than elsewhere in Islam at that time, is evident in the praise that other Arab authors heaped on Ibn Nagrela. One of them, his courtier Munfatil, exclaimed:

"Instead of seeking God's pleasure by kissing the black stone in Mecca [the Moslems] should kiss thy hands, for they give luck. Thanks to thee I have received here all that I wished, and I hope that through thy [intercession] my desires will be fulfilled in the next world. When I dwell with thee and thy people I often confess the faith which prescribes the observance of the Sabbath—when I am among my own people, I confess it secretly" (134).

The Andalusian poets sometimes had other reasons for observing Saturday. Ibn az-Zaqaq of Alcira sang, "It is the day when I am with the one I love" (i.e., his Jewish male paramour). "Isn't it most extraordinary that, being Moslem and *hanif*, the best day for me is Saturday?" (135)

Doubtless the contemporary reader will prefer to az-Zaqaq the poet Ibn Alfaxa, who dedicated a funeral ode to the son of Ibn Nagrela. "For me," he wrote, "fidelity is a religion and it orders me to weep for this Jew" (136).

A Jew who is a powerful minister and at the same time a military chief is certainly unusual in the history of the Dispersion. One day, after having escaped from great danger,

Ibn Nagrela swore to give thanks by writing a new commentary on the Talmud. He kept this promise, and the treatise, *Hilkata Gibbarwa,* was authoritative for several generations. Another of his works, the *Mebo ha-Talmud,* is to this day included in the large editions of the Babylonian Talmud (137). But in the course of his wars and his battles this learned doctor of the Law displayed the same wiliness and cruelty as his enemies. In a poem written for the traditional Saturday reading and the edification of children, he exhorted the gravediggers to dig a particularly deep grave for the enemy he had just beaten. And in a letter to his son he advised him:

> Announce good things to the hater with your lips,
> But inwardly beware of his deeds.
> Keep his offenses in your heart.
> When you find the possibility to kill him, do so speedily! (138)

This was the man who considered the usual title of *nasi—* chief of the Jews—unworthy of him and instead substituted *nagid*—prince—a man whose authority was recognized by all the Jews of Spain and even by many beyond its borders. He corresponded with the Jewish sages of Babylon and was the patron of the most highly regarded rabbis of his time, such as the illustrious philosopher Ibn Gabirol. After his death in 1058 his son Joseph ibn Nagrela succeeded him. But the good fortune of this Jewish family had long aroused envy. Emulating Ibn Hazm, the poet Abu Ishak of Elvira exclaimed:

"The chief of these apes has enriched his home with marble incrustations, he has had fountains built from which runs the purest water, and while he has us wait at his door he mocks us and our religion. If I said that he is as rich as you, O my king, I would say the truth. Ah! Make haste and set him aside and offer him in holocaust, sacrifice him, he is a fat ram. Do not spare his parents and allies; they too have amassed huge treasures . . ." (139).

In 1066, during a brief popular insurrection, Joseph ibn Nagrela was crucified by the crowd, and a large number of Jews was assassinated. There is evidence that those who survived had to leave Granada for some time.

Jewish and Arab writings of the time are rich in details about the career and exploits of such Judeo-Moslem heroes as Hasdai ibn Shaprut and the Ibn Nagrelas, but the social and economic life of the Jews of Arab Spain is less well-known. Sometimes a rabbinical source gives us a gleam of knowledge: thus, Maimonides' *Responsum* tells us that somewhere in Spain there was a mine or silver foundry which belonged to several Jewish and Moslem associates, the profits or receipts of which went to the Jewish partners on Fridays and to the Moslems on Saturdays (140). The inexhaustible *Geniza* of Cairo contains documents recording commercial transactions between Jews in Egypt and Jews in Arab Spain (141). Moreover, the proximity of Christian Europe contributed a great deal to the prosperity of those natural intermediaries between the two civilizations—the Jews. For that matter, from the ninth century onward the Jewish community of Saragossa (near the French border) is mentioned in various historical documents: around 825 the emperor Louis the Pious accorded a privilege to the merchant Abraham of Saragossa; in 839 it was Saragossa where Bodo, the emperor's deacon who converted to Judaism, took refuge and was circumcised (142). (This is another evidence of the social prestige of Spanish Judaism at that time.) Two centuries later, after the fall of the caliphate of Cordova, Saragossa and neighboring Tudela, also on the Ebro (the birthplace of the great philosophers Judah Halevi and Abraham ibn Ezra), became for some time the principal centers of Jewish culture. The king of Saragossa, al-Muktadir, had as minister the Jew Hasdai Abu'l Fadl, who was a great lover of philosophy and a sometime poet. He favored Arabic for poetry and finally converted to Islam. At that time Saragossa had a Judeo-Arab philosophical school that had grown up under the protection of Yequtiel ibn

Hassan, a predecessor of Abu'l Fadl (under King Mundir II). Around 1060 the Arab chronicler Ibn Sa'id, known as Sa'id of Andalusia (perhaps a pupil of Ibn Hazm), listed five Jewish thinkers of Saragossa whom he considered worthy of mention, and his commentary is one more evidence of the precise knowledge and insight that so many of the old Arab writers have displayed. He expressed it thus:

"And this [Jewish] nation, to the exclusion of all other nations, is the house of prophecy and the source of apostleship. The majority of the prophets—may God's blessing and peace rest upon them—came from them. This people lived in Palestine. In that country reigned their first and their last king, until they were finally banished by the Roman Emperor Titus. He destroyed their kingdom and dispersed their union. They were . . . dispersed in all directions, so that there is no place in the inhabited parts of the world where Jews would not be found, be it East, West, South or North. . . . When they were dispersed in different directions and began to mingle with the nations, a few of them aspired to the study of speculative sciences and evinced zeal for intellectual accomplishments, so that some individuals succeeded in attaining what they wished from the several branches of learning" (143).

It must be admitted that this description of the Jews by Ibn Sa'id is still completely valid.

One of the five Jewish thinkers of Saragossa listed by this wise contemporary is the illustrious Ibn Gabirol, the author of the philosophical treatise *Mekor Hayyim* (*Fons Vitae;* it has come down to us only in its Latin translation). Known as Sulaiman ibn Yahya by the Moslems, Ibn Gabirol became Avicebron for the Christians, and under this name he had a profound influence on the scholasticism of the Middle Ages.[2] Conforming to the views held by the Arab philos-

---

[2] It was only around 1850 that the Orientalist Salomon Munk was able to establish that ben Yahya, Avicebron, and Ibn Gabirol were the same person.

ophers of his era, Ibn Gabirol belonged to the Neo-Platonic school. Among the principal Christian theologians inspired by him were William of Auvergne, who thought he was a Christian and called him "prince of the philosophers" (144), and Duns Scotus. In Jewish thought, on the other hand, there are no traces of his system—which was difficult to reconcile with the fundamental concepts of Judaism because of his underlying pantheism—except among certain cabalists. (Some have also attempted to detect echoes in Spinoza (145).) Ibn Gabirol (who also wrote admirable synagogal poetry) was described by the historian Graetz as "the first philosopher of the European Middle Ages" (146). In any case, he was the first Western Jew who was a philosopher in the full sense of the term and who developed an original system. Thus, in a way that was typical of the tolerance of Spanish Judaism, of its somewhat "modern" mentality, the first among its illustrious sons enriched universal thought while remaining sterile for Jewish thought in the strict sense of the word.

His contemporary, the physician Isaac ibn Saktar (known as Yizhaki), submitted the Scriptures to the critique of reason (a form of scholarship that, as we have already seen, was quite common in the land of Islam) and observed that the passage of the book of Genesis which mentions the kings of Israel (36:31) had probably been written by someone other than Moses, who had died well before. This is an argument to which the first "freethinkers" of modern times returned when they attacked the Holy Scriptures. In the following century, similar considerations were developed by the great universal spirit, mathematician and theologian, poet and astrologer Abraham ibn Ezra. He was the first exegetist to hint that the book of Isaiah was the work of two different authors. This curious person—simultaneously a rationalist and a mystic—played a leading role in the history of Occidental thought. In fact, that eternal wanderer spent the major part of his life in Italy, France, and England, teaching mathematics, Biblical exegesis, and the hidden movements of the stars in the course of his peregrinations, so that his astrological treatises, copied and translated into all languages, contributed to making his name known and helped propagate the principles of critical reason in Europe (147).

The Jewish authors of this period preferred Arabic for their philosophical writings and Hebrew for their poetry. They cultivated all the secular arts with the exception of the plastic arts, which both Jews and Arabs shunned because of the Biblical prohibition. The traditional currents of Jewish thought also found illustrious proponents. Thus, Isaac ben Jacob Alfasi (Isaac of Fez) composed a manual of Talmudic law that complemented the work of the *geonim* of Babylonia and was adopted by all the rabbis of Spain. Bahya ibn Paquda wrote a famous manual of asceticism, the treatise "Duties of the Heart," modeled on the precepts of Moslem mysticism "in a measure unparalleled even in the medieval literature of the theologians" (148). Its influence extended all the way to the Ashkenazi Jews of the north.

Just as elsewhere in the lands of Islam, traditional concerns coexisted with a strong universalist or assimilative current among the Spanish Jews. The polemicist Ibn Hazm even stated that "while they were convinced of the truth of Islam, the chiefs of the Jews would not admit it out of ancestral pride and the desire for temporal domination; I have observed this among many of their great men" (149). Whatever the case, many Jewish scholars were characterized by a disdain for their own heritage and servile imitation of the Arabs. We have as proof the treatise *Book of Consideration and Memories,* which the great poet Moses ibn Ezra composed in Arabic to combat such tendencies (150). In it, he stresses the principal symptom of assimilation, the neglect of Hebrew. He states that "Hebrew has been forgotten, corrupted, because it has fallen into disuse"; that "its beauty has disappeared and it is held in low esteem because of its sobriety and summary lexicon." Ezra's apology was quite timid. Typical is the conclusion:

"All that I have written up to this point I consider an introduction to prepare the reader to understand what I am going to say now. The figures of speech of which I have spoken conform perfectly with Hebrew; but there are also figures that our language cannot absorb; it is not capable of it and that is why we cannot imitate Arabic literature at all.

"The Arabs then should not criticize our sacred Scriptures; they should not think that we are not aware of Arabic rules; nor that only the Arabic language contains admirable phrases and words; nor that Hebrew is devoid of all these things. Although our Sacred Scriptures do not follow certain of the rules of Arabic poetry, nevertheless they contain numerous elements reflecting the majority of these rules. . . ."

We shall also quote this charming anecdote that Moses ibn Ezra tells in another part of his treatise:

"Once, when I was young, in my native land, one of the most renowned Moslem sages (he was one of my friends and benefactors), a great student of his religion, asked me to recite the ten commandments in Arabic. I immediately perceived his intention, which was none other than to belittle the manner of expression. I then asked him to recite in Latin (which he knew fluently) the first sura of the Koran. He tried, and realized how the beauty was disfigured by a defective manner of expression. He then understood the reason for my request, and did not repeat his own."

Moses ibn Ezra was well equipped to become the champion of Judaism among the scholars of the time. He was both "a great scholar of the Law and of Greek sciences" (151). In his writings he quoted pertinently Socrates and Plato, Diogenes and Aristotle. And above all, he was the earliest of the great Judeo-Spanish poets.

We shall pause a moment longer with his illustrious friend Judah Halevi, because this man symbolizes his time and because his life and his work clearly illumine the conditions and the problems of a Spanish Jew of the great era.

Born in Tudela (152) around 1070 or 1075, Judah Halevi

led an adventurous life against a background of wars and upheavals. The first half was spent in the Moslem kingdoms of the northeast and the south of the peninsula, where he practiced medicine. At the beginning of the twelfth century the invasion of Andalusia by the Almoravides from Morocco forced him to seek refuge in Christian Castile. In a letter that dates from that era, he described the "huge and hard" Christian lords with whom he dealt: "I look after Babel, but it remains sick." In numerous elegies the sensitive soul of the poet tried to interpret the peregrinations of Israel through his own wandering life. "Is there a single place in the East or the West where we can rest our head? How long, my God, will I be devoured by the burning flames which you have made my judges?"

At this time he was under the protection of Joseph ibn Ferrizuel, known as Cidellus (Little Cid), a minister and favorite of Alfonso VI of Castile and one of the first Jewish dignitaries to control the destiny of Christian Spain. A bilingual poem which he dedicated to his patron, a *muwashshah,* was written in Castilian but set down in Hebrew script:

Responde, mio Cidello! venid
con bona albixiara [presents]
como rayo de sol exid
en Guadalajara.

Thus the prince of the Jewish poets is also the earliest Spanish lyric poet whose name has come down to us (153).

Later, perhaps after his friend Solomon ibn Ferrizuel (the nephew of Cidellus) was assassinated in 1108, he returned to Moslem Andalusia. He does not seem to have found peace there. His visionary soul's mystical quest finally inspired him to do something that was as senseless to his contemporaries as it is rich in meaning for distant posterity: he decided to settle in the Holy Land, which had been in the hands of the Crusaders for several years. His friends seem to have tried to dissuade him. He upbraided one of them:

Your intentions have come to me
But their honey hides their thorns
You say that we have nothing to do at Jerusalem
   which is in the hands of perverse and uncircumcised people.
Should we not revere the house of our God
Should we then only care for our friends and our families?
. . . Reflect, my friend, reflect and observe,
Avoid the snares and the ambushes.
Do not let yourself be seduced by the science of the Greeks
   which produces flowers but does not bear fruit. . . .

He departed around 1140. The voyage and the perils of the sea inspired some of his most beautiful poems. But he does not seem to have reached his destination safely. It is known that he spent many months in Cairo and Alexandria, feted and entertained by his admirers. Then all traces of him are lost. (There is a version that says he was killed by a knight under the walls of Jerusalem, but this is only a legend.)

Judah Halevi's poetic message and even his biography spoke of the millenary hopes of Israel. But because of his culture and his style he remains a son of his time. There is nothing more revealing in this regard than the great treatise he wrote against the ravages of assimilation, entitled in Arabic "Book of the proof and the argument for the defense of the despised religion," but better known under the name of *The Kuzari.*

Judah Halevi was a scholastic philosopher, and one of our contemporary exegetic scholars of *The Kuzari* (H. Wolfsohn) (154) even considers him a precursor of contemporary thought. The German, von Herder, once compared his work to Plato's *Dialogues,* not only from the point of view of form but also because of the spirit motivating it. The two principal interlocutors, Haver, the Jewish sage, and the king of the Khazars whom Haver is trying to convince of the pre-eminence of Judaism, speak the same language. Their dialectic is the same, just as if they had been nourished by the essence of the same culture, to the point where it has been claimed that long passages are borrowed from Saint Augustine (155).

A theological discussion, *The Kuzari* naturally reflects all the theological discussions that took place at that time. Influences of Greek thought and of Moslem theology can be detected, particularly that of the illustrious Ghazali. It centers largely on the question of knowing if the universe was created or if it pre-existed for all eternity. But once this tribute is rendered to the great philosophical problems of the time, Haver becomes a historian and apologist. In particular he attributes intellectual supremacy in all domains of knowledge to Judaism—in medicine and in the other sciences of nature, in astronomy and in music. He returns to this on several occasions. It is wrong, he insists, to attribute to the Greeks and the Romans the discovery of the laws and the precepts that King Solomon already knew by his divine virtue. (One Flavius Josephus reasoned similarly; more subtly, certain modern apologists are doing the same thing before our very eyes.)

Here now are other arguments. How can one reconcile for the skeptics (Jews or non-Jews) the fact that the Jews were God's Chosen People with the fact of their Dispersion and the state of abasement that the Almighty imposed on his people for centuries? Haver recalls that earthly triumphs cannot serve as criteria of truth, either for Christians or Moslems, because both glorify humility (the passion of Christ or that of the Prophet's companions) and warn against the pride of the powerful of this world. For both possess part of the truth. Thus, throughout the polemic, which is carried on in a climate of courteous intellectual honesty, Haver renders his due to the ethical value of Christianity and Islam. And that Israel was chosen is, in his eyes, just as beneficial for non-Jews as for Jews, for as possessor of the revealed truth Israel spreads it, in some form, to all the other peoples. The Dispersion "is a secret and wise design of God; thus, wisdom hidden in seeds is buried in the ground, where, invisible to sight, it seems to merge with soil and water—but in the end it transforms soil and water into its own substance; purifies the elements and bears fruit. Thus the nations pave the road to the expected Messiah, which is the fruit, for all will be His fruit, and if they recognize Him all will be but one single tree . . ." (IV, 23).

Here we have one of the most interesting aspects of Judah Halevi, which is typical of Jewish thought in general when it develops within a Judaism that is wide open to the outside world. The stress then is laid more on the meaning that "the sufferings of Israel" hold for all men, and the universal mission that is incumbent on the Chosen People (156).

Such concepts have often portended the death knell of Judaism. In Andalusia the golden age could not last much longer. In 1147 it was invaded by the Almohades of Morocco, an intolerant, sectarian people who imposed Islam by force. Those of the Jews who did not resign themselves to the humiliating and dangerous condition of the Anusim had to leave Andalusia for the more tolerant climates of Castile, Aragon, and Provence. There is little information on the fate of those who remained; no historian has yet studied what became of them. On the one hand, according to an Arab chronicle, they played a leading role fifteen years later in the course of an abortive insurrection against the regime of the Almohades. On the other hand, Ibn Aqnin (Maimonides' favorite disciple) says that they made great efforts to please the Almohades and even continued to observe the rites of Islam when they were no longer forced to, but that they did not find grace in the eyes of the Moslems. Actually, in two instances at the beginning of the thirteenth century these converts were made to wear a distinctive insignia (157). We can suppose that they constituted a community that was Jewish and Moslem at the same time, similar to the sects we have described in the preceding chapter. This may explain how Ibrahim or Abraham ibn Sahl of Seville could at once be both the head of the Jewish community and one of the best-known and most ribald Arabic poets of his time (158).

When in the middle of the thirteenth century the fall of the Almohade dynasty made pretense unnecessary, there is no trace of a massive return to Judaism. Ibn Aqnin compared the Anusim to an incurable disease with which the Jews of Andalusia were stricken, attached to them "like smoke follows fire, like the shadow follows the needle of the sun dial" (159). But in Granada a Jewish community once more came into being openly. In the fourteenth century the physician Abraham ibn Zarzal, a friend of the illustrious Ibn Khaldun, flourished there; he later entered the service of King Peter the Cruel of Castile. In 1391, after the great massacres that bloodied Christian Spain, a certain number of Jews took refuge in Granada. In 1465 an Egyptian voyager mentioned the doctor of Malaga, Moses ibn Samuel ibn Yahuda, among the eminent men he met there and praised his wisdom (160). At the time it fell to the armies of the Catholic Monarchs in 1487, Malaga contained 450 Jews. They were taken prisoner and later they were ransomed by the Jews of Castile (161). In 1492, after the fall of Granada, the surrender stipulated that the Jews could practice their religion and enjoy the same rights as the Moslems. But three months later they had to follow the Jews of Christian Spain into their final exile.

six

La Reconquista

The first reliable information about the Jewish settlements in the northern part of Christian Spain goes back to the ninth century (162). It is obvious that these Spanish Jews enjoyed the same prestige and the same privileged position the Jews enjoyed in Carolingian France. In the middle of the ninth century, there was already a thriving community in the county of Barcelona. It maintained relations with *Gaon* Amram of Babylonia, who, around 870 or 880, sent to Spain a *siddur* (prayer book) written by him. At the same time Emperor Charles the Bald entrusted a Jew named Judas or Judacot (*Juda hebreus, fidelis noster*) with carrying a message and the sum of ten silver pounds to Bishop Frodoin of Barcelona. The few documents and contracts we have from the ninth and tenth centuries show that in Asturias, León, and Castile, as well as along the frontiers of the Pyrenees, the Jews devoted themselves to commerce, buying and selling lands and cultivating them on a perfectly equal footing with the Christians. Typical in this regard is an article of the kingdom of León's *fuero* (common code) of 1020, which stipulated that a farmer who wished to sell a house he had built on someone else's land had to have its price estimated by four honest appraisers, two Christians and two Jews. As far away as Coimbra, there is mention around 900 of a Jewish proprietor of a hamlet (*curtis*). As we will see, the *wergeld*—the blood price to be paid for the murder of a Jew—was sometimes the same as the amount stipulated for the life of a knight or a cleric. Starting in the second half of the eleventh century, at the beginning of that Spanish crusade known as the *Reconquista,* the condition of the Jews in Christian Spain improved even more, and their importance did not diminish but rather increased.

. While in Christian Europe the Crusades marked the beginning of a decline of the Jews and directly contributed to that decline, in thoroughly Islamized Spain the first phase of the *Reconquista,* which lasted for several centuries, actually favored an upsurge of Judaism unequaled in the history of the Dispersion. For the *Reconquista,* that permanent eight-centuries-long crusade, was at the same time something quite different, particularly in the beginning. Thus, in considering the fate of the Jews, it is important that we look at the background and briefly describe the millenary epic that began as a vague, meaningless brawl and became the *gesta Dei per Hispanos,* the crusade which achieved its aims (unlike the Crusades of the East—but that is perhaps the internal logic of a crusade carried to the ultimate, the paradox of a sated quest that then led to the persecution of one part of Spain by the other, as we shall see below).

It is customary to say the *Reconquista* began immediately Islam took root in Spain. We have already seen how in the course of their swift advance the conquerors permitted Christian enclaves to survive in the north of the peninsula. As late as the tenth century they still regarded the people of these barbaric kingdoms with disdain: Ibn Hazm and Sa'id of Toledo compared them to the blacks of the Sudan or the Berbers, impervious to all culture. But they agreed that they were formidable warriors. In the course of the innumerable obscure wars that bloodied the first centuries of Islamo-Christian coexistence, Moslem and Christian principalities formed ephemeral alliances which reflected the interests or the grudges of the moment and sometimes degenerated into wars of everyone against everyone else. "Old lies, old concessions, old grievances linked each Andalusian kingdom to each kingdom of the North. Each Moslem prince had at some time allied himself to a Christian king to raid the fields, attack the city, slaughter the subjects of another Moslem, and vice versa. . . ." That is how an excellent student of North African affairs described the beginnings of the *Reconquista* (163).

՚ However, the Christians of Spain were fighting under the banner of a patron saint, Saint James (Santiago), whose mortal remains were said to have been transported miraculously from Palestine to the shrine of Santiago de Compostela, in the extreme northwest of the peninsula. In the network of legends that were woven about this gentle apostle, he became the younger brother and even the double of Jesus, and at the same time a knight in shining armor, doubtless inspired by the warrior figure of Mohammed (164). The shrine of Santiago de Compostela soon became one of the principal sites of pilgrimage for all of Carolingian Europe, and thus the influence of the young Christian culture began to counterbalance that of the caliphate of Cordova, so that the people of Castile or Aragon became more aware of their Christianity. This was how the confused skirmishes slowly began to evolve into a "holy war,"[1] a concept that was then applied retroactively to the whole undertaking at the same time as its epic incarnation—El Cid Campeador—was promoted to the rank of Paladin of the Faith (which his biography hardly seems to warrant).[2] Monks (especially the Cluniacs) and knights from beyond

---

[1] It seems that the expression "holy war" was applied to the *Reconquista* for the first time by don Alonso de Cartagena, the Castilian representative to the Council of Basle (1434) while trying to demonstrate Castile's pre-eminence over England: ". . . even if the lord king of England makes war, his war is not holy for . . . it is directed neither against the infidels, nor for the exaltation of the Catholic faith, nor for the extension of the boundaries of Christianity, but for other reasons. . . ." The fact that this first ideologist of militant Spain was the son of Rabbi Solomon Levi of Burgos, and a convert to Catholicism, is very typical of Spanish history.

[2] Despite all the talent displayed by R. Menendez-Pidal in his brilliant essay of rehabilitation (*La España del Cid*), it seems to me that R. Dozy, in the last century, displayed a healthier regard for historical reality on this subject.

the Pyrenees contributed a great deal to this evolution in the eleventh century, as more and more of them came to reform Spanish religious life or to lend a hand to the combatants. But it took time for their influence to penetrate. For example, it was relatively late before the act that best expresses the spirit of the Crusades, the vow and the taking of the cross, was adopted by the Spanish knights; it did not become common until the beginning of the thirteenth century. Similarly, it was not until 1212 that the Christian kings of Spain were able to overlook their old grievances and unite into a general alliance against the Moslems. This resulted in the decisive victory of Las Navas. And it seems likely that the great military orders that were later to play such an important role in Spanish history—St. James, Alcantara, and Calatrava—were not an original creation but imitations of the orders of the Holy Land (165).

True, since the ninth century, obscure churchmen of Navarre or León had exhorted the Christians to expel the Saracens and re-establish Visigothic Spain, but in Islamized Spain, the Spain of the Three Religions, these ideas scarcely took root. Centuries of in-depth Christianization were necessary for Spain to find itself and become imbued with the fundamental precepts of Christian Europe. As we have indicated, these precepts seem to have grown even more ingrained once the Infidels who had to be battled, conquered, and eliminated were no more than a memory—but what an obsessive memory—on Iberian soil. Was this a crusade of Don Quixote against the windmills? Or a holy war against the corpses of those it had been necessary to kill? The last part of this volume will linger at length on this tragic imbroglio, from which Spain, which had been a haven of tolerance in the Middle Ages, emerged the most intolerant country of Europe.

The decisive period of the *Reconquista* lasted for two centuries, from 1045 to 1250. The Christians advanced in several waves and were driven back by the counteroffensives of

Islam. On two occasions, around 1085 and around 1145, the Moslems called for aid from their coreligionists of North Africa, who were organized into militant sects—Tuareg nomads (the Almoravides) or mountain Berbers (the Almohades). Both times they made the Christians retreat northward. The Almohades in particular, as we have already mentioned, were noted for their fanaticism and intolerance, and their arrival forced many Jews to take refuge in Christian lands—Castile and Aragon (and, on the other side of the Pyrenees, in Languedoc and Provence).

The kingdom of Castile, in particular, which had borne the main burden of the battle over the centuries, became the principal place of refuge. Once the land was conquered a government had to be formed and people induced to settle the new territories, which were often deserted and devastated (the length of the Duero, a ravaged and almost uninhabitable area—a sort of no man's land—served as a buffer between the two adversaries). To encourage settlement, the princes accorded franchises and privileges to new colonists, even going so far as to appeal to common criminals. "They would have welcomed the devil in person," wrote a contemporary historian (166), adding, "thus they received the Jews with open arms." But other provinces fell into the hands of the conquerors intact, with their motley population of Moors, Jews, and Christian *mozarabes,* and the problem of organizing and administering them took precedence over resettlement.

As the Christian kingdoms pushed their borders southward, they re-established much of the former social and economic organization of the conquered lands, which means that many institutions of Moslem origin were adopted, with only slight modification, by the sovereigns of Christian Spain. The Jews were essentially the intermediaries in this adaptation. The princes of the *Reconquista* found them to be devoted and reliable allies, technicians familiar with the situation and the possibilities the reconquered areas offered, some having even exercised administrative functions during the Moslem domination. In sum, they were experts whose role was similar to that of Western technicians in underdeveloped countries today. Americo Castro's image is even more descriptive when he compares the reconquered lands and cities to a California—a San Francisco, Los Angeles, and San Diego—reoccupied by Mexicans . . . (167). That does not mean to say that the luxurious way of life of the old lords of Toledo, Cordova, or Valencia did not seduce the conquerors and obtrude on them. Once more in history it was the conquered who imposed their customs, their way of life— in a word, their civilization—on the conquerors. To a certain extent, one might say, Christian Spain became re-Islamized at this time. And as the Jews were the principal agents of this transformation, it would also be true to say (as S. de Madariaga has said) that Spain became Judaized. This term is necessarily vague, but it has the advantage of highlighting the great originality of Spanish medieval history, which has resulted in the distinct physiognomy of Spain today.

After the *Reconquista,* the Spanish kings called themselves Kings of the Three Religions (the first to use the expression seems to have been Ferdinand III, king of Castile), but under the circumstances the position of the Jews was rising to the same extent as that of the Moslems was declining. After the capitulation of Toledo in 1085, the Moors were guaranteed immunity of life and property, but later most had to leave. When Toledo was captured in 1115, only the Jews, and not the Moslems, were authorized to live inside the city walls. The same thing happened three years later after the capture of Saragossa (168). In Tortosa, in 1148, orchards, vineyards, and olive groves abandoned by the Moors were distributed among the Jews (169). The charter of Cuenca, promulgated twelve years after the capture of that city (1190), made the differentiation particularly clear: in detailing the rules for economic and social life, it took into account only Christians and Jews, mentioning the Moors in just a few general passages (170). In fact, to an extent the Jews took the place of the ruling Moslem class that had been driven out, while the Moors, who were split—according to a concept borrowed from Islam—into "Moors of Peace" and "Moors of War," found themselves cast right to the bottom of the social scale.

Juridically the Jews enjoyed the same rights as the Christians.[3] In fact, they ranked right after the king and lords on the social scale, a position that reflected the extraordinary importance and variety of their socioeconomic functions. According to one Arab geographer, they formed half the population of Barcelona in the eleventh century; according to another, Tarragona was "a Jewish city" (171). For the most part, they controlled commerce, industry, and handicrafts. The devastation of the *Reconquista* had resulted in the ruin of manufacturing and the abandonment of silver and other mines; the Jews revived them. In the conquered territories they lent great impetus to viniculture, which was traditionally frowned upon in Islamic lands. As landed proprietors they were constantly on the lookout for ways to enhance the value of their land (172).

Most important, at this time they formed the administrative cadres of Christian Spain. They were diplomats and financiers, the indispensable adjuncts to the kings. They inspired and executed their policies and minted coins with Castilian and Arab legends (173). The persecution of the Almohades was an added guarantee of their loyalty. Did they take part in the battles directly? An Arab legend tells us that on the eve of the battle of Zalaqa a three-day truce was declared to allow the Moslems to celebrate Friday; the Jews, Saturday; and the Christians, Sunday (174). According to a twelfth-century German rabbi, "It is customary in Spain for the Jews to follow their king on campaigns" (175). It seems,

---

[3] This does not mean "equality of citizens before the law," for there were different laws for Christians, Jews, and Moslems. But collectively, the Jewish "nation" or community was placed on equal footing with the Christians. Cf. Baer, *Toldot* . . . , pp. 61–2 and the numerous texts he cites in his two collections.

however, that they were not obliged to do regular military service but only to defend the cities, and so it was only as volunteers that they went out on campaigns (176). This must have been the case of the Jews Axicuri, *arbalétrier,* and Vellocid, *arbalétrier à cheval,* who took part in the division of the Andalusian spoils in 1266 and, along with ninety other Jews, received gifts of houses at Jerez de la Frontera (177). The Jewish favorites of the kings were given sumptuous gifts, vast lands *cum montibus et vallibus,* whole villages with their fields and their pastures. In the cities, despite prohibitions dating from the days of the Fathers of the Church, they built synagogues which were as high and as beautiful as the Christian churches. In many places they took over abandoned mosques and consecrated them to the Jewish religion. (Later some of these became churches. Even to this day, certain Spanish children think a synagogue is "a mosque consecrated to the Christian religion" (178). And, in fact, wasn't it incumbent upon the Jews to transmit the Arab heritage to Christian Spain?)

What was the attitude of the Christian Church toward such a precipitous Jewish growth?

The popes soon became concerned. As early as 1081 Gregory VII requested Alfonso VI of Castile "not to appoint Jews to positions of authority and command over Christians" (179), the first manifestation of an anxiety we shall encounter time and time again. But in Spain itself churchmen great and small seemed to have accommodated themselves to the situation very realistically. The archbishop of Toledo (primate of the Spanish Church) decreed equal rights for Jews and Christians in Alcala de Henares, won from the Moors in 1118 (180). The economic position of the Jews was such that, directly or indirectly, they were the major source of revenue for the Spanish Church. The kings often assigned to the Church taxes collected from the Jews or from lands they had settled. There were close business relationships between the Church and Jews who administered ecclesiastical properties, collecting taxes on them or leasing them out to others. Jews even made loans accepting religious articles as collateral, and in principle, when they themselves were landowners, they were required to pay the tithe and other Church taxes just as the Christians did (181). Spanish churchmen took advantage of the situation, justifying themselves—as the archbishop of Toledo did—by pointing out that it was necessary to keep the Jews in Castile so that some day they could be converted as the prophets had predicted (182). Meanwhile, the Jews even had to share such costs of the Church as the illumination of the altars (183). Conciliar deliberations relating to the Jews were rare before the fourteenth century, and those that took place were principally concerned with the collection of the tithes on the lands "which the Jews, detested and dishonest, have bought or are going to buy from the followers of Christ . . . for it would be unjust if the Church were to lose those tithes which it enjoyed before the arrival of the Jews . . ." (184).

, Foreign churchmen, particularly the French who had flocked to Spain at that time, apparently had other ideas on how to treat unbelievers. One of them, Dom Bernard, a Cluniac who was the first archbishop of Toledo, would not permit the great mosque to remain consecrated to the Moslem religion, as had been stipulated upon the capitulation of the city, and, against the will of the king, he turned it into a cathedral (185). It was the same with the knights who came to battle the Saracens. On several occasions (in 1066, in 1090, in 1147, in 1212) they stopped along the way, incited by holy anger and greed, to sack the rich Spanish Jewish communities. Each time, order was re-established by a population that still did not know the spirit of the Crusade and obeyed the royal orders. But from these encounters Spanish Christians learned that on the other side of the Pyrenees Jewish lives were not worth much; as for the Jews, they recognized the familiar danger "between Edom and Ishmael." In 1066 Pope Alexander II congratulated Count Ramon Berenguer I of Barcelona "for the wisdom which he had shown in preserving from death the Jews of his terri·

tories, for God does not rejoice in the shedding of blood, and does not find pleasure in the distress even of evil men" (186).

Other Jewish massacres occurred during popular uprisings that took place during times when the throne was vacant: in Castile in 1109, after the death of Alfonso VI; in León in 1230, after the death of Alfonso IX. These uprisings were directed against the king and against the men of power and do not seem to have been specifically anti-Jewish (187).

seven

The Golden Age

Spain of the Three Religions

"The Tartars . . . are swarthy little men like the Spaniards," reported the monk Guillaume de Rubruquis, when he
was sent to Mongolia by Saint Louis to negotiate an alliance
with the great Khan (188). In fact, there is every indication
that in the twelfth and thirteenth centuries the Spanish
population looked very much like Asiatics, in strange contrast
to the people of medieval Europe. They retained, or rather
they had adopted, the costume of the Moslems. "Although
the Spaniards had reduced the power of the Moslems by
arms in the thirteenth century," the great Spanish encyclopedia states, "sculptures and miniatures show that they
very willingly adopted their style of dress" (189).

Doubtless there were differences in the dress of the Christians, the Jews, and the Moors, but we know little about
them. We do have some information about the Jews, for in
1215 the Fourth Lateran Council prescribed that Jews (and
"Saracens") living in Christian lands wear a distinctive
badge precisely so that they could be recognized as such,
and because the Jews were trying to evade this requirement. In Aragon, as we can see from documents, it seems
that they were already recognizable because of their tradition of wearing distinctive cloaks, and that they themselves
valued this distinction highly (190). In Castile the badge
seems to have been all the more necessary as there were no
distinctions of this type (191), but the Jews absolutely

refused to wear it, going so far as to resort to threats, and the Holy See finally had to give in. This can be seen in a letter from Pope Honorius III to the archbishop of Toledo (1219): ". . . The Jews are so seriously wrought up over that which was decided with regard to them . . . that some of them choose rather to flee to the Moors than to be burdened with such a sign. Others conspire because of this, and make secret agreements. As a result, the king, whose income in large measure derives from these very Jews, can hardly raise his expenses and serious misfortune may befall the kingdom" (192). At around the same time, the Council of Valladolid (1228) demanded that the Castilian Jews be forbidden to wear capes similar to those the clergy wore "with the result that strangers and travelers often treat them with undue reverence and accord them sacerdotal honors . . ." (193).

This clothing question gives us an inkling of the extraordinary distinctiveness of Spain of the Three Religions, structured in the Middle Ages along Oriental lines. Its inhabitants did not fail to practice that species of nation-to-nation fraternization which the kings demanded of them in the name of economic and political imperatives. Of their good relations there exist highly diverse examples, as curious as they are eloquent.

- On the secular and political level: to celebrate a victory or a new king's accession to the throne, Christians, Jews, and Moslems expressed their common joy with processions and hosannas or songs of welcome, examples of which can be found in the eleventh century as well as the fifteenth, literally on the eve of the expulsion of the Jews. Thus, in Toledo in 1139, when Alfonso VII made his triumphal return after his victory over the Almoravides, ". . . the three peoples, Christians, Saracens, and Jews, came out to meet him with lutes, citharas, drums, and numerous other instruments, singing praises to God and the conqueror, each in his own language, *unusquisque eorum secundum linguam suam* . . ." (194). In 1414 in Saragossa, after the coronation of Fernando de Antequera as the new king of Aragon, ". . .

the Jews dressed like the Christians, danced and played, their minstrels before them, running through the streets, showing their joy, and finally entering the palace of the Lord King . . ." (195). In 1497 and consequently *after* the expulsion of the Jews from Spain, the daughter of the Catholic sovereigns who had just married King Manuel of Portugal was similarly received by the Jews when she arrived in Lisbon (196).

But such fraternal accord was not reserved for special events. It was evident in everyday life, and sometimes even in certain aspects of intimate life. For example, as far as hygiene was concerned.

Spain at that time was still ignorant of the medieval "horror of baths." It inherited from Islam, and partially retained until the end of the Middle Ages, the institution of public baths (although certain Castilian kings judged them debilitating and dangerous) (197). The use of these baths was regulated by municipal *fueros*. In certain cities different days were assigned to men and women; in others, such as Zorita and Cuenca, Mondays and Wednesdays were reserved for women, Thursdays and Saturdays for men, and Fridays and Sundays for Jews; in still others, such as Tortosa, where the baths were known for their luxury, there was no schedule of this sort (198), from which we can assume that no separation was practiced—neither of sexes nor religions—men and women, the circumcised and the uncircumcised, in all innocence washing together in the same water.

The Castilian general code, known as *Las Siete Partidas* (we shall return again to this basic document), acting against a licentious custom that had already troubled the first Fathers of the Church, stipulated that *"ningunt judio non sea osado de bannarse en banno en uno con los cristianos"* (199). That such a prohibition had to be repeated in Castile in 1309, 1412, and 1465 (200) leads to the conclusion that it was not very scrupulously obeyed.

In addition to the custom of common baths, there was also that of common meals. True, the Jews, most of whom followed the dietary prohibitions of the Torah, were not easy guests to entertain in this regard. So it was up to their Christian friends to bend to their rules, like the Aragonese lord who had a Jewish butcher slaughter a cow on the occasion of his son's wedding so that he would be able to send a few choice morsels to those of his friends who followed the Law of Moses. This was not an isolated case (201). Obviously, it was easier to follow the rules of medieval courtesy when the situation was reversed, and the Jews did not fail to send their Christian friends food and drink on the occasion of their family feasts, something that the Church, by virtue of a tradition which was already very old (and which, again, was mentioned in *Las Siete Partidas*) (202) opposed. Typical of this was a synodal decision of the diocese of Valencia (1263) that forbade the clerics, under pain of excommunication, not only to accept wine from the Jews but even "to deliberately buy their wines" (203), with the usual exception "for an urgent situation"—a reminder that the Jews by preference devoted themselves to viniculture.

Despite prohibitions of this sort, on innumerable occasions the Christians, Jews, and Moors of Spain of the Three Religions brushed aside all barriers in their social relations. The frequency and the severity of punishment imposed for sexual relations show that this ultimate barrier, too, was regularly crossed. We shall return to this point later.

Jewish men and women participated in Christian baptisms as godfathers and godmothers, *compadres* and *comadres* (204), and the Christians did the same at circumcisions. In New Castile it was even customary to invite Jewish singers to Christian burials to have them chant *endechas*, the traditional funeral songs (205).

Such practices also give some clues about religious life. For here, too, the Spanish people followed customs that the clergy succeeded in eliminating only after a secular battle (the past still weighs on the present and makes it more understandable). Thus, Spanish Christians did not miss an opportunity to listen to the sermons of rabbis reputed for their eloquence, even on the eve of the 1492 expulsion (206). Nor was the reverse unusual. There was even a custom of praying or holding nocturnal vigils together, which a conciliar decision of 1322 described in the following terms:

  "An evil has become rooted in certain dioceses; the unbelievers are mixing with the faithful while the divine offices are being celebrated in the churches, with the result that they are often disturbed and the faithful are prevented from performing their devotions. At the nocturnal vigils which the piety of certain simple souls has introduced into the churches, indescribable outrages are committed beneath a laudable outward appearance. In any case let us forbid them strictly. It is condemnable to allow the unbelievers into these vigils and to keep them there, or to have them raise their voices or their instruments in chorus. Henceforth, he who does not take the preceding into account in his relations with the unbelievers will be forbidden entry into the churches in his lifetime and will be denied a Christian burial after his death . . ." (207).

Proceedings instituted in 1313 against a Jew of Taust, in Aragon, who "attended a vigil in the church of Saint Bartholomew of Taust, in the company of Christian men and women of the city, who performed there by dancing a dance and kicked the altar, abusing and insulting the Christian faith" give an idea of these nocturnal vigils. It is characteristic that the offender was reported to the judge by the Jews of Taust (208).

But the custom of common devotions seems to have been deeply rooted in medieval Spain. Again, in 1449, to exorcise a plague that was raging in Andalusia, the Jews of Seville, with the permission of the archbishop, organized a solemn procession of the Torah scrolls through the streets of the city, following the procession of the Christians' Blessed Sacrament (209). The incident aroused the indignation of Pope Nicholas V, but it does not seem to have been unusual

(210). Living together in a tight community, these Spaniards of the past extended the good relations they enjoyed with their neighbors to the God of these neighbors—the common God of Abraham and the Father common to all three peoples.

Nothing better expresses that state of mind than an unpublished chronicle about Alfonso XI of Castile quoted by Americo Castro, in which he relates an unfortunate expedition that the sons of the king, Don Pedro and Don Juan, launched against the Moslems (211). The king of Granada had signed a truce with the Christians and was forced to pay them tribute. But on the insistence of the pope, the sons of the king broke the sworn pact and invaded Moorish territories. They were beaten, and in the course of the battle the infante, Don Pedro, was killed. The anonymous chronicler, after having related these facts, comments:

". . . of all that had happened to Don Pedro, his men remember this: he had broken the pact which had been signed with the king of Granada, and transgressed the sworn faith which God established among the peoples; and his men suspected that this was the reason he had met death . . . for the Almighty knows only the truth, and never executes judgment without reason."

It was of little importance that the disloyal combatants were Christians and of equally little importance that they had broken the truce on the insistence of the Vicar of Jesus Christ on earth: God, the common Father of all just men, did not spare them for it and accorded the victory to the Moslems.

We have seen that this broad-mindedness, this extraordinary tolerance, stemmed basically from the need for public order in Christian lands where a large part of the population —the most productive strata economically—was not Christian. The same need for public order and stability gave rise to certain barriers that were curiously incompatible with the spirit of the Gospels (and with their letter): in the Spain of the Three Religions, where all the religions were respected, changing from one religion to another, even converting to Christianity, was either forbidden or made very difficult.

The exercise of each religion was officially protected by the government and even regulated by it. As far as the Jewish religion was concerned, the Castilian code of *Las Siete Partidas*, for example, after first recalling that it was necessary to let the Jews live among the Christians as reminders of the Crucifixion, went on to state that the word *judio* "was derived from the tribe of Judah, which was the noblest and most powerful of all," the one from which the kings were selected and the one which always attacked first in battle (a concept dear to the hearts of Spanish Jews; no doubt they lent a hand in the drafting of the code, regardless of its ecclesiastical inspiration). After this demonstration of how typically Spanish concepts were mixed with canon law, the measures of protection were decreed. "For the reason that the synagogue is a place where the name of God is praised, we forbid any Christian to deface it or remove anything from it, or to take anything out of it by force . . . or to place any hindrance in the way of the Jews while they are there performing their devotions according to their religion. No force or compulsion shall be employed in any way against a Jew to induce him to become a Christian; but Christians should convert him to the faith of Our Lord Jesus Christ by means of the texts of the Holy Scriptures, and by kind words . . ." (212).

There were provisions in other codes aimed at making the Jews themselves respect the Law of Moses: "It is forbidden for any Jew to read the books which speak [ill] of his Law, which are [directed] against it, or to possess such books; these books must be burned before the door of the synagogue" (213).

By order of the king and Christian law, the Jews were required to observe their Sabbath and their feasts: "And the Jew . . . who transgresses the Sabbath or a Holy Day will pay thirty maravedis. . . . And if on the day of Saturday

he carries a weapon, he must pay twenty-eight maravedis.
. . . And if a Jew rides horseback on a Saturday or a Holy
Day, the horse will be taken by the lord and [the Jew] will
pay thirty maravedis for each Sabbath or Holy Day he rode
horseback . . ." (214). (One can see the profile of a Spanish Jew, knight, and swordsman.) The fine was collected by
the royal treasury, and thus the crowned protectors of the
Jewish faith showed themselves most jealous of its purity, to
such an extent that at the beginning of the thirteenth century a rabbi of the city of Daroca, in Aragon, had to pay a
fine of a hundred and five maravedis for not having sharp-
ened his knife *segunt tachana de judios* (according to Jewish
rule) before the ritual slaughter of an animal (215). More
severe was the punishment of that headstrong Majorcan Jew
at the end of the fourteenth century who, *en menyspreu de
la sante fe catholica et de la ley mosaica* (in contempt of the
Holy Faith and the Mosaic Law), had said Moslem prayers
with his slaves. But this did not prevent him from also violat-
ing the law of Mohammed, since he ate pork and drank
Christian wine (216). In 1294, on orders from the king, the
bailiff of Valencia searched for Jews who had "broken Jewish law" (we do not know how) and taken refuge "among
powerful [Christians]" (217).

A Jew had to behave as a good Jew in all things; the
Spanish Church even forbade him to become a Moslem, and
vice versa. Conciliar decisions were explicit on the subject:
in Aragon, the Council of Tarragona decreed in 1234 that
"no Saracen, man or woman, could embrace Judaism, and no
Jew or Jewess could become Saracen; those who did so
would lose their liberty" (218). In 1252, after conquering
vast territories in Andalusia, Castile passed similar decrees
(219).

The situation was evidently more complex as far as conversion to Christianity was concerned. The Spanish Church
could not refrain from trying to convert the unbelievers
but—at least before the thirteenth-century emergence of the
great Franciscan and Dominican preaching orders and the

efforts they made in Aragon—in practice it made very little effort. As a result nothing was done to lead a Jew to baptism, and many things contributed to deterring him. In the first place there was the poverty that awaited him, because in accordance with an old custom his possessions would be confiscated by the royal treasury. It was only in the thirteenth century that this practice began to be questioned. In 1242 James I of Aragon made a show of renouncing it, declaring that from then on no convert would lose his property or his inheritance, "for even as they merit the grace of God, so shall they be known to have ours, whose duty it is to imitate His good will and favor." He was highly praised for this by Pope Innocent IV (220). But it was only a gesture without practical significance. As late as 1322 the Council of Valladolid described the situation of the new converts in Castile as follows:

"After having been baptized [they] are generally forced to go begging, because of their poverty, and certain among them abandon our holy faith for this reason. It is thus necessary to furnish what is needed in the hospices and the charitable institutions. . . . Those who could be capable of learning a profession should be directed by the rectors of the hospices to learn professions . . ." (221).

The fact that neophytes were reduced to begging was the beginning of the converts' status as outcasts. In the Spain of the Three Religions, conversion was a scandal and the convert was the target of open hostility from both his old and his new coreligionists. Considered a renegade by the one group, he was a *tornadizo* for the other. This state of affairs was also reflected in *Las Siete Partidas*, which forbade the Jews to kill or wound the converts and forbade Christians to remind them of their lineage, enjoining them to the contrary, to accord them *todos los oficios y los honras que han los otros cristianos* (222).

Actually, before the fourteenth century the conversion of a Jew was quite an exceptional event. Those who took this step were often those who had nothing to lose, such as that

Barcelonan Jew who was convicted in 1022 of having fornicated with a Christian woman and was baptized the following year (223). Those of the converts who could read became clerics and tried to catechize their former coreligionists. For a long time they were the only ones who dedicated themselves to this thankless task, men such as Moses Sefardi (the illustrious Pedro Alfonso or Ildefonso) at the beginning of the twelfth century and his contemporary, Samuel the Moroccan (224).

Just as rare seem to have been Christian converts to Judaism, or even Moslem converts (most of the latter were slaves). Although such actions necessarily had to be kept secret, some cases have come to our attention. A rabbi of Aragon, enumerating the prayers to be recited on such an occasion, added: "And this, I have observed, is the practice which is followed here" (225). Shortly before his death in 1312 the archbishop of Tarragona took action against several Jews who were not satisfied with merely diverting Christian neophytes from the straight path but had helped Christians from Germany to be circumcised. In this particular case the offenders got off with heavy fines (226).

In sum, in Spain the medieval concept that each member of society had to remain in his place was applied in the Moslem manner, meaning that it was extended to the realm of religion. For the present it is important to describe the Jews' extraordinary political influence.

A famous legend that has given rise to a vast literature tells of the love of Alfonso VIII of Castile (d. 1214) for the beautiful Rachel, "*La Fermosa*," to whom he remained faithful for seven years, and it attributes the power and prestige that the Jews enjoyed in the court of Castile at this time to this love affair. But the Jewish courtiers did not need such romantic complications—a sort of Spanish Queen Esther— to gain the confidence of the kings. When the Castilian lords felt it was good politics for Urraca, the daughter of Alfonso VI (d. 1109), to marry the king of Aragon, they had this dynastic plan submitted to the king by his faithful Cidellus (the Jewish minister referred to in Chapter 5) rather than propose it themselves. And two centuries later a king of Aragon addressed these deferential terms to Yuçaf de Ecija, Jewish minister of a king of Castile:

"Don Alfonso, king of Aragon, to you Don Yuçaf de Ecija, *almoxarife* [collector of revenues] of the very powerful king of Castile. Greetings to the man whom we love and in whom we have confidence. We inform you that a few days ago we had the accident of illness but, praise be to God, we are well cured. We inform you because we know that you are anxious about our health and our well-being. As we desire to be entertained by the musicians of the king of Castile, those which are from Tarragona, the one who plays the cithara and the one who plays the lute, we beg you to request of the king that he send us these musicians, and we thank you very much for this service" (227).

Charged with the pleasures of the princes as well as their profits, the great Jews of Toledo and Barcelona acted as permanent brain trusters for the Spanish kings, accompanying them on their incessant travels. In Aragon the need for this function began to diminish at the end of the thirteenth century; in Castile, where the Arabic influence was stronger, it continued until the fifteenth century. The fact that a real Christian bourgeoisie was either absent or slow to develop, as well as the fact that the kings mistrusted the nobility, explains the persistence of this state of affairs, something which Juan Manuel, the nephew of Alfonso X (called the Wise) and Spain's first political thinker, understood. In his *Libro de los estados* he strongly emphasized that the "merchants" rather than the nobles and the clergy be entrusted with the conduct of affairs of state (228). This famous prince, "the most accomplished Spanish type in the fourteenth century" (A. Castro), considered his doctor, Don Salomon, as his only true friend, and he said so openly in his will, and less openly in his book *De las maneras del amor* (229). Heeded and respected by the powerful, Jewish doctors were among the principal links between Jews and Christians.

Another aspect of the activities of the Jews of Castile was their civilizing and educating function, which the clergy filled in other parts of Europe. Thus, beginning with the thirteenth century, the vernacular took the place of Latin in administrative and juridical acts, for the Jews bore a marked aversion to Latin. This was the origin of classical Castilian (230).

One aspect of these cultural activities deserves a more detailed description, for it was essential to the rise of Christian Europe. We are speaking of the role the Spanish Jews played in transmitting the knowledge of the ancient world and of the East.

There were other points of contact between East and West in the Mediterranean, such as Sicily, which had also been taken over by the Arabs, and Byzantium. But Spain was the principal entry point for arts and sciences, doubtless because in Spain the principal intermediaries—the Jews— were both numerous and educated. The Moslems did not always look with favor on these intellectual borrowings. Early in the twelfth century an Andalusian Moslem wrote: "Neither the Jews nor the Christians should be sold scientific books, with the exception of the books which treat of their laws, for they immediately translate them and pass themselves off as the authors, they and their bishops" (231).

Translating was systematically carried on for three centuries, particularly at Toledo. One early translation academy was headed, from 1030 to 1070, by the canon Domenico Gonsalvo, assisted by the Jewish chronicler Abraham ibn David (Abendauth). They themselves translated Avicenna's *Treatise of the Soul,* with the Christian translating into Latin the text that had first been put into vulgar Castilian by the Jew. Beginning with Aristotle, other ancient or Arab philosophers were translated in the same way, and the Koran was translated by "Maestre Pedro," a Jew of Toledo.

The body of technical and scientific knowledge of the ancient world penetrated into Europe in much the same way, as did, it seems, the Indo-Arabic numerical system and the idea of zero. The same thing happened with lighter reading: a collection of Oriental tales, translated as *Disciplina Clericalis* by the Aragonese convert Pedro Alfonso at the beginning of the twelfth century, enjoyed tremendous popularity across Europe, from Sicily to Ireland, and furnished themes for the English popular theater and the French fabliaux.

In the following century, around 1260, the work of the Toledo school was resumed at the instigation of Alfonso the Wise, this time in more original guise. Isaac ben Said or ben Cid, cantor of the synagogue of Toledo, was ordered to calculate the astronomical tables known as the Alphonsine Tables, which remained authoritative until the sixteenth century and were the ones used by Copernicus.

The king charged some writers to produce a *grande y general estoria* in Castilian. Typically, he also ordered that the majority of these works be translated not only into Latin but also into the principal vulgar European languages (232).

During this time there were close relations between Christian theologians and Jewish rabbis in Barcelona. The scholar Arnaud de Villeneuve, a student of the cabalist Abraham Abulafia, seems to have been so strongly influenced by him that he was accused of being a secret Jew (233). The famous Franciscan Raymond Lull was also a member of this group. A manuscript of his dedicated to the principal rabbis of the city, "Master Abram Denanet [ben Adret], Master Aron, Master Salomon, and the other Jewish Sages who are in the *aljama*," has been discovered (234). His *Dialogue of the Three Sages* (Christian, Moslem, and Jewish), perhaps inspired by *The Kuzari*, remains the pinnacle of medieval humanism and tolerance.

But at the same time and in the same city, and sometimes with the assistance of the same scholars, the Dominicans created an Institute of Oriental Languages with a view to converting the unbelievers, and Raymond Martin, who also numbered some rabbis among his friends, wrote his *Dagger of Faith* (*Pugio Fidei*), which remained a source of inspiration for anti-Jewish polemicists until the dawn of modern times.

One may feel that these phenomena were closely linked, and the most distinguished student of this subject, I. Baer, has written: "Among the European countries, Christian Spain was the one distinguished at the same time by its religious fanaticism and by its religious tolerance" (235). And, we add, the first term flows from the second. This was the peculiar dialectic of Spanish history.

The Jewish Nation of Spain

As late as the twelfth century there were still Jewish farmers working their lands in Spain, and even Jewish agricultural colonies, but the majority of the Jews lived in "castles," or fortified villages, under the direct protection of a prince. Sometimes the Jewish communities were responsible for keeping the castles in good repair and for fortifying them, their charters authorizing them even to defend these castles by force of arms against all attackers, whatever their religion. Many Spanish cities, which were later populated by Christian bourgeois, either natives or *émigrés* from the other side of the Pyrenees, originated in these castles. In the surrounding countryside were the lands of the rich Jews; sometimes their domains covered vast areas (236).

Within the castles the Jews mixed freely with the Christians and worked at the same trades. As far as their number is concerned, it is impossible to make any estimate for the eleventh and twelfth centuries; the most that can be said is that in the beginning they formed the bulk of the bourgeoisie. In Spain the Christian bourgeoisie formed slowly and late, and the first elements seem to have been *émigrés* from across the Pyrenees. Afterward, according to the best estimates, there were nearly three hundred thousand Jews in the fourteenth century, representing a quarter or a fifth of the total urban population (237). Just as the Christian artisans and merchants did, the Jewish artisans and merchants organized into guilds or corporations for the defense of their professional rights, especially when the Christian organizations began to compete with them. They had their own religious institutions and chapels—a home for Jewish tailors in Perpignan, for example, and a synagogue for Jewish weavers in Calatayud. Such "professional apportionment" was maintained until the 1492 expulsion, and an edict that King Juan II promulgated in 1443 precisely to protect the Jewish artisans against the jealousy and competition of the Christians gives us an excellent idea of the wide range of Jewish professions:

"But it does not follow therefrom, that they are prohibited to contract, buy, sell, or exchange any goods and wares among, and with Christians; nor are trades and useful handicrafts forbidden to them, as clothesmen, silversmiths, carpenters, barbers, shoemakers, tailors, clothiers, milliners, braziers, bridle makers, saddlers, ropemakers, potters, curriers, basketmakers, money-changers, and all other similar trades, mechanical arts, and useful handicrafts, in which they use manual labor and work" (238).

Such occupations were particularly typical of the communities in the small cities, far from the courts of princes with their speculations and intrigues. At Talavera de la Reina in Castile, where there were sixty-eight people in the Jewish community in the thirteenth century, the local Jewish specialty was basket weaving. In addition, there were three goldsmiths, two shopkeepers, a few doctors and farmers, and numerous artisans, blacksmiths, harness makers, tailors, and cobblers. I. Baer, who gathered these data from Castilian fiscal archives, also compiled numerous tables for the majority of the other Spanish Jewish communities that were similar to this in every way (239).

Thus it is not surprising that the first Spanish historians of the Enlightenment, in trying to determine the reasons for the Spanish decadence, attributed it to the expulsion of the Moors and Jews who were the only ones in Spain who had cultivated the arts and crafts (240).

The reality, of course, was more complicated: it is no less so now that it can be examined with the aid of certain figures. In 1294, in the kingdom of Aragon, the Jews alone contributed 22 per cent of the fiscal receipts and returns of the royal treasury. We know that in Castile (for which no precise figures are available) this proportion was even higher (241). Let us recall that in Paris in 1292 the Jewish share of the total was only 1 per cent. (Cf. Vol. 1, p. 77.)

These receipts reflect taxes and assessments paid by rich and poor Jewish families, and the great majority were of modest means, as we can see from the crafts they practiced. The financiers and moneylenders represented a tiny minority, especially as medieval Spanish economic conditions were less favorable for lending at interest than those of France or England. It was only at the end of the thirteenth century that such transactions became common in Spain. How deeply rooted the Jews were in Spanish life can also be seen from the stability of their residences. There are family names that appear again and again down through the centuries (242), so we know that fathers and sons of Jewish families lived in the same place for generations, in contrast to the incessant Jewish peregrinations in the rest of Europe. In Spain the Jews were free to "grow and multiply," and thus they could attain and maintain such a population density. Elsewhere, the Jews, sociologically speaking, constituted a wandering, marginal group; in Spain they constituted the backbone of social and economic life. "At the same time they were Spain and they were not," Americo Castro has observed significantly (243).

They were not, in fact; and they would not become so as their country slowly evolved from a trinational state on the Oriental model toward a homogeneous Christian state on the European model. We shall return later to this evolution of the Spanish "Christian nation."

As far as the "Jewish nation" was concerned, with its roots deep in Iberian soil, its "Spanishness"—all of this existed concurrently with a strong internal differentiation, due primarily to economic differences. In numerous *aljamas* (communities) the Jews (just as the Christian townsmen) were statutorily divided into three classes according to their wealth: the *mans major*, the *mans mijana*, and the *mans minor* (upper, middle, and lower class, respectively). Above all, there were certain rich and powerful Jewish families connected with the royal court, a sort of special class of Jews, who were declared "free" or "franchised," that is, exempt from community jurisdiction and from payment of taxes. At times the king even levied a special tax on the community for the benefit of these families, in addition to prohibiting the communities from persecuting and excommunicating them (244).

Thus, a Jewish oligarchy developed, which was lax about following the rules of the Torah and looked down on the community from which it had sprung. The communities, for their part, treated such influential coreligionists—their natural protectors—with every consideration. In the fourteenth century a Castilian rabbi even composed a special Talmudic treatise for their use, modifying or simplifying many of the requirements of the Law, for they were incompatible with the life of a courtier (245).

It was particularly within this oligarchy that the customs of the Arab era were perpetuated and certain character traits defined which have left their imprint on Spanish Jews in general. These customs and character traits are worth examining in some detail, because for centuries they continued to exercise a fascination on the Jews who were expelled as well as on Spain, which had rid itself of the Jews at such tragic cost.

- Let us first note that, especially in Castile, the Jewish nation remained Arabic-speaking for a long time. Even when Castilian was substituted for Arabic as the everyday language, Arabic remained the language of culture and erudition, the key to philosophy and science. There was also a practical reason for this: "Remember that the great men of our people attained fame and high rank only through the writing of Arabic," Judah ibn Tibbon (the founder of a celebrated dynasty of translators) wrote to his son around 1190 (246). The German rabbi Yehiel ben Asher, exiled to Toledo around 1305, had to learn Arabic to be able to perform his ministry (247). All throughout the fourteenth century, administrative acts and rabbinical *responsa* were written in fluent Arabic in the *aljamas* of Castile and Aragon (248).

Especially in the great oligarchic families, this retention of Arabic went hand in hand with a tribal pride that was also derived from the customs of the Orient, and gave birth to a specifically Judeo-Spanish exclusivism.

Even the Christian legislators agreed, as we have seen, that the Spanish Jews were of illustrious descent. According to the scholar Rabbi Moses Arragel, who translated the Old Testament into Castilian at the beginning of the fourteenth century, the Spanish Jews had always excelled all other Jewish communities "in lineage, wealth, virtue, and learning" (249). Such claims were justified by identifying Spain as the land of the Sefarad, in which, according to the Old Testament, the children of Jerusalem, the flower of ancient Judaism, were exiled. Spanish Judaism was considered to have descended either from the Jews exiled by Nebuchadnezzar or from those exiled by Titus. In any case, according to the historian Ibn Verga, it was of royal stock (250). The great families of Toledo and Barcelona even claimed direct descent from King David. Moreover, these families jealously defended their reputation and the purity of their line (251). (Later, apostasy did not in any way diminish this tribal pride. According to the converts baptism had improved the nobility of their blood.[1] After his baptism in 1391 the most

[1] Thus Moses Diego de Valera, chronicler of the Catholic sovereigns, wrote: ". . . not only do I respond that they retain their nobility or their

famous of them, Solomon Halevi of Burgos, wrote a "discourse on the origins and the nobility of his line." The conclusions his distant descendants drew from it will be discussed later; certain variants of these stories were actually used by the grandees of Spain of Jewish stock, as diplomas *ne plus ultra* of nobility.)

, Such claims to nobility climaxed a life style that was radically different from that of the Jews of Europe, those outcasts of Christian society. An episode in the famous romance of chivalry, *Amadís de Gaula,* shows a Judeo-Spanish knight insulting Christian and Moslem knights (252); the historical improvisations of Heinrich Heine were thus not unfounded. The Spanish Jews, we have seen, carried arms and, on occasion, used them to wreak bloody vengeance on an enemy—Jewish or Christian. Artuset, a Catalan troubadour, learned this bitter lesson, for according to the troubadour Bertrand de Born he was killed by the friends of a Jew whom he had killed (253). The history of the Spanish Jews is full of incidents of this sort. Sometimes pious motives were involved: in 1313 Jews of Borja, most of them artisans, attacked with stones and swords two Franciscans who were leading a young Jewish boy to baptism (254). Sometimes the motives were political: in 1380 several Jewish notables, jealous of the favor that Henry of Castile showed his treasurer, Joseph Pichon, beheaded the latter in his house, to the great indignation of the king and the chroniclers of the time (255).
- Within the *aljamas* these violent customs found their expression in cruel physical punishments and even in the death penalty, which the Talmud expressly prohibits.[2] It went

---

hidalguerie after having been converted, but I say that they increase it. . . . Speaking of the Jews, Deuteronomy says: 'What other nation is as noble?' " (Epistles of D. de Valera, *Bibliofilos Españoles,* XVI, pp. 206–12.)

' [2] The custom astonished the rabbis from the other side of the Pyrenees. "When I first arrived here," wrote the German rabbi Yehiel ben Asher, "I asked in amazement by what legal right Jews could today legally convict anyone to death without a Sanhedrin. . . . In none of the countries that I know of, except here in Spain, do the Jewish courts try cases of capital punishment." (Cf. A. A. Neuman, *op. cit.,* Vol. 1, pp. 138–39.)

hand in hand with a remarkable lack of inhibition in many other areas. I. Baer cites the case of a father and son who quarreled over the charms of a beautiful Moorish slave; the son burst into the synagogue of Figueras, sword in hand, and tried to kill his father. These Karamazovs of Jewish Spain were far from unusual. Sexual relations with Christian or Moorish women were so frequent (despite the brutal punishments imposed by the *aljamas*, such as cutting off the nose) that the rabbis advocated, as the lesser evil, recourse to Jewish prostitutes, and they existed in numerous Spanish cities (256). Other rabbis who opposed such practices, in accordance with the Old Testament, tried to direct the virile impulses of their flock into another direction. Polygamy, which had never been forbidden to the Spanish Jews, was widespread (thus the most famous Spanish Talmudist, Hasdai Crescas, whose first wife was sterile, piously married a second) (257). Above all, concubinage was legalized, and the rabbis even went so far as to distinguish between two sorts of concubines: the *hachoukah*, the "desired one," a free concubine, and the *pilgechet*, the "mistress," to whom the lover had bound himself by a promise of betrothal (258). Here, the customs of the Spanish Jews were not very different from those of the medieval Christians, to the great scandal of the rabbis across the Pyrenees (259).

The lack of faith of numerous Spanish Jews was an even greater scandal. This lack of belief was particularly common among the great Jews of Castile and reconquered Andalusia, who continued to cultivate Greco-Arabic philosophy and either followed its precepts or cultivated no philosophy at all, forgetting their religion and its morality in the turmoil of the adventurous life they led at court.

The vast currents of thought that converged under the name of Averroism (among the Christians) or Maimunism (among the Jews) furnished, if the need arose, the justification for trampling on religious observance. The basic idea was that the Torah could be taken literally by simple people, but for the true sages it was but an allegory, a system of "double truth." Illuminated by the light of divine reason, these men were not constrained to conform to the rites or to abstain from what was prohibited. Step by step, numerous libertines of this era—men who were liberated in every sense of the word—broke their ties with Judaism and remained Jews in name only, merely because they considered it unnecessary or unprofitable to be baptized. A Jewish poet who had frequented these circles and led a life of festivities and debauchery, late in life reflected on what he had done. He described his former companions as follows:

Sinners abound, miscreant rebels—
Jews so-called, who cherish Christian lore—
Who walk in darkness, from Moses' Law estranged;
Who transgress the sages' precepts,
Too blind to esteem the Hebrew faith.
Exceeding rare is the night in Talmud study spent.
"*Aleph-Bet* will suffice us," they say, "with a bit of script.
Hebrew we need not know; Castilian is our tongue, or
    Arabic . . ."(260).

Philosophical heterodoxy even contaminated certain rabbis, such as the one quoted by H. Graetz who publicly questioned the prohibition of pork on the grounds that hygiene did not justify such a prohibition (261). But generally the rabbis did their best to fight against the craze for Greek science and, from their point of view, its disastrous consequences. In conformity with a *herem* (edict of excommunication) promulgated in 1305 by Rabbi Solomon ibn Adret of Barcelona and immediately extended to all the Judeo-Spanish communities, the study of "Greek works," with the exception of medical treatises, was forbidden to Jews under twenty-five years of age, whose minds would still be too malleable. "The knowledge of man," proclaimed Ibn Adret, "cannot be compared to the omniscience of God. Born of dust, man cannot have the pretension to judge his creator, to say: He can accomplish that, but he cannot accomplish this; for, in this way, his spirit will in the end turn entirely away from the faith" (262). A century later, at a decisive time for the future of Spanish Judaism, the great Hasdai Crescas complained that no one dared to put in doubt the arguments of "the Greek [Aristotle] who has dimmed the eyes of Israel in these our times" (263).

The rabbis were certainly right; the questions raised by men with a speculative turn of mind concerning the commandments of Sinai led others, who were more down-to-earth, to draw the most dangerous practical conclusions. This was facilitated by the intimate footing of the Jews and Christians.

This intimacy made it possible for interested parties to denounce a Jew or a whole community to the Christian authorities for the most varied offenses: fiscal fraud, political intrigue, transgression of divine law (Jewish or Christian), or, on the other hand, overzealous application of the Law of Moses (which went against Christian sentiment); the pretexts furnished by daily life were numerous. Jewish informers, apostates from their faith, were legion. The struggle against them was a permanent concern of the Jewish communities, and it constitutes an essential thread in the history of Spanish Judaism. The *aljamas* were accorded royal privileges to flog the informers, to cut off their limbs and their tongues, and to put them to death. "Item, as there are certain Jews of bad behavior and unruly speech, who mingle with the Christians and the Moors, those who are called *malsins* in Hebrew, cause great scandals and evils . . ." says the text of one such privilege of King Martin of Aragon dated 1400 (264). The kings were all the more willing to safeguard public morality because they were sure of gaining on all scores: the execution of an informer was taxed one thousand sueldos in the above-mentioned case, for example; the privilege was only accorded in consideration of a substantial present; a well-founded denunciation could bring in even more.

These struggles have left their traces, even in modern Spanish (*malsin* means "slanderous," *malsinar* means "to inform," etc.).[3]

The *aljamas* then had to fight on several fronts at the same time—against the abuses of the liberated oligarchy, against the philosophical contemners of Judaism, and against actual renegades. These internal conflicts were simultaneously religious and social, for to a large extent the distinction between religious laxity or indifference and traditional piety corresponded to the distinction between rich and poor. While the upper classes remained open to the influence of Greco-Arabic rationalism, the lower classes developed their own forms of popular mysticism that paralleled the spread of Christian mysticism (and perhaps partially imitated it). This accounts for the upsurge of cabalism and the success of the *Zohar*. The eternal human need to find a reason for the misery and injustice of this lowly world and to reconcile them with divine wisdom stimulated cabalistic speculation and calculations and the belief in an imminent redemption, to which Jewish piety was attracted. The cabalists denounced the depraved customs of the rich, "worshippers of the golden calf and idolatrous . . . orthodox in idolatry . . . priding themselves on coming to the synagogue head held high, dagger in the belt, pockets filled with clinking coins" (265). They consoled the poor by promising that they alone would have a place "in the world to come." But even in this exclusive domain we can see the assurance of the Spanish Jew, living as equal in the Christian world. Thus it is no surprise that the most influential of the Spanish cabalists, Abraham Abulafia, did not hesitate to go to Rome in

---

[3] The situation was not unlike modern times. The arguments and facts used to discredit Judaism often came from Jewish sources, with the concurrence of Jews, converted or not. Certain Jewish reactions, the reactions of "assimilated Jews," were the same. Thus, just like the reform German rabbis of the nineteenth century, certain Spanish rabbis counseled against reciting the Kol Nidre on Yom Kippur because that prayer, which accords absolution to perjurers, could discredit Judaism.

1281 to convert the pope to Judaism (only to land in prison). For rich or poor, mystics or libertines, these men all regarded themselves profoundly and naturally as Spaniards, equal to the Christians.

Anticipating what is to come, we quote here the sharp retort of a marrano who had returned to Spain after the 1492 expulsion. When an inquisitor asked him why he had immigrated: "If the king, our lord, had ordered the Christians to become Jews or to leave, some would have become Jews and others would have left. And when those who left felt lost, they would have become Jews to be able to return to their native land, all the while remaining Christians at heart and will and deceiving the world . . ." (266).

The Subreconquista

In line with the medieval order of things, it was incumbent upon the Spanish clergy to instruct the people, to explain the world to them, and to teach them to love Good and avoid Evil, in the Christian manner. At the beginning of the *Reconquista* the clergy was singularly lacking in the requisite qualifications for such a task. In the Christian principalities of the north the clergy was in general crude and rough, sometimes literally illiterate. Moreover, during the wars against the Moslem enemy a good number of them were not content to exhort their faithful to the battle, but set themselves up as examples and took up arms, contrary to what befitted their state (267). (Doubtless this was the origin of the traditional combativeness of the Spanish clergy and the resulting warlike Christianity of a Saint Domingo de Guzmán, a Saint Vincent Ferrer, and so many other champions of the conquering church.) As to that part of Spain in Moslem control, the Christian clergy there had its own customs, born of secular servitude, and, as in Syria or in Egypt, followed its own Oriental rite, which was here called the *Mozarabic* rite.

At the beginning of the *Reconquista* this clergy was little concerned with the Jews and was hardly troubled by the prosperity and haughtiness of the deicides as long as they remained useful allies in the battle against the Moors. This battle mobilized all spiritual energies and polarized sectarian enmity. Here, as in so many other ways, the Spanish clergy retained its own traditions for a long time. Rome was far away, and generally the European cultural influences remained negligible for many years.

According to the Spanish historians it was at the end of the eleventh century that Christian Spain became aware of its true vocation, finally tearing itself from the Moslem cultural sphere and joining the European concert of nations. The growing participation of the Franks in the battle against Islam seems to have been a determining factor in this.

"It is notable," writes Sanchez-Albornoz, "that the massive immigrations of northerners—princes, knights, monks, bourgeoisie, and laborers—which inundated Christian Spain during the last third of the eleventh century, and the parallel increase in the pilgrimages to Santiago de Compostela, led the Spanish lands to adopt the ideas, feelings, practices, institutions, customs, artistic and literary forms, etc., from beyond the Pyrenees. Along with the immigrants and the pilgrims came new religious concepts, born in France . . ." (268).

Actually, it was a time of real reform of the Spanish clergy, thanks particularly to the methodical work of the Cluniac order, whose monasteries proliferated all over the Iberian Peninsula at that time. For its part, the Holy See showed a growing interest in Spain. At its insistence the king of Aragon ordered in 1071 that the Latin rite be substituted for the Oriental *Mozarabic* rite in his realm. After the capture of Toledo in 1085 the king of Castile followed suit. Thus began the Spanish people's slow assimilation of the principles and customs of medieval Christianity, which A. Castro has described with the subtle phrase "internal reconquest," or *subreconquista* (269).

However, during the time that the *Reconquista* itself was at its peak and the Christian military apparatus was supported by a commissariat that was essentially Jewish, no one in the Spain of the Three Religions thought of meddling with the traditional structures. As we have already pointed out, the princes of the Church and the heads of the military orders followed the lead of the kings in employing Jews as administrators and financiers and maintained the most cordial and varied relations with them—as in the case of that Inquisitor General of Aragon at the beginning of the fifteenth century whose trip to Avignon to receive his doctorate in theology was paid for by the Jews of Saragossa (270). The Church claimed its tithe not only from the Christians but also from the Jews and Moors: in 1359 the Council of Tortosa forbade Christians to associate with Jews who refused to pay it (and those alone), thus indirectly excommunicating them. But at the beginning of the thirteenth century the Church of Castile imposed another tax on the Jews, a special levy curiously named Tax of the Thirty Deniers (after the thirty pieces of silver of Judas), although its actual amount varied and was not related to the figure thirty. However, it became customary to exempt certain *aljamas* from this tax, and, it seems, the powerful *aljama* of Toledo tried to have itself exempted on the grounds of the known antiquity of its settlement, which absolved it of all responsibility for the Crucifixion. Thus it is seen how legends of this sort also can have their practical applications (271).

This tax, and above all its name, is one evidence of how the Church began to move toward the prevailing European views on this subject. In Aragon in particular these views began to hold sway quite early. In the middle of the fourteenth century, after the conquest of Valencia and the Balearic Islands, the clergy there concerned itself very seriously with the conversion of the infidels. In 1242, with the support of Pope Innocent IV, Dominicans and Franciscans obtained authorization from the king to preach in the synagogues. On these occasions, bands of Christians excited by the spectacle often interrupted, and these sermons generally degenerated into scandals and brawls (272).

We have already mentioned that the Dominican order had founded a regular missionary institute in Barcelona. Ramon Penaforte, confessor to the king and their former general, succeeded in organizing a great public Judeo-Christian debate in that city in 1263, similar to the one that had taken place in Paris in 1240. The Christian champion, the Dominican convert Pablo Christiani, was opposed by the wise rabbi of Barcelona, Moses ben Nachman. After the debate, which lasted nearly a week in the presence of the king, each camp claimed victory; the result was that the Jew, who had displayed amazing candor,[4] was banished from Aragon and left on a pilgrimage to Palestine.

In Castile, where the Jews were more powerful, the preaching orders did not manage to complicate their lives with such spectacles. The clergy there contented itself with reviving from time to time the pontifical instructions on the wearing of a distinctive badge—with no effect—and trying to prevent intercourse between Christians and infidels. As a

[4] Here is a charming little bit of Moses ben Nachman's argument: "Of a certainty the doctrine which you believe and which is a dogma of your faith cannot be accepted by reason. Nature does not admit of it. The prophets have never said anything that would support it. . . . That the Creator of heaven and earth and all that is in them should withdraw into and pass through the womb of a certain Jewess and should grow there for nine months and be born a small child and after this grow up to be handed over to his enemies who condemn him to death and kill him, after which, you say, he came to life and returned to his former abode, neither the mind of Jew nor of any man will sustain this. . . ." Addressing himself particularly to the king, Moses ben Nachman added: "Isaiah said: 'They shall beat their swords into plowshares . . . nation shall not lift up sword against nation, neither shall they learn war any more.' But since the days of Jesus up to the present, the whole world has been full of violence and rapine, the Christians more than other peoples being shedders of blood and revealers likewise of indecencies. And how hard for you, my lord the king, and for those knights of yours, if they should learn war no more." (Cf. O. S. Rankin, *Jewish Religious Polemic*, Edinburgh, 1956, pp. 191–92.)

Christian bourgeoisie developed, the problem of the money-lenders became another source of conflict. Thus, in 1307, on the strength of instructions sent by Clement V to the Spanish clergy, certain clerics and laymen of Toledo considered it their right to stop paying installments on their debts. On learning of this the king declared he was astounded at such unheard-of actions and came to the defense of his Jews, ordering that in the future, instructions or messages of this sort be given directly to him (273). Thus the lines were drawn, with the king and his indispensable Jews on the one side, the Church and the Christian population of the cities on the other.

The populace, however, took even longer than the Church to become aware of the particular nature of the Jews. In the twelfth century that masterpiece of the popular Spanish epic, *Poema del Cid*, was written. In one of its episodes two Jews appear, Raquel and Vidas, and the gallant hero plays a bad turn on them: he borrows six hundred maravedis from them and leaves as security two coffers supposedly of jewels but actually filled with sand. Financiers and moneylenders of their state, Raquel and Vidas find themselves derided as such, but at no moment can one perceive any particular religious or even "racial" animosity.

Quite the contrary, for there are some versions of the epic in which the Cid, once his fortunes change for the better, hastens to reimburse the "honorable Jews" Raquel and Vidas, apologizing to them profusely and covering them with flowers. (Moreover, it is only on this single occasion that Raquel and Vidas are described as Jews; in all the other passages or versions of *The Cid* where they appear, they are only recognizable as such by their names and their profession.) In sum, such a description, while true to life, does not foreshadow any trace of a particular prejudice (274).

Things were different a century later when a less spontaneous and more edifying literature developed. The deacon Gonzalo de Berceo, the first Castilian poet whose name is known, describes many Jews in his religious poems, especially in his most popular poem, "The Miracles of the Holy Virgin." He describes them very subtly: some are odious and remain faithful to the Talmud; others are virtuous and convert to Christianity, which means that the poet considers them "salvageable" in accordance with the concepts prevailing in all of Europe at that time.[5]

The same could be said of the *Cantigas* of King Alfonso the Wise, which date from the same era, some fifteen of which are concerned with the subject of the Jews. While one finds in these pieces both Jews who are allied to the Devil and the prefiguration of the theme of ritual murder (the action of which is situated in England, where the first legend of this sort was actually born), one also finds Jews who are most sympathetic. The majority of these, after many trials, end up by converting, some after having been mistreated by Christian bandits and some after having been condemned to death by their *aljama*. One can see that the king, who was indisputably the author of the *Cantigas*, took his subjects from daily life and distributed light and shadow quite impartially. Having echoed the legend of ritual murder,

---

[5] Among the themes treated by Gonzalo de Berceo, that of the Jewish moneylender or usurer, the future Shylock, is particularly informative. In Berceo, Shylock is prefigured by a rich anonymous Jew of Constantinople (called Abraham by other European authors of the time) who is inclined to cheat but is not fundamentally bad, and who converts at the end of the story (Miracle XXIII, "The Paid Debt"). Later, this character became worse from version to version and from century to century, as Christian anti-Semitism increased, to culminate in the implacable moneylender of Venice, whom only the genius of Shakespeare could imbue with any humanity under his heinousness. However, in the first Christian version of the legend that goes back to the beginning of the Byzantine Empire, Abraham-Shylock is a good man, an honest and generous Jew, whose final conversion is only the crowning touch to his many virtues. It must be added that the primitive Christian legend was merely the adaptation of a Talmudic Midrash in which the celebrated sage Rabbi Akiba played the leading role. "Thus gold is turned into vile lead." In this case the dialectic of Christian anti-Semitism is particularly clear. (Cf. "The Legend of the Divine Surety and the Jewish Moneylender" by Benjamin Nelson and Joshua Star, *Annuaire de l'Institut de Philologie et d'Histoire orientales et slaves*, 1939–1944, Vol. 7, pp. 289–338.)

Alfonso the Wise returned to this theme in *Las Siete Partidas* (VII, 24, 2): "And because we have heard that in some places Jews celebrated, and still celebrate, Good Friday, which commemorates the Passion of our Lord Jesus Christ, by way of contempt—stealing children and fastening them to crosses and making images of wax and crucifying them, when they cannot obtain children—we order that, hereafter, if in any part of our domains anything like this is done, and can be proved, all persons who were present . . . shall be seized . . . and after the king ascertains that they are guilty, he shall cause them to be put to death in a disgraceful manner, no matter how many there may be" (275). "And because we have heard. . . ." The legend, born in Norwich, England, in 1144 (cf. Vol. 1, p. 58) had managed to cross the Pyrenees. But if Spanish Christians whispered about it, it was not until the end of the fifteenth century that a great trial for ritual murder was actually held in Castile, as the prologue to the 1492 expulsion (while in Aragon such affairs began to crop up at the end of the thirteenth century).

· In 1309 a *fuero* promulgated by the king of Castile reflected the progress of the *subreconquista* and the decline in the status of the Jews. According to this *fuero* there was no longer the same price on the life of a Christian and the life of an infidel: a Christian who killed an infidel had to pay a fine of one hundred maravedis; an infidel who killed a Christian had to pay with his life (276).

Part Two

Toward Unity
of the Faith

---

eight

The Decline

The Mounting Danger

In the course of the fourteenth century, anti-Jewish sentiment crystallized and expanded all across the Iberian Peninsula; by the end of the century there were large-scale
massacres in most Spanish villages. Catalonia and Aragon,
just below the Pyrenees, were the first theaters of these
bloody episodes; in Castile the explosion came only in 1391,
and the movement then spread across all of Spain. But it did
not reach Portugal, at the far end of the peninsula—an
added proof, if necessary, of how important the influences
and examples from the other side of the Pyrenees were in
this matter.

In 1321 it was in Aragon and in Navarre that the mad
"Shepherds' Crusade" of France ended; after massacring the
Jews at Jaca, Montclus, and Pamplona the Crusaders were
dispersed by Aragonese troops. In 1348, during the great
plague called the Black Death, the people of Barcelona and
neighboring cities blamed the Jews for this disaster and tried
to burn and pillage the *aljamas*. The same thing was going
on in Germany and in France (while in Castile there was no

trouble of this type). But order was quickly restored by the authorities. The kings did their best to protect the Jews against the increasingly numerous attacks by agitators. From obscure documents we can sometimes see the details of how anti-Jewish agitation built up until the fire flared at the end of the century. For example, when there were disturbances in Gerona in the spring of 1331, the king ordered the general bailiff of Catalonia to make an investigation and to punish the guilty. In his circumstantial account the bailiff stated that at Lent a band of tonsured clerics and young students had tried to burn the *aljama*. A week later, "excited by the music of a minstrel beating the drum," the students had thrown stones at a Jewish burial. At Easter the situation worsened. On Holy Thursday some thirty clerics and schoolboys, led by the canons Vidal de Villanova and Dalmacio de Mont, had tried to tear down the gate and break into the *aljama*. The bailiff of Gerona, accompanied by some armed men, had tried to restore order. When he was attacked by a hail of stones, he prudently retreated and posted himself at some distance. The rioters gathered sticks and piled them before the gate, sprinkled oil on them, and set them on fire. Then, while the Jews and police fought the fire together, another canon succeeded in calming down the rioters and they finally dispersed, so that a general massacre was avoided. In his report the general bailiff related how the citizens of Gerona who gathered at the scene were vocal in their disapproval; he also noted that the band of troublemakers included several children aged twelve to fifteen, if not even younger, all belonging to the Gerona chapter (277).

⸱ This meticulous report, faithfully recording the facts and the actions of the rioters, and even their cries—their slogan was that the Jews should be forbidden to circulate freely in the city—clearly shows the almost statutory anti-Semitism of the lower clergy, or, more precisely, the fundamental role played at the time of the anti-Jewish disturbances by the numerous men of the lower classes who gravitated to the churches and monasteries—young students or seminarians, servants and common laborers, even minstrels and beggars.

The pretext put forth by the troublemakers—to forbid the Jews to circulate in the city and mix with Christians—corresponded to one of the principal demands formulated by the ecclesiastical councils at the time, demands that were immediately adopted by spokesmen for the middle classes for motives which were anything but theological.

The relationship between purification of the faith and class or caste interest is particularly clear in Castile, where from the end of the thirteenth century the growing middle class acquired a voice, being allowed to name representatives to the legislature, or Cortes, and to authorize taxes. In 1313 the Council of Zamora demanded that the Jews be required to wear a distinctive badge, that they be forbidden to circulate in public from Wednesday night to Saturday morning and during all of Holy Week, that they be forbidden to work Sundays, and so forth. These demands were repeated by the Cortes of Palencia six months later, by that of Burgos in 1315, Medina del Campo in 1318, and others over the years (278). Demands of more immediate practicality, calling for a general moratorium on loans contracted with Jews that had fallen due, were added. The king either tried to avoid answering such demands or made promises he then did not keep. As we have already mentioned, the great Jewish bankers of Toledo and Seville who controlled all the financial channels of the kingdom remained all-powerful in the court of Castile. Their names appear in the chronicles in rapid succession. Some met a tragic end, for they lived in the atmosphere of an Oriental seraglio with its intrigues and plots, and they battled ferociously against the Christian favorites when they were not battling among themselves.

In fact, the situation of the Jews in Castile was not seriously affected until the second half of the fourteenth century. From 1355 to 1366 a relentless civil war pitted the legitimate King Pedro the Cruel against his bastard brother Henry of Trastamara; the latter finally won. Each called in foreign mercenaries, the troops of the Prince of Wales for Pedro and those of Bertrand Du Guesclin for Henry (this was during one of the truces in the Hundred Years' War), and each, in order to defray the expenses of war and to pay the soldiers, had his regular Jewish financier. But the great majority of the Castilian Jews, loyalists by prudence as well as by tradition, remained faithful to the legitimate king. Henry tried to gain the support of the clergy by using this fact to smear his opponent as "the Judaized king," a man completely dominated by the Jews and their ambitions, who "confided all his secrets to them and not to his close friends and blood relatives" (279). The myths of war began to inflate; little by little the "Judaized king" became the "Jewish king," a Jew who was substituted for the legitimate infant at the time of his birth (and thus much more illegitimate than King Henry) and who, moreover, had plotted with his Jewish friends to kill his first wife, a French princess.

The country was ravaged by the war and thus most willing to attribute all its misfortunes to the Jews. These stories were also carried by Du Guesclin's men back to France, where they enjoyed a considerable vogue and were included in many chronicles and many legends, contributing to the version still believed today, that King Pedro was a "depraved king" while Henry was a "virtuous king." But we know that generally it is the winning side which writes history.

Virtuous or not, Henry of Trastamara knew how to come to grips with reality. When, after the end of the civil war, the Cortes met in Burgos and once more demanded that measures be taken against the Jews, and in particular that taxes henceforth be put in the hands of Christian tax collectors, the king answered that he would willingly give them preference, even on terms which were less advantageous to him, but that Christian financiers or experts were not to be found in his kingdom. The Cortes also demanded that all Jewish officials or "intimates" be removed from the royal court. The king did not deny that he allowed some Jews "to come and go in his household," adding that he did not see any reason to isolate them, but he promised to be careful that the Jews were never given too much authority over the Christians (280).

The king was only defending the ancient privileges and rights of the Crown. Actually, the civil war had dealt the *aljamas* of Castile a blow from which they would never recover. In 1369 a royal edict took note of their difficulties: ". . . Our *aljamas* are poor and needy. For a long time they have not been able to recover the sums which are due them . . ." (281). Some had been put to the sword by the foreign mercenaries; almost all had been pillaged, and the local population, the *pueblo menudo*, had also had a hand in this. Above all, the prince, traditional protector of the Jews, seemed for the first time to have sided against them, having been carried to power on a wave of anti-Jewish agitation.

Henceforth the Cortes, which had grown in influence at the end of the war, made the Jewish question one of its great issues. Returning to the subject in Toro in 1371, it described the principal ill from which the kingdom was suffering as follows:

". . . Because of the great liberty and power accorded to the enemies of the faith, especially the Jews, in our whole kingdom, in the royal household as well as in the houses of the knights, the squires, and the nobles, and because of the high offices and the great honors which they enjoy, all Christians are forced to obey them and fear them and bow deeply to them, so that the councils of all the cities and of all places and all people are captives of the Jews and subjugated to them. Be it because of the honors which are accorded them in the royal household and in the houses of the great, be it because of the revenue and offices which they hold, for whatever reason, the Jews, evil and rash men, enemies of God and of all of Christianity, cause numerous evils and sow corruption with impunity, so that the greater part of our kingdom is tyrannized and ruined by the Jews, in contempt of the Christians and our Catholic faith . . ." (282).

After drawing this somber picture, the Cortes of Toro reiterated the usual demands: no Jewish officials or tax collectors; the wearing of a distinctive badge. They also demanded that Jews be prohibited from riding horseback or dressing luxuriously and that they be obliged to change their name if it was a Christian one.

- The king granted this last demand, as well as the demand that the Jews wear a badge. Actually, the very vehemence of the Cortes' remonstrances was an index of the decline of Jewish power in Castile after the disastrous civil war. Before that, such an extreme tone would have been unimaginable. Thus the myth of Jews drunk with power, thirsty for the blood of Christians, was popularized and spread abroad at the very time Jewish influence was shrinking and the status of the Jews was declining. Doubtless this happened *because* their status was declining and because their power and their pride were sufficiently shaken so that henceforth one could vilify and detest them without danger.

Chancellor Lopez de Ayala, who had early abandoned King Pedro and joined King Henry, repeated the theme of Jews as bloodsuckers in his famous and cruel satire *Rimado de Palacios:*

> Here come the Jews all alike
> And present their detailed writings
> To drink the blood of the poor people
> Promising jewels and gifts to the courtiers (283).

The degradation of the Jews at that time is reflected in the *Proverbios Morales* of Rabbi Santos (deformation of "Shem-Tov") of Carrion, one of the classical masterpieces of Spanish medieval literature. The rabbi-poet moralizes melancholically:

> The rose has no less fragrance
> Because it blooms on thorns
> Wine has no less delicacy
> Because the vine climbs from the ground

The vulture is not less worthy
Even if he was born in a vile nest
Nor the good precept
Even if a good Jew says it.

Let us note in passing that the author, in his irony, shares
the views of his audience (Jewish or Christian). He compares the Jews to "vile" vultures, also victims of prejudice.
That means that for this rabbi Spanish culture took precedence over Jewish culture; the language of the Cid, in fact,
was more familiar to him than the language of the Bible. A
great poet in Castilian, he was a fairly poor versifier in
Hebrew (284).
ˑ Starting in 1370 the classical anti-Jewish regulations of
the Middle Ages, whose application had been so long deferred in Castile, were put into effect in rapid succession. Of
particular consequence to the *aljamas* was the suppression of
their juridical autonomy in 1380; the royal edict recalled
that captivity was the natural lot of Jews, since with the
coming of Jesus Christ they had lost their sovereignty. The
liberties that had been granted them in Castile were termed
sins and scandals (285). The right to complete jurisdiction
over their people was then withdrawn from the Jewish
communities, and the cornerstone of their power collapsed.
A few years later the Council of Palencia, sitting in the
presence of the Cortes, introduced the policy of segregated
housing for Jews—that is, a ghetto—a policy whose application would not be long delayed (286). Parallel with this,
there were frequent annulments of the interest on debts, or
partial annulments of the debts themselves, to the benefit of
the Christian middle class and the detriment of Jewish
creditors.
ˑ Faced with these humiliations and woes, Spanish Judaism
reacted quite differently from the Jews beyond the Pyrenees.
The Jewish communities did not close in on themselves or
turn the walls of the ghettos into an impassable barrier. Far
from leading to a fanatic religious zeal, the persecutions

tended instead to temper their religious ardor. The deep roots the Jews had put down in Spain, their familiarity with the local customs and culture, plus the latent skepticism of many intellectuals for whom security was well worth a Mass, all converged to orient them toward the convenient solution of baptism. The knowledge of the Christian and Moslem dogmas contributed to this, as well as a philosophy that taught the relativity of all things. Ibn Verga, one of the best Jewish chroniclers of the time (to whom we shall return again), had one of his characters say:

". . . Everyone knows that the various religions exist only thanks to the representations which one makes of them. The Jew thinks that there is no teaching and religion better than his and considers those who believe something else to be imbeciles. The Christian, on the contrary, believes that the Jew is nothing but an animal in human form, and that his soul will go to the depths of hell. As for the Moslem, he will say that hell is full of both of them. . . ."

This from the pen of a Jewish polemicist whose characters clearly serve as spokesmen for him! (287)

In short, the intercourse between Christians and infidels that had so disturbed the Spanish clergy now made its missionary work that much easier. For the moment it was still a matter of individual cases rather than a mass movement, but these cases were becoming more and more frequent. The convertors, who for the most part were converted Jews themselves, were no longer preaching in the wilderness. The most successful was Abner of Burgos, a wise doctor who had practiced philosophical skepticism for many years before becoming sacristan of the Cathedral of Valladolid. In his many writings he knew how to marshal the arguments that would best impress his contemporaries, proofs based on the philosophical doctrines of the time or concordances drawn from the cabala. He was "the master ideologue of the apostasy," the founder of a school and a prototype at the same time (288).

The early successes of Christian propaganda can be seen from various examples. In Castile during the civil war "many were those who left the ranks of our community, after the sufferings that they endured . . ." noted Rabbi Samuel Çarça (289). In 1380 a Cortes petition noted that "numerous Jews and Jewesses who have turned toward the true faith of God" had to be protected from persecution by their old or their new coreligionists (290). The same year Rabbi Shemtov Shaprut noted sorrowfully: "Many of our coreligionists are abandoning our ranks and pursuing us with their arguments, trying to prove the truth of their [new] faith to us with the aid of verses of the Holy Scripture and of the Talmud . . ." (291). We know that these apostates were recruited principally from among the cultivated or rich Jews, while the plain, common people—that is, the majority—still held to their simple faith. But the learning and social prestige of the early converts threatened to make them models to be copied.

Portugal, at the far end of the peninsula, was the only place not yet affected by the general evolution. In the fourteenth century both the lives of the Jews and the organization of their communities were still modeled along old Oriental lines: the king named the great rabbi and supreme judge who was also in charge of levying taxes. This veritable prince of the Jews sometimes also exercised the functions of general treasurer of the kingdom. As elsewhere, the clergy protested against Jewish domination and the people began to murmur, but such agitation was a long way from being translated into direct action.

In the course of the coming centuries Portugal was destined to become the principal land of refuge for the Spanish Jews.

Vox populi, vox Dei

Seville, the old Roman capital, had again become the most populous and the richest of the Spanish cities by the end of the Middle Ages. The Jews had been active in repopulating it during the *Reconquista* and thus were assured of a particularly strong position. The richest were part of the municipal administration, which was exceptional even in Spain; numerous others carved out a career for themselves in the royal court, in the affairs of state (292).

Since 1378 the archdeacon of Ecija, Ferrant Martínez, former confessor of the queen mother, had been preaching against the Jews in Seville and stirring up the Christians against them, "putting them in horror of these people" (293). On his own authority he had arrogated the right to settle disputes between Christians and Jews as ecclesiastical judge. When the king, "fearing that there would be evil and harm for bodies and souls," ordered him to cease his agitation, he paid no attention. Comparing himself to the prophets of Israel, to Isaiah, to Jeremiah, and even to Moses, the greatest of all (for he had not been afraid to brave the anger of the pharaoh), he replied: ". . . I cannot keep from preaching and saying of the Jews what my Lord Jesus Christ said of them in the Gospels. . . ." Besides, he was convinced he was acting in the best royal interests. Were not the Jews defying and cheating the kings and princes of the earth just as they had once defied God and lied to Him? These were the explanations he gave to the king, but in the course of his anti-Semitic sermons Ferrant Martínez added some others: a Christian who harmed or killed a Jew would be causing the king and queen no displeasure; quite the contrary. This he knew from a direct and certain source, and he himself guaranteed it. (The king was indignant: "You, who belonged to our household, how dare you say such things?")

The fact is that for more than twelve years Martínez continued his agitation with impunity, telling his flock to expel the Jews from the cities and villages and to demolish their synagogues. Powerless to stop him except perhaps from time to time by gifts (an obscure dispute on the subject of a piece of cloth pitted Martínez against the spokesman of the *aljama* in 1388), the Jews feared the worst. The agitator's fame began to spread all through Spain. But his preaching does not seem to have led to any bloody excesses before the summer of 1391. It is true that the available documents only reflect a few aspects of his campaign and that the gaps give pause for thought: Who was protecting him—or was in collusion with him—so that he was able to defy both his king and his archbishop at the same time?

Both of them, Juan I, king of Castile, and Barroso, archbishop of Seville, died a few days apart at the end of 1390. The archbishop's seat remained vacant for a long time; the successor to the throne, Henry III, was scarcely ten years old. The Sevillian agitator took advantage of the interregnum to intensify his campaign. The results were not long in coming: on June 6, 1391, after a few skirmishes an unruly crowd stormed Seville's Jewish section, and all the Jews who did not hide in time were called upon to convert. The majority hastened to embrace the Cross; the rest were massacred on the spot.

Like a forest fire, in a few weeks of that summer the conflagration ravaged all of Spain.

Starting in Seville at the beginning of June, in less than a month the riots spread to most of the other Andalusian and Castilian cities (294). They reached Aragon the following month and the Balearic Islands and Catalonia in August. How did the flame leap from place to place? There is every evidence that agitators trained by Martínez went from city to city inciting the populace. A boat transported a band of agitators from Seville to Valencia and Barcelona to give the signal for the uprising. In Saragossa the principal leader was the nephew of the archdeacon himself. Martínez managed to gain credence for a rumor that the kings and even the pope were secretly behind him; and the ambivalent attitude of Clement VII did nothing to contradict this. In Valencia the mob attacked the *aljama* with cries of "Martínez is coming! Death or holy water for the Jews!" In Barcelona they cried: "Long live the king and the people. The fat ones wish to destroy the little people!"

Under such conditions the movement quickly became a

sort of peasant uprising in which all classes of the Christian population finally participated. "The eagerness to plunder the Jews grew greater each day," Chancellor Ayala noted laconically. Believing they were doing pious work pleasing to God and the king, the mob pillaged and massacred with full peace of mind. Nowhere could the authorities bring in troops against them; once the fire had started, it was impossible to extinguish it.

On the contrary, the riot generally ended naturally after the Jews of an *aljama* converted. "Let the Jews become Christians and all tumult will cease," wrote the administrators of Perpignan to Juan I of Aragon. It was in vain that the kings wrote comminatory letters to their cities trying to save the *aljamas*. Juan of Aragon in particular, a wise prince, a friend of learning, surrounded by excellent Christian and Jewish advisers, was farsighted, and his messages show not only an elevated sense of his royal duties but also a far better understanding of theology than the majority of the Spanish prelates possessed at the time. In each message he insisted that respect be shown the "free will" of the Jews, and he called the forced baptisms "horrible crimes." "If they do not voluntarily accept Christianity, they will be more deeply sunk than ever in their error," he wrote to the administrators of Lerida. "Neither civil nor canonical law permits conversion by force. Those who interfere in this matter, either by persuasion or in any other way, endanger themselves with both God and man," he wrote to those of Perpignan (295).

But all this was in vain. A holy fury had seized the soul of the people; yesterday's friends and neighbors were now mere infidels; the spirit of the *Reconquista* had been unleashed. At Cuenca the municipal counselors had the church bells rung to give the signal for attack (296). At Tortosa the signal was a minstrel beating a drum (297). The people rushed to the *aljamas* "as if they were going out to wage a holy war at the king's command," noted a Christian eyewitness (298).

A modern historian sees in these events "the community of

feelings of the Spaniards, a symptom of the unity of the Hispanic people" (299), meaning, therefore, their taking a stand in favor of hating the Jew. However, at the time, numerous Jews found shelter in the homes of Christian burghers. Great lords let them take refuge in their castles, but they had to pay for it "and were left very poor," noted Ayala, "for they had to make large gifts to these lords for sparing them from such a great tribulation." The Jews also gave large gifts to the pope in Avignon, Clement VII, to keep him from giving his public blessing to Martínez (which it seems the pontiff was about to do, for the queen of Aragon begged him to abstain from making any reckless gesture or issuing a rescript or bull in favor of the rioters) (300). As for his condemning the massacres, there was no question of doing so at a time when Christianity was torn by the Great Schism.[1]

Hundreds of Jews stood firm in the face of these trials and died "to sanctify the Name" in accordance with ancient tradition. For example, this happened in Toledo in the case of the Talmudist Judah ben Asher, grandson of the German rabbi, and his students; in Barcelona Jews committed suicide by the dozen; as one man, those of Gerona refused to abjure their faith. But in the majority of the *aljamas* panic and apostasy were in the air.

Those who did not succeed in hiding or fleeing Spain accepted baptism, and many rabbis themselves set the example. Seized by a sheeplike panic, the Jewish masses followed them. This clerical treason is not surprising. Centuries of thought and philosophical doubt were behind it, paving the way for conversions dictated by ambition or despair, by prudence or cowardice. But although individual motives

---

[1] It must be recalled here that from 1378 to 1417 two and later three popes ruled over Christianity, opposing each other mercilessly. Spain recognized the authority of Clement VII of Avignon, whose chief adviser was the Spanish cardinal Pedro de Luna. In 1394 de Luna succeeded Clement VII under the name of Benedict XIII. He later played a leading role in the history of Jewish persecution by staging the great Disputation of Tortosa.

may often have been extremely complex, they still led to the same brutally simple result.

The Jewish intellectuals of the time were well aware of that complexity. Writing to a friend who had converted, the doctor Joshua Halorki listed four possible reasons for his conversion:

"Did you perchance lust after riches and honors? . . . Or did the study of philosophy cause you to change so radically and to regard the proofs of faith as vanity and delusion, so that you therefore turned to things more apt to gratify the body and satisfy the intellect without fear and anxiety and apprehension? Or, when you beheld the doom of our homeland, the multitude of the afflictions that have recently befallen us, which ruined and destroyed us . . . did it then seem to you that the name of Israel would be remembered no more? Or perhaps the secrets of prophecy have been revealed to you and the principles of faith . . . and you saw that our fathers had inherited falsehood . . . and you chose what is true and established?" (301)

After long years of hesitation Joshua Halorki himself was finally baptized in 1412. Immediately hastening to furnish the customary token of his sincerity, he then became, under the name of Jeronimo de Santa Fe, the keenest convertor of his generation. The behavior of his friend and correspondent Solomon Halevi, who was converted in 1391, was more subtle. The epidemic of conversions of that year was dominated by this unusual and powerful figure.

To this day the memory of Solomon Halevi, rabbi of Burgos, alias Paulus de Sancta Maria, bishop of that same city, is abominated by Jews and revered by Spaniards with equal fervor (302). Doubtless this philosopher and master of his fortunes would have smiled disdainfully at both the rancor of the one and the pious praise of the other. Born into an illustrious family of Talmudists and statesmen, Solomon Halevi had a solid grounding in Jewish studies and early in life completed the course of all the knowledge of the time; Christian scholasticism was familiar to him, as were philosophy and astrology. As a man of many parts he also enjoyed the game of politics and was the diplomatic adviser to the court of Castile. His keenest interest, however, ran to pure speculation; in accordance with the precepts of Aristotle he sought happiness in the meditative quest for truth. Some of his intellectual preoccupations can be seen in the correspondence he exchanged with Joshua Halorki:

"Be he Jew, Christian, or Moslem, does not reason force the wise man to compare his religion to that of others? But how, under such conditions, can one who is not certain of having chosen the proper path find peace of mind? Short of being basically unjust, God cannot forbid such comparisons and quests, for this would be to forbid those who are born in error from tearing themselves away from it and finding truth. . . ."

Obviously such speculations, which were common among the learned Jews of the time, were hardly calculated to strengthen one's faith, whatever it might be.

Other speculations probably captivated the mind of Solomon Halevi during his long tenure as a diplomat in France, where he had occasion to debate at leisure with Christian theologians. It is obvious that Saint Thomas Aquinas' proof based on the permanence and the power of the Christian Church made an impression on him. The study of Aristotle presented him with the same argument in another form: that a slave can be neither happy nor wise. After having escaped from the Burgos massacres of 1391, how could a man of this caliber do anything but convert?

As a prudent man he chose the name of Paul, in memory of the apostle, and the surname of Santa Maria to further his claim to resplendent bonds of relationship, for as a member of the tribe of Levi he claimed to be of the same lineage as the Holy Virgin (303). He had a long and magisterial career, accumulating honors of state and church, until in the end he was able to control the majority of the Castilian episcopal seats. When he died in 1435, in the odor of sanctity, his tomb was a site for pilgrimages (304). For several generations his numerous descendants in their turn were prominent in all domains of Spanish life (305). Among the various writings he left to posterity is an anti-Jewish polemic, "The Debates Between Saul and Paul on the Jews." His former coreligionists saw him as the principal architect of anti-Jewish edicts—which does not mean that he favored the *conversos;* on the contrary, he tried to avoid associating with those like him, to block their progress and keep them away from the court (306). Here, too, this unusual man was farseeing.

The Rout of the Aljamas

It goes without saying that it was a rare Jew who felt comfortable in the difficult role of Christian in spite of himself. Most were repelled by the Masses and devotions; "bad Jews, they became even worse Christians."[2] Some continued to practice Judaism in secret—almost openly, in fact, for the Castilian Inquisition did not yet exist. In any case, as the storm abated there was indescribable confusion in the *aljamas.* Spanish Judaism suddenly found itself split into two enemy camps. For the Jews, the converts were renegades, traitors, unless they allowed themselves to be carried back into the bosom of Judaism. For the converts, the Jews took on varied and contradictory meanings, of which the clearest was that they were a living reproach, a permanent reminder of the converts' past apostasy and their present hypocrisy, of their doubly ambiguous situation.

However, the most solid of human bonds—ties of family, business, or close friendship—survived among the members of the two camps. The converts naturally continued to follow the same trades and to live in the same houses as before

2 "Regarding these new Christians, most of them practiced Judaism in secret; others were men with neither God nor law; bad Jews before, and even worse Christians afterward." (Menendez y Pelayo, *Heterodoxos,* Vol. 1, p. 630.)

their baptism. There were numerous divorces between couples who now had different religions. It was a situation likely to engender extreme tension and to breed hatred. The effects were not slow to appear. In many Spanish cities, from the day after their baptism the *conversos* became the most ardent persecutors of the Jews. "The Jews of your *aljama*," Henry III wrote to the municipal authorities of Burgos in July, 1392, "have informed me that when they were attacked they left their homes in fear of death and took refuge in the houses of the best of you, where they live today in your safe custody, not daring to return to their houses in the *aljama*, for fear that certain Jews who now have become Christians will persecute them and do them much harm . . ." (307). Again, in 1394 the *conversos* of Perpignan incited the crowd against the Jews and prevented them from returning to their former homes (308). Conflicts of interest aggravated and embittered these hatreds. Once an *aljama* had split in two after the conversion of some of its members, to whom did the community assets belong? There were all sorts of machinations and incredible coercion, on which the few remaining documents sometimes shed some light. Thus, in Jerez, where around fifty heads of Jewish families were baptized in June, 1391, the converts on August 20 of the same year donated to Fray Pedro, bursar of the Dominican monastery, the Jewish cemetery "with all the buildings which are located on it . . . because of the numerous benefits which we have received and receive each day from you, who inform us and instruct us in the holy Catholic faith, insuring the health of our souls . . ." (309). There was a similar instance in Lerida, where seventy-eight Jews had been massacred in the summer of 1391: the cemetery went to the *conversos*, and the synagogue was turned into a church and dedicated to "Saint Mary of the Miracle" (310). However, in both Jerez and Lerida, a large Jewish community survived. The exact conditions under which they were dispossessed is not known, but they can be imagined. Across all of Spain, despite the desperate protestations of the Jews, synagogues were turned into churches (at Toledo, those of Santa María la Blanca and Santa María del Tránsito are still there for tourists to admire) (311). But if the Church was gaining on the one hand, it was also losing on the other. For example, the Dominican monastery in Madrid was deprived of the annual income of three thousand maravedis from the *aljama,* which had been completely wiped out (312). In New Castile the confusion reached its peak in 1395, when the archbishop of Toledo tried to name his personal physician, Maestre Pedro, a convert, as supreme judge of the Jews of his archdiocese. Although the majority of the Jews of Toledo objected, Maestre Pedro was nevertheless accepted by some of them, creating a great uproar in the synagogue (313).

The days of Spanish Judaism seemed numbered. Was it still possible to rebuild it? The most illustrious of those who did not despair and who tried to ward off the impending disaster was the rabbi of Barcelona Hasdai Crescas, who was both a man of action and a great thinker.

Supported by the king and queen of Aragon, Crescas tried to reconstruct the great communities that had been destroyed. In May, 1393, the king accorded him exceptional powers to establish new *aljamas* in Barcelona and Valencia, settle sixty Jewish families in each city, and furnish them with money, resorting to force if necessary. Moreover, in all the cities of the kingdom of Aragon, tax exemptions were granted to the Jews and amnesty was promised to those who had secretly taken refuge abroad. New constitutions were drafted to limit the outrageous rights of the former oligarchs within the *aljamas* and to divide the tax burden more equitably. Crescas, whose only son had been massacred in Barcelona, set an example by marrying his second wife in the spring of 1393 with the king's permission—symbol of a new growth and increase of the Children of Israel (314). At the same time attacking what for him was the root of the evil, he wrote treatises in which he demonstrated the impossibility of rational knowledge or intellectualization of religion—an allusion to the attraction of the philosophical reasoning of Maimonides and his successors. More and more, his speculations on the creation of the universe by God led him to attack Aristotelian physics with a vigor that would later win the admiration of Spinoza (315). Trying by every means to fan the flame of Judaism, he also wrote a treatise in Spanish, intended for the masses, of anti-Christian polemics, only fragments of which survive.

But the many efforts of this sage could not turn events from their ineluctable course. The man of action was powerless to revive the *aljamas* of Barcelona and Valencia. The thinker found no following. A contemporary relates how in the court of Aragon Hasdai Crescas met Paulus de Sancta Maria, who tried to engage him in a theological discussion. Where is a Shakespeare to depict that encounter between the unbending champion of the decimated Jewish line and the leader of their successors, the yielding converts?

After the popular explosion of 1391 the surviving Jews enjoyed a brief respite. But henceforth missionary frenzy was in the air in Spain. From the moment it took charge of the shattered or restive souls of the *conversos,* the Church was tormented by the bad example that the free and openly declared Jews set for them. Some converts, especially those who like Paulus de Sancta Maria had gone into the Church and made a career of it, did their utmost to combat this and issued numerous warnings. Twenty years later it was the clergy's turn to enter the fray. And even those churchmen who were Christian enough to condemn the massacres of 1391 soon instigated others.

This was the case with the greatest preacher of the time, Saint Vincent Ferrer, whose flaming eloquence was then arousing the whole Western world. His sermons, which all the Jews were forced to attend, did not fail to recall that Jesus as well as the Virgin Mary had been Jewish and that nothing would displease God so much as baptisms obtained by force; that it was vital for the Church to convert the Jews, but that this had to be accomplished by gentle persuasion and kind words. In his vivid image: "The apostles who conquered the world carried neither lance nor knife! The Christians should not kill the Jews with knives, but with their words!" Meanwhile, it was important always to keep them at a safe distance and to isolate them in the ghettos, for fear of their pernicious example (316). This is what the saint preached from city to city, all across Aragon, Castile, and Gascony, leaving his innumerable listeners in ecstasy thanks to his miraculous gift of tongues[3] and brandishing the anathema of excommunication against those who had anything to do with the Jews.

· After he passed through, terror reigned in the *aljamas*. Any means to convert recalcitrant Jews—prison, hunger, torture—seemed right to Christians under the spell of Vincent Ferrer's words. Charged by the king of Aragon to find out what was behind these unbelievable events, his son investigated the details in person and then wrote: ". . . may Your Highness now know of these persecutions and what means were used so that they could proclaim that the Jews were converted by the light of the Holy Ghost" (317). (The infante was all the more indignant in that his own messenger narrowly escaped being torn to pieces by the unruly crowd.) The king himself, who was a great admirer of the saint, stated that "following the preaching of 'Maestre Vincent' there are some who without thinking make attempts, commit various misdeeds, and engage in plots against the Jews . . ." (318). Finally, at the mere news of his arrival whole Jewish communities took refuge in the mountains and forests, while others took the path of converting en masse.

---

[3] Saint Vincent Ferrer's miraculous gift of tongues was only partial. Without being able to speak languages he did not know (as, for example, the apostles did at Pentecost), he succeeded in making his own language (Catalan) perfectly understandable to an audience that did not know it at all. This is according to the *Dictionnaire de Théologie catholique*, Paris, 1950, Vol. 15, Part 2, p. 3040. Obviously, under such conditions the intentions of the saint were not always completely understood by his listeners, and they interpreted his words in their own way, relying on his gestures alone. (On Saint Vincent Ferrer, see also Volume 1 of my *History of Anti-Semitism*, pp. 144–45.)

⊘ At the beginning of 1412 Saint Vincent Ferrer succeeded in having a new statute passed in Castile concerning the Jews, the statute of Valladolid (319), forbidding them, among other things, to sell or give food to Christians, to have Christians work in their fields, to preface their names with the title "don," to change domicile, cut their hair, or shave their beards. As to their clothing, three articles of the statute were concerned with it: their attire had to be humble, of rough cloth, and naturally it had to include a highly visible, distinctive badge. On all these points Castile had now caught up with the rest of Europe.

⊘ Vincent Ferrer, who made and unmade kings, was one of the confessors of Pope Benedict XIII. This pontiff, one of the protagonists of the Great Schism, was in difficulties. Two other popes opposed him; the Council of Pisa had excommunicated him; his successful rival Martin V had called him the "son of the Devil." In 1412 he resolved to do a glorious deed and convert the Jews en masse, by showing them as vividly as possible how foolish their belief was. This demonstration has gone down in history under the name of the Disputation of Tortosa (320).

The demonstration took nearly two years. The champion of Christianity was the learned doctor of the pope, the convert Joshua Halorki, mentioned previously. The wisest rabbis of Aragon were summoned to oppose him and to admit that if the Talmud were read correctly and honestly, it would confirm that the Messiah had already appeared in the person of Jesus. Joshua Halorki defended his Christological commentaries zealously; the rabbis—there were fourteen of them—opposed him valiantly. A great deal of subtle argument issued from both sides. It is disconcerting to read the discussion today, for although the topic is a serious one, it reminds one of the debates on the sex of angels.[4] But

---

[4] Among other things, Halorki tried to demonstrate that Jesus was the Messiah by appealing largely to the methods of cabalistic exegesis, based on the numerical value assigned to the letters of the Hebrew alphabet, and more generally on the principle according to which each comma, and even

the real spectacle was the audience. One to two thousand spectators attended each session. Some came from far away, especially the Jewish visitors who had been commanded to attend and who, at the close of each colloquy, got up and declared that the arguments of the Christian had convinced them and demanded to be baptized on the spot. After which they were sent back to where they had come from to sow the good seed. Three thousand Jews at least—this figure was attested to by a notary—filed through the baptistries of Tortosa between January, 1413, and November, 1414, particularly after eighteen members of the Caballería family, the most illustrious Jewish family of Aragon, were collectively converted in January, 1414. It was, indeed, an impressively contrived spectacle, and the memory of it is still alive in the local traditions (321).

Bullied and threatened, most of the rabbis who submitted to this brainwashing finally gave up and humbly begged in the summer of 1414 that they be allowed to return home. They declared themselves "ignorant, insufficient, of slender knowledge, incapable of continuing to discuss the Talmud and its holy and wise authors" (322). The pope and Halorki claimed victory and stated that the rabbis had "disavowed the Talmud." There was even a rumor that they had been

---

certain traditional spelling errors in the sacred texts, had their hidden meaning. Thus, for example, Isaiah 9: 6–7 says about the Messiah: "A son is given unto us . . . that the government may be increased, and of peace there be no end, upon the throne of David. . . ." To increase (in Hebrew, *lemarbe*) is written with an error consecrated by tradition: the *m* (*mem*) instead of being an ordinary open *mem* (numerical value forty) is a closed or final *mem* (numerical value six hundred). From this Halorki concluded first, that the closing of this *mem* symbolized the virginity of the Mother of God, and second, that its numerical value was related to the six hundred years that had elapsed between Isaiah and Jesus. It must be assumed that he himself was not the author of such interpretations or speculations, for they were current in convert circles. Let us briefly point out the parallel between these methods of cabalistic exegesis (which were later cultivated in Central Europe) in attributing a hidden meaning to each comma and *lapsus calami* of the "Biblical discourse" and the present methods of the sciences of man, particularly those of psychoanalysis.

converted, a version which the majority of the Christian authors accept (323). However, two rabbis, who were more stoic than their colleagues, continued the fight to the end and returned home heroically undefeated.

/ But the objective sought by Halorki and by the antipope was in large part attained. When he was condemned by the Christians at the Council of Constance a short time later, Benedict XIII could at least claim that he had defeated the Jews. From Perpignan to Cadiz they were converted by the thousands. Whole communities were wiped from the face of the earth, to the jubilation of Christian hearts. Signs appeared in the heavens: the king of Aragon himself wrote to Saint Vincent Ferrer that 122 Jews of Guadalajara, in Castile, having perceived a miraculous cross in the clouds, converted immediately in March, 1414 (324). It is possible that this time there was an even greater number of "New Christians" than in 1391; in the Jewish chronicles 1391 remains "the year of persecutions and oppression" and 1413–14 "the year of apostasy." "It is not even certain that a thousandth of the race of Jews who came from Jerusalem to Spain still survive," exclaimed the chronicler Ibn Verga (325).

nine

The Impasse—Marranism

Ibn Verga's cry of distress, while obviously an exaggeration, shows the pessimism that reigned in the *aljamas* after the blows they suffered at the hands of Vincent Ferrer and the antipope. Before disaster struck at the end of the century, however, the Spanish Jews were to enjoy a new period of calm, which lasted even longer than the preceding one. The Great Schism having come to an end, in two bulls dated 1421 and 1422 Pope Martin V reiterated that a forced baptism was not a Christian baptism and strongly condemned the persecutions, and for their part the kings of Castile and Aragon again assumed their traditional role as protectors of the Jewish faith, to the extent of their ability. But the situation had changed radically.

Before discussing the new and unsettling state of affairs that resulted from the events of 1391 and 1410–14, let us take a look at the social and economic background of the time. According to the best estimate, at the beginning of the fifteenth century Spain (with the exception of the small kingdoms of Granada and Navarre) had a population of 8.5 million people. Nearly seven million of these were rural, and 500,000 of the rural population were Moriscos—Moslems. The urban population exceeded 1.5 million (according to the same Spanish historian, Juan de Regla) (326), of which 10 per cent were aristocrats and upper class and 70 per cent were lower class (*pueblo menudo*).

"The gap that existed between the aristocracy and the common people," this author went on to note, "was to a large extent filled by churchmen and Jews. With the exception of a minority of high dignitaries of the Church and a perceptibly larger number of wealthy Hebrews, these constituted a true middle class. . . ." This class, which was Christian in the other European countries, gave birth to the modern bourgeoisie that developed so weakly and so tardily in Spain.

In speaking of this class the author does not specify if he has in mind the Jews and the converts together or only the "avowed Jews." And it is all the more difficult to determine the proportion of each because the line between the two had become blurred; thus, the precise definition of a Jew seems impossible to determine retrospectively.

Actually, in the cities of Castile and Aragon the three official creeds of what had been the Spain of the Three Religions had been replaced by a multiplicity of cults that may not have been clearly established denominations but were at least "existential situations" which engendered an ever-increasing variety of attitudes, practices, and rites. We shall attempt to outline these below.

Let us begin with the traditional "public Jews," the last outpost of those who were faithful to the Law of Moses. In Castile especially, where they still retained some of their former prerogatives (327), they tried to revive their communities and even to turn the trials they had gone through to some benefit. As pious Jews they did not seek to shirk their own responsibilities; and as Jews who were culturally assimilated to their environment they did not merely question their insufficient piety, their sins against God (as their brothers in Germany and France had done after similar trials), but they also questioned their conduct toward their persecutors, the Christians. The chronicle of Ibn Verga, written at the end of the fifteenth century, is full of reflections of this type (and, from this point of view, is not unlike the self-criticisms of certain "assimilated" Jews on the eve of the Hitler era). Thus, Ibn Verga attributed the following judgment to the philosopher Thomas: "I have never seen a reasonable man hate the Jews, but the lower classes hate them and they have their reasons: first, the Jews are proud and aspire to dominate, forgetting that they are exiles and slaves . . . second, when they arrived in this kingdom they were poor and the Christians were rich, while today the situation is reversed, for in the pursuit of profit the Jew is intelligent and cunning. . . ." In another passage Ibn Verga had a Christian king enumerate "six causes of anti-Semitism": "Why do the Jews teach their children to sing, they who should weep and remain in mourning all their lives? . . . Why do they have their children learn to fence, they who do not go to war? . . . Why do they wear princely garments, which serve to incite hatred and envy toward them? . . ." And so on. In accordance with this state of mind representatives of the *aljamas* of Castile, meeting at Valladolid in 1432, adopted stringent rules, prescribing in particular a strict separation of Jews and Christians and declaring war on luxury and ostentation. It is true that the course that things had taken contributed in itself to this austerity: the great Jewries of Toledo and Seville were no more; Judaism survived mainly in the medium-sized and smaller cities. For their part the Christian officials of certain cities treated the avowed Jews the same way they treated avowed prostitutes—as untouchable, except in certain circumstances or needs essential to life; throughout all of Spain there was no worse insult than *judío*. . . .

Nonetheless, certain Jews who were unconcerned with religion resisted conversion for reasons that had nothing to do with religion. In fact, the freethinkers had not disappeared, and the recent disasters of Israel merely served to reinforce their skepticism. But certain of these emancipated philosophers recoiled before baptism, it seems, for fear of the treatment the Church accorded to unbelievers. In the belief that a façade of Judaism constituted the lesser danger, they remained Jews not out of religion but out of irreligion (328).

Much more Jewish at heart were the converts who could

not forgive themselves their temporary lapse and who aspired to become full Jews again. Moving to North Africa or Portugal was the most satisfactory solution, and this was what the rabbis advocated. But such action was not within the reach of all; expatriation was strictly forbidden, and in addition it was expensive and hazardous. Those who re-solved to go abroad were ex-Jews motivated by a strong religious fervor, and by preference they went—and here again we see the historical intertwining of religion and commerce—where economic conditions were propitious to them, their situation predisposing them to international trade. The weaker ones remained in Spain and passed their religion on from father to son, all the while allowing them-selves to be baptized: this was how the marranos originated. They kept apart from the Christians and preferred to asso-ciate with the avowed Jews, their actual spiritual leaders. Some were circumcised as adults. Before the ascension of the "Catholic monarchs," Ferdinand and Isabella, this en-tailed no mortal risk. The customs of the time being what they were, these Judaizers even found accomplices within the Spanish clergy; a bull of Pope Nicholas V tells us that there were some priests, old hands at selling indulgences, who lost no time making a profit from the situation by encouraging the neophytes to Judaize, provided they bought their dispensations in advance (329).

Certain events were calculated to fortify the determina-tion and the hopes of the converts in spite of themselves. This was particularly true when Constantinople fell to the Turks in 1453. In certain marrano circles this victory of the "Ishmaelites," which made a profound impression on all of Europe, was seen as presaging the imminent fall of "Edom" and the imminent deliverance of Israel (reminiscent of the impression the victory of Stalingrad made on the occupied people of Europe in 1943). An active conventicle of mar-ranos at Valencia, confident that the Messiah had just ap-peared on a mountain top near the Bosporus, prepared to immigrate to Turkey: ". . . the blind goys do not see," said a zealot from the group, "that after we have been subject to them our God will now see to it that we dominate them. Our God has promised us that we will go to Turkey. We have heard that the Antichrist is coming; they say that the Turk is he, that he will destroy the Christian churches and will turn them into stables for the beasts and that he will bring honor and reverence to the Jews and the synagogues. . . ."

Some members of the group succeeded in reaching Constantinople, and others were making ready to join them when they were stopped by the Aragonese Inquisition in 1461. It came out in their trial that some were primarily interested in regaining their spiritual health, while others were primarily interested in gaining their fortune. When the tribunal asked one of the accused if a certain friend of his had become a Jew (that is, if he had been circumcised), he answered: "No, but he became rich," and all the codefendants burst out laughing. Another, who had been seen in Venice and Cairo dressed in "Judaic garments," protested that he had only worn them for the good of his business (330).

But this vigorous commercial optimism is only one facet of the complex and ever-varying countenance of the marranos. Practiced in secret, their Judaism became adulterated; the need to preserve the secrecy and the duplicity that were foisted upon them led to tragic internal conflict. A marrano prayer with syncretic Judeo-Christian accents found in the archives of the Inquisition shows this terrible anguish: "Lord, I have failed Thee by my meanness and my unworthiness, ruled by my evilness and by my treason in spite of myself. Thou, who hast visited me in true justice and hast cherished me like a son, see how I have fallen in a tribulation so great and so perilous, from which I cannot arise or escape. Knowing my guilt, I turn to Thee, Lord, repentant, sighing and weeping, as a son turns to his father, begging Thy holy mercy for forgiveness, that Thou mayest raise me from the great torment and the great tribulation into which I have fallen. . . ." The cry of a shattered soul, this long prayer ends suddenly with an invocation to Jesus of Nazareth, probably added to throw the Inquisition off the scent (331).

Distortions of quite a different sort were the hateful and ludicrous de-Christianization ceremonies prevalent in certain *converso* circles. We know of these only from the archives of the Inquisition, so it is impossible to separate the true from the false—i.e., the anti-Christian passion of the marranos from the extravagant imagination of their torturers —but to the extent that they may have been authentic, such practices as the fastening of a crucifix to the buttocks, the cudgelling of a statue of Jesus, and even ritual sacrifices are strong evidence of a Judaism adulterated by the effects of baptismal water.

There was an idea current in marrano circles at the time that nothing suited them better than the peace of the monasteries, and many became monks, particularly in the order of Saint Jerome, the richest in Spain in those days (332). Others went to the papal court to practice their religion by wangling a mission from a monastic or military order, for example (333) (so many, in fact, that the Roman populace ended up believing all Spaniards were Jews). And then there were the marranos who were grandees, with skeptical minds and lukewarm convictions. The well-known statesman and jurist Pedro de la Caballería, one of the converts of Tortosa, was a typical example of this. In 1450 he too ended up proving the orthodoxy of his faith and his knowledge of theology by writing the treatise *Zelus Christi contra Judaeos, Sarracenos et Infideles*. This only made him all the more free to Judaize from time to time, less out of conviction than sentimentality. Evidence of this came to light after his death; according to the archives of the Inquisition he had confessed it to a Jewish scholar. The latter had asked: "My lord, how could you have become a Christian, you who are so versed in our Law?" And "Maestre Pedro" had answered: "Imbecile, with the Jewish Torah what more could I have ever been than a rabbi? Now, thanks to the 'little hanged one' [Jesus] I have been given all sorts of honors. I am in command of the whole city of Saragossa, and I make it tremble. What is there to keep me from fasting at Yom Kippur and observing your holidays if I feel like it? When I was a Jew, I did not dare observe the Sabbath and now I do anything I want" (334). It was particularly men of this sort who filled the courts of Spain in those days and arranged for their daughters with their rich dowries to marry "Old Christian" lords.

Pushing irreligion even further, other *conversos* professed an aggressive atheism. Certain of them formed a conventicle that is known to have existed at Medina del Campo around 1460. They possessed books and "Hebraic writings" revealing "the secrets of the past, what Abraham, Jesus, and Mohammed were and the spirit that animated these three impostors." They were even so bold as to recruit proselytes, to whom they taught that the Gospels were nothing but deceit and fraud and that there was nothing beyond birth and death. "In this world you will not see me grieve, in the next you will not see me executed": that, it seems, was their motto (335). Even if atheism was not completely unknown in medieval Europe, this is doubtless the first historical mention of an "atheistic sect" in the bosom of Christendom. Rabbis and staunch Catholics bore them the same implacable hatred.

Finally we come to the *conversos* who became sincere Christians after a generation or two. It goes without saying that this category too was well represented; there were even bishops and other high Church dignitaries of Jewish stock. But nothing would be more useless than to hazard even the slightest guess on how many there were. Let us quote the estimate of Fernán Pérez de Guzmán, an observant and thoughtful gentleman who played an active part in the political life of the times. He deserves to be read at length:

"I am going to put forward certain reasons to counter the opinion of those who, without distinction or difference, absolutely condemn that nation of New Christian converts of today, saying that they are not Christians and that their conversion was neither good nor useful. And I, with all respect for those who say this, say that of course, people who have lived all their lives under the other Law, who were born under it and believed in it, and especially those who were submitted to the New Law by force, without due admonitions and exhortations, cannot be as faithful Catholics as those who are Christians from birth. For these reasons, there is no cause for surprise if some are not Christians, especially the women and the obtuse, rude, and ignorant men, for an educated and literate man is better able to grasp the truth than an ignorant one, who believes only in the faith he inherited from his father, and for that reason alone [that it is the faith of his fathers]. But I do not believe this is true of all the New Christians as a whole; I believe that among them are people who are good and devoted, for the following reasons: first, I believe in the virtue of the holy baptismal water, which cannot be sprinkled and lavished without any result; second, I have known and I know good *conversos,* who of their own free will lead an austere life in the religious orders; third, I have seen them work and wear themselves out in the monasteries, reforming dissolute and corrupt orders, and others, such as the honorable bishop [Paulus de Sancta Maria] and his honorable son Don Alfonso, bishop of Burgos, who have produced writings of great utility for our holy faith.

"And if some say that these works have been done only out of fear of the kings and the prelates, to find grace in their eyes, I answer that there is not that much zeal for our faith today that they would have done so for that reason, and that these days it is easier to gain the hearts of kings and prelates by gifts than by devotion and virtues . . ." (336).

This judgment reminds us that many *conversos* became men of the Church, a category that bore the closest resemblance to their former social status. But perhaps nothing was more uncomfortable at the time than being a sincere Christian *converso,* for where could these people find refuge?

Viewed with suspicion by all sides, what could they do to justify themselves? There were some who tried to exonerate their Jewish ancestors, and it was at this time that the legend that the Jews of Spain had tried to prevent the Crucifixion first appeared (337). Others cast slurs on their brother *conversos;* thus, the *conversos* of Old Castile claimed that those of Andalusia were Jews or worse but that they themselves were good Christians (338). True, such arguments were not necessarily proof of sincere Christian faith; they were more a matter of defending a group interest, of a "battle against anti-Semitism" in the style of the times.

Thus we return to the question of which ideology was prevalent among the *conversos.* Even if there are no precise figures on the subject, we are left with the impression that the majority no longer believed in the God of Israel and practiced some Christian rites without any conviction, out of superstition or out of prudence, sometimes even mixing in a residue of Jewish rites. Considered as Jews by their contemporaries, but without much belief in either God or the Devil, they had become "Jews by chance," "alienated Jews" before their time. Their history no longer meant anything to them; they had no faith to relieve or ennoble their suffering; their guilt was without sin and without redemption.

Remarkable evidence of this hopeless situation still exists, for the *conversos* who were literate poured it out in the poetry of circumstance that was in style at the time (339). Thus, one of the greatest Spanish poets of the century, Antonio de Montoro, wrote to Queen Isabella at the time of her accession to the throne:

> I have said the Credo,
> I have prayed to the pot of fat pork,
> I have heard Masses and I have prayed
> And still I have not been able to wipe out
> The lineaments of a *confeso.* . . .
> I have prayed with devotion
> And I have counted the beads

But I have never been able to lose
The name of a common old Jew.

His fault, then, was that he came from Jewish stock. This concept of an original stain comes out even more dramatically in another of his poems, composed the day after a great massacre of *conversos* in his native city, Córdoba.

. . . [Our persecutors] will not shrink
From massacres, flight and banishment
Because they want [our destruction]
By flight, blood and fire. . . .
And despite our losses and our tribulations,
Our injuries and our exiles
We would have been content
If they had pardoned us
For we want to pay taxes
To be slaves and to serve
To be poor, unfortunate, detested
But at least to be alive . . . (340).

That being of Jewish blood was unfortunate and shameful, all the authors of the time, both "Old" and "New" Christians, agreed. It was even one of the common themes of the collections of lyric poetry, the *cancioneros*, of the fifteenth century. The *conversos* responded in different ways. Some concealed their origin when possible. For example, during a heated poetry contest Gonzalo Dávila and Anton de Moros each in turn called the other a Jew, at the same time protesting the purity of his own Christian lineage (341). Others did not hide what they were—doubtless because they could not—and denounced their rivals in verse, much to the amusement of their protectors and the public. This is what Antonio de Montoro did—and not without a certain dignity—writing to Juan Poeta: "We belong to the same race; you and I are Jews. The offenses done to you are mine; the shame I suffer is yours." He also reproached Rodrigo de Cota for serving pork to his old parents on Saturday (342).

As for the poets of uncontestably Old Christian lineage, they could vaunt it to the fullest. For example, the Count de Paredes described the unsettling effects of the presence of Juan Poeta at a solemn procession in Valencia in 1470: "From the moment he entered the cathedral, the holy statues and the holy rites were transfigured: the pilgrims' medals became *rouelles,* the papal bull a Talmudic scroll . . ." (343).

This shows how Spanish public opinion had finally failed to distinguish between converts and Jews. If any distinction at all was made, it was to the advantage of the traditional Jew. After all, he was a familiar sight; he had been part of the Spanish scene since ancient times. The *converso* was too disturbing and too exasperating; he was the one the people tended to blame for everything that went wrong: "this abhorred, damned and detested genus and state of baptized Jews and its damned line" according to one author of the time; according to another, it was much more necessary to wage an unremitting battle against them than against the notorious and manifest infidels (344). Anything that had to do with them was necessarily bad; they were even criticized for their cooking. The priest Andrés Bernáldez, chaplain to an inquisitor, summarized this in his famous chronicle as follows:

". . . they never lose their Jewish way of eating, preparing their meat dishes with onions and garlic and cooking them in oil, which they use in place of lard, so that they will not have to eat pork fat; and oil with meat is something which gives the breath a very bad odor; and their houses and their doorways smell very bad because of this way of cooking, and they themselves attribute their Jewish odor to these dishes" (345).

As we know, Spain later became used to this "Jewish odor." Salvador de Madariaga, among others, thinks that cooking in oil is a legacy from Spain's Jewish past (346).

As a result of all this a remarkable theological evolution began. The most rabid detractor of Jews of that period, the Franciscan Alfonso de Espina, made a list in his treatise

Fortalitium Fidei ("Fortress of the Faith") of all the vices and all the crimes of which the Jews were then accused inside and outside of Spain. He told the following story of their expulsion from England: the king had compelled all the Jews to convert; but entertaining doubts about their sincerity, he had set his throne on the seashore between two tents, one of which held the Torah and the other the Cross. Then he said to the converted Jews that they could go into the tent they preferred. They rushed toward the scrolls of the Torah; the king then had his men slit the throats of some and exiled the rest (347). The lesson to be drawn from this story is evident: it would not do to doubt the virtues of holy water even though it had no effect when applied to Jewish foreheads, so it was necessary to conclude that the Jews were evil by their very nature and not only because of their beliefs. Therefore, de Espina submitted that there were two types of Jews, public Jews and hidden Jews, and that both had the same nature. Thus, by means of an implacable dialectic, the ill fame of those who had become Christians in spite of themselves or out of conformity redounded on the Jews, whom earlier Spanish theologians had merely reproached for their erroneous beliefs. The ball bounced back again, and new accusations were brought up against the Talmud and Jewish traditions; inquisitors claimed that the Jews were ritually bound to commit perjury, to kill a Christian every day, and so on (348). Such an atmosphere was enough to excite people's imaginations to such a point that the myth of a "Jewish world conspiracy" was able to take root.

This shows particularly clearly how *sectarian* hatred could turn into *racial* hatred. The popes of the time and the sensible Spanish prelates cautioned against attempts on Christian universalism; Pope Nicholas V, in his bull *Humani generis inimicus*, and Bishop Alonso of Cartagena (the son of Paulus de Sancta Maria), in his "Defense of Christian Unity," recalled that redemption was equally accessible to all human souls—all to no avail. What power did theologians have against passions? And from that time on the passions of Spain were to follow their implacable course.

In this anarchical period of Spanish history, at the end of the reign of Juan II and during the reign of Henry IV, hatred of the *conversos* led to numerous excesses, attacks, and massacres, such as the Córdoba massacre that Antonio de Montoro spoke of; history books are full of the details. The *conversos* defended themselves by force of arms, and sometimes even took the offensive; for some, it was a battle between two political camps or factions. But what is striking about this ferocious struggle is the *conversos'* lack of determination and even their passivity, despite their number and influence. At no time did they band together to form a united front in the face of mortal danger. They lacked, among other things, the stimulus of a common ideology and faith. Meanwhile, a collective ideology and will crystallized spontaneously in their enemies' camp. Following the first of the massacres—in Toledo in 1449—the city officials published an ordinance that gave a long enumeration and description of the crimes of the *"conversos of Jewish lineage"* and recalled particularly that this line had turned the city over to the Moslems more than seven centuries before, and then prescribed:

"We declare that all the said *conversos,* descendants of the perverse line of the Jews . . . in reason of the above-mentioned heresies and other offenses, insults, seditions, and crimes committed by them up to this time, should therefore be held as disgraceful, unfit, inept, and unworthy of holding any office and public and private benefit in said city of Toledo and in its lands . . . to give witness and faith as public notaries or as witnesses . . . to have domain over Old Christians in the holy Catholic faith . . ." (349).

Spanish racism was on the march.

ten

The Inquisition

Machiavelli, in *The Prince,* designated King Ferdinand the Catholic as the ideal monarch: "We have in our own day Ferdinand, king of Aragon, the present king of Spain. He may almost be termed a new prince, because from a weak king he has become for fame and glory the first king in Christendom, and if you regard his actions you will find them all very great and some of them extraordinary. . . . Besides this, to be able to undertake greater enterprises, and always under the pretext of religion, he had recourse to a pious cruelty, driving out the Jews from his kingdom and despoiling them. No more miserable or unusual example can be found." (Was Machiavelli alluding here to the Jewish blood that flowed in the veins of the king (350)?)

⌐ Indeed, Ferdinand and his wife, Isabella of Castile, the "Catholic monarchs," had unified their country, put an end to anarchy, and in a very short time turned Spain into the most powerful land of Europe. They had re-established order, wiped out banditry, reconquered Granada (the last Moslem enclave on the peninsula), and undertaken the colonization of the New World. And finally, by expelling the Jews they had achieved the religious unification of the country, thanks to the Spanish Inquisition, whose imprint on Spain is still visible. Chapter 9 has shown us the seriousness of the disease; now we shall see the horror of the cure.

⌐ The Inquisition, it must be recalled, was not a Spanish creation. There was a sort of advance justification for it as far back as Saint Augustine, who said that "moderate perse-

cution" (*tempereta severitas*) was permissible for turning
heretics back to the straight path (351). In fact, it had been
founded by the Holy See in the thirteenth century, and it
was especially in France, after the battle against the
Cathars, that it first became active, which explains the air of
embarrassment displayed by some French historians who
are generally laudably objective when speaking of it. Thus,
when it was instituted in Castile more than two centuries
later to purge *conversos* suspected of practicing Jewish rites,
it functioned according to principles and techniques that
were already tested. But the Spanish inquisitors were distinguished for their particular ferocity, and they turned their
instrument into a state within a state that was not abolished
until the nineteenth century. Conservatives all over Europe
regretted its abolition: "It is the Inquisition which saved
Spain, it is the Inquisition which immortalized it!" Joseph de
Maistre exclaimed at the time (352). The Castilian Inquisition effectively molded Spanish life and customs, its shadow
still hangs over the country, and its apologists on the other
side of the Pyrenees still speak of it longingly.

 Our generation has had the unpleasant privilege of seeing
more such "police of men's souls" develop in what are called
totalitarian states. The historical conditions under which
they have appeared are different, and they espouse different
principles, but their procedures have not changed much. For
ultimately, beyond differences in institutions and structures,
what is involved is the most basic psychological relationship
there is—the confrontation of one person with another.

In this regard one could say that Communism is a more
universalist faith than Christianity. As the Church pro-
claims, "Outside of the Church, there is no salvation"; those
who have not been baptized are, in principle, lost souls even
when they are not to blame. This means that a Jew or a
Moslem is something quite different from a Christian, while
for the Communist all men of reason are equally redeem-
able, even if the proletarian is more predisposed to such
redemption because of his "class consciousness." But the

Inquisition regarded the baptized Jew, the *converso*, as a Christian heretic and not as a Jew, and thus the comparison is valid.

A group of harsh and determined men who were convinced that they possessed the revealed truth, men with the power to coerce at their disposal, tried to force their beliefs on other men who still held to their convictions, even if they were only negative ones ("we do not believe a word you say; eternal salvation does not exist"). Beyond the desire for power, beyond the elimination of a dangerous heresy by those in power, or beyond even the vulgar profit motive, it was in this confrontation, in the attempt to violate the secrets of a disarmed adversary's soul, that the crux of the tragedy lay. And it could be that the tragedy was enhanced by the unavowable doubts of the inquisitor himself, doubts that he sought to exorcise by making his antagonist justify him. For the conversion to Christianity of the frank and self-avowed doubter would be justification indeed. It is this that underlies brainwashing techniques, the "conjunction of coercion and persuasion"; it is very much the same in all eras, in all latitudes.

Making the adversary suffer weakens his strength to resist, degrades him, reduces him to a state of near-infantilism: that is the coercion. Then, after he is receptive and open to suggestion, so to speak, he is gently catechized, the hope of deliverance is dangled before him: that is the persuasion. And, if necessary, the whole process can start all over again: he can languish in doubt and foreboding for months, his friends and relatives can be called to testify against him (and vice versa). And, in this way, a man can be broken, made to worship the gods he ridiculed a short time before, turned into another man, a "new" man.

The operation is not always successful. According to a famous saying, religions are like nails: the harder you hit them, the deeper they go. But if you hit too hard, the nail disappears into the wall—sometimes even cracking it. In the case in point, the Spanish Inquisition, some were broken by it, and some were strengthened in their resistance. And the whole edifice of what was once the glorious Spanish Empire finally crumbled under the impact of the blows dealt to Judaism, which reverberated from generation to generation.

゜ One of the first concerns of the Catholic monarchs, who acceded to power in 1474, was to attack the general relaxation of morals and the religious anarchy. The clergy demanded the establishment of the Inquisition, which had never before existed in Castile and which, in Aragon, did not display excessive zeal. The Jewish and *converso* counselors of Ferdinand and Isabella, some of whom had taken part in the negotiations that preceded their marriage, tried to foil the plans of the Spanish clergy and appealed to the Holy See. Even with their influence and their gold they only succeeded in gaining a few years. In 1478 a papal bull was promulgated instituting the Castilian Inquisition; in 1480 the first tribunal began to function in Seville. At the same time, measures were taken to segregate the *conversos* from the avowed Jews, who were considered their corrupters. And as Andalusia was the principal seat of marranism, all its Jews were expelled in 1483.

゜ As we have said, the Inquisition functioned according to time-tested principles, but from the start these were applied with particular cruelty in Spain (according to L. Pastor, the historian of Catholicism, it was "a question of life or death for Catholic Spain") (353). Once it was established in a city, the inquisitorial tribunal first invited the heretics to give themselves up: that was the "Edict of Grace" generally fixed at a period of thirty days. People who presented themselves to admit that they had practiced Judaism then had to denounce all the Judaizers they knew, and they were treated as "first-degree suspects." They were spared torture and imprisonment; their sins were atoned for by flagellation and public humiliation (wearing of the infamous and grotesque *sambenito*) and by the partial confiscation of their belongings. Moreover, throughout their lives they were forbidden to hold any office or exercise any honorable profession or to wear formal dress.

Next, the tribunal invited the good Catholics to expose the suspects they knew of. A Christian even was obliged to go so far as to denounce his father and mother, and he was assured of impunity, for the names of the witnesses for the prosecution were kept strictly secret. A special edict enumerated thirty-seven points by which heretics could be recognized: celebration of the Jewish holidays or dietary or other laws; consumption of meat during Lent; omission of the phrase "Glory be to the Father, and to the Son, and to the Holy Ghost" at the end of a psalm; and so on. From that starting point the faithful went further and further, and a chronic "espionitis" in religious guise began to prevail in Spain. Let us take a look at the archives of the Inquisition. Did the so-called Aldonça de Vergas smile on hearing the name of the Holy Virgin? She is then a *conversa* and a heretic. Did Blanca Fernandez hear her neighbors speak to each other and not understand what they were saying? Then they were speaking Hebrew, and she denounced them. Cooking with oil, commonly considered as an infallible sign of Judaism, was perhaps the most frequent cause for denunciation. Ordinary meanness joined forces with the obsession with sin, and consequently, especially after the Inquisition had become an integral part of Spanish life, the archives contain depositions like the following:

"Juana Perez, wife of Zeoai Bernal, deposes that after she had heard the edict on the subject of people who have eaten of the Jewish cuisine, her husband told her that when he was a child a Jew gave him a piece of cake, which he gave to another young child who ate it. Her husband refusing to bear witness on this subject himself, she presented herself so as not to be troubled by scruples."

Inquisition of the Canary Islands
26 February 1578 (354)

Such denunciations made it possible to pursue those "second- and third-degree suspects" who were reluctant to put the rope around their own necks. Thus it was necessary to constrain them to do so. As with all police of men's souls, the Inquisition and its procedures were conceived in pursuit of that supreme moment, confession (inquisitorial procedure as opposed to accusatorial procedure). "Heresy being a sin of the soul, the only possible proof is confession," wrote Eymerich, the author of the best-known inquisitorial manual. He who confessed saved his life; he who persisted in denying went to the flames, and a sixteenth-century observer, Francesco Pegna, went so far as to praise the execution of the innocent who were falsely condemned: "If an innocent is unjustly condemned, he has no reason to complain about the Church's sentence, which is based on sufficient proof, and what is hidden cannot be judged. If false witnesses have caused him to be condemned, he should accept the sentence with resignation, and rejoice in dying for truth." Thus we enter the special private domain of ecclesiastical hypocrisy, to which unlimited possibilities were opened by the promise of eternal salvation, justifying the tortures and the autos-da-fé. As the Church was anxious to proclaim its horror of shedding blood (*Ecclesia abhorret sanguinem*), the impenitent heretics were burned at the stake so blood would not flow. And keeping its hands even cleaner, so as not to stain them at the time of the execution, the Church turned over or "released" the condemned prisoners to the "secular arm" for execution. Combing through the texts, commentators succeeded in justifying the Inquisition and its executions with the aid of quotations from Christ, according to the Gospel of Saint John.[1] We must

---

[1] "I am the vine, you the branches. . . . He who does not dwell in me is thrown away like a withered branch. The withered branches are heaped together, thrown on the fire, and burnt." (John 15, 5–6.) From this Henri de Suse and Jean d'André concluded that the heretic, who does not dwell in the Church, should be burned. As for Saint Thomas Aquinas, he compared the heretics, corrupters of the faith, to counterfeiters, corrupters of money, and demanded the same punishment for them.

admit that today's police of men's souls no longer have such resources.

‹ To elicit a confession the Inquisition applied torture; water was the most usual, but there were also a great many others, such as deprivation of sleep. The torture was alternated with kind words, which were also supposed to convince the accused to confess and to denounce his accomplices. The inquisitorial manuals, those *sui generis* catechisms, prescribed saying: "I pity you, when I see you so abused and with a lost soul. . . . So do not assume the sin of others . . . admit the truth to me, for, as you see, I already know everything. . . . In order that I may be able to pardon you and free you soon, tell me who led you to this error." If that was still not enough, if the accused still held fast, the judges had third parties intervene, the eternal prison trusty or else "worthy people" from the outside, charitable souls instructed to visit the prisoners and comfort them so as to gain their confidence.

‹ It should be pointed out that these refinements were unknown to the Castilian Inquisition in its first period (that of Torquemada), for it held a series of proceedings with only a handful of inquisitors and innumerable suspects. There were only some ten or twelve tribunals, and the justice they dispensed could only be summary. Among those subject to their jurisdiction were also the dead, no matter when they may have died; judgment was passed on their skeletons, and their bones were burned. Since they could no longer testify, their descendants had to do so for them—and be stripped of their inheritance in case of posthumous conviction. Here, the profit motive was the strongest. To justify such plundering the inquisitors resorted to the Old Testament: in punishment for their disobedience, were not Adam and Eve, those first human heretics, expelled from Paradise, as well as their descendants, and was that not a confiscation? (Moreover, the *sambenito* was compared to the animal skins in which they dressed after their fall, when they knew they were naked. Thus, one can see that for the theoreticians of the

Inquisition, original sin and heresy ended up as the same thing.)

. Counting the number of heretics burned by the Inquisition of Torquemada as being of the order of one to two thousand, one can say that the Holy Office was far less bloody than the twentieth-century police of men's souls. And in fact, the only prisoners who ended on the funeral pyre were those with the strength of mind to continue saying No to their tormenters to the last and to refuse to confess, plus the relapsed or impenitent heretics. This explains why only a small percentage were actually executed. The majority accepted "reconciliation" with the Church and were sentenced to life imprisonment or shorter terms after marching in processions and undergoing innumerable public humiliations, as well as having all their property confiscated. Not only material ruin but social ostracism also was handed down to the posterity of the condemned: his children and grandchildren were forbidden to wear gold or silver and to hold public or ecclesiastical office. Thus, we see the beginning of a legal hereditary discrimination that was extended in the following century, under the name of "Statutes of Purity of the Blood," to every Spaniard who had (or was presumed to have) a drop of Jewish blood. Let us add that on different occasions the Holy See tried to restrain the excesses of the Castilian Inquisition, but with little success. As early as the beginning of 1482 Pope Sextus IV wrote to the Catholic monarchs that the activities of the tribunal of Seville were too often dictated "not by zeal for the faith and concern for the salvation of souls, but by cupidity and the profit motive" (355). But the papacy quickly lost the power to make such observations. The inquisitors were royal officials, named by the Crown; the Counsel of the Supreme and General Inquisition, or *Suprema*, became a vital cog in Spanish life.

' As we have said, the first tribunal to be established was in Seville, the center of the principal marrano stronghold. Ibn Verga recounts how an inquisitor one day said to the governor of the city: "My Lord, if you want to know how the

conversos celebrate the Sabbath, climb the tower with me."
When they had reached the top, the inquisitor said: "Lift up
your eyes and look at all these houses where *conversos* live;
as cold as it is, on Saturdays you will never see smoke
coming out of their chimneys, for on that day the *conversos*
do not light a fire" (356). Ibn Verga tells also how one of his
relatives, the cabalist Judah ibn Verga, when he learned that
the Inquisition had been established in Seville, placed three
pairs of doves in the window of his house. One pair had been
plucked and slaughtered and bore a label that read: "These
will be the *conversos* who will be the last to leave"; the
second pair, plucked but still alive, bore the inscription:
"These will leave second." The third pair, which still had
their feathers, bore the inscription: "These will be the first to
leave" (357). Anyone who knows the pattern of political
emigrations of recent years will agree that the anecdote has
not lost its timeliness.

The *conversos* of Seville did not do much to defend themselves: according to the chronicler Bernáldez a conspiracy
that they plotted was denounced by the daughter of one of
the principal conspirators, who was in love with an Old
Christian (358). The majority tried to placate the inquisitors by lavish signs of Christian fervor and with offerings
and gifts, like the rich *converso* Mesa, who had the
quemadero, the principal place of atonement in Seville,
decorated with four statues of prophets, an act that did not
spare him from later being burned there himself (359). For
seven years the purge raged. Five thousand *conversos* finally
accepted reconciliation after the customary punishment and
humiliation. Seven hundred impenitent and relapsed heretics were burned (360).

In 1483 Tomás de Torquemada was named Inquisitor
General for all of Spain. While the Sevillian Inquisition
continued its work, tribunals were established in other Spanish provinces. In Aragon Torquemada's excesses resulted in
popular uprisings in Valencia and Teruel in which numerous
Old Christians participated, and in a *converso* conspiracy in

Saragossa to assassinate the inquisitor Pedro de Arbues, Maestre de Epila (later canonized). Terror was countered by terror. The extremes to which the Aragonese Inquisition went are perhaps best illustrated by the trial of Brianda de Bardaxi, a rich *conversa* of Saragossa and a pious Catholic if ever there was one, who was, however, guilty of having observed a Jewish fast when she was a child, of not liking bacon, and of once having given four coins to a Jewish beggar. This was sufficient to justify seven years' imprisonment, innumerable tortures to make her confess more, and the confiscation of a third of her property. Her principal accusers were her tenants, Beatriz and Gilabert Desplugas, also *conversos*; the wife was burned as a heretic in 1486, the husband as a relapsed heretic in 1502 (361).

Toledo's turn came in 1486; in all, there were 4,850 reconciliations there in four years and fewer than two hundred *conversos* were burned. In the capital the Inquisition was the least heavy-handed (362). Doubtless, political and economic considerations had something to do with this; at a certain level of wealth and influence a *converso* could count on the protection of the kings and the Holy See, and he became unassailable. Typical was the case of Alfonso de la Caballería, the vice-chancellor of the kingdom of Aragon, whose father was the high official previously mentioned; Alfonso was much more attached to Judaism and the Jews than the skeptical Pedro. Despite the overwhelming evidence collected against him by the Inquisition of Saragossa, his trial dragged on for nearly twenty years and finally ended in 1501 with an acquittal on orders from the papacy (363). But these were individual cases, and just as Göring exclaimed that it was up to him to decide who was Aryan, the Catholic monarchs arrogated the right to say who was Christian. As a statesman, Ferdinand pursued a policy ruinous for Spain, and therefore he was all the more pleased that the confiscations guaranteed him the funds necessary for the war on Granada. When the municipal authorities of Barcelona complained about the economic crisis the inquisitorial terror had unleashed, the king answered: "Before consenting to the establishment of the Inquisition in the cities of our kingdom, we considered the harm this could cause crafts-men and commerce. But in our great zeal for our holy faith, we have placed the service of the Lord well above all our other interests, whatever they may be" (364). Thus, the Catholic monarchs' Christian zeal permitted them to finance a short-term policy of glory. (One steals better when one steals with good conscience; just as Jewish travels repre-sented an intertwining of religion and commerce, the anti-Jewish persecutions constituted an intertwining of religion and brigandage.) The upheavals in economic life caused by the Inquisition were common knowledge at the time, and foreign ambassadors did not fail to mention them.[2] Today, nearly all Spanish historians agree it was the Inquisition that stifled the "bourgeois revolution" in Spain.[3]

It contributed also—at least during the early years—to the return of the *conversos* to Judaism. In their distress they appealed to God, to a God who could not be the Christ in whose name they were being burned, to a God who could only be the ancient God of Israel. "Be baptized and go see how they burn the New Christians!" was the ironic epigram of an old Jew confined in the jails of the Inquisition,[4] who

[2] In 1523 Andres Navajero, ambassador of Venice at the court of Charles V, noted the following after visiting Granada: "When the Catholic monarchs conquered this kingdom, they promised the Moors that the Inquisition would not be allowed there. . . . But on the eve of my arrival it was estab-lished. This could easily ruin the city, for the privilege of not having the Inquisition for forty years has meant that all sorts of people settled here to live in safety. Now this will be very prejudicial to the beauty and the growth of the city, for these people have built beautiful houses and are very rich merchants."

[3] "The lack of capital, particularly aggravated by the expulsion of the Jews and by their exodus occasioned by the Inquisition prevented industriali-zation from moving forward. . . . The void created in the field of large-scale mercantile activities by the flight of capital caused by the establishment of the Inquisition and by the expulsion of the Jews could not be filled by the indigenous population. . . ." (*Historia social y economica de España,* Vol. 2, pp. 474 and 475.)

[4] Benito Garcia in the trial of La Guardia.

had been converted forty years earlier. There were free-thinkers who had cared little about Judaism during times of tolerance but who now recited the *Shema Yisrael* on the funeral pyre as a sign of supreme defiance. There were good Catholics who became Jews out of hatred for the Inquisition (the grandson of Jeronimo de Santa Fe was one of them) (365). Brainwashing is a double-edged sword that promptly arouses rebellion in the soul it seeks to crush. It took long generations for the Inquisition to extirpate all trace of Judaism from Spanish soil, and it succeeded only at the price of ruinous effort.

ᐟ Under these conditions the first problem of the Inquisition was the Jews who were authorized to remain Jews, the so-called public Jews. They hampered the effectiveness of the Inquisition in various ways. First of all the simple fact of their existence added an extra note of absurdity to forbidding the "hidden Jews" to doubt the mystery of the Trinity and to eat meat during Lent. But it goes without saying that it was not their mute presence alone which created problems, for the public Jews could not refrain from playing an active role in the tragedy of the *conversos*. Much as they hated the renegades, they felt a kinship with their brothers who were struggling in the coils of the Inquisition and cursing Christianity. The records of the era are full of proceedings brought against Jews who tried to keep others in the bosom of Judaism and who helped the *conversos* practice Judaism. Thus, they too found themselves under the jurisdiction of the Holy Office. In addition the Castilian Inquisition lost no time in imposing the duty of sacred denunciation on the Jews: the rabbis were required to enjoin their faithful, on penalty of the most solemn excommunication, to report any Judaizing *conversos* they knew of to the inquisitors. "Oh, how that sword of excommunication wrought havoc among the Spanish Jews!" a contemporary exclaimed. "Wherever they turned [they] found hardship and misfortune! By means of these accusations the Spanish king had many thousands of the marranos burned and confiscated innumerable fortunes, using the money for the war against Granada" (366).

One can imagine the dilemma of the Jews who were bound by conflicting oaths and duties. On the eve of the 1492 expulsion the rabbi of Saragossa, Levi ben Shemtov, presented himself to the inquisitors and revealed to them the confidences one of his faithful had made a few years before on the subject of the heretical conduct of Alfonso de la Caballería, the secret protector of the Jews of Aragon. Despite the solemn excommunication he himself had proclaimed, he had ordered his informant to keep silent, for though the Law of Moses required that oaths be sworn to nothing but the truth and that the ban should be enforced, the Talmud permitted relaxation of the ban when the security of the whole Jewish community was at stake. Convinced that the lives of the Jews depended on Maestre Alfonso, he had released his informant from the oath to reveal everything to the Inquisition. But now that the fate of the Jews was sealed due to the publication of the Edict of Expulsion and the informant had died in the meantime, he felt that the ban should no longer be violated and swore that he was not reporting this out of hatred or quarrel but out of concern for the sworn truth (367). A few weeks later Rabbi ben Shemtov embarked on the path of exile and took refuge in Portugal (368).

Other rabbis were accused of having actively promoted the return of the *conversos* to Judaism. This was the case of Abraham Alitienz, of Huesca, who was indicted for having performed circumcisions in the course of de-Christianization ceremonies and was condemned to the flames in 1490. A statement he presented in his defense tells a great deal about the theses propagated by the Inquisition on the eve of the expulsion of the Spanish Jews: "The fiscal procurer has produced two levels of accusation. One is universal; it says that the Jews in general have always been bad and perverse, dedicating themselves to evil practices against God and against the world. The other is individual and concerns the crimes of which I stand accused, and especially the crime of de-Christianization. As to the first, it is not my intention to reply to it, as that quarrel has been picked with us many times and we have always answered it satisfactorily. I will then merely humbly reply to the second. . . ." And, basing himself on the Talmud and on Maimonides, the rabbi demonstrated that Jewish tradition did not recognize any anti-Christian practices, "these things which are abusively born in the imaginations of these witnesses who have testified against me . . ." (369).

There was no longer any way to extricate themselves from the crisis. Once more in the course of their history the Jews, against their will, played the Church's game by assuming, on the *political* level, the role of tempters and sworn enemies of the faith, which Christian *theology* had designated for them from its earliest beginnings. To win its battle it was now incumbent on the Inquisition to demonstrate convincingly that "the Jews in general have always been evil and perverse, engaging in evil practices against God and against the world," so that they could then be driven off Spanish soil. The medium chosen for this demonstration was a spectacular trial; here, too, the techniques of the police of men's souls have not changed.

At the end of 1490 six Jews and five *conversos* of La Guardia, near Toledo, were accused of having tried to ruin Christendom through black magic, in which a consecrated host and the heart of a crucified child were used. The accusation against one of them, Yuce (Joseph) Franco, read:

" . . . His soul embittered and depraved, he went in company with several others to crucify a Christian child on a Good Friday, in the same fashion, with the same animosity and cruelty as his forefathers had for our Savior Jesus Christ, tearing his flesh, beating him and spitting in his face, covering him with wounds, crushing him with blows and turning to ridicule our holy Faith. . . . He mixed its heart with a consecrated host. With this mixture, Yuce Franco and the others expected that the Christian religion would be overturned and destroyed, so that the Jews would possess all the property which belongs to the Catholics, that their race would grow and multiply while that of the faithful Christians would be extirpated forever . . ." (370).

The records of the La Guardia trial furnish curious details on the way the lawyers were instructed to spy on and provoke the accused and on the various procedures used to make the prisoners testify against one another.[5] After a year of this treatment it seems that all had given satisfactory confessions except the indomitable *converso* Benito Garcia, who affirmed that "from the time they poured water into his nostrils, he was totally de-Christianized." Although he also agreed that the Jews who had turned Christian were antichrists, he proclaimed in the courtroom that Torquemada was the greatest antichrist (371). But while the inquisitors went to a great deal of trouble to obtain spectacular confessions, they were particularly negligent as far as material proofs were concerned: the allegedly crucified victim had neither name nor face, no one had reported the disappearance of a child, the body was never found (although the confessions contained a description of the place where it was buried), and no attempt was made to identify it. However, that ectoplasm, the anonymous "Holy Child of La Guardia," later became the object of a devout cult and was celebrated by numerous poets and writers (such as Lope de Vega). Even today, certain Spanish Catholic historians affirm that the crime really took place (372).

The verdict was pronounced on November 15, 1491; all the accused were found guilty and burned the following day. Copies of the sentence were sent to all the Spanish cities, and in Barcelona they were translated into Catalan.

---

[5] The lawyers named by the court had to swear to reveal to the inquisitors all confessions and other information that their clients might give them. In prison, in addition to using trusties the inquisitors devised other ways to make it easy for the accused to communicate with one another in order to eavesdrop on their conversations.

The congenital ignominy of the Jews had been demonstrated judicially. The last act of the tragedy was now to follow.

On January 2, 1492, the Catholic Ferdinand and Isabella solemnly entered Granada; the *Reconquista* had been achieved. On March 31 of the same year they signed the Edict of Expulsion of the Jews of Spain. The edict gave many reasons:

> "We have been informed by the inquisitors, and by other persons, that the mingling of Jews with Christians leads to the worst evils. The Jews try their best to seduce the [New] Christians and their children, bringing them books of Jewish prayers, telling them of the days of Jewish holidays, procuring unleavened bread for them at Passover, instructing them on the dietary prohibitions, and persuading them to follow the Law of Moses. In consequence, our holy Catholic faith is debased and humbled. We have thus arrived at the conclusion that the only efficacious means to put an end to these evils consists in the definitive breaking of all relations between Jews and Christians, and this can only be obtained by their expulsion from our kingdom" (373).

The Jews were given four months to liquidate their businesses and to sell their lands and property, but they were forbidden to export money and precious metals. Thus, they had to leave before July 31. (On August 2 Christopher Columbus' three caravels left for the discovery of America; the three most important events of Spanish history took place in the space of a few brief months.) The Jews, who still had powerful representatives at court, naturally tried to have the edict abrogated or postponed, but it was in vain that they offered the treasury huge sums of money. A last-minute baptism was the only thing that would allow them to remain on the soil of the mother country. During the weeks preceding the exodus the Spanish clergy undertook an energetic missionary campaign that was often crowned with success. According to a Christian observer at Segovia, "As the time approached, the Jews left their houses and scattered in the fields, hoping for a postponement. The Jewish cemetery was full of these miserable people. Some people of our city, concerned for the salvation of their souls, took advantage of the occasion to preach sermons and demonstrate to them their blind lack of belief, in face of so much evidence and so many centuries of calamities. Some converted, and the event gave its name to the place, which still today is called the Prado Santo; the others left the kingdom" (374). According to a Jewish witness, "Numerous Jews, great and small, and even rabbis, remained in the country, preferring to change their Law to that of the God of the country. At their head was the rabbi Abraham Seneor, rabbi of all the Spanish communities, with his sons and all his relatives and many thousands of other Jews. Only a segment of the Spanish rabbis preferred martyrdom and left . . ." (375).

But the example of the highest-placed Jew in Spain, the "court rabbi" Abraham Seneor, whose baptism was celebrated on June 15 in the presence of the king and queen, was not followed by all. In fact, popular imagination soon transformed his apostasy into martyrdom; it was said that Queen Isabella had sworn to destroy all the Jewish communities if her favorite was not baptized (376). The most reliable estimates say that nearly 150,000 Jews accepted exile (the majority went to Portugal) and that only fifty thousand preferred a last-minute conversion (377). Ten years of inquisitorial terror had done more to revive the Jewish faith than all the centuries of exhortations by the rabbis. A veritable ecstasy took hold of their hearts; their tribulation was compared to the flight from Egypt. It would be followed, it was said, by a promised land of glory and honor. Others added that it would not be long before Spain recalled her children, so certain exiles, after selling their property, buried their money in the soil of the mother country (378).

This was the atmosphere of the great departure, which is described in Bernáldez as follows:

"In a few months, the Jews sold all they could; they would barter a house for a donkey and a vineyard for a small piece of cloth or linen. Before leaving, they married off all their children of more than twelve years, so that each girl had the protection of a husband. . . . Then, trusting in the blind hope that God would lead them to the Promised Land, they left their homes, great and small, old and young, on foot, on horseback, on asses or other beasts or in wagons, some falling, others rising, some dying, others being born, others falling sick. There was no Christian who did not pity them; everywhere they were invited to conversion and some were baptized, but very few, for the rabbis encouraged them and made the women and children play on the timbrel . . ." (379).

It seems, nevertheless, that the great majority of the Christian population was little moved by the exodus of the Jews. True, there are few descriptions; a sort of silent terror hovered over the land. It was preferable not to dwell on the departure of the Jews. With the exception of Bernáldez, who, it should be recalled, was the chaplain of the Inquisitor General, the Spanish chroniclers of the time hardly mentioned the subject and did not allow their feelings to show (380). Four years later Juan del Encina, the father of Spanish drama, wrote in a poem: "We no longer know in this kingdom what Jews are" (*que cosa sean judíos*) (381).

The disappointments and sufferings that befall exiles is a classic theme in Jewish historiography. We shall not dwell on it. A single glimpse will suffice. A Genovese chronicler, Barthelemy Seneraga, described the desperate cargoes of Jews who left the country by sea as follows:

"It was a sad sight to see. The majority were exhausted by hunger and thirst. . . . One would have said that they were ghosts: pale, shrunken, hollow-eyed, one would have thought them dead if they had not moved from time to time.

A great number of them died on the pier in a place which was set aside for them, not far from the market. . . ."

And this is the conclusion this Christian came to:

"Their sufferings would seem praiseworthy for anyone who is of our religion, but they are not without cruelty if we consider them not as animals, but as human beings, created by God in His image" (381a).

That was, in effect, the attitude of the time, even in enlightened Italy of the Renaissance, where a Machiavelli and a Guicciardini could express nearly the same views.

Meanwhile, the epilogue to the drama was being played in neighboring Portugal.

King John II had admitted the exiles, charging them a tax of eight crusadoes a head on condition that they would leave the country within eight months on boats he would provide. One group did set sail for Africa, but the majority could not or would not. When the allotted time ran out, the king began to sell these Jews as slaves. His successor, Manuel I, ordered them set free, but shortly afterward a marriage was arranged between the young king and the infanta of Spain, and the Catholic monarchs made the total Christianization of Portugal one of the conditions for this marriage. As expulsion would have meant immediate disaster for the economic life of the little country, forced baptism was the only solution compatible with Portuguese political ambitions. At Easter, 1497, the situation came to a head. Children were torn from their parents and taken to the baptismal fonts; their parents, numbering several thousand (and including native Portuguese Jews), who did not follow them willingly were forced to submit a few weeks later. In the case of the émigrés from Spain, they had already proved themselves faithful to the Law of Moses. Many committed suicide, and there were other atrocious incidents as well. Certain Portuguese churchmen disapproved of these measures. "I have seen," the bishop of Algarve related thirty years later, "many dragged to the font by the hair, and the fathers clad in

mourning, with veiled heads and cries of agony, accompanying their children to the altar, to protest against the inhuman
baptism. I have seen still more horrible, indescribable violence done them" (382). "A sacrilegious farce, motivated by
the most vile and sordid material interests"—that was the
judgment of Menendez y Pelayo in the nineteenth century.
There is probably no other example in Christian history
(unless you go back to Charlemagne and the conversion of
the Saxons) of such complete disrespect for the sacrament of
baptism. The pope, Alexander VI (Rodrigo Borgia), tried to
limit the damage, his zeal stimulated by the gold of the
emissaries of the Portuguese Jews. Consequently, as a last
homage to free will a remarkable compromise was adopted
in Lisbon: unlike their counterparts in Spain, baptized Jews
in Portugal would be free to live as Jews, even being allowed
to assemble to celebrate their services. They were also free
to enrich themselves if they possessed any commercial ability,[6] a solution that could not have been more advantageous
to the royal treasury, for it could extort contributions on all
occasions. This state of affairs lasted for half a century, and
the whole Portuguese population was caught up in frenzy.
Furious pogroms took place from time to time; the one in
Lisbon, in 1506, resulted in more than a thousand victims.
Finally, an Inquisition copied on the Spanish model was
introduced into Portugal in accordance with a papal brief of
1536, and it began to smite as implacably as its counterpart.

[6] In 1564 a Venetian ambassador described the situation as follows:
"Nearly sixty-five years ago, King Manuel of Portugal converted the Jews
who were in his kingdom to our holy Catholic faith. These Jews were poor,
and after having become Christians, they became rich, for thanks to the
benefits of the faith they became doctors, specialized surgeons, and began to
traffic in all merchandise just as the other Christians. Thus the increase in
their wealth and their native lack of belief led them to return to Judaism,
secretly observing in their houses all the Jewish ceremonies, teaching
Judaism to their children and maintaining a synagogue in the city of Lisbon, where they celebrate their services as they do in Rome, meanwhile
confessing and conforming to Christian customs." According to Graetz,
Vol. 9, Appendix 5, the author of this anecdote was G. Soranzo. Whoever
he was, he confirms the wisdom of the Venetian ambassadors.

The paradoxical interlude of the Portuguese "public marranos" had various consequences that we shall discuss later. It allowed the marrano communities to adapt to the Christian mask; and as this mask was worn only lightly, they achieved unparalleled vitality. The long years of toleration seem to have constituted an unequaled tonic, to the extent that crypto-Judaic traditions still persist in contemporary twentieth-century Portugal, as we shall see below.

It is worth reflecting on the comparison between Spain and Portugal. With their rigid principles the Catholic monarchs offered the Jews the choice between Judaism in exile and Christianity in Spain. The choice was cruel, but in their own way the monarchs showed a certain respect for the beliefs of others. Today, the hatchet of war has still not been completely buried between the Jews and Spain, and this very resentment forms a bond that even makes one suspect a sort of disappointed love on both sides. The Portuguese policy was just as cruel and, moreover, it was perfidious and devoid of principle: as such, it does not seem to have left any particular traces on the tablets of the prodigious historical memory of the Jews.

eleven

Spain's Fateful Hour

The Citadel of Faith

What did Spain lose when it expelled the Jews? The Huguenot emigration from France, to which it may be compared, did not have disastrous consequences, either short or long range, although it might be blamed for a certain slowness in the development of some aspects of the French economy. In Spain the expulsion itself was probably less responsible for the stagnation or decadence of the country than were the conditions placed on the converts and their descendants. And the results of this were apparent only after a good many years.

At first, the departure of the Jews did not seem to change Spanish life at all. Of course Spanish historians today judge it differently. "The expulsion," Vicens Vives has written, "eliminated from society the only groups capable of developing the first thrust toward capitalism in Castile. In numerous cities it undermined the sources of prosperity. It also put an enormous amount of wealth into circulation, most of which went to finance the foreign policy of the Catholic monarchs, while the rest was dissipated at the hands of the aristocracy" (383).

But at the time, even such realistic observers as Machiavelli and Guicciardini felt that the Catholic monarchs had done something eminently useful for their country. Henceforth, for nearly a century Spain was to march from triumph to triumph; the gold of the Americas was to flow into its treasury, to the amazement of Europe; Charles V was to assume the imperial crown; and the sun was never to set on the Spanish Empire, as a proud motto recalled. In 1492, the year when the Jews were expelled, Spain was on the threshold of grandeur.

Among the national institutions of the time, the Inquisition, responsible for eradicating all possible forms of heterodoxy, was to become one of the most typical—and one of the most popular. For fifty years historians have argued about whether it was a royal or an ecclesiastical instrument. It was neither, or it was both at the same time. Above all, it was profoundly Spanish. It was a sort of rallying point where ambition and fanaticism converged; it was a form of government and a moral standard. It inspired terror, but the common Spaniard regarded that terror as good and salutary. Great and small, nobles and beggars, witnessed the autos-da-fé, and it became customary to have these dramatic lessons of true Christian faith coincide with the solemnities of the court, such as accessions to the throne or royal marriages. It should be noted in this regard that heretics were not burned at the autos-da-fé; the ceremony, which was sometimes inaugurated by the king himself, consisted of a procession of hundreds of condemned prisoners ("penitents"), carrying candles and wearing their grotesque *sambenitos*, toward the site where the auto-da-fé was to be held (in Madrid, the Plaza Mayor). There the verdicts were read aloud. These processions lasted from morning to evening and, if necessary, continued the following day. The pyres were set up elsewhere, generally in a suburb of the city, in a place called the *quemadero* (from *quemar*, "to burn"). But the punishment itself was also open to the public and attracted great crowds of people avid for gratification. A manuscript of the time tells of the consternation of the people of Seville in 1604 when the king canceled an auto-da-fé at the last moment: "A general feeling of internal sadness took hold of everyone, as if each were wounded; for the cause of God has such strength that each wanted to come to its defense. This event showed the love, the respect, and also the fear that they felt for the Inquisition" (384). (The inquisitors protested and the auto was held a few days later, "to the great joy of Seville and the whole province.")

This affection that the Spanish people felt for the Inquisition over the centuries makes it easier to understand why even today it has its defenders in Spain. Of course, even the most zealous defenders express some surprise in noting that the trials of certain Judaizers lasted for decades.[1] Even more striking are the remarks of a sixteenth-century bishop to the effect that burning was the only suitable punishment for heretics without property, "for they do not know shame, and one cannot confiscate anything from them" (385). But this merely serves as a reminder that we should not measure triumphant Renaissance Spain with a twentieth-century yardstick.

Was the Spanish Inquisition the incarnation of absolute cruelty? It has been established that generally its prisons were far from being secret dungeons, the *in pace* of legend. Rich prisoners arrived accompanied by their servants; poor prisoners did their own cooking and sometimes even worked in the fields during the day. Rich and poor alike could receive visitors; and if inmates were literate, they were permitted to read and write. When the prisoners found their prisons too cramped, the inquisitors sometimes rented houses in the city to lodge them. Those sentenced to life imprisonment were generally confined in monasteries if they belonged to the clergy; if not, they sometimes were able to serve their sentence at home (386).

The conditions always depended a great deal on the seriousness of the accusation or offense, and the Judaizers

---

[1] Professor Lopez Martinez, author of the study cited previously on the Castilian Judaizers, an apology for the Inquisition crammed with anti-Semitic professions of faith, cites the case of a trial that took place in the inquisitorial tribunal of Toledo from 1485 to 1537, and writes in this regard: "There are some cases that we can no longer understand today." (*Los judaizantes castellanos y la Inquisicion en tiempo de Isabel la Catolica*, p. 328, note 130.)

had to expect the worst—just as the Jews did in the twentieth-century Nazi prisons or concentration camps.

Not all of the accused were tortured. Where torture was used, it was worse for the innocent than for the guilty, because the whole inquisitorial system was based on free and spontaneous confession—much to the distress of the innocent who had nothing to confess. We have already described the singular problem of confession; now we shall give a concrete example.

, What follows is an extract from the report on Elvira del Campo, a good Christian according to all the witnesses, but accused of not eating pork and of putting on clean linen on Saturdays (Toledo, 1568):

"She was carried to the torture chamber and told to tell the truth when she said that she had nothing to say. She was ordered to be stripped and again admonished, but was silent. When stripped, she said: 'Señores, I have done all that is said of me and I bear false witness against myself, for I do not want to see myself in such trouble; please God, I have done nothing.' She was told not to bring false testimony against herself but to tell the truth. The tying of the arms was commenced. She said, 'I have told the truth; what have I to tell?' She was told to tell the truth and replied, 'I have told the truth and have nothing to tell.' One cord was applied to the arms and twisted, and she was admonished to tell the truth but said she had nothing to tell. Then she screamed and said 'I have done all they say.'"

The proceedings of the torture session, recorded by a notary, continue, meticulous and inflexible; according to the rule, up to sixteen turns of the cord on the arm were permitted:

"Another turn was ordered. She cried: 'Loosen me a little that I may remember what I have to tell; I don't know what I have done; I did not eat pork for it makes me sick; I have done everything; loosen me and I will tell the truth.' Another turn of the cord was ordered. . . . She was told to tell in detail truly what she did. She said: 'What am I expected to tell? I did everything—loosen me for I don't remember what I have to tell—don't you see what a weak woman I am? Oh! Oh! my arms are breaking.'"

After the sixteenth turn of the rope another torture was administered:

"She was then ordered to be placed on the *potro* [rack]. She said, 'Señores, why will you not tell me what I have to say? Señor, put me on the ground—have I not said that I did it all?' She was told to tell it. She said 'I don't remember—take me away—I did what the witnesses say.' She was told to tell in detail what the witnesses said. She said . . . 'Señor, remind me of what I did not know—Señores, have mercy upon me—let me go for God's sake—they have no pity on me—I did it—take me from here and I will remember what I cannot here.' . . . She was told to declare it. She said, 'I don't know how to say it—I have no memory—Lord, you are witness that if I knew how to say anything else I would say it. I know nothing more to say than that I did it and God knows it.' . . . She said, 'The Law of which the witnesses speak—I don't remember what Law it was—cursed be the mother that bore me. . . . Oh! Oh! they are killing me—if they would tell me what—Oh, Señores! Oh my heart!' . . . She clamored for confession, saying that she was dying. She was told that the torture would be continued till she told the truth and was admonished to tell it, but though she was questioned repeatedly she remained silent. Then the inquisitor, seeing her exhausted by the torture, ordered it to be suspended" (387).

At the next torture session the unhappy *conversa* agreed that her dislike for pork was not accidental, that it had the significance of a Jewish rite. The inquisitor agreed that she knew nothing else about Jewish Law, so she ended up with her life and the customary penances.

⸱ The traditional symbol of the Inquisition is still the pyre, on which thousands of human beings were burned alive because they denied the divinity of Jesus or because they diverged from Catholic dogma in some way (as on the existence of purgatory). The fact that the pyres were erected in the suburbs of the cities and not in the main squares did not make the execution any less cruel (although certain modern apologists make a great deal of this point). And the fact that most of the condemned were strangled before being burned, a favor they owed to a renunciation *in extremis,* is also a rather strange moral argument—unless we recall that the executioners believed that beyond the flames of the pyre they were sparing their victims the eternal flames of a hell in which they themselves believed intensely. But what was the total number of burnings between 1480 and 1834 (the date when the Inquisition was definitively abolished)? Llorente, the renegade inquisitor, who was in a position to know more about this than anyone else (for he was in charge of the complete archives of the Inquisition) (388), estimated it at 341,021. The accuracy of the figure is suspect; in fact, as shown by the Lutheran Ernst Schäfer, a scholar who has refused to take sides, it is the result of a superficial extrapolation and should be reduced by at least two-thirds (389). Thus, the real number of executions was probably on the ɔrder of one hundred thousand, and the number, after the great initial slaughter, decreased from year to year. The majority, whatever their offense, were descendants of Jews who had more or less accepted baptism.

The "crime against faith," like the "political crime" of our time, turned out to be a very flexible concept, and it was not long before the Inquisition had to concern itself with very diverse matters. Before going into this, let us consider a few other aspects of the Spanish police of men's souls.

First of all, the techniques of espionage and investigation. For this the Inquisition established a network of "familiars," or well-placed people, some of whom belonged to the best aristocratic families and whose total number in the following century was put at more than twenty thousand (390). They were not paid; instead, a medal or plaque served as a sign of gratitude, a much sought-after distinction, for it was both evidence of Spanish "racial purity" and a way of evading arrest and the secular police, since no matter what their offenses the familiars were responsible only to the tribunal of the Inquisition. "They had," a historian of the last century wrote, "in a way divided the nation into two camps: the denouncers and the denounced" (391). Again, it must be remembered that the denounced, or, more precisely, the denounceable, considered this state of affairs as normal and even salutary.

These outside agents facilitated the work of the Inquisition itself, which a French traveler described in 1603 as follows:

"The procedure is to invite everyone, for recompense and fear of excommunication, to inform against those who they know have said something against the faith . . . and to place numerous detectives and spies in the field who are everywhere and gather what they see and hear on the subject to report it to these men so that they can seize the offender if the case warrants, or else write it on the red paper and stop him if he continues.

"If he flees and is a person of consequence, information about his size, hair, age, color, and general description is circulated throughout the country, and one of the other master detectives is put on his trail, and he will be found without fail, no matter where he may go" (392).

ᵛ And in fact, a heretic, especially if he was prominent, was followed wherever he went. Servetus, the illustrious Spanish theologian who discovered the circulation of blood, was tracked down in France by the Inquisition because of his anti-Trinitarianism; he then sought refuge in Calvin's Geneva (and thus his pyre was lighted by the Reformationists). The noble Alonzo Diaz went to Germany to find his brother who had become a Lutheran and killed him with his own hands "to prevent, at the price of a crime, numerous other and worse forfeits" (393).

Let us now consider the archives of the Inquisition. Obviously it did not have the cross-indexed card catalogues and the computerized sorting that the police of our time use. But in addition to the dossiers of its trials and reports of its informers, it did make use of genealogical lists of the families of *conversos* and related families, all a priori suspects. In the beginning there was a *visita del partido* (visitation of the district) each year. An inquisitor accompanied by a notary had to visit each locality to proclaim the "Edict of Grace," bring the genealogical lists up to date, and inspect the condition of the *sambenitos* (394). In fact, the garments of shame, while serving for the edification of the masses, had the singular fate of becoming a sort of tool, a *sui generis* type of archive.

This piece of crude and rough cloth, decorated with various emblems (most often the cross of Saint Andrew, but in the case of those condemned to death the devils of hell), was something the "reconciled" penitent had to wear on certain days or for his whole life, according to the sentence. It marked him as someone the masses should watch and sometimes prevented him from finding work (395). After the death of its wearer the *sambenito* was displayed in the church of his district as a perpetual warning, so that the children of the town and their children would know of his infamy and realize that his descendants were still suspect. Sometimes the exhibit was mobile, and the *sambenitos* made the rounds of all the churches of the diocese (396). Some villages petitioned that these rounds be stopped or that the *sambenitos* be left to rot instead of being kept in repair, for the families suffered the consequences of the heterodox views of an ancestor for centuries (397). But as late as the end of the eighteenth century an Englishman named Clarke saw them on exhibit in the cathedral of Segovia (398).

In common usage the word *sambenito*, after first referring to the garments of shame, came to mean the man who had worn them and his children. If they were good Spaniards in that Spain so concerned with its honor (and we are approaching the pages that treat of the bond between Spanish pride and the infamy of being Jewish), the distress caused by such reproofs was boundless.

"The *sambenitos*," the Venetian ambassador Sorranzo related in 1602, "are a type of men who nourish an indescribable private hatred against the king, against the Crown, against the government, against justice, and against everyone indiscriminately. They are descendants of persons condemned by the Inquisition. This condemnation, which is passed on to their posterity, means that by no fault of theirs, but because of the sin of another, these people are not only excluded from the benefits or advantages accorded others, but are also marked with perpetual infamy. They live in torment, despair, and rage. Just as the marranos and the Moriscos, they are driven by that distress which even in vile and abject souls creates a spirit of furor and passion. They are ready for any rebellion . . . but the very rigor of justice and of the Inquisition makes any demonstration impossible for them, no matter what it may be" (399).

On the other hand, a true crypto-Jew, a Portuguese marrano, for example, could be scornful toward what for him were merely Christian grimaces. A witness related with indignation how, at the time of an auto-da-fé in Valladolid, a "Portuguese" dressed in a *sambenito* decorated with the cross of Saint Andrew walked "without faltering or pain," exclaiming, "Isn't Saint Andrew as honorable as Saint James? Why should this burden be heavier for me than the other?" (400) A Jew could at least admit aloud that he was Jewish. Among the victims of the Inquisition it was not those who scorned Christ who were subjected to the whole gamut of tortures in its repertoire; they were spared certain exquisite varieties of moral suffering.

In fact, if a good Catholic was accused of heresy and denied his guilt, protesting the purity of his faith until the end, he became a *negativo* and was burned. But if he gave in and confessed to an imaginary sin, he saved his life—at the price of perjury and dishonor for his family. According to theology, only the first solution would assure the salvation of his soul, and the archives of the Inquisition give us a glimpse of these indescribable stories of martyrdom[2] just as they contain many a confession of imaginary sins supposedly committed by marranos.

"We must find an effective remedy," wrote a courageous inquisitor, "for the deceit in the midst of which (through no fault of its own) the Inquisition lives, as one sees numerous evil people being absolved and numerous good people being condemned by the malice of witnesses. A good many others flee because they know that someone has said something against them, or because they fear that someone will . . ." (401).

The confessions of the accused were duly recorded before a notary, and the perfection of the form made up for the abundancy of errors within; for it must be said, once and for all, that the proceedings of the Spanish Inquisition, the punctilious formalism of the examinations, the precision and minutiae of the informations, are reminiscent of the bureaucratic pedantry of the totalitarian police of our era. "*Summa injuria, summum jus,*" one could say; for terror engenders an admirable exactitude.

Let us turn now to the enemies and the victims of the Inquisition.

For nearly a half century the Inquisition's activities were limited almost entirely to the struggle against Judaism. For it goes without saying that the expulsion of the Jews was not enough to turn all the *conversos* into good Christians. Around 1500, Messianic movements appeared throughout Andalusia, despite—or because of—inquisitorial terror.

---

[2] "Those who resisted to the end and went to the stake, asserting their Catholicism, were unquestionably good Christians who preferred the most frightful of deaths rather than admit that they had been heretics and confess and abjure heresies that they had never entertained, for if they were really guilty there was nothing more to be gained by denial than by the defiant avowal of their beliefs. Cases of this kind were by no means rare. . . . The Church will never know how many martyrs of this kind the Inquisition furnished to its roll of uncanonized saints." (H. C. Lea, *A History of the Inquisition in Spain,* Vol. 2, pp. 585–86.)

However, such manifestations of marranism only increased the repression. At Córdoba the inquisitor Lucero took advantage of this situation to intensify the terror and to attack Moriscos and Old Christians, confiscating their property and distributing their possessions to his friends. He went so far as to accuse the archbishop of Granada himself, the venerable Hernando de Talavera. The Andalusian nobility threatened an uprising, and after numerous intrigues, the Inquisitor General, Cardinal Cisneros, dismissed Lucero from his post in 1508 (402). The days of the incorruptible Torquemada were in the remote past; in a few short years the Andalusian Inquisition had become a hotbed of blackmail and graft.

Nevertheless, these excesses dealt formidable blows to crypto-Judaism; after 1530 the autos-da-fé became less and less frequent for lack of Judaizers. During the second quarter of that century, new categories of enemies of the faith increasingly claimed the attention of the inquisitors. These were at the bottom of the social scale—the Moriscos of Granada, who had been baptized by force—and they were at the top—the Lutherans and other followers of the Reformation, who, although not numerous, were considered as particularly dangerous. Spain at that time became the bastion of militant Catholicism, and in the eyes of the Inquisition the Protestants were virtually Jews in a new mask. It is worth pausing on this point.

The connection of the Reformation with the humanist movement, with its rediscovery of the ancient sources, the first strides in philology and the translations of the Bible, should not be forgotten. Before the Protestant schism, Spain's intellectual elite had participated in this movement enthusiastically, and no other than the Inquisitor General Cisneros himself had assembled a team of Hebraists and Hellenists, who around 1515 produced the text of the famous Polyglot Bible. In the words of Cardinal Cisneros, it was a matter "of checking the books of the Old Testament against the Hebrew text and those of the New Testament against the Greek text,

so that each theologian could go back to the sources themselves" or, as other humanists put it more simply, "of seeking
the Hebraic truths" (403). But soon Luther was to show the
world the consequences that could be drawn from interpret-
ing these truths; it also seems that certain Judaizers used the
Castilian translations of the Bible to teach their children
about the Law of Moses. These translations were thus prohibited and placed on the Index, and rigorous censorship of
books became one of the major tasks of the Inquisition, an
area in which it showed such proficiency that, according to
an inquisitor at the end of the eighteenth century, the Bible
had become an object of horror and detestation for the Spaniards.[8]

Under these conditions any attempt to reflect on the
sacred texts was prohibited, and the simple desire to read
them could legitimately be considered as Jewish, since these
texts were Jewish. Thus, one sees again how, when it became
the common patrimony of the whole West, the revelation on
Sinai contributed to the persecution of the Jews and the
disparagement of the Jewish name. And thus it was that
when the persecution of humanists began in Spain, the son
of the Inquisitor General Manrique wrote to his famous
friend Luis Vives: "For now it is clear that [in Spain] one
cannot possess any culture without being suspected of
heresy, error, and Judaism. Thus silence has been imposed
on the learned . . . [and] they have been filled with great
terror . . ." (404).

But it was particularly with the accession of Philip II in
1558 that the situation worsened and Spain became a sort of
totalitarian country. The Protestants were harshly persecuted (two small conventicles had been discovered in Seville

---

[8] This inquisitor, Villanueva, wrote in 1791: "The zeal with which the
Holy Office has tried to keep the Bible out of the hands of the common
people is well-known, with the result that the same people who once
sought it, now regard it with horror and detestation. Many care nothing
for it and are ignorant of its very existence." (Cited by H. C. Lea, *Chapters from the Religious History of Spain*, Philadelphia, 1890, p. 56; see
also p. 44, chapter "The Scriptures.")

and Valladolid). The archbishop of Toledo, Carranza, was prosecuted and died in prison because he had published a "commentary on the catechism," certain passages of which seemed open to dispute. Importation and possession of prohibited books became a crime punishable by death. Spanish students were recalled from foreign universities and required to appear before the Inquisition (which was also charged with surveillance of all foreigners living in Spain) to ascertain if they went to Mass, confessed, knew the prayers, and behaved as good Catholics. "One could say," Marcel Bataillon has written, "that Spain was gathered behind a sort of *cordon sanitaire* to prevent some terrible epidemic"—and the chief virus of this epidemic was the Jewish virus. This was the era when the prominent theologian Santotis, at the Council of Trent, defended the thesis that Protestantism was nothing more than a return to Judaism. Other theologians went further, affirming that Judaism was at the root of all heresies, including Islam.[4] From this the inquisitors drew the obvious conclusion by searching for the Jewish ancestry of Lutherans and other heretics, and imputed it in order to render more serious the charges against them.

Take, for example, the following passage from the death sentence of Pedro de Cazalla, head of the Lutheran conventicle of Valladolid:

"The aforesaid Pedro de Cazalla, descendant of the line and caste of converted Jews, by his father on both sides, and by his mother, Dona Leonor de Vivero, by her mother, being of the opinion that by the passion and the merits of our Redeemer Jesus Christ all sinners will find themselves redeemed without the necessity of any good works or any penitence . . ." (405).

The theologian Luis de León, one of Spain's enduring

[4] See Appendix B, the philippic of the bishop of Segorbe against the Moriscos of Spain, those uncircumcised people, "worse than the Jews, who conserve and retain the Law of Moses, while living and persevering in the sect of Mohammed." (Cf. also N. Lopez Martinez, *op. cit.*)

glories, was interrogated by the Inquisition around 1570 because he had expressed doubts on the infallibility of the text of the Vulgate of Saint Jerome. One of his inquisitorial investigators wrote in this regard: "Let the accused not have the audacity to say . . . that the Holy Spirit revealed to him, who is not so holy, nor even Old Christian, that which He hid from the glorious Saint Jerome" (406). It happened, in fact, that a Jewish great-great-grandfather of Luis de León, who was born around 1375 and died in his eighties, had converted in 1415; in 1491 the Inquisition discovered that he had Judaized after his baptism, condemned him *post obitum,* and caused his bones to be burned. This was the source of a never-ending series of vexations for his children, and it had its repercussions on the fate of Don Luis, who was unaware of the whole thing. But the Inquisition itself was meticulous about keeping its genealogical entries up to date. Such a case is a good illustration of the predicament of a Spain crossbred with Jews and Moors, where it was commonly accepted, as we shall soon see, that the Jewish virus was transmitted genetically (which in today's terms would make it a sort of pathological gene).

But even this conviction, this suspicion that hung over the New Christians even when they were not *sambenitos* in the proper sense of the word, predisposed them to bitterness and doubt, so that actually they did tend to be less orthodox than the Old Christians. They were townspeople and generally literate, and thus doubly receptive to new ideas. This created a vicious circle that confirmed the accepted notion of the noxiousness of Jewish blood.

As for the real crypto-Jews, the Spanish marranos, inquisitorial terror depleted their ranks to such an extent that they had almost completely disappeared by 1570–75. But in 1580 an accident of history again placed the battle against marranism uppermost among the concerns of the Castilian Inquisition and reinforced the Spanish obsession with the Jews.

In 1580, after King Sebastian was defeated and killed in

Morocco, Portugal was united with Spain. The Portuguese Inquisition, which had functioned for some thirty years, now redoubled its ardor, and at the same time it became much easier to cross the Spanish border. As a result, a great number of Portuguese marranos, more confirmed in the practice of crypto-Judaism than the Spanish *conversos,* spread over the whole peninsula. More adept in the battle against the Inquisition, they maintained a sort of permanent lobby in Rome that made substantial contributions to the pontifical treasury to obtain collective pardons from which the rich Judaizers in particular benefited, while the poor and unfortunate were burned. The result was that the Spanish people came to believe that being Portuguese was synonymous with being Jewish. This leads us to the following question: What did Renaissance Europe think of the Spaniards, the Portuguese, and the Jews?

ᵟ If ever there was a term whose origin gave rise to much controversy over the centuries, it was "marrano"; for Christian Europe the word itself was as intriguing as the condition it described was upsetting. As far back as 1637 the Spanish monk Jerome de la Cruz discussed all the possible etymologies (407). In 1925, in an epochal publication, the Italian philologist Farinelli settled the question (the term *marrano* came from the old Castilian word for "pork," which came in turn from the Arabic *mahram,* "prohibited"), and in the course of his scholarly work he became interested in certain views prevailing at the time (408). It seems that in the sixteenth century, the century of Spanish preponderance in Europe, public opinion, especially in the many countries dominated by Spain, suspected the people of the Iberian Peninsula of being more or less Jewish. This was particularly true in Italy, whose people had good cause to reach conclusions so wounding to Spanish pride. The first and most obvious of the reasons for this was the very existence of the Inquisition, whose terrifying reputation had soon spread beyond the borders of Spain. If a Christian country needed to fight so ferociously for the purity of the faith, it could only be because this faith was shaky; and with this reasoning as a starting point, as far back as 1506 the Venetian ambassador Querini wrote that the Inquisition "is more than necessary, for they Judaize in Castile just as elsewhere in Spain; a third of the townspeople and the merchants there are marranos" (409). Moreover, as the only Spaniards that numerous Italians of this time knew, unless they had come across the Spanish troops on campaign, were the marrano or Jewish refugees, this ignominious suspicion had quickly spread through the conquered nation (410). The Italian pamphleteers lamented the fate of their country, subjugated by the odious marrano sect. As early as 1500 the epithet was applied to Pope Alexander VI, Rodrigo Borgia, who was of Spanish origin; half a century later Pope Paul IV railed against the Spaniards, "those heretics cursed by God, seed of Jews and marranos" (411); at the end of the century the Italian prelate Camille Borghese justified the severity of the Spanish Inquisition by "the mixture in this kingdom of Moors, Jews, and New and Old Christians" (412). And in Italian popular parlance, unbelief, or shaky faith, was called a "Spanish peccadillo." In sum, the people thought that all Spaniards were Jews, just as in the nineteenth century they thought that all Britons were tourists.

But this was true not only for Italy. In the course of the century Spain became the number-one enemy of France. When the anti-Spanish phobia attained its peak around 1590, innumerable pamphlets appeared (one of which was the famous *Satire Ménippée*) vilifying the overpowerful neighbor. *L'Anti-Espagnol,* one of the most popular, inveighed against the Spaniards as follows: ". . . cads of Castile, bastard Catholics, half-Jews and half-Moors scarcely removed from the synagogue and the Koran" (413). According to the memoirs of Vincent Carloix, "The Spaniards were marranos before they were Christians!" (414) According to Bonaventure des Périers, "Marranism is in such great vogue that anyone who likes bacon had better stock up on it, for it will be forbidden us one day" (415). In *Gargantua* the adolescent Pantagruel is not given Spanish arms because "his father hated all these hidalgos, as drunk and marranized as the devil" (416). Without stating that all Spaniards were of the Jewish race, the majority of the French of the time attributed origins to them that were murky, to say the least. As late as 1680 the French dictionary of Pierre Richelet contained the following definition: "*Marrano:* abusive term which we call the Spaniards and which means Mohammedan (he is a marrano)."

Throughout Europe, country by country, it would be easy to find many more examples. Thus, Erasmus writing to his friend Wolfgang of Capito: "If the Jews abound in Italy, in Spain there are hardly any Christians . . ." (417). Or Luther exclaiming: "I would prefer to have the Turks as enemies than the Spaniards as suzerains; the majority are marranos, converted Jews" (418). From the seventeenth century on, suspicion about the origin of everyone from the Iberian Peninsula, without distinction, came to refer especially to the Portuguese. In their spitefulness the nations could see clearly enough under the circumstances, as we shall soon see. Around 1700 various Portuguese authors described this distressing state of affairs, e.g., the Jesuit Father Antonio Vieira: "Portuguese and Jew have become synonyms"; the Rabbi de Pinhas Nieto in Leghorn: "The majority of the Europeans confuse Portuguese and Jews, and the kingdom is thus discredited . . ." (419).

But what was only a pin prick for little Portugal was an intolerable blow against Spanish grandeur at a time when the cult of honor, the craze for knighthood, and the obsession with the "purity of the blood" had become the major preoccupations of Hispanic life. The suspicion naturally arose that there could be a link between the frenzy with which the Spaniards cultivated their nobility and glorified the splendor of their origins, and their bad reputation abroad. They themselves were not unaware of this and complained bitterly: "I do not know," wrote Diego de

Hermosilla, "why this misfortune has struck Spanish nobility, so highly qualified and held in such wretched esteem, because of the ignominious name of marranos which the other nations persist in applying to the Spaniards" (420). Similarly, Fernandez de Oviedo: "Foreigners have no right to call all Spaniards marranos . . . for all the Christian nations, there is not one where the origin of nobles of good and pure caste is better known, nor where they are as concerned with the faith; these are all things which remain hidden in the other nations" (421). For their part, those Spanish authors who advocated relaxing the statutes of "purity of the blood" stressed their harm to the national reputation and thus gave unpleasant publicity to the very evil they sought to circumscribe. According to the Dominican Augustin Salucio, Spain was considered as a land of marranos, whose inhabitants must be either vile or mad to dishonor themselves so (422). One of his emulators said that the statutes made Spain the laughingstock of the other nations, and because of them the Spaniards were called marranos (423).

There is reason to believe that the defenders of the New Christians were not painting an entirely false picture and that the passion with which the Spaniards persecuted the traces of their Judeo-Moslem past contributed to the annoying reputation they had acquired. But in reality we are faced with a very complex social evolution. On the one hand, in its zeal to eliminate all heterodoxy, Catholic Spain had acquired a number of the characteristics of a totalitarian country, before the term was invented. On the other hand, in addition to the avowed heretics, the persecutions created a category of statutory suspects that included the converts, their descendants, and, generally, the Spaniards of "impure" blood, or presumed as such, who were credited with an irresistible tendency to heresy, due to their ancestry. Legislated racial discrimination—for the statutes of *limpieza de sangre* were nothing else—was established against them, the first example in history of legalized racism. There is no better way to demonstrate the relation between the inquisitorial persecutions, the national obsession with "pure" blood, and the peculiarities of social and economic life of the peninsula than to outline the history of the statutes in question. Certain conclusions will be inevitable.

The Cult of
Purity of the Blood, or Iberian Racism

We have seen that the first decrees eliminating the *conversos* from social life were promulgated after the rebellion of the Old Christians of Toledo in 1449. That is typical: the statutes of "purity of the blood," so un-Christian in principle, were conceived and imposed by public opinion. The power of the state was content to validate them; the Church did the same, not without some resistance. The semantic evolution reflects the increasing ascendancy of racist concepts. The term "New Christian," or *converso*—which originally simply meant a Jewish or Moorish convert—was finally extended to mean anyone who had a Jewish ancestor. Let us point out here that in practice the descendants of the Moslems suffered little discrimination: on the one hand they were considered as being of "pagan" and not Jewish stock; on the other, most of them belonged to the peasantry and did not compete for honors and offices. (It is impossible to say if either of these two factors would have been sufficient in itself or if the combination was necessary (424).)

After the Toledo incident, numerous guilds in various cities decided not to admit New Christians. There were also cities, particularly in the Basque country, that denied them residence (425). Thus, the movement originated among the urban middle class; at a time not far removed from the mass conversions of the Jews, the status of Old Christian was established by common consent and did not require a system of genealogical proofs. Although the nobility was generally more hesitant, the orders of chivalry followed the movement: as early as 1483 the order of Alcantara demanded the proof of purity of blood for its members; that of Saint James did the same in 1527, with an express waiver for the descendants of Moors (426). The custom also began of excluding New Christians from the benefits of the pious foundations and of refusing them admission to the *colegios mayores,* the colleges from which the ruling class of Spain was recruited. It was in these nurseries of future ministers and future prelates that the admission requirement of purity of blood later became so meticulous and extravagant. There were some delicate cases: the College of Santa María de Jesus, cradle of the University of Seville, had been founded in the fifteenth century by the *converso* Santaella, needless to say without any restrictions on students from the same background as the founder. A restrictive clause was added in 1537 with recourse to forgery (427).

As far as the Church was concerned, the situation varied from order to order and from province to province. The order of Saint Jerome was the first, at the end of the fifteenth century, to introduce restrictive clauses; the Franciscans did the same in 1525; with the Dominicans each monastery determined its own practices; we shall discuss the case of the Jesuits later. Generally, discrimination was less rigorous than among the laymen, and most of the orders admitted *conversos* from families that had been converted for four generations. In the case of the regular clergy the practice was even less uniform, and if there were dioceses in which a New Christian could not become a choir boy, there were others in which nothing could prevent his becoming bishop (428). Was this relative liberality a tribute to the fundamental principles of Christianity or was it due to the positions the New Christians had achieved in the Church during preceding generations? Here, again, it is impossible to say.

Toward the middle of the sixteenth century the statutes of purity of blood acquired the force of law. In 1536 a local quarrel led Charles V to take the side of the Old Christians and to accord imperial sanction to the statutes. But the decisive episode was the purging of the chapter of Toledo in which the New Christians were firmly entrenched.

The man who declared war on them, Juan Martinez Siliceo, archbishop of Toledo, typified the Old Christian mentality. He was born into a family of simple laborers. After an adventurous youth (he had run away from home at the age of sixteen) he studied theology in Paris and was then chosen as tutor to the infante Philip (the future emperor Philip II). In 1544 he became archbishop of Toledo. Throughout his life he nurtured a fierce hatred toward the *conversos.* Doubtless he was predisposed to this because of his humble origins; in fact, men like him, who succeeded thanks to merit and not to birth and who were still looked down on by the hereditary aristocracy, often tended to look for other credentials of nobility. The observation that has been made about racism in other places summarizes an essential aspect of Spanish racism: if all the Old Christians could not be *hidalgos,* "sons of someone," all, by definition, were at least *limpios,* "of pure blood."

After plotting for some three years, Siliceo succeeded in completely winning the emperor over to his views, in having the statutes approved by the pope, and in having his principal opponents, the pro-Jewish aristocrats of Toledo, imprisoned. Although it was a long time before the polemics were over, the New Christians had definitively lost the battle.

Nothing is more revealing than the arguments Siliceo advanced in favor of the statutes in a long memorandum he presented to Charles V. His scriptural reasons were drawn mostly from the Old Testament, as was natural; thus, he recalled that the ministry of the Temple was entrusted exclusively to the tribe of the Levites, and compared the *conversos* to the Ammonites and to the Moabites who were excluded from the assembly of the Eternal. But he was also adept at finding arguments in the New Testament. The very fact that Christ came among the Jews, he exclaimed, showed that He had recognized their perversity and wanted to bring His healing where it was most needed; he quoted Matthew:

"Those who are well have no need of a physician, but those who are sick" (9:12). This verse referred to the tax-collectors, but even the life of the disciples of Jesus furnished Siliceo with arguments to demonstrate the congenital perversity of the Jewish race. Had they not abandoned their Lord on the eve of the Passion?[5] As to the Jewish origins of the Mother of God, the theology of Siliceo simply ignored them, and as if anticipating the "Aryan Christ" of Nazi theology, he came very close to calling Jesus an Old Christian. Finally, he compared the pious Old Christian faith to the sterile erudition of the New Christian clerics in a way that is also reminiscent of certain clichés of modern anti-Semitic propaganda, of which one is tempted to call Archbishop Siliceo a great unrecognized precursor.[6]

The Toledo affair created a stir throughout Europe. In Paris, Henri Mauroy, professor of Holy Scriptures at the Sorbonne, published a long treatise in 1552 in which he came to the defense of the "descendants of the patriarchs converted to the true faith" and easily demonstrated that Catholicism and racism were incompatible. Perhaps the hispanophobia of the time contributed to the success of his *Apologia*, which was reissued in 1562 (429). In Spain itself the Dominican Domingo Baltanas was so daring as to sustain a similar thesis in a pamphlet, *Sobre la discordia de las lineas* (1556), in which he placed the descendants of the Gentiles on the same footing as the descendants of the Jews, "for the one is no different from the other, neither in origin nor in guilt for the death of the Son of God." He then listed the great families of converts—the Sancta Marias, the Coronels, the Talaveras—and related the benefits they had bestowed on Spain. Too bad for him that he did, for he was

[5] Matthew 26:56; Luke 14:50.

[6] Also attributed to Archbishop Siliceo was the *Correspondence of the Jews of Spain with the Jews of Constantinople,* one of the most widespread anti-Semitic forgeries of the sixteenth century. (Cf. the unpublished thesis of A. A. Sicroff, *Les Statuts de pureté du sang en Espagne aux XVIe et XVIIe siècles*, Paris, 1955, p. 360.)

accused of heresy and condemned to perpetual seclusion in 1563 (430). In 1572 the Inquisition forbade all discussion and polemic about the statutes of purity of the blood (431). The only man who was able in his lifetime to ignore the taboo of *limpieza* with impunity was Ignacio de Loyola. High birth as well as missionary genius made this founder of the Jesuit order immune to the racist contagion. He once even exclaimed that he would have considered it a great grace to be of the same blood as Christ. Disregarding the opinion of his time, he chose a *converso*, Diego de Lainez, to succeed him and another, Juan de Polanco, to serve as his secretary. After his death the Society of Jesus maintained this position for more than thirty years in the face of many pressures. Finally, in 1592 it capitulated, adopted the statutes, and expelled all the New Christians, going so far as to falsify the genealogy of Diego de Lainez posthumously. Thereafter, the Spanish Jesuits were distinguished by their rigid application of the statutes (432).

The problem of purity of blood stirred Spain up too much for the Inquisition's prohibition of public discussion to be fully respected. Writings pro and con continued to circulate underground. We shall not linger on this curious literature but content ourselves with a few words on the theses of Escobar del Corro, the most extreme of the champions of the statutes. According to him, the relation between the body and the soul was perfectly rigid, and moral attributes were transmitted genetically in the same way as physical characteristics. Denying free will, this Christian proclaimed that no matter what they did, the *conversos* were irremediably tainted. This "anthropology" led him to lament the misfortune of Spain, exposed to the Jewish contagion until the end of time, "subjugated by the Sabbath-worshippers and their infected progeny" (433).

But how to track down this contagion? Once the indignity of Jewish blood had become an article of law, it was important to know how to establish legally who was Old Christian and who was not. In this regard, the lowborn had the advantage of being impossible to investigate, as there were no marriage registers or interest in their ancestry. As to the nobility, its Jewishness had been brought to light the very year Siliceo entered the fray, by the famous *Tizón de la nobleza española,* a pamphlet attributed to Cardinal Mendoza y Bobadilla, which showed that all the great families had intermarried with Jews. Even as late as the nineteenth century this scandalous chronicle was reprinted some ten times (434).

Whatever the accuracy of the genealogies of the *Tizón,* it is not necessary to say that pure blood was a myth and there was no Spaniard who did not have at least one circumcised ancestor. Those who were recognized as Old Christians were those for whom there were no records to charge against them or whose genealogy did not go back very far. The matter often became sort of a game of losers win, for the children of unknown parents were sure to come out on top.[7] In practice, at the time of admission into an order or a college, an investigation was made at the expense of the applicant, particularly in his birthplace, to establish that he "did not belong to the Jewish race." If such an inquiry was a hardship, it was because it was necessary to pay not only the investigators but also the witnesses, and to silence malicious tongues and professional blackmailers. In fact, some Old Christians were numbered among the rejected; certain *colegios mayores* even rejected applicants who were victims of false rumors because, like Caesar's wife, they had to be above reproach (435). There were also families known to be of Jewish stock who slipped in among the select. The most unusual case was that of the Sancta Maria family, admitted to

---

[7] Perhaps there is a relationship between the problems that the investigations into the purity of blood posed and a custom that Mme. d'Aulnoy described as follows in her account of a trip to Spain: "One thing which is quite unusual . . . is that the foundlings are noble, and they enjoy the title of *hidalgos* and all the privileges attached to nobility, but it is necessary for that, that they prove that they were foundlings and that they were nourished and raised in the hospice where they put children of this sort." (Paris, 1699, Vol. 3, p. 129.)

the benefits of pure blood because they were supposed to have descended from the same family as the Holy Virgin, as the cedula of royal dispensation expressly said.[8]

In studying the procedures of these investigations we get a glimpse of all the string pulling, subtle pressuring, and pitiless blackmailing that went on. It is not too much to say that the power of certain inquisitors as well as many illustrious careers and many sudden downfalls was linked to the possession of certain documents or certain lists (such as those Marcel Bataillon described in regard to the New Christians of Segovia (436), which went unmentioned). For many things were surrounded by a padded zone of silence. As a sort of racial nobility, *limpieza* was a much more serious matter than *hidalguería* (social nobility).

A memoir published around 1600 said on this subject: "There are two types of nobility in Spain: a major, which is *hidalguería*, and a minor, which is *limpieza*. . . . In Spain a commoner who is *limpio* is more highly esteemed than a *hidalgo* who is not *limpio*" (437). It is noteworthy that the literature of the Spanish Golden Age, which accorded such an important place to themes of honor and the "major nobility," completely avoided the question of the "minor nobility" except in the comic and picaresque genres. These were full of such allusions, which shows the taboo that surrounded these questions and the aura of obscenity associated with it (438).

When, toward the middle of the sixteenth century, the statutes of purity of the blood acquired the force of law, the New Christians of Spain constituted 4 or 5 per cent of the population of the country (439) and formed a sort of social

[8] The cedula in question was published in 1604 by Philip II, in benefit of Don Pedro Osorio de Velasco and other descendants of Don Paulus de Sancta Maria. It was founded "on his miraculous conversion . . . on the ancientness of it . . . and on the nobility of his blood, the accepted tradition being that he descended from the line of Our Lady. . . ." (Fr. Cantera Burgos, *Alvar Garcia de Santa Maria,* Madrid, 1952, p. 280.)

class or caste, bourgeois and literate, quite closely linked to the "major nobility," often living in its shadow or serving it, but forbidden all social advancement for lack of "minor nobility." Because of this, their life in Renaissance Spain was a continuing tragedy. "An equivocal smile, a glance, a conversation about the military orders or the *colegios mayores,* trivial, often involuntary, incidents ceaselessly fed the flame in which they consumed themselves in rancor and resentment. Men bred in the cult of honor, swift to draw their swords to avenge the slightest affront, were powerless before the opprobrium which now weighed on them. Today it is hard to imagine the life of a provincial *hidalgo* who had a blot on his genealogy. Some sought refuge in piety and resignation; others were more impatient and persisted in lashing out and resisting, in pursuit of a rehabilitation which only time and oblivion could assure them." This is how the burden of the *conversos* was described by their best historian, Dominguez Ortiz (440). Certain old writings show their distress even more vividly. "In Spain," wrote a Franciscan in 1586, "there is not so much infamy in being a blasphemer, robber, vagabond, adulterer, sacrilegious person or in being infected with any vice as in having descended from the line of the Jews, even if one's ancestors had been converted for two or three hundred years to the holy Catholic faith. . . ." And farther on: "Who can be blind to the point of not seeing that there is not in Spain any *converso* who would not prefer to have descended from paganism rather than Judaism, and most would give half their lives for such an ancestry. For they have a horror of this line which was handed down from their parents . . ." (441).

Taking into account the important cultural role played by the New Christians, this bitterness and its heartbreak doubtless contributed to molding the lineaments of "tragic Spain." Their influence is today being studied by historians (Marcel Bataillon and Dominguez Ortiz, Americo Castro and Salvador de Madariaga). Genealogies of men who were the glory of their nation, such as Luis de Léon, Luis Vives, and even Cervantes, have been prepared or disputed.[9] But in investigating the relationship between the racial drama of Spain and its present state, one is confronted with problems about which little is known, problems that are extremely complex.

What is known is that the obsession with the purity of blood masked a latent civil war that Luis de Léon hinted at when he compared "a kingdom where some have too many honors and others too many affronts" to "a sick body, where the humors don't get along with each other" (442). Already, in the nineteenth century the great Menendez y Pelayo considered that "this internal racial struggle was the principal cause of the decadence of the peninsula" (443). Today, Dominguez Ortiz elucidates that idea as follows:

"The proofs of *limpieza* and nobility rested essentially on the testimony of witnesses, and thus the status of every man depended on the opinion of others and not on his wealth or his individual qualifications. Insinuation, insult, or calumny could cause such great evils that they had to be expiated by death. There were theologians who justified putting the calumniator to death, because he threatened *honor*, which was much more precious than life. As he had to depend on the opinion of others, the Spaniard (especially the *hidalgo*) lived in a state of agony and excitability which reflected his internal insecurity. The peace of knowing his own value was

---

[9] The question of the origins of the great Spaniards of the Golden Age has been definitively resolved in some cases, and in others still is the object of certain, often shaky, hypotheses. While, for example, the *converso* origin of Fernando de Rojas, author of *La Celestina*, or the great mystic Teresa de Avila has been clearly proved, the Jewish ancestry of Christopher Columbus or of Cervantes, which de Madariaga maintains, has been disputed by other authors. And were there specific influences in the "*converso* spirit"? Bataillon has wondered whether "the religious and moral inspirations of the Prophets did not reappear in them, developing into a Messianic anxiety." Ortiz has the merit of showing that "common nuances existed, if not in all, at least in a great number, but that these were the result of their social condition and not due to a racial factor."

lacking and, carried along by the current, he placed more value on appearances than on realities" (444).

The mania of nobility extended to all classes of society, since all Spaniards, except for the *conversos*, could claim the "minor nobility" of blood and did not fail to make a great deal of this claim. This was the origin of customs among the common people that astounded foreigners, and travelers' tales are full of the details: all the peasants said they were of noble blood; instead of working, artisans strutted with swords at their sides. "This is their profitless honor, which causes the sterility of Spain," concluded one of these observers. These are the origins of Spanish pride and the unique national type, the *caballero*.

"One does not see a carpenter, a harness maker, or any other shopkeeper who is not dressed in velvet and satin, like the king, a great sword, a dagger, and a guitar hanging in his shop," noted Mme. d'Aulnoy (445).

"The common people and tradespeople who cannot avoid working to earn their livelihood, do it negligently, generally with a cloak over their shoulders if their occupation permits. . . . Most of the time they sit before their shop disdainfully; if they succeed in amassing 200 or 300 reales, they are noble; there is no reason to do anything until these are spent and then they return to work to earn some more," noted Barthelemy Joly (446).

It reminds one also of so many of Cervantes' characters, beginning with Sancho Panza, "of good birth and at least an Old Christian" (447).

If instead of considering these questions from the standpoint of social psychology, we approach them from that of economic history, the salient fact is that the New Christians were concentrated in certain occupations—commerce and crafts—the occupations of their Jewish ancestors, on which then devolved a double discredit. These trades were progressively abandoned, for the New Christians had a tendency to leave them in the hope of making it easier to hide their origins, while the Old Christians tended to avoid these occupations above all. "When commerce was a sin in our eyes, in whose hands was it? In those of the Jews!" Capmany, the first Spanish economist, later exclaimed (448). In the sixteenth century the Moriscos and numerous foreigners filled the void, but all the Moriscos were expelled in their turn in 1609. We shall see below how commerce and impure blood finally became synonymous. It is not surprising that a country which held the "mechanical arts" in such low esteem and considered commerce a sin eventually fell into decadence. When the Spaniards themselves finally became aware of it, it was too late. The mirage of the silver and gold of the Americas, a sort of added curse, had merely masked and aggravated the process of impoverishment.

It was under these conditions that the Iberian Peninsula stood apart from the march of time and the great upsurge of capitalism. From this point of view, there is nothing more striking than the contrast between Spain of the Counter Reformation and Puritan or Calvinist England and the Low Countries, the centers of the Industrial Revolution and of the modern world. But while a whole school of scholars has attacked the problem of how the capitalist spirit was born on the shores of the North Sea, at the opposite pole historical research is still undeveloped. No Max Weber has appeared to investigate, as it deserves to be investigated, the relationship between the ethic of Iberian Catholicism, the cult of purity of blood, the absence of the mercantilist or capitalist spirit, and the resulting decadence.

Part Three
The Marrano
Epic

twelve

The Marranos of
Portugal

Whereas the Castilian Inquisition succeeded in completely uprooting Judaism, the Portuguese Inquisition, in a sense, became perhaps one of the instruments of its conservation. It is true that at the time it was created in 1536, the Portuguese marranos were singularly well equipped to fight for their survival.

We have seen that they were descended in the main from Spanish Jews who had preferred exile to apostasy. Once this choice was made, their numerical importance—more than 5 per cent of the Portuguese population—gave them added unity. At a time when little Portugal was becoming the pioneer in overseas trade, the Jews were in on the ground floor to take part in it and develop it, so that they constituted a religious caste that was also a pseudoracial caste, and at the same time a sort of merchant guild with world-wide branches. The different names by which they were known in Portugal reflect these three aspects: the *Cristãos Novos* (New Christians) were also *homens de nação* (persons of the nation) and *homens de negocio* (businessmen). They arrived as foreigners, speaking a different dialect, and this "otherness," which was an added barrier to their mingling with the Christians, became more and more accentuated: Castilians in Portugal, they were later to become Portuguese in Spain, and in the end they imposed their language and their customs on a whole segment of the Mediterranean Dispersion. As for their religion, behind the Christian façade that by this time had become inevitable, it evolved into a sort of syncretism that their historian, Cecil Roth, has called the "marrano religion" (449).

Roth tells us that certain crypto-Jews of Portugal ultimately retained nothing of Judaism except the belief that salvation (conceived in the Christian manner) was possible under the Law of Moses and not under the law of Christ, and that they had their own saints, "Saint Esther" and "Saint Tobit." The theology of the majority was not quite this summary; however, condemned to feign the Christian way of life, the marranos had to renounce the obvious signs and tangible manifestations of Judaism, of which circumcision was first and foremost—the most obdurate had themselves circumcised on their deathbeds (450)—and Hebraic books. For scripture, they had only the Christian Bible, and while they rejected the New Testament, they paid close attention to the Apocrypha. Some even found in them absolution for their apostasy, a sort of blank check to worship foreign gods outwardly while remaining faithful to the God of Israel in their secret hearts.[1]

· In fact, the Portuguese marranos, unlike their Spanish predecessors of the fifteenth century, faithfully complied with all the rites of Catholicism, going to Mass and confes-

---

[1] The apocryphal *Epistle of Jeremy to the Exiles* contains the following passage, which the marranos applied to their own case: "But now shall ye see in Babylon gods of silver, and of gold, and of wood, borne upon shoulders, which cause the nations to fear. Beware therefore that ye in no wise become like unto the strangers, neither let fear take hold upon you because of them, when ye see the multitude before them and behind them worshipping them. But say ye in your hearts: 'O Lord, we must worship Thee.'" (4:7.)

sion, and they had every right to pride themselves "on living a very Christian life" (451). They were so deeply immersed in this way of life that later, in the Protestant Low Countries, they revealed that they were secret Jews only when they were threatened with expulsion as Catholics (452). Their camouflage was so good that Josel of Rosheim, the "regent" of the German Jews who visited the great marrano center of Antwerp in 1536, could write: "It is a land where there are no Jews" (453).

This basic insincerity, this permanent transgression of both the Commandments of Sinai and the law of Christ, contributed to a feeling of guilt that was evinced in frequent fasts and to a sort of selectiveness in the Jewish ritual and the holidays that reduced marrano tradition to a familial cult.

While Yom Kippur was scrupulously observed (transformed into *Día Pura* [Day of Purity]), holidays such as the New Year or Pentecost sank into oblivion. Of Purim, the marranos retained only the Fast of Esther, of little importance in the Jewish ritual but a pillar of the marrano faith. It is easy to understand that the Jewish queen who concealed her origins even from her husband, revealing them only in the hour of danger, would become the principal heroine of the marranos. Another Apocryphal text, the Prayer of Esther, became the great marrano prayer (it is the prayer that Racine transcribed quite faithfully in *Esther*: ". . . I whom you keep among the infidels, you know how much I hate their criminal feasts . . . this pomp to which I am condemned, this diadem in which I must appear, / Alone and in secret I trample them under my feet . . .").[2]

How was the marrano tradition transmitted from generation to generation? It was obviously not something that

[2] It should be recalled that the Apocrypha were writings which were not part of the Jewish canon of the Old Testament but which appeared in the Greek translation of the Septuagint version, the source, through the Vulgate of Saint Jerome, of the Catholic translations of the Bible that inspired Racine to write *Esther*.

could be taught to children, certainly not until they were old enough to hold their tongues. Thus, it was generally held off until adolescence, and the rite of Bar Mitzvah, or religious maturity, even seems to have been turned into a sort of initiation. Often it was the task of the mother of the family; generally speaking, crypto-Judaism was perpetuated thanks to the women who in time became veritable priestesses, the *sacerdotisas*, of the last marranos of the twentieth century. This preponderant role of women is described by an exile of 1492: "Many of those renowned for their wisdom, if not almost all of them, allowed themselves to be baptized in this bitter year, while the women and the humble folk gave their property and their lives for the sanctification of the Divine Name" (454).

But marranism was perpetuated not only because of this obscure fidelity of the women and the humble folk, but also through the considered choice of young people or mature men whose protests it expressed or whose doubts it reflected. The marranos' background was sometimes very mixed, or even Old Christian. We learn this from the archives of the Inquisition, so concerned with establishing the genealogy of the accused as precisely as possible, and we see it also in marrano tradition, in the veneration of martyrs such as the Franciscan monk Diego da Assumpção, who had only a single Jewish ancestor and was burned in 1603, or the *Desembargador* Gil Vaz Bugalho, an Old Christian who belonged to a Messianic sect and was burned in 1551 (455). There were compelling reasons for marranism to resurge and propagate itself in the most diverse ways among the New Christians of Jewish stock. For some, it was testimony of fidelity; for others, it expressed a conflict between generations, the Judaizing son opposing the faithful Christian father. According to his famous biography this seems to have been true for Uriel da Costa, who left his Christian home in Portugal to become a Jew in Amsterdam, then turned to a sort of natural religion, and ended his days a

suicide. "What devil pushed me towards the Jews?" he asked
at the end of his autobiography (456).

Marrano instability and distress were also evinced in the
frequent Messianic movements, in the effort to remedy in
the here and now an unbearable state of affairs, which,
moreover, truly corresponded to the political situation of the
Jews of the peninsula and to the memory of the Jewish
leaders of former times. Let us consider David Reubeni, a
Jewish adventurer of unknown origin, who presented himself to the court of Pope Clement VII in 1524 as an emissary
of a Jewish kingdom of the East and proposed an alliance
against the Moslems. The pope took him seriously, referring
him to the king of Portugal, where he went in a ship flying a
Jewish flag. Believing the hour of deliverance had come, the
marranos were jubilant and even mounted an attack on the
inquisitorial prison of Badajoz. One of them, Diego Pires,
became a Jew under the name of Salomon Molcho and
joined Reubeni. Between 1524 and 1532 they traveled together through Europe with visionary plans, even being
received by Charles V, but finally they ended on the pyre.
Such ferment, with its political and nationalist aspect, seems
typical of the marrano mentality, a mentality that is so
difficult to grasp, for marranos could survive only by confusing things, by passing for what they were not.

If the situation of the marranos could provoke dreams of
this sort (dreams that, as we shall see, could lead far), it was
even more conducive to the spirit of commercial enterprise.
During the sixteenth century, adventurous Portuguese "businessmen" swarmed over all the countries of the known
world, and these pioneers of capitalism on the march created
a network of new trading relationships. They did not go
abroad merely to flee the Inquisition and to be able to practice Judaism in peace, as a certain naïve historiography
would have it. Neither, after studying their coastal routes
and their enterprises, would it be correct to turn their condition into an abstraction and neglect their beliefs, as over-

sophisticated scholars of our time tend to do. All things considered, business, through various detours, could keep alive what was doubtless a fairly tepid faith in the hearts of numerous great exporters and merchants. As a matter of fact, the role that clan and family relationships formerly played in commercial life should not be forgotten. To be a marrano meant also to be affiliated to a vast secret protection and mutual-aid society. And later, to return to open Judaism in Salonica or Amsterdam was also to join a powerful commercial consortium, and these *sui generis* naturalizations were often followed by remarkable religious revivals. To be a marrano meant especially to wage a permanent battle against the Portuguese Inquisition. A few words about this Inquisition are fitting here.

The negotiations between the Roman Curia and the Portuguese Crown that preceded its establishment lasted more than thirty years, and they constitute a curious page in the political customs of the Renaissance. The length of these negotiations is easily explained: neither of the parties involved wanted to kill the goose that laid the golden eggs, and the threat of an Inquisition was much more effective than an actual functioning Inquisition for blackmailing the rich and industrious businessmen. But a threat cannot be brandished indefinitely; imperceptibly, step by step, the apparatus of the Portuguese Inquisition was set up. In 1542 King John III, who had become resigned to establishing it, informed the pope of his point of view on the whole affair with admirable frankness. He wrote that the New Christians constituted an important part of his population, the most useful part of all. He recalled that, thanks to them and their capital, commerce, industry, and the public treasury had been growing before they were persecuted, adding that there was no reason to hate them, for they had always served him loyally and zealously. And he concluded: "How can one dare to require me to cut the throats of my own flock?" (457) It then became a matter of fleecing the marrano lambs rather than slitting their throats, and there were numerous applicants for the shearing. In Portugal the king named his own brother, the infante Don Henrique, as Inquisitor General in 1539. In Rome there was no shortage of candidates for such a profitable nunciature. When the vessel transporting the belongings of the nuncio Capodiffero was shipwrecked on the way to Italy, the Portuguese ambassador was jubilant: "It is not without reason that this boat, laden with the spoils of the blood of Our Lord Jesus, and presents offered by his enemies, has sunk in the sea" (458).

In Rome the tariffs allocated to influential persons were well-known (459).

Perhaps the marranos did not profit enough from this situation. Unfortunately for them, they did not always agree among themselves. The most determined left Portugal; the others tended to solicit individual pardons and exemptions for themselves and their families rather than participate in collective action. In the final reckoning the marranos were betrayed by their own agent in Rome, the converted soldier of fortune Duarte da Paz. When, after ten years of useful services, he could not collect the sums due him, he felt himself Christian at heart and denounced the marranos to the pope. "If they say," he wrote, "that I am acting not out of zeal for the faith but out of spite, because they have not paid me my due, I appeal to God who knows my motives, and to those who know me. I repeat that for money they would kill each other and to keep it they would become the best Christians in the world. Divine pity has made them behave the way they have with me; for ingratitude and bad faith make good men evil, and if I have become evil, I hope to become good by the grace of Jesus Christ" (460). Later, this former protégé of the king of Portugal and knight of the Order of Christ returned to Judaism and finally went to Turkey where he embraced Islam.

Starting in 1536, the Inquisition began to reign in Portugal with ever-increasing furor, tracking down the unfortunate marranos in cities and villages, forests and mountains. The pyres began to blaze: relatives of those who were burned were often not even allowed to know why the New Christians were dying, what invocation was on their lips. . . . After burning some twenty of them on October 14, 1542, "under a splendid blue sky," the redoubtable inquisitor of Lisbon praised their bravery: "Nothing astonished me so much as to see the Lord give such steadfastness to the weakness of flesh; children attended the burnings of their parents and wives those of their husbands and no one heard them cry out or weep. They said farewell and blessed them as if they were parting to meet again the next day" (461). In fact, after the establishment of the Portuguese Inquisition the function of the marranos remained the same as it had been in the past. Their money continued to flow through the same channels, into the Inquisition or the treasury of the Holy See, which dispensed individual and collective graces and pardons.

The most enterprising traveled a great deal for their business, going to the Low Countries, Turkey, or the Indies and back, so there was close liaison with the marrano colonies abroad. Always on the alert, the Portuguese Inquisition kept an eye on these movements and these relationships and maintained its dossiers with the same precision as its Spanish counterpart. For two centuries it kept records of the marranos dispersed all over the world and registered their professions, their wealth, and their customs, thanks to the depositions of its victims, its witnesses, and its spies. Some of its reports contained hundreds of names. Dossiers of forty thousand trials (most of which still await the curiosity of historians) have been preserved in its archives, making it possible to reconstruct the lives of the victims through the accounts of their torturers, those classic annals of persecution triumphant.

' After the initial flare-up the Portuguese Inquisition generally avoided senseless executions and was conservative about sentencing people to burn, in contrast with the hecatombs of Spain.

‚ This relative moderation was opposed by the Portuguese populace with its inexpiable hatred. The marranos were rich, they were persecuted, they were Jews, or considered as such; and on top of all this their Judaism was secret! The rites attributed to them were enveloped in a disquieting mystery. Rarely have so many conditions been present to drive hatred to a frenzy.

‛ The huge Lisbon pogrom of 1506 was followed by many other excesses. The state of excitement was not always carried to its conclusion. For example, in Lamego in 1532 there was a rumor that the king was going to establish the Inquisition. Immediately the Old Christians rejoiced, saying that they would no longer need to build houses because they would take over the Jewish houses. They met to divide the anticipated spoils equitably, or to draw lots for them. One declared that he was going to force his vines the better to burn the marranos; another, that he was going to sharpen his sword the better to cut their throats. That very evening the mob headed for the street where the marranos lived but was dispersed at the last moment (462). Ten years later it was learned that an inquisitorial tribunal would be established in Lamego. An ode of thanksgiving attributed to an anonymous poet circulated throughout the city and was recopied dozens of times. It described how the marranos would go to the pyre, divided into two groups, one of which was to sing and the other to dance. "Let us thank God that we shall see in our time the punishment of this race of infidel and heretical dogs. Let us raise our voices in chorus to thank Him for this favor. Let us pile up the branches so there will be enough wood at the hour of the holocaust" (463).

It goes without saying that, just as in Spain, a statute of racial discrimination was promulgated in Portugal. Actually, the *homens de la nação* had become a cursed race, made conspicuous by persecution and hatred to the point where the Portuguese historian Saraiva wrote that this race was a myth created by the Portuguese Inquisition (464).

Certainly Saraiva went too far, and the genesis of what he calls the "marrano myth" goes back, as we have seen, to the glorious *aljamas* of earlier times; but it was the dungeons of the Inquisition that gave this myth its definitive form. They literally forged the marrano mentality in the course of a secular struggle, a secret war where no holds were barred, in the name of a faith that was degraded by both sides equally, so that the two camps and their weapons provoke the same repugnance and the victims are to be judged as severely as the executioners.

We shall see below how and under what conditions the marranos fled abroad. Those who did not have the means or the energy for this remained in hiding in the most desolate corners of Portugal, where vestiges of marranism have been preserved to this day. After 1580 many crossed into Spain. In Seville, the hub of trade with the Indies, there were nearly two thousand "Portuguese businessmen" around 1640 (465). At the same time in Madrid, the most enterprising competed with the Genoese bankers in financial dealings with the court. Through all of Spain, intermittently until the middle of the eighteenth century, they fed the pyres of the Spanish Inquisition.

As to those who continued to lead a secret existence in Portugal, their social and intellectual level continued to decline, as the Inquisitors did not fail to note. At an auto-da-fé in 1705 an archbishop inveighed against them as follows: "Miserable relics of Judaism! Unfortunate fragments of the synagogue! Last vestiges of Judea! Scandal for the Catholics, laughingstock of the Jews themselves! . . . You are the laughingstock of the Jews because you do not even know how to obey the law under which you live" (466). Over the generations marranism had lost its dramatic substance. Immigration to the Protestant countries continued, drawing the stronger ones away from Portugal. For the masses, rejection of Christianity became nothing more than a secret and peaceful anticlericalism. In 1773 the Marquis of Pombal, the energetic reformer of Portugal, eliminated all legal distinction between New and Old Christians with a stroke of his pen.[3] The Inquisition had lost its principal *raison d'être* and declined quickly, until it was finally eliminated completely in 1821. But the marrano religion did not disappear. It continued to survive in the shadows, combining the public Christian observances with secret Jewish rites, and while, all during the nineteenth century, the Jews of Europe thought that all trace of Judaism had disappeared from the peninsula, the Portuguese marranos for their part thought they were the last and only Jews in the world. They were rediscovered in the twentieth century, after the First World War. It was then learned that they had split into two groups (not unlike the situation that had prevailed since the Renaissance): the one, faithful Christians, were nevertheless still considered as Jews by the rest of the population; the others, fewer in number, considered themselves Jewish. Under the leadership of their old *sacerdotisas* they continued to observe certain Jewish holidays, reciting old prayers in Portuguese and privately denying the Christ whose divinity they celebrated in the churches. There were several thousand of them living in the backlands of northern Portugal, humble artisans or peasants, for the most part illiterate. Around 1925 the big Jewish organizations of France and England became interested in this lost tribe of glorious Sephardic Judaism and tried to establish a sort of Jewish mission in Portugal. But the rediscovered Jews were not particularly enthusiastic about this, and the efforts were fruitless. Was it because they "imagined that this God could only be worshipped clandestinely, and they considered a public profession of faith as a sort of profanation?" (Cecil Roth) Or had the descendants

---

[3] How can we resist quoting the legendary tale: The king of Portugal, Joseph I, had ordered that every Portuguese who had any Jewish ancestors at all wear a yellow hat. A few days later the Marquis of Pombal appeared in court with three such hats under his arm. The king was astonished and said to him: "What does all this mean?" Pombal answered that he wanted to obey the orders of the king. "But," said the king, "why do you have three hats?" "I have one for myself," replied the Marquis, "one for the Inquisitor General, and one in case Your Majesty wishes to cover himself."

of those who had been forced to be marranos become—like the Donmeh of Salonica, whom we shall discuss in the next chapter—voluntary and deliberate marranos? Even today, there are those who practice Judaism in their own way in modern Portugal. Very little is known about them. Let us merely point out their curious explanation for why they are called *Judeus* (Jews). "We are called *Judeus*," they say, "because we help one another [*ajudarmos*]" (467).

thirteen
The Marrano Dispersion

The 1492 expulsion, which drove tens of thousands of Jews
out of Spain and into Barbary, Turkey, and the few Christian territories that allowed them to enter, was followed by a
slow but steady marrano exodus which continued for two
centuries. In Portugal, where such departures were sometimes legal and sometimes clandestine, they were generally
the object of financial transactions. In Spain they were
always perilous, for they aggravated the suspicion of Judaism. But certain circumstances could facilitate clandestine
emigration. For example, in 1609–14, at the time of the
expulsion of the Moriscos, a certain number of Portuguese
crypto-Jews and Spanish *conversos* slipped into their ranks
and crossed the Pyrenees. It is interesting to note that the
entry of the Moriscos into France was negotiated by the
marrano Lopez, the future confidant of Richelieu. A short
time before, the question of letting fifty thousand families of
Portuguese marranos, "prudent and industrious people,"
settle in France had been considered (468).

The marranos received their biggest welcome in Turkey,
which had been trying to attract Jews from the Iberian
Peninsula since the conquest of Constantinople. According
to Rabbi Moses Capsali, Sultan Mohammed II made the
following proclamation at that time: "Hear, descendants of
the Hebrews who live in my country. Let each who desires it
come to Constantinople, and let the remnant of your people
find asylum here." And, the chronicler continued, "throngs
of Jews flocked to Constantinople from all directions. The

sultan put homes at their disposal and they settled there."
After the expulsion from Spain, Sultan Bajazet is said to
have exclaimed: "You call Ferdinand a wise king, he who
has made his country poor and enriched ours!" (469) According to the French ambassador d'Aramon (1547), "Constantinople is inhabited principally by Turks, then by an
infinite number of Jews, that is, marranos who were driven
out of Spain, Portugal, and Germany. They have taught the
Turks every handicraft, and the majority of the shops belong
to Jews." His contemporary and compatriot Nicolas de
Nicolay stated: "Among [the Jews] are very excellent
workers in all arts and manufactures, especially the marranos
who have recently been banished and chased from Spain
and Portugal. To the great detriment and shame of Christianity, they have taught the Turks numerous inventions,
artifices, and machines of war, such as how to make artillery,
arquebuses, cannon powder, cannon balls, and other arms.
Similarly, they have set up a printing shop, never before
seen in these regions" (470).

But even more than Constantinople, it was Salonica that
became the great Jewish community of the Levant and the
principal marrano refuge in the sixteenth century. The rabbis recommended aiding them to become good Jews again at
all costs. The famous Samuel of Medina even sanctioned
deceit and abuse for this pious motive;[1] other learned men
did not hesitate to proclaim the repentant marranos as better
Jews than the most pious of Jews. When some twenty mar-

---

[1] The case was as follows: "Ruben," a marrano who had returned to
Judaism, induced his friend "Simon" to follow his example and to come
and join him in Turkey. He promised to lend him two thousand florins
on his arrival and advanced three hundred of them. It was agreed that
Simon would keep this money if Ruben did not keep his promise. Simon
came to Turkey. Ruben refused to give him the remaining seventeen
hundred florins and demanded the advance back. The case was brought before Samuel of Medina. He ordered Simon to reimburse Ruben with the
three hundred florins, for he "had acted to save him from hell and to
bring him back under the wing of the Shekinah." (Cf. H. J. Zimmels, *Die
Marranen in der Rabbinischen Literatur*, Berlin, 1932, p. 52.)

ranos were burned in Ancona in 1556, the Jews of Turkey responded with an attempt at international boycott. But return to Judaism was not always easy. Ordinary Jews disapproved of the marranos and referred to them—supreme insult—as *Kistanios*.[2] Even in Islamic lands (where it was more convenient to be a Jew than to be a Christian) marrano ambiguity was not easy to bear. According to J. Nehama, the historian of Jewish Salonica, the city "was teeming with families with an indefinite religious situation, half Christian, half Jewish. . . . There were those who did not know what they were, for they had not been able to adhere to a single doctrine since childhood, and they vacillated between one faith and the other, their souls injured. . . . There were even those who returned to their ancestral religion and then were overcome by a longing for Catholicism, and went back to it." This author goes on to cite curious examples of such inverse marranism (471). For these people were Jews externally and Christians internally. There were also unbelievers who adopted Islam for the sake of appearance, some of whom carved out illustrious military careers in the service of the sultan (472).

The effects of this confused situation will be described below. Let us point out once more that there are no popular or official persecutions in the annals of the Jews of the Ottoman Empire. Their situation as a "nation," often exposed to despotic rule, remained what it had been in the Middle Ages, and we have said enough on this topic at the beginning of this book. In both the economic and intellectual domains this situation reflected the general stagnation of the Moslem world until the twentieth century.

Numerous marranos also settled in North Africa, close to the Iberian Peninsula. The Spanish and Portuguese authorities made every effort to keep them from reaching the Turks, the traditional enemy, and some of them arrived in

---

[2] As *Kistanios* and not as *Kristianos* to avoid pronouncing the name of Christ.

the Levant or Barbary only after long years of extensive detours and prolonged stays in Italy or Flanders. Others never reached their destination, either because the Inquisition intercepted them or because local possibilities and prospects attracted them along the way.

Several factors governed the marrano peregrinations, the most important of which were the laws and business opportunities. Later, Parisian businessmen were to say: "They are particles of quicksilver, which run, lose their way, and on the slightest slope reunite into a bloc" (473). The mystics acted as mystics, and the merchants acted as merchants. Some headed for the places where they could practice Judaism freely, others were attracted by the great commercial centers; thus, according to the circumstances of the moment, the marranos settled in Antwerp, Venice, Ancona, Salonica, and Bordeaux in the sixteenth century and in Amsterdam, Hamburg, and London in the seventeenth, all the while continually swarming to the New World. All the Christian governments (with the exception of those of their countries of origin) soon came to see what financial profits could be reaped from them, and received them with open arms, often granting them many privileges. The Holy See had set the example by welcoming them in 1525 to Ancona, the gateway to the East. There was no port of any size where they did not settle, and like an international guild of maritime trade, they even included in their colonies marranos who were good Catholics. The report of an Inquisition informer who was sent to France in 1632 to investigate the settlements contains several details on this curious subject: in Bordeaux there were a marrano priest and his brother and two or three other persons who were also Catholics; in Rouen "out of twenty-four or twenty-six houses, eight to ten were Catholic"; in Antwerp "there was a bit of everything"; but in Amsterdam there was only one single Catholic marrano aided by those of Rouen (474).

We have already pointed out that there was inverse marranism in the Islamic lands, where, as an exact counterpart to the resurgence of Judaism among the Portuguese or Spanish *conversos,* there was a resurgence of Christianity among the third or fourth generation Jews of the marrano line.

But whether they were Jews, Christians, or downright unbelievers, the marranos remained singularly Spanish through all of their tribulations, as though, mistreated and mistrusted wherever they went, they were attempting to retain their enduring and profound identity. A Jewish Spain was perpetuating itself beyond the borders of Spain. It was Castilian (or Portuguese) that resounded in the streets of Salonica, Leghorn, and Amsterdam; it was Castilian, written in Latin characters or Hebrew script, that the marranos used for writing to each other or publishing their works. Discarding the Christian mask did not change this custom at all. This singular fidelity to the Spanish language, which became the Ladino of the Sephardim, was not the only or even the most striking evidence of their profound Spanishness. In the course of a commercial litigation in 1601 the Jews of Venice declared that "although driven from Spain, they did not consider themselves any the less subjects of the Catholic king" (475). Were they merely astute merchants without faith or law? But in 1641 it was the marranos of Rouen who aided the Spanish prisoners after Rocroi (476); it was other ex-marranos in Fez in 1578 who were humane to the Portuguese captives, remnants of the defeated army of invasion (477).

In 1736, after a Spanish garrison had left Leghorn, the French agent sent the following message to Paris:

"The Jewish nation is losing a great deal by losing the Spaniards, it being unbelievable the good treatment which it enjoyed and the disinterested justice which the Spaniards dispensed on the occasions which presented themselves, to the confusion of the people of the country who expected that, as in Spain, they would be the scourge of that nation here too. And the Spaniards admit aloud that in this country it has been only the Jews who have treated them well and served them faithfully" (478).

Which shows that when Spanish Jews and Spanish soldiers were abroad—that is, when both were exiles—they saw each other as compatriots, a human note which recalls that relations between Spaniards and marranos did not consist solely of persecution on the one hand and resentment on the other. There are other examples of this. For instance, recently published documents on Spinoza show that there was a sort of group or club in Amsterdam where "Portuguese" who had returned to Judaism and Spanish voyagers passing through the city conversed amicably and discussed theology (which the latter reported to the Inquisition on their return to Spain) (479).

Under these conditions it is easier to understand how so many marranos could go to Spain on business under a Christian mask and how Madrid or Lisbon could employ marranos as diplomatic agents and consuls, sometimes even conferring titles on them for their loyal services (480). A certain Cansino, native of Oran, was rich enough to be able to come to Madrid in 1656 openly as a Jew; "loving Spain very much," he offered the king a loan of eight hundred thousand ducats without interest (481).

This profound Spanishness of the marranos came out in many other ways. In such matters as the persecutions and trials of the unbelievers and heretics of Amsterdam, the "Dutch Jerusalem," or the humiliating repudiations and penitences imposed on a Uriel da Costa, one suspects the influence of the Inquisition (482). The ancient tribal pride of the Spanish Jews survived all vicissitudes; until the seventeenth and eighteenth centuries they continued to claim royal descent from David (483). Their scorn for the other Jews—German or Polish—was proverbial. (Held in suspicion by Christian society, didn't they regard themselves as more Jewish than anyone else?) They were careful to keep these others at a distance. In an answer to Voltaire, who aimed many shafts at the Jews and Judaism, Isaac de Pinto said: "M. Voltaire cannot be ignorant of the scrupulous exactness of the Portuguese and Spanish Jews not to inter-mix in marriage, alliance, or any other way, with the Jews of other nations. . . . Their variance with their other brethren is such that if a Portuguese Jew in England or Holland mar-ried a German Jewess, he would of course lose all his pre-rogatives, be no longer reckoned a member of their synagogue, forfeit all civil and ecclesiastical preferments, be absolutely divorced from the body of the nation, and not even be buried with his Portuguese brethren. . . . This is the cause of those distinctions and of that elevation of mind which is observed among them, and which even their breth-ren of other nations seem to acknowledge." (Voltaire agreed with him.[3])

In fact, a Portuguese who married a "Teuton" would find himself banned, if not anathematized. In the great syna-gogues of Amsterdam and London, German Jews had re-served for them special benches separated by barriers. In Venice the Portuguese had the German and Levantine Jews expelled from their quarter, the *ghetto vecchio* (484).

Thus, even after their return to open Judaism the mar-ranos retained the manners and the attitudes that had once served as a mask, conducting themselves as persons of dis-tinction, dressing fashionably, and wearing wigs. "They do not wear beards," wrote de Pinto, "and do not affect any distinction in their clothing. Those who are well off pursue elegance and ostentation to the same extent as the other nations of Europe, from whom they differ only in religion." Thus they have been called "pioneers of assimilation." Here

---

[3] "The lines you complain of," answered Voltaire, "are cruel and unjust. There are among you very learned and respectable persons. . . . As you are a Jew remain so. You will never cut the throats of forty-two thousand men because they pronounced the word Shibboleth wrong, nor destroy twenty-four thousand men for having lain with Midianite women. But be a philosopher. This is my best wish to you in this short life." (*Letters of Cer-tain Jews to Monsieur Voltaire*, ed. A. Guenee, Cincinnati, 1845, pp. 37–8 and 54–6.)

is how the preaching brother Labat, disapproving as the good monk he was, described the ostentation of the Jews of Leghorn: "They are free there, they do not wear any beard to distinguish them from the Christians. They are not confined to their neighborhoods. They are rich; their business is extensive. Almost all have farms from the prince and they are protected to the point where it is proverbial in Tuscany that it would be better to beat the grand duke than a Jew. This only makes them all the more odious to everyone else. But they laugh at this, and I do not believe that there is any place in the world where they are more arrogant and more haughty. . . . They love ostentation, especially on the occasion of their weddings" (485).

And Brother Labat went into detail about the pomp of Jewish marriage ceremonies, honored by the presence of the grand duke and held in a ballroom "paved with bars of silver as thick as a thumb." A more benevolent witness, the English navigator Thomas Coryat, was surprised by the elegance and refinement of the Jews of Venice, ". . . such goodly and proper men, that I said to my selfe our English proverbe To looke like a Jewe (whereby is meant sometimes a weather beaten warp-faced fellow, sometimes a phrenticke and lunaticke person, sometimes one discontented) is not true. For indeed I noticed some of them to be most elegant and sweet featured persons . . . I saw many Jewish women, whereof some were as beautiful as ever I saw, and so gorgeous in their apparel, jewels, chaines of gold, and rings adorned with precious stones, that some of our English Countesses do scarce exceede them . . ." (486).

This splendor, too, was a part of the Old Christian mask, a mask that would remain with them. A pride that was completely Spanish; a fidelity to Judaism that did not preclude a longing for Christianity; the traditions or the carry-overs from the secret life; the searing bitterness of Christian spite—these were the contradictory forces that shaped the elusive profile of a marrano. A seventeenth-century Portuguese poet, João Pinto Delgado, who returned to open Judaism in Amsterdam, described another marrano trait admirably. "There, where Lusitania borders Andalusia," he wrote, "is the land which was the cradle of my birth. When I arrived at the age when one knows how to distinguish good from evil, it was the humble and dangerous boundary of my thoughts. Humble, because I could only dedicate a few hours to the exercise of science; and dangerous because my parents had already planted in me the seeds of the very holy law, the fruits of which would be delayed as long as the situation kept me from grasping them in my hands to nourish myself. This anxious fear which clutched my mind made me see the others as different from what they were, timidly hiding the truths under false appearances, distinguishing the signs leading to investigation which could lead to the loss of the three greatest blessings of this world: honor, life, and fortune" (487).

"Loss of the three greatest blessings of this world," whence unending tension at all times; "see the others as different from what they were," whence acuity of thought and search for hidden truth; thus the traditional Jewish critical spirit was carried to its pinnacle.

Spaniards reviled by Spain; Christians for show, but against their will attracted by the seductions of the Church; Jews by intention and heart, but yielding with difficulty to the yoke of the Law and despising their brothers' strict Mosaicism—such were the contradictions and the cleavages of the marrano soul. One is tempted to try to penetrate it to its deepest crevices, but this soul is the most unfathomable of all: fertile in prodigious exploits as well as in nameless villainies, rich in the possibility for sublime heroism and sordid realism; the epitome of the human soul, but what an epitome! Any generalizations would be false by definition, for the marrano condition could justify the behavior of a *hidalgo* as well as the behavior of a usurer; for a marrano was at once a potential Talmudist and a potential conquistador, as prompt to succumb to Messianic delirium as to sink into total nihilism. The only valid generalization is to say that all human potentialities could be accomplished and be lived with increased intensity. Thus, the best one can do is to illustrate the marrano condition with a few individual or collective destinies and adventures.

The Duke of Naxos

The story of the marrano dispersion in the sixteenth century is dominated by the Mendes family, or rather the Mendes clan. Two Mendes brothers, Francisco and Diego, the first living in Lisbon and the second in Antwerp, started a company that became the chief spice importer for northern Europe; like the Fuggers and the Welsers, they also lent funds to the kings. Another of their activities, perhaps the most remunerative, seems to have been the transfer of marrano capital and property from Portugal to Flanders and from there to Italy, as the case might be; but for the most part this matter must remain a subject of conjecture. It is known, for example, that agents of the firm in London supplied letters of exchange on Antwerp to marranos who were passing through, and that the escape route to Venice functioned with the aid of the famous Antwerp printer Daniel Bomberg. Moreover, the Mendeses were the principal suppliers of funds for the marrano lobby in Rome (488).

After the death of the two brothers, Francisco's widow, Beatrice de Luna, became the veritable head of the firm. She was joined by her nephew, João Miquez, known as Juan Micas. The boy, who was an intimate of the imperial court as companion and fencing partner of the future emperor Maximilian, was knighted by Charles V. His contemporaries praised his noble bearing and elegant manners. "He comported himself in humane and dignified fashion in all things . . . [a man who is] more fitting to be a Christian than a Jew," noted one of them. "There are few persons of account in Spain, Italy, or Flanders who are not personally acquainted with him," wrote another. "He deserved it all, for he was a gentleman, expert in arms, well read, and a friend of his friends." And still, he was only a Jew, adept at playing the Christian game but with origins that remained his Achilles heel. In the machinations and struggles of high finance, the supreme argument of the firm's royal debtors when they wanted to obtain postponements or new credits was denunciation to the Inquisition; thus, in 1532 Diego Mendes was accused of heresy and had to spend several months in prison, and in 1540 several of his friends and correspondents were arrested. Particularly embarrassing for the clan must have been the plans for a marriage between Brianda de Luna, cousin and future wife of Juan Micas, and the favorite of Charles V, Francisco de Aragon. This would have put the family fortune into the hands of Old Christians. The emperor and his sister, Queen Mary of Hungary (who had been promised the modest commission of two hundred thousand ducats by the suitor!), were most insistent that the wedding take place. Thus, in 1544 the Mendes family decided to leave. The women went directly to Venice; Juan Micas joined them there two or three years later after first liquidating the Antwerp firm and engaging in new business dealings with the Crown of France in Lyons and that of Germany in Ratisbon.

The peregrinations of the clan were still not over, and for the most part we do not know the reasons behind them. From Italy they continued to wage the marranos' secret war against the Inquisition, and they did not decide to leave Christian territory until 1553, when the intensification of the Counter Reformation made their position too risky. Preceded by Juan Micas, the whole tribe (some forty persons including the servants) finally made their way to Constantinople, where the sultan welcomed them with open arms. There they immediately returned to Judaism. Juan Micas became Joseph Nasi, Beatrice de Luna became Gracia Nasi. And to some extent their activities changed in nature. Like a dowager queen, Gracia Nasi dedicated herself to pious works: surrounded by rabbis, she concerned herself with the defense and glorification of Judaism. Joseph Nasi, whose piety was not his dominant feature, gained the favor of the sultans and became a political force for all of Europe to reckon with.

But whose game was he playing? It is easy to see what was behind him: thanks to the international marrano network and to the personal friendships of the man who had been Juan Micas, for some fifteen years Joseph Nasi was the best-informed man of Europe, and his confidential information, reinforced by his gifts, made him a one-man "pressure group" with a great influence on Ottoman foreign policy, even to the point of deciding on declarations of war and peace settlements. What is impossible to determine is for *whose* benefit the man was working at any given moment. Certain coordinates, however, are clear enough.

Joseph Nasi, who had been introduced to the Ottoman court by the French ambassador to Rome, the Seigneur de Lansac, became a sworn enemy of France as a result of litigation about 150,000 ducats he had lent to Henry II around 1549. According to the French allegations, one could dispense with rendering his due to a marrano, "for the laws of the kingdom do not permit Jews such as the said Joseph Nasi to do business or traffic in anything; but they order that all their goods be confiscated" (489). The reasoning thus was "diamond cut diamond": since you deceived us by hiding the fact that you are a Jew, we will deceive you by not paying you back. Such reasoning, it must be agreed, was bound to exasperate the marrano creditor. After many ups and downs, Nasi finally took triumphant revenge in 1568 by having the sultan confiscate merchandise carried to the Levant under the French flag and keep it until the debt was paid. This resulted in a brief conflict between France and the Sublime Porte, settled by the treaty of October, 1569— the original of which was written in Hebrew. Who knows if this odd detail is not just one more way the Jew was trying to vex the Very Christian King? (490) As a result the French diplomats' grudge against him was redoubled, and they tried to overcome him "by putting Miquez in a pique." They wanted to make him lose his head so that they could avenge the French king "by revealing Nasi's treason to the sultan," and proposed to do this by "taking from his desk . . . an infinity of letters which he writes regularly to the pope, the king of Spain, the duke of Florence" (491). But the plot, in which a Jewish secretary of Nasi's participated, was easily thwarted by this virtuoso of Ottoman intrigues.

As durable as his hostility toward France seems to have been his sympathy for the cause of the Protestant rebels of Flanders. The advice and encouragement he sent to the Calvinists of Antwerp, among whom were a number of his old friends, played their part in the events that led to the mission of the Duke of Alba and the insurrection of the beggars of the Low Countries. "As regards the Flemings," wrote the seventeenth-century historian Strada, "Miches' letters and persuasions had no little influence on them. By this news, courage was generally heightened; and it was resolved in the Consistory of Antwerp that since there was such a promising opportunity to strengthen the enterprise, they should raise as much money as possible . . ." (492). More than once in the course of the sixteenth-century religious struggles the Calvinists were aided by Jews, and William of Orange himself sought their assistance. Moreover, among the instigators of Flemish resistance in 1566 were the influential marranos Marco Perez, Martin Lopez, and Ferdinando Bernuy (493).

The relations of Joseph Nasi with the Crown of Spain seem to have been complex in quite a different way. Philip II called him "the one who contributes the most to the enterprises prejudicial to Christianity and who instigates them," in other words, the invisible orchestrator of an anti-Christian plot. But when the secret Spanish agents in Constantinople, the commandant Juan Barelli and the Greek patriarch, undertook to kidnap Nasi and send him back to Spain dead or alive, Philip II prohibited killing him. Whatever the reasons behind this scruple, they did result in certain considerations on Nasi's part. He made every effort to dissuade the sultan from launching an expedition against Spain at the time of the Morisco rebellion in 1570 and suggested that he attack the Venetian possessions instead. Perhaps he was in the pay of Philip II, as the French agents continually stated, recalling that he was, after all, a "native Spaniard." We do know that he carried on a secret correspondence with the king of Spain, but there are many things we still do not know about this matter. The fact is that at the end of 1570 Nasi asked Philip II for a safe-conduct for himself and his retinue of "seventy persons, some Hebrew, some Turks" to come to Spain. He begged "to be pardoned for having during some time used and practiced Hebraic law, having been constrained and forced to do so." Was this a serious intention or a mere pretense? He did not neglect to request exemptions from customs duties for the goods he wanted to import. Philip II was inclined to agree to this extraordinary reconciliation. For two or three years it was the subject of secret Spanish dispatches, but then, for reasons which again are unknown, it never took place (494).

On behalf of whom, then, was this great adventurer working? On behalf of himself, of course, all the while serving his master the sultan. But there is every indication that in doing this he was pursuing a visionary plan of his own invention. His great design seems to have been to surpass his childhood companions, to erase all the affronts suffered by his line by assuming a Jewish crown. To become king was his patent ambition. To base his power not on the favors of a sultan whom he had to flatter but on the bravery of an army under his command; that must have been his dream of power.

On different occasions and in different ways he had acted as protector of the Jews. In 1556, when Pope Paul IV had ordered twenty-five marranos burned in Ancona, Gracia Nasi and he had tried to make the Holy See repent by organizing the international boycott of the port of Ancona. This attempt failed, for reasons that are too complicated to go into here. However, it marked an effort to remedy the situation of the marranos by force, that is, in the Christian manner. Earlier, during his stay in Italy, Nasi had requested Venice to put an island at the disposal of the homeless marranos. Strada has written that the refusal of this request turned Nasi into a mortal enemy of the Venetians. In 1561 the sultan made him a grant of the city of Tiberias and the surrounding lands to create a sort of Jewish homeland or refuge; he set about rebuilding the city, surrounded it with a wall, and tried to establish industry there, despite the protestations of the apostolic legate in Palestine, Bonifazio di Ragusa, against "the arrival of these vipers more deadly than those which haunt the ruins of the city." According to de Petremol, the French ambassador, it was this costly enterprise that made him claim his due from France; "Miques," he wrote, "has received permission from the Grand Signior . . . to build a city on the shore of the Lake of Tiberias wherein Jews only are to live. In fact, he proposes to begin his achievement here by this renewal, having the intention so far as one can judge of proclaiming himself king of the Jews. This is why he is demanding money from France so insistently" (495).

But this project was unsuccessful for lack of the spontaneous response from the Jewish masses to his "political Zionism," in advance of its time. Few Jews came to settle in Tiberias. "Little practical encouragement could be forthcoming from the rabbis, immersed in hair-splitting casuistry; or from mystics, convinced that the Redemption could be hastened only by permutations and combinations of the Divine Name; or even perhaps from fugitive Marranos only too happy if they had succeeded in saving their own bodies" (Cecil Roth). A political man and a great lord, Joseph Nasi was not a messiah in any sense.

He nevertheless continued to weave his plans. In 1566 the new sultan, Selim II, made him a gift of the island of Naxos and the title of duke, but this was merely a fief and not a kingdom. When he urged Selim to declare war on Venice in 1570, the campaign began with the conquest of Cyprus. Nasi expected to become king of that great island, which is a steppingstone to Palestine. But the capture of Cyprus resulted in an alliance among Venice, the Holy See, and Spain and culminated in the great Turkish naval defeat at Lepanto. As a result Nasi fell into semidisgrace. Nevertheless, he still kept up his hopes; once again, in the summer of 1572, he believed himself on the verge of being named governor of the island. But his star had fallen. Other Jewish favorites supplanted him in the sultan's favor. He died in 1579, rich and powerful but no longer an influence on affairs of state.

His name, which had been a continual topic of European diplomatic correspondence for fifteen years, was to fire men's imaginations for many years after his death. Through Christopher Marlowe's *Jew of Malta* he contributed to the crystallization of the image of Shylock, the merchant of Venice. His life was also transposed to the stage by others, but perhaps only a Shakespeare could define certain of his traits. One is reminded of the famous tirade of the Venetian moneylender who does business with the Christians without difficulty, all the while remaining anathema to them: ". . . I am a Jew. Hath not a Jew eyes? Hath not a Jew hands, organs, dimensions, senses, affections, passions? . . . If you prick us, do we not bleed? If you tickle us, do we not laugh? If you poison us, do we not die? And if you wrong us, shall we not revenge?" That last, in fact, was probably one of the motives in the soul of this personality.

Israeli historiography is not wrong when it considers Joseph Nasi as the great precursor of Zionism. But the uprooting of the marranos was still not able to lead to a collective adventure in which each would have made the decision to change his fate in the name of a purely worldly ideal. To colonize Palestine without the aid of the Messiah was absurd, almost sacrilegious as far as rabbinical tradition was concerned. The Jews continued to go to Palestine to die, not to live. In the following century the marranos' desire for deliverance took the form of a powerful Messianic movement that swept all of Judaism along in its path and led, among other repercussions, to a dramatic relapse: certain marranos took up a deliberate and voluntary marranism.

The Sabbatians

In Safed in Palestine, not far from Tiberias, where Joseph Nasi had attempted to create a Jewish state, and at about the same time, a cenacle of cabalists had formed. Most of them were exiles from Spain trying to hasten the redemption of the universe through prayer, study, and fasting. Their hopes and their mystical concepts were carried to all the countries of the Dispersion, and from generation to generation the coming of the Messiah seemed ever closer to the Jews and ever more certain. Finally, all the necessary conditions coincided and a Messiah appeared.

In 1625 or 1626 the Judeo-Spanish merchant of Smyrna Mordecai Zevi had a son, born Ab 9 (the day on which, according to tradition, the Messiah would be born). The young Sabbatai seems to have suffered from psychiatric problems. He had a sort of split personality, a Dr. Jekyll-Mr. Hyde condition; in his second state he committed sacrileges that he then regretted in his first state and could not understand. In the words of one of his intimates, "He then again became a normal man and regretted the strange things that he had done, for he no longer understood their reason. But he had understood their reason when he committed these acts" (496). In 1648, the year the *Zohar* had predicted the dead would rise and the Messianic age begin, Sabbatai committed the supreme transgression in the synagogue of Smyrna by pronouncing in a loud voice the sacred Tetragrammaton, the ineffable name of God. He was excommunicated, and years of wandering ensued. Finally, he arrived in Jerusalem, where another prophet, Nathan of Gaza, convinced him to proclaim himself Messiah. His cracked brain was only asking to be persuaded. Moreover, he had the

physical appearance for the job: the august stature, the unc-
tion, the manner; but he seems mainly to have been a puppet
whose strings were pulled by other false prophets. He soon
had rich worshippers, and the good tidings gradually spread,
attracting numerous believers, especially among the marranos whose faith was shaky. The more Sabbatai denigrated
the Law of Moses, the more they were convinced, "for,"
argued Nathan of Gaza, "if he were not the Redeemer, these
deviations would not occur to him; when God lets His light
shine over him, he commits many acts which are strange and
wonderful in the eyes of the world, and that is proof of his
truth" (497). Thus it was a matter of the *credo quia
absurdum* of the ancient theologians. It is also noteworthy
that the eccentricities of Sabbatai and his imitators, who
sinned in the name of a sort of mystical defiance, resulted in
acts or transgressions similar in nature to those that continued to torment the marrano conscience.

Moreover, Sabbatai's messiahship, which before long was
accepted as an established fact for numbers of Jews all over
the world, aroused the greatest fervor in marrano or ex-
marrano colonies. It was generally agreed that 1666 would
be the year of redemption, which was in accordance with a
millenarian concept of Christian origin. In fact, numerous
Protestants, especially in England, also believed in Sabbatai.
In December, 1665, the scholar Heinrich Oldenbourg wrote
from London to his friend Spinoza: "All the world here is
talking of a rumor of the return of the Israelites, dispersed
for more than two thousand years, to their own country.
Few believe it, but many wish it. . . . Should the news be
confirmed, it would bring about a revolution in all things." It
seems that the financiers were less skeptical than the philosophers, for the odds on the London Exchange were 10 to 1
that Sabbatai would be king of Jerusalem in the next two
years. As to those who were chiefly interested—the future
Jewish subjects of this king—in Hamburg the Portuguese
community forbade making wagers pro or con on his imminent reign, for betting would imply doubt. And doubt was

no longer admissible. The delirium continued to spread, and most rabbis rallied to Sabbatai, except in Poland; skeptics were persecuted, and blood flowed in many places. Throughout the whole marrano dispersion, from Amsterdam to Leghorn, from Salonica to Fez, as the fateful day approached, rich and poor alike began to liquidate their assets and make ready to leave for the Promised Land, and throughout Europe the mystical Jewish fervor caused international trade to languish (498).

Sabbatai himself—who had introduced a number of new holidays and, in accordance with the predictions of the *Zohar,* had begun to release his followers from Jewish observances—chartered a boat in the beginning of 1666 to go to Constantinople in order, he announced, to make Sultan Ibrahim cede his throne to him. The tragicomedy that followed is well-known: the sultan had him arrested and, to put an end to all the excitement, gave him the choice of embracing Islam or being burned alive. Sabbatai opted for Islam and shortly afterward addressed the following message to his followers in Smyrna: "God has made me an Ishmaelite; He commanded, and it was done the ninth day of my regeneration" (that is, of his coming).

This meant that he had not renounced his messiahship at all. In fact, the dialectical resources of the cabala made it possible to interpret his apostasy mystically and to represent this supreme treason as supreme proof of messiahship, as the indescribable passion of a Redeemer who, the better to expiate the sins of his people, had himself committed the greatest sin of abjuration. This deception thus became his martyrdom and his power. The verses of the prophet Isaiah on the "man of sorrows whose sufferings bring peace to man," which the Christians apply to Christ, were applied to Sabbatai Zevi by his followers. The marrano Abraham Cardozo even taught that because of Israel's sins, all the Jews had been spiritually destined to become marranos but that God's grace had saved them from this awful fate by imposing this supreme sacrifice on the Messiah, for only the soul of the Messiah is strong enough to bear this fate without harm. One can see how the history of the marranos made them receptive to such teaching: "That the Messiah should by the very nature of his mission be forced into the inescapable tragedy of apostasy was a doctrine ideally made to provide an emotional outlet for the tormented conscience of the marranos" (Gershon Scholem).

Nevertheless, when the news of Sabbatai Zevi's apostasy spread across the Dispersion, the Messianic fervor died down and the majority of the Jews returned both to their senses and their former occupations. Others continued to worship the Messiah Sabbatai in secret while acting as good Jews. "The moderate schools of Sabbatianism," writes Scholem, "achieved the miracle of living in the continuous paradox of devout fulfillment of the Law and belief in the impending approach of a new era in which such fulfillment would be meaningless." In short, the time had come and it had not come, and Scholem gives us a glimpse of the link between the great half-deluded attempt, the provisional abandonment of the Law of Moses, and the laicization of the Messianic hope that was later to characterize the great ideological currents of Jewish life at the time of the emancipation. But it is the "radical wing" of Sabbatianism that interests us here as one of the possible outcomes of the marrano adventure.

Radical Sabbatianism consisted of the imitation of the Messiah Sabbatai in all things, but first and foremost in abandoning the observances of Judaism. After various adventures Sabbatai Zevi himself, as well as those of his faithful who (according to the accepted expression) had "assumed the turban," were exiled to Albania, where the false Messiah died in 1676. His messiahship immediately became a sort of family asset and his brother-in-law Jacob Querido ("well-loved") proclaimed himself Sabbatai's son and his reincarnation. His proselytizing among the Sabbatians of Salonica was so effective that a thousand of them collectively assumed the turban in 1683. Thus, we have the birth of a sect of voluntary marranos, the Donmeh ("apostates" in Turkish). They were double apostates, as much from Islam as from Judaism, and, consequently, were equally scorned by both. For the Ten Commandments of Moses they substituted the eighteen rules of Sabbatai Zevi. The second rule commanded belief in Sabbatai ("who is the true Redeemer; there is no salvation outside of him"); the sixteenth and the seventeenth, that one must follow the observances of Islam in all things ("everything which is seen from without must be accomplished"); but it was forbidden to contract marriage or make any alliances with the Turks ("for they are an abomination and their women are reptiles"). The second coming of Sabbatai and the end of time were announced in the following terms: "These eighteen rules I have prescribed because the throne is still not firm enough for Israel to take vengeance on Satan and his legions. At that time everything will become equal; nothing will be prohibited and nothing will be permitted; there will be no impure and no pure; and all will recognize me from the lowly to the great" (499). These rules were recited in Ladino to the secret gatherings of the sect along with the Song of Songs, its principal hymn, and its other prayers and psalms; Castilian was thus the Sabbatians' sacred language. The Messiah and his successive reincarnations bore the name *Santo-Señor*.

The eighteenth rule, which was perhaps a bit ambiguous, prescribed that "fornication not reign among you; although this be a precept for the creature one must nevertheless be reserved on this point because of the thieves [Jews]." It seems, then, that out of fear of the Jews of Salonica, Jacob the Well-Loved had still not realized certain consequences to which voluntary marranism led. He died in the course of a pilgrimage to Mecca, and his sect divided first into two and then into three subsects, each with its distinctive features and customs. That of the *Kapanjis,* or "knights," composed primarily of wealthy businessmen, seems to have gone the furthest in instituting occult saturnalias to celebrate the holiness of sin starting with the transgression of the Law. At the annual Feast of the Lamb, a sort of holy communion to which only married people were admitted, the lights were extinguished and wife swapping was practiced; the children thus conceived were reputed to be holy. Apart from this, the knights, just as the other Donmeh sects, were distinguished by their exemplary lives, by their charity, and by their solidarity.

In the middle of the eighteenth century an offshoot of the sect blossomed in Poland. Jacob Frank, a charlatan with a dominating and sadistic temperament, had spent his youth in Turkey and had been initiated into the Donmeh cult.[4] When he returned to Poland, he declared himself the reincarnation of Sabbatai Zevi and God the Messiah and pushed the doctrine to its ultimate consequences. His theology proclaimed that the only effective way to redeem the world was to combat the forces of evil with evil (the germs of this concept can be found among many cabalists). Thus, he advocated sinning, lying, stealing, fornicating, wronging one's neighbor, and adopting all the existing religions one after the other and ridiculing them as the means of reaching the total freedom of the reign of the Messiah. The doctrine of this evil genius had certain things in common with ancient Gnosticism and necessarily implied "metaphysical anti-Semitism in its profoundest and most effective form" (Scholem). Frank recruited several hundred worshippers among the Polish Sabbatians. The sect was combatted by the Jews, and it counterattacked by making accusations against the Talmud and by spreading the legends of ritual murder. Its members were collectively baptized around 1760, and this seemed to promise an interesting future; but the rabbis were finally able to demonstrate to the bishops that the Messiah the Frankists pretended to adore under the name of Christ was in reality only the *Santo-Señor* Jacob

---

4 His real name was Jankiev Lejbovicz; he was given the surname of Frank in Turkey because he came from the foreign "Frank" country.

Frank himself. Then it was the Church's turn to persecute the Frankists and, after many avatars, they ultimately blended into Catholicism. Certain illustrious Polish families, particularly that of Adam Mickiewicz, are descended from this line.

As to the Turkish Donmehs, they led a more peaceful existence, even growing and multiplying, for their number was put at one thousand at the end of the seventeenth century, four thousand at the middle of the nineteenth century, and more than ten thousand at the beginning of the twentieth century. The Donmehs played an important role in Salonican life and took an active role in the revolution of the young Turks: one of them, Mohammed Djavidbey, became prime minister of Turkey on the eve of the First World War. After the war they settled in Turkey like the other Moslems of Thrace, in accordance with the Treaty of Lausanne on the exchange of populations. Since then it has become difficult to follow the fate of the sect. Does it still exist? Are there still believers who pray on the beaches of Turkey to beg for the return of Sabbatai, who cry out the ritual appeal to the Messiah: *Sabbatai Zevi, we await thee*? Before the last war Turkish newspapers sometimes engaged in polemics on this subject. The writer Alah Adhi Govsa, author of a work on Sabbatianism, stated that the sect continued to lead its underground life and furnished certain disturbing details in support of this. An ex-Donmeh publicist, Zadeh Mohammed Rouchdi, assured that there was nothing to this and produced his arguments to the contrary. Thus, in Kemalist Turkey, the old debate between the inquisitor and the marrano was renewed, a debate the accused always loses because his argument, whether he speaks the truth as a Moslem or lies as a Donmeh, has the same content and cannot convince his listeners.

In fact, it seems that Sabbatai Zevi is now only worshipped by a few old people, but that the Donmeh, held together not by faith but by the memory of this secret cult, still constitute a sort of surviving caste which is not without influence in Turkey—a sociological phenomenon whose persistence is limited, as certain parallel cases show, to two or three generations.

Spinoza

In the seventeenth century, Amsterdam, the commercial capital of the West, became the site of the largest marrano colony of Europe. Although they did not play as decisive a role in the economic growth of the Low Countries as is sometimes attributed to them, the "Portuguese" excelled in certain branches of commerce, such as the importation of colonial sugar, spices, and tobacco and trade in precious stones. They maintained particularly close ties with the New World, with both the Dutch colonies and the Spanish possessions where so many of their brothers were at the time trying to escape detection. In Amsterdam itself they created a Jewish book industry that was unrivaled in the Dispersion, and they also published translations of the Bible for the use of Protestants. Starting in 1675, a Jewish paper, *Gazeta de Amsterdam,* was founded, which, as was typical of its readers, covered all subjects except those of Jewish interest. We have already mentioned that the "Portuguese" looked down upon the humble German Jews who had come to settle in their quarter of Amsterdam, and avoided mixing with them. These, in return, cast doubt on the scholarship and piety of the "Portuguese," and one of them even stated that it was "easier for the Sephardim to become sick, lame, and blind than to become Jewish scholars" (500). He was certainly exaggerating, and excellent doctors of the Law were educated in the "Dutch Jerusalem," but it took generations for the ex-marranos to become completely Jewish again.

The crucial problem was posed by the dialectic of the return to Judaism itself, for on the one hand, the marranos' apostasy was a source of remorse and discomfort for them, and on the other, it was not easy for them to reassume the yoke of the Law and bow to the ancestral observances after a hiatus of several generations. Thus, the communities were torn by conflict, for they were concerned about the good behavior of their members partly from religious zeal and partly from simple caution that they not give the Christian authorities any grounds for the dangerous accusation of impiety. We have seen how the contradictions in the lives of the marranos led certain of them to the Sabbatian heresy and the glorification of their apostasy. But others followed the lead of the two theologies, Jewish and Christian, in questioning the rival creed and ended in doubt and unbelief. This was all the more likely because traces of the Spanish skeptical tradition had survived all the vicissitudes and continued to inspire polemics and battles of ideas that did not cease to plague their uprooted posterity.

What is the true nature of God? And what is man himself? What is meant by "soul"? Is there a hereafter? Perhaps no human group through all of history has sought after the absolute as fervently as the marrano intelligentsia. These discussions continued ceaselessly before the doors of the synagogues, and perhaps no one was so fascinated by them as the young Baruch Spinoza, student of the Etz Chaim rabbinical school of Amsterdam.

There was nothing, however, that seemed to predestine the young Talmudist to shake the foundations of all the traditional beliefs and become the prototype of the "Jewish demystifiers" of modern times. He was born in Amsterdam in 1633 into a family that was similar to many others. His father had practiced Catholicism in Nantes before settling in the "Dutch Jerusalem," where he returned to Judaism and founded a business. It has often been claimed that as a child Spinoza witnessed the humiliating punishment of Uriel da Costa in the synagogue, but there is no corroboration of this. His family was comfortable and respected; when he arrived at the age of reason, young Baruch aided his father in his business and even took part in the administration of the firm after his father's death in 1654. As late as 1655 he made a gift to the poor people of the synagogue. As his writings demonstrate, his Jewish education was first-rate; actually, we have few details about his youth, but we do know how the great crisis of his life erupted after, doubtless, a slow maturation in the shadow of the rabbinical school.

Around 1655 a seductive personality appeared in Amsterdam, "bold of speech, friend to what is new, insane in his reasonings, searcher after paradoxes and, what is even worse, abominable in his behavior," like so many of his fellows (501). This man, Dr. Juan de Prado, was born in Córdoba and educated in Spanish universities. He had returned to Judaism in the Low Countries in 1638, and afterward he took great pleasure in sowing philosophical doubt in the souls of the young Jews, a practice that, however, did not keep him from collecting subsidies from the communities. That of Amsterdam threatened to cut off his allowance and demanded a public retraction, which the flexible marrano readily agreed to, only to relapse later. There was even a question of sending him to the colonies, "giving him very generous aid."

Of course Juan de Prado was not Spinoza's philosophical mentor, but Spinoza was involved in the scandal thus created. However, the soul of young Baruch was of a different stamp from that of his seducer; refusing to compromise and scorning the pension that was offered him to "turn him from the false path," he allowed himself to be excommunicated so that "he was cut off from the people of Israel" and had to break with his family and his community.[5] He is next found at the University of Leyden as a free auditor, and "in the

---

[5] Spinoza's excommunication took place on July 27, 1656. It must be admitted that he displayed great prudence and did not begin to air his heterodox views until after liquidation of the family business in March, 1656, had made him safe from the pressures of his coreligionists and even perhaps assured him of modest economic independence. On the subject of Spinoza's excommunication, cf. "Le cas Spinoza" by Jacob Gordin in *Evidences*, No. 42, Paris, 1954. For biographical details on this part of the philosopher's life, see *Spinoza et Juan de Prado* by I. Revah, Paris, 1959.

house of Don Joseph Guerra, a knight of the Canaries who was living in Amsterdam to be treated for his leprosy," we find him frequenting a group made up of more or less free-thinking Jews and Spaniards intoxicated by the air of liberal Holland. When they returned to Madrid, two of these reported to the Inquisition some details about Spinoza as well as the beliefs he professed. He regretted not knowing Spain and had said that he longed to visit it. However, Prado and he "missed the subsidy which they were given in the synagogue and the communication with the other Jews." This did not prevent them "from being satisfied to be in the error of atheism, for they thought that God existed only philosophically speaking and that souls died with the bodies, and thus they had no need of faith." It was at this time that Spinoza must have written his *Apology,* which has since been lost, full of attacks against Jews and Judaism (he inserted certain passages of it into his *Theologico-Political Treatise*). But above all, he completed his studies, assimilating all the knowledge of the time, from the classics of antiquity all the way to Descartes, whom he could have passed in the streets of Amsterdam as a child.

An incident that is still unclear—a fanatic Jew seems to have attacked him with a knife—made him leave Amsterdam in 1660 and withdraw first to the suburbs of Leyden and later to Voorburg, near The Hague. Here he remained in the company of a few Dutch friends and admirers as well as passing strangers who were attracted by his growing reputation as an erudite scholar and sage. After paying him a visit, Leibnitz called him "the Jew of The Hague who is predicting the revolution which is rising in Europe." The French Prince of Condé, commander of the French army, invited him to his headquarters. Judging from the friends and protectors in high places whom he succeeded in cultivating, Spinoza's charm and brilliance must have been irresistible. A pension from the illustrious John de Witt, as well as some bequests, allowed him to pursue his meditations free from want; besides, his tastes were modest. In accordance with the precepts of the Talmudists he learned a trade and spent his leisure time polishing lenses. Essentially, his style of life and his virtues conformed to the wisdom of his ancestors;[6] like many other philosophical geniuses, from Pascal to Kierkegaard, he never married, and he was not known to have had any relationships with women. His gift for philosophical concentration and his love for pure knowledge must have made his solitude easy to bear.

His appeal to the "natural lights of reason" was dynamite for the traditional order of his era despite all the precautions he took to hide the ultimate implications. *Caute* (prudence) was his motto: the only notable work he published in his lifetime—and he published it anonymously—the *Theologico-Political Treatise* (*Tractatus Theologico-Politicus*), an argument in favor of freedom of thought, caused him many problems. In the words of his detractors, the work "was manufactured in hell by a renegade Jew." And in fact, wasn't it his destiny to live not only at the crossroads of all the cultures—Judaism and Christianity, Spain and the Low Countries—but also of all the fanaticisms—those of the inquisitors who were set against his lineage as well as those of his brothers who cursed him?

He died of consumption in 1677 at the age of forty-four. Shortly before his death he threw into the fire a translation of the Old Testament on which he had been working, as if this had been a senseless enterprise. His other works, in particular the *Ethics*, were published posthumously and anonymously at the expense of an unknown admirer.

---

[6] This was brought out by the Spinoza scholar Dunin-Borkowski in the following terms: "Prudence in human relations and love of peace; sobriety and mastery of the instincts; regard for others and love of his fellow man; mistrust of flatterers; great esteem for study and knowledge as well as for manual labor; resignation in the face of the eternal laws of nature—these are the most salient character traits of the philosopher that all his biographers list. Were we to gather the most beautiful ethical precepts of the Talmud and of the Midrashim, we would find exactly the same ideal of virtue." (St. von Dunin-Borkowski, *Der Junge Spinoza,* Münster, 1910, p. 132.)

Spinoza's philosophical system is still alive and continues to attract adherents as "the most imposing conceptual edifice which has ever been constructed by a human brain" (502). Historically, his grandeur lies in having revealed to enlightened Europe of the seventeenth century, in a form adapted to the understanding of the times, "Jewish wisdom," that is, the moral wisdom and the religious philosophy of the Talmud, developed by the Jewish theologians of the Middle Ages. His pedagogical genius was to put this message in the form of a geometrical demonstration, even if, actually, this was a Procrustean bed. He signed this revelation with his name and thus became immortal. True, in recognizing his debt to the rabbis, rather debatable authorities for his followers, he would have discredited his undertaking (the only one of whom he spoke with praise was Crescas) (503). The wisdom of the moral life remains the most vital part of his *Ethics*.[7] Similarly, in the *Theologico-Political Treatise*, where he shattered the foundations of revealed monotheism, there were few observations or criticisms regarding the contradictions of the Holy Scripture that were not borrowed from Abraham Ibn Ezra, from Rashi, or from that Maimonides who served as the target of his irony. Moreover, when in this work he attacked the notion of the Chosen People of Israel, he put himself in the line of the ancient

[7] According to H. A. Wolfson, Spinoza was a continuator of medieval, above all, Jewish, philosophy: "If we could cut up all the philosophic literature available to him into slips of paper, toss them up into the air, and let them fall back to the ground, then out of these scattered slips of paper we could reconstruct his *Ethics*." Wolfson adds that the very Talmudic precision of the philosopher's style is sometimes a source of obscurity and misunderstanding and has made possible the very diverse interpretations that have been made of his thought for three centuries. (H. A. Wolfson, *The Philosophy of Spinoza*, Cambridge, 1932, pp. 3 ff.)

Here is how another specialist, P. L. Couchoud, characterizes this aspect of the philosopher's thought: "His genius is first and foremost that of synthesis. The proper function of his thought seems to be to condense. It condenses books and foreign observations, it even condenses itself ceaselessly. It invents little and when it does so it is always at great effort. Rather it combines dissimilar elements." (P. L. Couchoud, *Spinoza*, Paris, 1902, p. 315.)

Jewish freethinkers (such as Hayawaih of Balkh, whom he must have known from the polemics of the Talmudists). From every evidence, the astonishing prerogatives accorded the "Chosen People" by Judeo-Christian tradition shocked and irritated him. He was addressing his Jewish contemporaries when he wrote: ". . . for he who thinks that his blessedness is increased by the fact that he is better off, or happier and more fortunate, than the rest of mankind, knows nothing of true happiness and blessedness, and the pleasure he derives from such thoughts, unless merely childish, arises only from spite and malice." And, further on: "The man who is pleased by such thoughts is pleased by the misfortune of another; he is therefore spiteful and wicked, and knows nothing either of true wisdom or of the peace of mind which true living involves." It will be noted that it was precisely this point which concerned him vitally: the denigration of his own line, leading to a virulent anti-Semitism, seems to have been the Achilles heel of the great philosopher.

One has only to read the different passages of the *Treatise* to see how he arbitrarily (for it is in no way required by the construction of the work) reverses the terms and makes the Jews responsible for the hatred the Christians bear them (he who wrote in the *Ethics:* "He who imagines himself to be hated by another, and believes that he has given the other no cause for hatred, will hate that person in return"):

"As for the fact that they have survived their dispersion and the loss of their state for so many years, there is nothing miraculous in that, since they have incurred universal hatred by cutting themselves off completely from all other peoples; and not only by practicing a form of worship opposed to that of the rest, but also by preserving the mark of circumcision with such devoutness" (*Chapter 3*).

"Hence the patriotism of the Jews was not only patriotism but piety, and it was so fostered by their daily ritual that it must have become second nature. . . . And this must have inspired in the Jews continued and ineradicable hatred, for a hatred which springs from great devotion or piety, and is itself believed to be pious, is undoubtedly greater and more persistent than any other. And the common reason for the continued growth of hatred, i.e., the fact that it is returned, was also present; for the Gentiles must have regarded the Jews with the most bitter hatred" (*Chapter 17*).

It is "the enemies of the human race" of Tacitus to whom Spinoza refers in another passage of the same chapter to imply that the Jews were struck by a sort of supernatural curse. Here he is in agreement with a certain historiography that goes back to ancient Gnosticism; it contrasts the cruel Jehovah of the Jews with the Redeemer of the Gospels. Moreover, in the nineteenth chapter the philosopher bases himself on the authority of the New Testament ("Again, the Jews could preserve the freedom they had won, and maintain complete control over the territories they held, only by adapting religion to the needs of their own state alone, and making a clean break with the rest of the world, as I have shown in Chapter 17, and this is why they were told 'Love thy neighbor and hate thine enemy.' See Matthew, Chapter 5, verse 43") to state that the Law of Moses taught hate toward non-Jews. (At this time in the Low Countries, the Socinian sect, falsifying the meaning of the text, was citing the Old Testament in support of such a thesis; as the first-rate philologist he was, without going so far, Spinoza multiplied the ambiguities and the approximations to demonstrate it.)

Looking at it a bit closer, one finds that this recurring anti-Jewish theme of the *Treatise* is like a counterpoint intermingling diverse readings on various levels. First of all, it seems obvious that Spinoza was concentrating his attacks on the Jews and the Old Testament, just as Voltaire would do later, because they were tactically the weakest links in the chain of traditional belief. On a second level, Spinoza is a subtle Talmudist speaking a second, esoteric language simultaneously with his explicit language: "He pretends to have demonstrated an idea but he manages to use such arguments and to cite such texts that the reader by himself discovers a whole different idea, a whole different consequence; and it is this second idea that Spinoza really wanted to demonstrate" (504). "There is" (in the words of the philosopher Wolfson) "a sort of dual authorship—an explicit author, who expresses himself in certain conventional symbols and patterns, and an implicit author, whose unuttered thoughts furnish us with the material for grasping the full significance of those symbols and patterns. In the case of the *Ethics* of Spinoza, there is, on the one hand, an explicit Spinoza, whom we shall call Benedictus. . . . Then there is, on the other hand, the implicit Spinoza, who lurks behind these definitions, axioms, and propositions, only occasionally revealing himself in the scholia. . . . Him we shall call Baruch." In other words, the marrano who admires Jesus. In a still deeper sense Spinoza's language is that of unappeased or disappointed love; one can detect the resentment toward the synagogue that rejected him. It is generally accepted that Spinoza borrowed the anti-Jewish passages of the *Treatise* quoted above from the *Apology* written after his excommunication, which makes it obvious that this polemic lies outside the search for eternal truth, the quest for the beatitudes of divine understanding. Incorporating them into the *Treatise* was an adventitious undertaking, but doubtless it was subjectively necessary. But in doing this, the sage who propounded "If we use our reason aright we can feel no hatred or aversion for anything" did not follow this precept but instead allowed himself to be guided by a dim feeling that he described in the *Ethics* as follows: "If anyone begins to hate a thing loved so that his love for it is clearly laid aside, he will bear greater hatred toward it on that very account than if he had never loved it, and the more so according as his former love was greater."

Such ambivalence corresponds to the situation of a man who, after having broken with the Jewish community, continued to be a Jew in the eyes of the world and could not but remain a Jew for himself even if he spoke of the "Hebrews" in the third person; and this contradictory situation confused his understanding to the point where it only allowed him to perceive things "through a cloud." This internal cleavage and intolerance toward their own line that we see among so many illustrious Jewish thinkers of modern times is illustrated here for the first time—and with what tremendous impact!—by the recluse of The Hague, whom Nietzsche once upbraided in these terms (in his poem "To Spinoza"):

Of "all in one" a fervent devotee
Amore Dei, of reasoned piety,
Doff shoes! A land thrice holy this must be!—
Yet underneath this love there sate
A torch of vengeance, burning secretly:
The Hebrew God was gnawed by Hebrew hate.
Hermit! Do I aright interpret thee?

Elsewhere Nietzsche did not hesitate to compare Spinoza to Jesus (505). There are few illustrious minds so worshipped by posterity—especially in Germany—as the man "who polished the lenses through which the Modern Age contemplates itself." And there are few in the history of ideas who have done so much to legitimize metaphysical anti-Semitism for generations of thinkers and theologians. It is as if the European conscience surrendered to a summary dichotomy, admiring the Jewish legacy through a figurehead that simultaneously served as a guarantee of the denigration of Judaism. Spinoza remains the herald of the new faith in man, the incarnation of the "side of peace and justice," which, according to Alain, "you will refrain from calling the Jewish side, but which will be that side nevertheless" (506). But, because he could not overcome his resentment, he could not render justice to the people from which he himself had sprung. His anti-Jewish polemic blazed the trail for the rationalist or secular anti-Semitism of modern times, perhaps the most formidable ever; and this justified a Hermann Cohen when he stressed "the demonic irony" of Spinoza resulting "from the tragic nature of his life, from the contradiction which existed between the spiritual and moral sources of his creative power" (507). Carl Gebhardt, the best modern editor and biographer of the philosopher, spoke of "the cleavages in the marrano conscience from which the modern conscience has sprung" and, as an epitaph, attributed to the marranos "who sought the meaning of the world in the world and not in God . . . the historical mission of producing an Uriel da Costa and a Spinoza" (508).

Modern Spain

Limpieza, Anti-Semitism, and the Inquisition

At the beginning of the seventeenth century, *la despoblación* became one of the major problems of Spain. "What land are we in? What king governs this realm, and why are all these villages so empty?" Tirso de Molina had one of his characters exclaim from the heights of the Pyrenees (509). The drama of the Spanish decline was part of the general economic crisis of the seventeenth century, but from the start it took an irreversible path. And the depopulation of the countryside was accompanied by the disconcerting spectacle of a kingdom that possessed all the gold of the Americas but was becoming impoverished before one's very eyes. Faced with such a paradox, one contemporary, Cellorigo, wrote as long ago as 1600: "If one does not find any silver or golden coins in Spain, it is because the country possesses them and it is its wealth which causes its misery, which is a veritable contradiction. . . . In reality, one would say that they have tried to transform this state into a land of enchanted men who live outside the natural order of things" (510). If it is true, as Jean Cassou has said, that "the absurd is a Spanish creation," then Cellorigo's is such an observation. Shortly afterward, Cervantes would give a name and a face to the prototype of the "enchanted men," the immortal knight of the sad countenance.

With a total population of some seven million people (511), Spain had well over a half-million nobles. Even if they were poor, they were surrounded by domestics, for it was more honorable to serve than to work. "By a singular eccentricity, to the Spaniards domestic service seemed less dishonorable than any other profession" (de Laborde) (512). Just as unproductive from the economic point of view were the members of the clergy, numbering some two hundred thousand. Professional beggars and thieves of all sorts, who inspired so many "picaresque novels," were nearly as numerous, and the mendicant orders served them as an august example.[1] "The beggars are even proud, and when they ask for alms it is in an imperious and domineering way" (Mme. d'Aulnoy) (512). "They seem rather to be doing you a favor by asking you for alms" (Frère Labat) (512). As to those who were forced to work with their hands, they kept this dishonor to a minimum. The tales of the travelers of the time abound in picturesque anecdotes on this subject, several of which we have already quoted, and today's Spanish historians agree: "The superlative cult of honor and the pejorative concept of work—'legal dishonor,' and, consequently, saving and the productive use of capital—sum up the impact of the aristocratic mentality on the social structure of seventeenth-century Spain" (513). In large part trade and handicrafts fell into the hands of foreigners, especially the French, everywhere but in Catalonia, and the French ambassador de Villars gave the reason for this exception: "The people there are very industrious, and in consequence there are few French" (514). The ethic of Catholic

---

[1] On this subject the author of a plan for Spanish reforms, Bernardo Ward, made the following shrewd observation in the eighteenth century: "The humility of a monk who could live a life of ease but subjects himself to a life of begging is doubtless a great example and worthy of esteem; but when the child sees that his mother, when she gives him the alms, also kisses the hand of the friar, the fact that mendicancy and veneration are united engenders, from the most tender age, an impression that imperceptibly inclines simple people who are incapable of distinguishing religious poverty from guilty beggarliness toward a lazy life." (*Proyecto Economico*, Madrid, 1782, quoted by Jean Sarrailh, *l'Espagne éclairée de la seconde moitié du XVIIIe siècle.*)

Spain led to the sanctification of idleness at the very time when the Calvinist ethic was leading to the sanctification of work. To the extent that the Inquisition extirpated the last vestiges of their Judaism, the Spanish *conversos* adopted these habits, and those who had amassed some money made every effort to put it into unproductive real estate (515).

- The only Spaniards to remain aloof from this were the Moriscos. Numbering about a half million, they were sober and industrious, and in the sixteenth century they became the vital force of the Spanish economy, making themselves rich and hated. In so doing, they brought upon themselves the fate of the Jews; in 1609–14 they in their turn were expelled for the greater triumph of a faith that would then be totally unified. Fernand Braudel said of them that they were "condemned to be rich" in Castile (516); it could also be said that in the absence of Jews they were condemned to fulfill the function of Jews, and we will return to this subject in the chapter we have devoted to them in the Appendix. Just as in the case of the Jews, the Spanish population was unanimous in proclaiming "the memorable expulsion and very just exile of the Moriscos" (Fray de Guadalajara), "the heroic resolution of the great Philip III" (Cervantes), and "a blessing followed by peace, security and all the felicities" (Bleda) (517).

- These were the customs of a century that lived according to the principle *cujus regio, ejus religio,* and Louis XIV did the same thing when he revoked the Edict of Nantes. In the case of Spain, however, the concern with religious unification could not be divorced from the obsession with purity of the blood and hatred of the Jews. Passions of this sort seem to be no more than a sort of folkloric theme, a theatrical setting with no relation to real history, a choice morsel for lovers of curiosities of the past or for the kind souls concerned with racism. But obsessions of this type precipitate the development of the great historical crises and even warp the course of history. Racial interpretations of history, which were particularly popular during the last century, were really just an obsession of the same type as *limpieza:* they culminated in a racist crusade, and the Hitler war would have been inconceivable without them. Memory of it still hangs over our world today, with its United Nations, its rapid decolonization, and its many problems with underdeveloped countries.

On this subject, why not make a few comparisons between the last white racists of our era and the Spaniards of the baroque? And as South Africa is not the Iberian Peninsula and the twentieth century is not the seventeenth, these analogies are all the more striking.

, "The Boers," Hannah Arendt states, "were the first European group to become completely alienated from the pride which Western man felt in living in a world created and fabricated by himself. They treated the natives as raw material and lived on them as one might live on the fruits of wild trees. Lazy and unproductive, they agreed to vegetate on essentially the same level as the black tribes had vegetated for thousands of years. . . . The poor whites in South Africa demanded and were granted charity as the right of a white skin, having lost all consciousness that normally men do not earn a living by the color of their skin. The Boers simply denied the Christian doctrine of the common origin of men and changed those passages of the Old Testament which did not yet transcend the limits of the old Israelite national religion into a superstition which could not even be called a heresy. Like the Jews, they firmly believed in themselves as the chosen people, with the essential difference that they were chosen not for the sake of divine salvation of mankind, but for the lazy domination over another species that was condemned to an equally lazy drudgery. . . . Whether racism appears as the natural result of a catastrophe or as the conscious instrument for bringing it about, it is always closely tied to contempt for labor, hatred of territorial limitation, general rootlessness, and an activistic faith in one's own divine chosenness" (518).

' We must refrain from oversimplifying and overschematizing, for the passages we have just quoted show the dissimilarities as well as the similarities. Moreover, the seventeenth century was the golden century of Spanish literature and art (which surprises some who believe in historical materialism), and the idea of Spain's being the chosen nation gave rise to a remarkable flowering of theological and political thought. Sanchez-Albornoz has written that the Jewish problem excited religious identity and accentuated Catholicism: "No other people was so sadly prepared for confronting the religious torments of the dawning modern era." According to Juan Regla, "The battle gave Spain and its clergy the absolute certainty of their spiritual superiority. To maintain it, they did not hesitate to uproot the nonconformist elements and to intensify their strictness with themselves, beginning with the proofs of the purity of blood and ending with the zeal with which the Holy Office guarded against the slightest deviation" (519).

Let us return to these essentially Spanish problems. In the seventeenth century the obsession with purity of the blood attained its peak. This was the era when "the roads of Spain were crisscrossed in all directions by commissioners in charge of investigations, the local archives were consulted time and time again, and the 'old people' of the villages had occasion to test their memories and their knowledge of family ties." Around 1635 the polemicist Geronimo de Zevallos became indignant about "the infinite number of people occupied in collecting information, procurers of honor and devourers of fortunes, squandering money which could have been better utilized for working the fields," while "men who should have considered their children and left them something consumed the fortunes which they should have bequeathed them in satisfying these pretensions, which is largely the reason for the depopulation of Spain, for in a family known as impure, the sons become priests or monks and the daughters nuns. . . ." Finally, he stigmatized "the men of lowly origin who not only want to equal but to surpass [the people of quality] thanks to an *acto de limpieza* [certificate of purity] which they could obtain easily because no one knew them, and which fills them with such vanity and such arrogance that there is not a noble *caballero* nor lord whom they would hesitate to discredit and cover with infamy as *no limpio.*" At the same time, an anonymous writer deplored "the innumerable perjuries of the witnesses who either out of affection and friendship or out of fear or self-interest say what the parties want them to say, and there are people who earn their livelihoods and make a profession of putting a word in all the reports, and if they are not paid they wreak such havoc that today everyone buys his honor, those who are *limpios* as well as those who are not, the latter to obtain it and the former to avoid losing it" (520).

These are not mere exaggerations of polemicists linked to the "noted" families. A curious exchange of correspondence between the bishop of Cuzco, Peru, Don Fernando de Vera, and his nephew Jacinto gives us a better glimpse of everyday life. In 1636 Jacinto, who was a cavalry colonel, applied for admission into the order of Saint John; such matters were a question of family honor. From Peru the uncle, as an experienced prelate, explained to his nephew how he should go about establishing the purity of his blood, how to recruit the witnesses, how to bribe the investigators, how to engage scribes. He sent him one thousand ducats to "negotiate" this delicate affair and ended his letter with the following words: "Our blood is certainly irreproachable, but that is not enough. It must be proved without fail" (521). In other words it was not enough to *be,* it was necessary to *seem!* Henceforth Spanish society was to know the *linajudo,* the person who dug out genealogies either because of some unwholesome passion or because of the desire for profit, collecting genealogies and making everyone around him tremble. "*Linajudo* from school with a big cap and a big beak, who spends his whole life ferreting out information," sang a ballad (522). In 1655 a company of *linajudos* from

Seville headed by the "noble and illustrious knight" Don Fernando de Leiba had a run-in with justice: "There were thirty-six to forty of them, with their notary, their attorney and other ministers . . . and anyone who did not come to them became the nephew of Cazalla, of Luther, and even of Mohammed," Barrionuevo relates in his *Avisos* (523). Compilations and lists of families with Jewish blood, on the order of the *Tizón de españa*, were known as *libros verdes* (green books). They proliferated despite all prohibitions against them, and today, in modern Spanish, the term *libros verdes* has come to mean not only books of genealogy but also defamatory books (524). The extensiveness of the proofs became more and more incredible as the abhorrence of infidel blood increased, to the point where we are told that an inquisitor, searching for the blemish of a heretic and not finding it in his ancestry, went all the way down to the wet nurse who had fed him and succeeded in establishing that she had had Jewish ancestors, which "gave him a great deal to reflect on" and doubtless assured him of intellectual peace of mind (525).

It is not surprising that the author who related this incident, Brother Geronimo de la Cruz, issued this appeal to Philip IV in 1637: "Why don't you banish from Spain the names 'Jews' and 'Moors,' for today the name alone does more harm than their presence did in the past!" An anonymous inquisitor stated in a memorandum to the king that nine out of every ten civil or criminal suits pleaded in Spain originated in a dispute relating to purity of blood. Another anonymous petitioner recalled that "the merchants, seeing that they do not enjoy the *honra* which they enjoy in other kingdoms, go abroad and then send for their relatives and their friends" (526). But all these petitions had no effect; to exorcise the myth of *limpieza* it would have been necessary to attack certain basic principles that were henceforth to govern Spanish life, and it is typical that the false genealogies and false chronicles which the New Christians produced to demonstrate that they had settled in Spain before the Crucifixion and that they had descended in a direct line from the Biblical patriarchs were used by Old Christian families to their advantage.[2]

We have already said that these questions came under a taboo which the authors of the time dared to touch only when they donned a comic mask. Their works are riddled with stings and allusions, some of which are very clear and some obscure. Thus, in his novelette *El Licenciado Vidriero* (Master Glass), Cervantes posts his hero by the door of a church: "Once as he stood at the door of a church he saw a husbandman go in, one of those who continually call attention to the fact that they are Old Christians. Behind him came one who was not in such good repute as the first, and Glass began to call out to the first: 'Sunday, wait until Saturday has passed.'" Just as revealing is another passage from the same novelette in which the Licenciado challenges a secondhand dealer with these words taken from the Gospel: "Daughters of Jerusalem . . . weep for yourselves . . . ," dealing in secondhand merchandise having been a most vile profession. More debatable is the meaning of the comedy *El*

---

[2] Sixteenth- and seventeenth-century tradition designated Tubal, the son of Japhet, who had taken refuge in Spain after the Flood, as founder of the Spanish race and sometimes went even farther back: "If you belong to the family of Christ as the Duke de Luna does, then you possess the highest possible credentials of nobility. But you could also be a descendant of Jews who were not deicides, and thus be one of the chosen race, for they believed in a single God instead of being polytheistic. For that it was necessary to be a *hidalgo* and, what is more, here is something that should not be forgotten: you should be originally from the Montana Valley [the province of Santander] and, by extension, from the north of Spain, Asturias, Navarre, etc., which after the Flood were peopled by Tubal, his companions and their descendants, who brought monotheism to Spain. That is why the top families claimed to have descended from Enoch, which means they claim a purer Jewish descent than most of the present Jews!" (Details kindly furnished by Ignacio Olagüe.) All during the first half of the eighteenth century the Spanish Carmelites quarreled with the Jesuits, who denied their claim that the Carmelite order had been founded by Enoch. (Cf. Lea, *Chapters from the Religious History of Spain*, p. 75, note 2.)

Retablo de Maravillas, in which the troubadours Chanfalla
and Chirinos invite the public to contemplate marvels that
can be perceived only by people of pure blood and legitimate birth. This means that no one dares to admit that he
has seen nothing and that therefore there was nothing to
see, and all the spectators vie with each other in their
ecstasy. This is the plot of Hans Christian Andersen's "Emperor's New Clothes," but it lacks the intervention of the
child who tells the truth. Did the subtle Cervantes thus wish
to make fun of the hypocritical bluffing on which the whole
system of *limpieza* rested? This claim has been made, and it
is entirely possible. Such allusions are equally frequent
among other authors. We find them in Lope de Vega as well
as in Tirso de Molina and Quinones de Benavente, but
always limited to comedy and satire (527). "This manifestation of *honra,*" wrote Marcel Bataillon on the subject of
limpieza, "is much more typically Spanish than the matrimonial vengeances of Calderon; and it is perhaps because of
this that no dramatist dared treat the subject seriously, to
write tragedies about purity of blood as they wrote tragedies
of conjugal honor" (528).

Later, the French philosophers of the Enlightenment did
not fail to poke fun at the Spanish racial complex: "Of those
who live in Spain and Portugal," wrote Montesquieu in the
78th Persian letter, "the most uplifted are such as are called
Old Christians; that is to say, such as are not descended
from the converts to Christianity made by the Inquisition in
later times. Those who dwell in the Indies are not less elated
by the consideration that they have the sublime merit to be,
as they say, white-skinned men. There was never, in the
seraglio of the Grand Seigneur, a sultana so proud of her
beauty as the oldest and ugliest rascal among them is of his
complexion of pale olive, when in a Mexican town he sits at
his own door with his arms folded. A man of such importance, a creature so perfect, would not work for all the
wealth of the world, and could never persuade himself to

compromise the honor and the dignity of his color by vile mechanic industry."

When Montesquieu wrote these lines, the statutes of purity of the blood were entering their last phase, perhaps the most paradoxical of all. Throughout the seventeenth century the Inquisition had been bursting with activity, and the flames of its pyres helped to reveal the nature of the discontented class of New Christians; even the frenetic efforts they undertook to escape their infamy contributed to exposing them to the public. In the eighteenth century there were fewer pyres for lack of Judaizers and heretics; the line between Old and New Christians grew so blurred that *limpio* came to mean a person who did not exercise a vile profession, and the distinction between *nobleza mayor* and *nobleza menor* disappeared completely. In popular speech *cristiano nuevo* became synonymous with gypsy, but appointments and promotions remained tied to the long and costly procedure of "proofs." Statesmen such as Carvajal and Floridablanca were powerless to abolish this custom (the latter became indignant over "the indecent and even infamous tag put on the converts and their descendants, so that a man's most sacred action, that is, his conversion to our holy faith, is punished with the same penalty as his greatest crime, that is, apostasy from it"). A 1772 law specified that a certificate of *limpieza* was necessary to obtain the title of lawyer, schoolmaster, or even notary. In certain localities, such as Villena, one had to present this certification to become a resident (529). The Inquisition finally disappeared after the Napoleonic whirlwind had swept through Spain, but the statutes still remained in effect. It was only in 1835 that they were abolished in the educational institutions under the jurisdiction of the Minister of the Interior, considering that "the noble and generous sentiments of the Spaniards make them refuse to reveal facts which could deprive innocent men and sometimes men of great merit of the means which the study of the sciences and the artistic professions offer them to gain their subsistence, and also considering that the expenses of the investigation constitute a sacrifice which the modest fortunes of numerous families cannot bear." Finally, an 1865 law definitively and generally abolished the "investigations" for contracting marriages as well as for entering into state careers (530).

Laws are powerless against customs. In Spain itself the old discrimination has sunk into oblivion, but this is not true of the Balearic Islands. In Palma de Mallorca today there are still several hundred Spaniards who are nicknamed *chuetas* (slices of bacon) because they are supposed to be descended from Jews. Just as their presumed ancestors, they are artisans and merchants. (It has been claimed that one of them, Juan March, is the richest man in Spain. He was Franco's banker.) The Catholic fervor of the *chuetas* is above all suspicion; there have been no autos-da-fé on the island since 1691. Laws promulgated in 1773, 1785, and 1788 were destined to mitigate the fate of these pariahs whom it was forbidden, under pain of imprisonment, to call *judios*, all to no avail; as late as 1911 Vicente Blasco Ibañez described their sad fate in his novel *Los Muertos Mandan* (The Dead Command). Later, after revolution and civil war, their ostracism was lifted and they were admitted into the army and the monastery; but in the schools of Mallorca the little *chuetas* are still the butt of their schoolmates' jokes. Islands have always been the last outposts of animal species and of human anachronisms (531). At present, a lingering memory of Judaism from time to time leads some Mallorcans to convert to the Law of Moses (532).

It is remarkable that Spanish racism, so violent in the Iberian Peninsula, was much milder on the American continent, where the conquistadors did not hesitate to marry the daughters of Indian chiefs and where the Inquisition that burned the Judaizing New Christians and other heretics of European origin left the forcibly baptized Indians in peace. The racial barrier was erected slowly, and it never became as impenetrable as in North America. Social discrimination fell mainly on the mestizos, those classless people, in accordance with the pithy colonial adage, "God made milk and God made coffee, but He did not make *café au lait*" (533). Which leads to the conclusion that the Spaniards were anti-Jewish first and racist later.

There is nothing more revealing than this anti-Semitism without Jews, for it lets us study the passion in its purest state as it continued to feed on itself without being affected by a troubled conscience on the one side and resentment on the other. Under these circumstances it became a sort of ritual attitude. Again, it is Cervantes who, in a short passage, shows that a Spaniard who wanted to have a clear conscience and make himself well regarded had to make a profession of hating the Jews. He shows us Sancho Panza doubting that a bachelor would slander him in the chronicle he is writing, and he puts into his mouth this profession of faith: ". . . and if I had no other merit save that I believe, as I always do, firmly and truly in God, in all that the holy Roman Catholic Church holds and believes, and that I am a mortal enemy of the Jews, as I am, the historians ought to have mercy on me and treat me well in their writings." This is the attitude of the character. Now let us look at that of the author. In Cervantes' stories, when the action took place outside of Spain, in Rome or among the Turks, there were a few Jews, and the misadventures he made these preposterous types undergo, the cruel farces he inflicted on them, provoked no commiseration in the author. If they were persecuted and debased, the fault could only lie in themselves, in their inconceivable obstinacy. Their ridiculous figures have no substance. How much more subtly and profoundly was the creator of Don Quixote able to evoke the tragedy of the Moriscos, the loyalty that poor Riconete retained for Spain, and the humble resignation with which he accepted his exile! (534)

While Cervantes merely reflected the customs of his time, Francisco de Quevedo contributed to molding those of generations to come. This satirical genius who feared nothing and no one had fallen into disgrace with the powerful minister, the Count-Duke of Olivares, and as a result harbored resentment toward him. When he got a hint that the duke was involved in financial negotiations with a group of rich Jews (Jews of Salonica it was commonly held; but most likely Jews of Amsterdam), around 1639 he wrote a vitriolic satire, *The Island of the Monopanti,* aimed at both the Count-Duke and his entourage (the *Monopanti*) and the Jews. Utilizing all the old myths and legends circulated during the preceding centuries by the anti-*converso* theologians and by "authorities" of the Inquisition, he secularized them to give them a more modern twist and described how the Jews, aided by the *Monopanti* (the future Freemasons), conspired to secure world domination thanks to their gold.

"Rabbi Saadias," the leader of the Jews, gathered together in Salonica delegates from all the Jewish communities of the world, from Rouen and from Oran, from Constantinople and from Amsterdam, and declared, among other things: "We have synagogues in the dominions of all these princes, where we are the principal element in composing of this confusion. At Rouen we are the purse of France against Spain, and of Spain against France. In Spain, concealing our circumcision by our habit, we supply that monarch with the stock we have at Amsterdam amidst his enemies. . . . The same we do in Germany, Italy, and Constantinople, and we have knit this indissoluble knot by placing the supply everyone expects in the hands of his greatest enemy. For we furnish money, lending for interest to one that plays and loses, that he may lose the more. . . ."

Moreover, Saadias advocated founding the triumph of the Jews on the "ruin of all others." It is typical that another conspirator, "Pacasmazo," quoted as his authority Niccolò Machiavelli, "who composed the thorough bass for our treble." The plot of *The Island of the Monopanti,* which Quevedo later incorporated in his masterpiece *The Hour of All Men,* which was further disseminated through such diverse works as Maurice Joli's *Dialogue aux enfers de*

Machiavel et de Montesquieu and by Hermann Goedsche's *Nach Sedan,* served the twentieth-century authors of the *Protocols of the Sages of Zion* as the basis for the contemporary version (535).

Doubtless Quevedo was ahead of his time, for during his lifetime anti-Semitic literature generally followed the old pattern, and the incredible grievances the pamphleteers continued to copy from one another were medieval rather than modern, or, if you prefer, religious rather than political. A bibliography of this material would be boring, so it is enough to say that the quantity of such works attests to the need they filled. One or two examples will suffice.

Drawing his inspiration from two successful authors, the Portuguese Costa Mattos and the Castilian Diego de Simancas, the friar Torrejoncillos in his *Centinela contra Judios* listed the innumerable sins, vices, hereditary defects, and crimes of the Jews and then stated:

"And for it to be so generation after generation, as if it were an original sin to be an enemy of the Christians and of Christ, it is not necessary to have a Jewish father and mother; one parent would suffice. It makes little difference if the father is not; it is enough that the mother be. It means nothing if she herself is not entirely; half would be enough. Even less. A quarter would do it. An eighth. And now the holy Inquisition has discovered that Judaism is practiced to the twenty-first generation."

Father Torrejoncillos then described the praiseworthy custom that was observed in the school of Santa Cruz de Valladolid every Good Friday. The students of the school met to discuss the Jewish guilt for the Crucifixion. Then the dean asked each his opinion on the Jews: "Beginning with the eldest, each was obliged to speak and to relate the case of a marked family, its location, and the way in which it was shunned; and then when all the students had said what they knew and had ridiculed the Jews, they concluded the meeting and left the refectory" (536).

It is easy to see how the obsession with purity of the blood led to a horror of the Jews, which in turn justified continuing the racial laws. Torrejoncillos wrote for all the Christian people; but here, in a juridical commentary published in 1729–32, the *Senatus Consulta Hispaniae* of Arredondo Carmona, a work intended for specialists, is a quick mention of the Jews: "After the death of Christ the Jews became slaves. Slaves can be killed, sold, and can also be expelled and exterminated. The Jews are infamous, abject, oppressed, and in a very vile state. The Jews are evil-smelling and obscene people. The Jews are odious even to those who do not know Christ. The Jews are like dogs and wolves. The malice of the Jews surpasses the iniquity of the devils" (537).

In addition to writings of this genre, an incredible variety of reminders and relics of all sorts perpetuated the sacred hatred of the Jews, such as the authentic thirty coins of Judas that a canon showed Casanova in a monastery (538). The hand of the Jews could be detected everywhere: in the testimony of a Moroccan ambassador who came to Spain in 1690, even the expulsion of the Moriscos was imputed to them! (539)

Of course, there were always men with a liberal bent, high-placed persons such as Olivares or Floridablanca, who did not share these beliefs. Let us now turn to these representatives of "enlightened Spain," one of the leaders of which, in the eighteenth century, was the Benedictine Benito Feyjoo. Like Voltaire, this universally recognized scholar did not disdain to enter into correspondence with the Jews on occasion. When one of them wrote from Bayonne to complain of the hatred the Spaniards bore the Jews, Feyjoo answered with a thirty-page letter in which he protested that the Spaniards were no worse than other nations, but admitted that the complaint was valid; that the superstitions in question were, however, those of the common people, of the *vulgo* alone; that as far as he was concerned he had always written against the fables which said that the Jews had a tail and Mephistophelean smell; that it was not true that their doctors killed sick Christians; that even the accusation of

ritual murder was unconfirmed. Then he added this significant paragraph:

‹ "The Hebraic nation has lived under the most miserable
oppression for seventeen centuries, dispersed across the
world without being able to form the smallest republic,
detested, scorned as very vile people, ignominiously driven
away from one place after the other, accused of the worst
extortions. Such a long and deadly calamity is particular to
the Jews, for there is no example of it in any other nation.
Therefore, it must be assumed that Providence had a very
particular complaint against the Jews. What could this complaint be, if not a crime very particular to the Jews, something which no other nation is guilty of—the death of
Christ?" (540)

While disengaging himself from the innumerable accre-
tions with which seventeen centuries of Christian faith had
encrusted dogma, Feyjoo still remained faithful to their
traditional substance; moreover, he denied the Copernican
system and maintained that the sun moved around an immo-
bile earth. (True, if he had affirmed the contrary, he would
have risked incurring the Inquisition's wrath.) (541)

‹ From generation to generation the Jews continued to be
for Spain the very symbol of subversion and blasphemy, and
not only were they strictly banned from the peninsula but in
1667 were expelled from Oran, the Spanish beachhead in
North Africa. We have mentioned the plans of Olivares, who
wanted to authorize some of the Jews to settle in Madrid to
take the Spanish finances in hand; in the face of indignant
public opinion and the opposition of the Inquisition, this
plan came to nothing. Later, the peace treaties of the end of
the seventeenth century exempted the great British and
Dutch merchants from inquisitorial jurisdiction, and these
privileged heretics were henceforth tolerated on Spanish
soil, but only on the condition that they were not Jews.

‹ During the following century tolerance was extended to
non-Catholic artisans and workers, but always with the
exception of Jews, "people who are in horror of the pure and

immaculate Catholicism of the Spaniards," a royal edict of 1797 stated in prescribing the maintenance of the *cordon sanitaire* against them. This edict was renewed in 1800, in 1802, and for the last time in 1816 (542). If these prohibitions had to be renewed so often, if in 1804 Charles IV threatened "with the severity of his royal and sovereign indignation" anyone who would preserve a Jew from the surveillance of the Holy Office, it was because there were always adventurous followers of Moses who did not respect these laws and penetrated Spanish territory fraudulently. Let us cite one of the last cases of this type, that of a merchant from Bayonne pursued by the Inquisition in 1804 in Santander. Beurnouville, the French ambassador, had to exert himself on this merchant's behalf to extricate him from his predicament; it was the first example in the nineteenth century of French action in favor of the Jews. Even after the abolition of the Inquisition in 1834 the *cordon sanitaire* was maintained; in 1854 the efforts of a German rabbi to have it abolished were fruitless. These laws were not repealed until the Spanish Constitution of 1869 (543).

At the present time some 8,500 Jews live in Spain. The largest community is in Barcelona. Spanish anti-Semitism, without having disappeared completely, has been pushed to two extremes—the least and the most cultivated. In the remote countryside the simple people still clothe the Jews with all the corporeal attributes of the Devil; the intellectuals yearn for a past that continues to blacken the Jews, the better to make the history and the figureheads of their nation shine.

Now let us consider the last panel of the triptych of Spanish anti-Semitism. In the preceding chapters we have discussed the Inquisition enough so that it is not necessary to describe it further. However, we must still emphasize its popularity and the stimulating aspect of its autos-da-fé, those great public celebrations that were for Spain of modern times what the mysteries of the passion were for medieval Christianity. Villages stopped their work, corporations got together to parade; what a way to inculcate in the people the fear and hatred of the enemies of Christ!

The preachers did not fail to hammer this theme home: "It is quite right for men to dedicate at least one day to avenge the offenses committed against God. Are there any sinners who are more the enemies of God and more worthy of punishment than those who follow the Law of Moses?" (Sermon at the auto-da-fé of Madrid, 1680) "An inhabitant of Asia, who should chance to arrive at Madrid the day of such an execution," wrote Voltaire, "would not be able to determine whether it was a rejoicing, a religious ceremony, a sacrifice, or a butchery; and it is indeed all these together. . . . Montezuma has been reproached with sacrificing the captives taken in war to his gods; but what would you have said if he had been spectator of an auto-da-fé?" It is true that other foreign authors of this time saw it differently and held the Inquisition in high esteem. Thus the Abbot Vayrac: "The policy of the Supreme Council as well as the other tribunals of the Inquisition is admirable. I despair of how to be able to convince my compatriots that circumspection, wisdom, justice, and integrity are the virtues that characterize the inquisitors." (Moreover, in France of the eighteenth century there was a Calas affair, in which those who were bankrupt were hung in effigy.) As to the intermediate opinion, let us quote that of Father François de Tule, who in 1699 witnessed a great auto-da-fé in Coimbra in which six *cristãos novos* were burned alive. After describing the ceremony at length, he concluded: "That is the manner in which the act of faith of the Inquisition is done. Some find fault with such a tribunal; thus, they have not wanted to have it in France. But there are pros and cons" (544).

We have mentioned how with the course of time the autos-da-fé became fewer and farther between. A last great blaze took place in 1721–27 after the discovery in Madrid of a conventicle of Portuguese bold enough to choose a rabbi and send him to Leghorn to study. All the inquisitorial tribunals were then set into motion to track down anyone who was practicing Judaism, and throughout Spain they found 820. Seventy-five were executed in person and seventy-four in effigy; most were of advanced age. After this massacre the Inquisition's zeal slackened, perhaps for lack of heretics, perhaps because times had changed, and around the middle of the century the English voyager Edward Clarke could write: "The Spaniards do not burn as the Portuguese do. . . . Today one hardly sees in Spain those bloody acts of faith and they have told me that there have not been any at all for more than twelve years." This does not mean that the Inquisition had stopped swinging into action at the slightest suspicion of Judaism. At the very time when Clarke visited Spain, the inquisitorial tribunal of Toledo was concerned with the case of a certain Manuel del Corral denounced in confession by his son—aged eight years!—an occurrence his confessor had hastened to report to the Holy Office. Display-ing a healthy prudence, the tribunal decided to take an oblique path and pursue del Corral not for the crime of heresy but as the guardian of his turbulent heir, who had mistreated a twenty-two-month-old little girl, and to wait and see what would happen next, meanwhile having the priest spy on the suspect's neighbors. The archives remain silent on the epilogue to this affair, which tells a great deal about the customs of the Inquisition at a time when it was losing its power of life and death over those within its juris-diction (545).

It only attempted all the more to enclose their lives in a net of police surveillance. Here is what a brave Protestant merchant from Strasbourg noted on the subject when he came to Cadiz on business in 1718:

"The number of spies of the Inquisition is considerable in Cadiz, and they actively watch the foreigners as well as the natives. And when they note a suspect word or act, they advise the inquisitor without delay. One of these spies came to pay a visit to me in my room, and he said all sorts of friendly things to me without my knowing who he was. He picked up my prayer book which I had brought along on the trip and began to leaf through it. But he also found some letters there, some itineraries, and various other information useful to a merchant coming from abroad, and as he did not know German (he chatted with me in excellent French) I told him that it was a travel guide and he accepted this answer. I mentioned this visit to my landlord, who assured me that my interlocutor was one of the privileged agents of the Inquisition. As I had several times remained in my room the whole morning, he immediately advised me to go out every morning from now on, since there were individuals in charge of watching foreigners and verifying if they went to Mass" (546).

Throughout the eighteenth century this is how the Inquisition in decline waged a fierce rear-guard action against dangerous ideas and their presumed bearers. We have seen that since the Renaissance it had forbidden the reading of the Bible; later it dealt with heretical books just as it had dealt with people, burning them with great pomp after parading them in a procession through the streets. It even reached the point where the crowd, not knowing whether a book or a man was involved, cried "Burn the Jews!" as the procession passed. This happened in Madrid in 1684, for example, when an anti-Jesuit pamphlet was burned (547). The censorship of the Inquisition was of unparalleled severity and thoroughness. Considering the *Index librorum prohibitorum* of the Holy See as overindulgent, the inquisitors soon created their own Index, but even works not listed in it were judged subversive, whether it was a matter of Galileo or Newton, of Descartes or Leibnitz. In 1768 the Count de Penaflorida stated ironically: "Who can pay any attention to heretical dogs, atheists and Jews like Newton, who was a terrible heretic, Descartes, who is materialistic as far as animals are concerned, a Leibnitz, who is God-knows-what, a Galileo, whose name proves he must have been some arch-Jew or proto-Hebrew. And others whose name alone fills one with horror!" Reading other no less illustrious thinkers could have grave consequences. In 1778 the civilian judge Pablo Olavide, who possessed the works of Hobbes, Spinoza, Montesquieu, and Voltaire and who had read them to his friends, was stripped of all his offices and condemned to eight years in seclusion in a monastery; his property was confiscated and his descendants declared ineligible to hold any office until the fifth generation. According to another enlightened Spaniard of this time even the study of exact sciences was dangerous: "The mere fact of hearing someone talk of oscillation, of cohesion of the parts, of percussion, and of elastic fibers and other similar physical terms was enough to have him declared formally a heretic and condemned to hell" (548).

We have seen that reading the Old Testament in Spanish was authorized in 1789. Thirteen years before the promulgation of this edict the Inquisition had published another, ordering the strict examination of all books, letters, and papers coming from France capable of conveying dangerous ideas. The *cordon sanitaire* against the Revolution became the great concern of the police of thought, to the extent that they purely and simply denied its existence. It was forbidden to mention the French situation in books and newspapers or to make the slightest allusion to it, even unfavorable (thus a pamphlet telling of the persecution of the clergy in France was confiscated). In sum, the Inquisition, that Orwellian ministry of truth, had undertaken to rewrite contemporary history in its own way. It had lost none of its bureaucratic meticulousness of earlier times; its instructions and edicts were communicated and applied from Mexico to the Philippines, and Lea cites the case of a priest of a small parish in Yucatan who "amid the solemnities of the Mass published the prohibition warning his little congregation of Indians and half-breeds not to read [a certain politico-philosophical work which had been published the previous year with the fictitious imprint of Philadelphia] and to surrender forthwith all copies in their possession." It must be believed that the Inquisition's popularity in Spain remained very firmly entrenched, for the "patriotic juntas" that drove the French out of Spain between 1811 and 1813 tried to re-establish it province by province (549).

After the Napoleonic tempest the Inquisition again took up the cudgels against dangerous ideas in an atmosphere of political instability that thenceforth would be chronic and punctuated by civil wars. In 1824 an edict ordered the Spanish population to submit all recent books to the priests to be checked. The Index of forbidden books was enriched by such titles as Bernardin de Saint-Pierre's *Paul et Virginie*. Finally the Inquisition was abolished in 1834.

Today it is still the subject of passionate polemics. To some, it is important to demonstrate its evil influence and to establish a direct link between its oppression and the present condition of Spain; to others, for whom this condition leaves nothing to be desired, its action was good and salutary. But both are reducing to a simple cause-and-effect relationship a historical process that was extremely original and complex. We have attempted to reconstruct a few meanders, and we hope that other researchers will chart their course. These questions are worth pondering, for they show how slowly but surely, over the centuries, customs are molded by beliefs to give rise to institutions that, as they become established, help to solidify the mental attitudes from which they sprang. This is true of Spain, and before trying to draw any general conclusion, we must remember that history never repeats itself—or never in quite the same way.

There is still an infinite variety of paths it can take. The one we have just described is strange nonetheless; it has carried us, starting with the Islamic customs and the conditions Islam placed on the Jews, through the Judeo-Arabic emancipation and its great figures and the Jewish ascendancy over Spanish life, to the religious crisis of fifteenth-century Spain and the actions of the Catholic monarchs, and from there through the inquisitorial system and the obsession with purity of the blood to the haughty, tragic, and miserable Spain of modern times!

The Jews of the
Holy See

The history of the Jews of the Holy See, which means, essentially, the Jewish community of Rome, is remarkable on several scores.

Over the centuries, the papacy tried to make the Christian governments respect the teachings of the Fathers of the Church on the subject of the Jews. These teachings had two facets, one of which was the necessity for conserving the remnants of Judaism, and the other, the equally necessary abasement of the Jews. On numerous occasions the popes protested strongly against the massacres and persecutions of the Jews; on equally numerous occasions they warned the Christians against the Jews and their influence, and these warnings led innumerable Christian hearts to draw bloody conclusions. In sum, the role of the Holy See could be compared to that of a regulator: hostile to the Jews when their position equaled or even surpassed that of the Christians (during the early Middle Ages, for example, and, more subtly, in the nineteenth century), and favorable when their position declined too greatly and became hellish (for example, at the end of the Middle Ages or at the time of Hitler's persecutions).

Where it exercised temporal power, that is, in the Papal States, throughout all of the Middle Ages the papacy seldom applied its own decrees to the full advantage of the Jews; starting with the Counter Reformation, however, it took these decrees very seriously and established a kind of model Jewish community. Rome, the only great European city from which the Jews were never expelled, remained an oasis of peace for them, but only at the price of unparalleled degradation. Here again we see the regulator at work, behind which we can also detect a certain attempt at preservation. Exceptional in these respects, the case of the Jews of the Holy See is also interesting in another regard.

The influence of the papacy on the fate of the Jews was linked to the dream of establishing the ideal Christian city on earth, in which they would have been *sub ecclesia* despite their *extra ecclesiam* status. Although this plan came to nothing, it had innumerable consequences of all sorts. In the first place, it had repercussions—if only because of geographical proximity—on the status of the Jews in the other Italian states, although outwardly their status seemed to have nothing in common with that of the Roman Jews. The Italian Jews as a whole were a case apart from the other European Jews. Their history in the Middle Ages was not a "vale of tears," and in modern times there was no "Jewish problem" in Italy, but religious Jews were harmoniously integrated with their compatriots. Today, for the man on the street in Rome or elsewhere, the Jew is more or less an amiable eccentric who is still waiting for the Messiah. Within the framework of the present study, we will not be able to review the various factors that have contributed to such an exceptional and fortunate evolution, in sharp contrast with the Spanish tragedy. If the actions of the Holy See were among these factors, we cannot always say with certainty that the popes always wanted it that way. However, in reading the following pages, it is important to bear in mind the interplay of influences between the situation of the papal Jews and those of the other Italian principalities or republics.

We do not know when the first Jews settled in Rome, but it was well before the Christian era, which allowed the Roman Jews—and old Italian authors after them—to state that they had had nothing to do with the Crucifixion.

According to one Talmudic tradition the Messiah was to be born and raised in Rome; according to another that was circulated widely, the Roman Empire was the fourth kingdom predicted by Daniel, which "will devour all the land and break it." Many other passages of the Talmud reflect the fascination that the Eternal City exercised over the ancient rabbis. Afterward, other legends were born within the Jewish community of Rome that were familiar and sometimes affectionate. One of them told the story of Andreas, or Elchanan, a Jewish child kidnapped from his parents, who ascended the throne of Saint Peter, all the while remaining a faithful Jew. Another attributed this hostage role to the apostle Peter himself, who was supposed to have pretended to be a Christian and penetrated into the heart of the Church in order to provide for the welfare of the Jews from that time on. This role of sublime archmarrano that devolved on the popes reflects the naïveté of popular imagination and also the hopeful trust the ghetto placed in its rulers, the bishops of Rome, and even beyond that, perhaps, a secret comprehension, a furtive wink of recognition, between Judaism and the papal sovereigns.[1]

Little is known about the tribulations of the Jewish community of Rome under the first Christian emperors at the time when the doctrine of the Fathers of the Church was finding its way into the codes of Theodosius and Justinian. At the end of the sixth century Pope Gregory the Great, who was trying to convert the Jews by kindness, submitted that none of the rights they had been given by Christian legislation should be taken away from them, but neither should any more be added. This formula (*Sicut Judeis* . . .) became the papal golden rule on the subject. When they mounted the throne of Saint Peter, most of the popes of the Middle Ages reproduced it word for word and accompanied

---

[1] In Hebrew, the pope is traditionally designated by the noun *Afifor*, the provenance of which is uncertain and has given rise to scholarly debate. The etymology *avi*–or *abi*–*pior* (Father Peter or Abbot Peter) proposed by Rabbi Berliner, the historian of the Jews of Rome, is likely.

it with commentaries, the essence of which was that the religion of the Jews should be respected and their lives protected. Other bulls of protection were issued in special circumstances, such as the Crusaders' excesses or the accusations of ritual murder. Jewish delegations hastened to Rome to solicit them (doubtless with presents, but this essential inducement was not necessarily the decisive one), and perhaps Judaism could not have survived without this protection from the Vicar of Christ. But even more frequent were the papal fulminations *against* the Jews, warnings about their influence and their usury, a concern to create a separation between Christians and Jews in the name of the eternal servitude of the fallen people.

There is something that is strange at first glance: whether the bulls were favorably disposed to the Jews or hostile to them, in nearly all respects they were based on the same grounds.

Let us take for example the thirteenth century, when the Holy See was at its peak of influence (550). In publishing the *Sicut Judeis* bull of protection, the glorious Pope Innocent III gave it the following preamble:

"Although Jewish perfidy is in every way worthy of condemnation, nevertheless, because through them the truth of our own faith is proved, they are not to be severely oppressed by the faithful. Thus the psalmist says, 'Thou shalt not kill them, lest at any time my people forget the Law,' or more clearly stated, thou shalt not destroy the Jews completely, so that the Christians should never by any chance be able to forget the Law, which, though they themselves fail to understand it, they display in their book to those who do understand."

A few years later Innocent III wrote to the Count of Nevers and inveighed against Jewish superstitions and usury, against the profits the princes derived from it, and against the custom of buying wine from the Jews and using it for the Christian sacrament. Here is the preamble:

"The Lord made Cain a wanderer and a fugitive over the

earth, but set a mark upon him, making his head to shake, lest any finding him should slay him. Thus the Jews, against whom the blood of Jesus Christ calls out, although they ought not to be killed, lest the Christian people forget the Divine Law, yet as wanderers ought they to remain upon the earth, until their countenance be filled with shame and they seek the name of Jesus Christ, the Lord. That is why blasphemers of the Christian name ought not to be aided by Christian princes to oppress the servants of the Lord. . . ."

Some of the other texts relating to the Jews contain interesting nuances, and some even imply that Judaism is a sort of demi-Christianity gone astray. Here is how Honorius III, the immediate successor of Innocent III, justified giving protection to Isaac Benveniste, the favorite of the king of Aragon:

"Although the perfidy of the Jews, condemned as they are to perpetual slavery because of the cry by which they wickedly called down the blood of Christ upon themselves and their children, has rendered them unworthy of the consolation of the Apostolic Throne, nevertheless, since we have learned . . . you [Isaac Benveniste] . . . conduct yourself in accordance with Mosaic law while quarreling with no one, and since out of a certain, even though wrong kind of religiousness, you beg for our protection and help, we . . . yielding to the prayers of our dear son in Christ, James, the illustrious king of Aragon . . . admit your petition and grant to you the shield of our protection."

This tone is even more marked in an exhortation that Gregory IX addressed to the bishops of France in 1233:

"Although the perfidy of the Jews is to be condemned, nevertheless their relation with Christians is useful and, in a way, necessary; for they bear the image of our Savior, and were created by the Creator of all mankind. They are therefore not to be destroyed, God forbid, by his own creatures, especially by believers in Christ, for no matter how perverse their midway position may be, their fathers were made friends of God, and also their remnant shall be saved."

But such solicitude should not make us forget that one of the functions of the Jews was to symbolize degradation and opprobrium. It so happened that the notion was conceived regarding a question which did not concern them at all. Thus, in 1234 there was a quarrel between the Cistercian order and the German bishops; feeling they were being persecuted, the monks appealed to Gregory IX and he, ruling in their favor, wrote that the Cistercians found themselves "in worse condition than even the perfidious Jews, who are by their own guilt condemned to perpetual slavery, and are received into our midst solely out of Christian pity and mercy."

One of the probable reasons for the privileged situation of the Roman Jews in the Middle Ages was their role as natural intermediaries between the papal court and the foreign Jewish colony, a role that must not have been unprofitable. In the eleventh and twelfth centuries there were Jews who achieved high office in the Curia, just as later the pope's Jewish doctor or his Jewish financial adviser became traditional figures in Roman life. Benjamin of Tudela, who visited Rome in 1160, found there "about two hundred Jews, who occupy an honorable position and pay no tribute, and amongst them are officials of the Pope Alexander, the spiritual head of all Christendom. Great scholars reside here, at the head of them being Rabbi Daniel, the chief rabbi, and Rabbi Yechiel, an official of the pope. He is a handsome young man of intelligence and wisdom, and he has entry of the pope's palace; for he is the steward of his house and of all that he has." A Jewish minister or adviser to the pope, whose position was similar to the advisers of the kings of Spain, was doubtless more dependable than a Christian minister, as he was not beholden to any of the Roman factions or families in those troubled times. In recalling the peaceful prosperity of the Roman Jews, one must also bear in mind the relatively good situation they enjoyed all over Italy. The wearing of the rouelle, in fact, was not imposed on the Roman Jews until the end of the thirteenth century, and it was often neglected during succeeding centuries; the pope's doctors and other Jewish dignitaries were generally exempt. At Comtat Venaissin the Jews could do much as they pleased with the badge of infamy.[2] This papal land was the only province of France from which the Jews were never expelled; let us point out a dossier of complaints written in 1532 by the deputies of Comtat under the title *Privilèges concédés aux Hébreux par les papes en haine des Chrétiens* (Privileges Conceded to the Hebrews by the Popes out of Hatred of the Christians). These Jews were certainly the "pope's Jews"; in 1510, during a conflict with Julius II, the governor of Provence took reprisals against them and against the clergy, excluding all the other inhabitants of Avignon.

As ruling the Jews was a matter that touched closely on the articles of faith, it was possible for the popes to permit themselves liberties in their own lands that they would have condemned anywhere else. Doubtless Jewish money did the rest. On this topic it is important to note that the Jews of Rome and the other Italian lands did not specialize in lending at interest until the fourteenth century—that is, much later than elsewhere in Europe, and under very different conditions; the Jewish lending offices were *sui generis* municipal institutions that functioned throughout all of Italy under a license granted by the Holy See. This curious state of affairs deserves closer examination, and we plan to return to it in a work of a more technical nature (551).

Probably no tenet has aroused as much discussion and dispute over the centuries as the Church's prohibition of lending at interest. It was based on several passages of the Old and New Testaments, in particular on the passage "Give to him that asketh thee, and from him that would borrow of

---

[2] According to a papal brief of 1494 the men of Comtat Venaissin would wear a circle of white thread which was scarcely visible; as to the women, the statutes of the city of Avignon prescribed that they wear earrings if they were married. On the subject of the Jews of Comtat Venaissin, see M. de Maulde, *Les Juifs dans les États français du Saint-Siège au Moyen Age,* Paris, 1886.

thee turn not thou away" of the Sermon on the Mount, to which Aristotle's maxim "Money does not engender money" came to be added. A verse from Deuteronomy (23:20: "To a foreigner you may lend upon interest, but to your brother you shall not lend upon interest") made it possible for the theologians of both religions to justify the lending of money by Jews to Christians and vice versa without transgressing the law. Again, there was far from unanimous agreement; in the innumerable works dedicated to this matter some theologians as well as some rabbis opposed this compromise for varied and often contradictory reasons. Thus, for certain scholars the Jewish lender was breaking the Law of Moses; he was a heretic of Judaism and should be treated as such. For others the Christian borrower was released *ex officio* from his promise to make restitution, for he had made a contract with an enemy of the Christian faith (*fides no servanda es ei qui frangit fidem*). Some rabbis who were opposed to usury referred to a passage of the Talmud (Baba Mezia, 70 b) to say that a person should not lend at interest because to do so would be to lower himself to the ways of the goyim.

As a general rule Jewish usury was a last resort, a means of adapting to the needs of life. These were particularly precocious and demanding in Italy, the cradle of medieval economic life. Contrary to what became typical in the countries across the Alps, in Italy the Jews never played a preponderant role in commerce. The pioneers of this commerce, the great merchants of the northern Italian cities, began to lend at interest at the same time, despite ecclesiastical fulminations, sometimes evading them by means of technical strategies of all sorts. We know that quite early they spread out across all of Europe and were known under the generic name of Lombards or Caorsins. In Italy itself the Jews were never powerful enough to compete with them, and until the beginning of the fourteenth century they confined themselves principally to crafts and small businesses. As a matter of fact, when Saint Thomas Aquinas discussed the "Jewish usurers," he cited Italy as an example of a country where the Jews worked with their hands. When Dante, in *The Divine Comedy,* described the usurers who were groaning in the seventh circle of hell, he evoked the great Florentine families of his time but did not mention the Jews, and it would be easy to cite many other literary allusions of this type, which are the most reliable indication of the Christian usuries of fourteenth-century Italy. (Thus, in a *novella* by Franco Sachetti, a priest who wants to make the world flock to hear his sermon announces that he will demonstrate that usury is not a sin.)

It goes without saying that if the prohibition against lending at interest had been obeyed to the letter, it would have made all credit impossible and consequently all trade of any scope. Besides, the Church was powerless to impede the development of economic life and thus resigned itself to coming to terms with it. The theologians changed the tone of their doctrines, admitted increasing numbers of deviations, and eventually recognized the usefulness of commerce. Consequently, a distinction was made, so that except for open and patent usury, commercial and financial activities of every sort acquired a cachet of perfect respectability. Where the fathers, especially in Italy, had got rich on usury and founded the great financial dynasties that Dante condemned to eternal flames, the sons abandoned this field and limited themselves to legal and honorable trade; other merchants, even smaller ones, tended to follow their example.

But in medieval economy (just as in every underdeveloped economy, poor in the means of production and poor in currency) loans were still indispensable (or seemed so, which is perhaps the same thing); in Italy of the Middle Ages the lending office became a national institution, just as the lottery bureau is in Italy today. From the Christian point of view, it was preferable, according to theology, for these lending offices to be run by Jews; from the Jewish point of view, there was a minimum of opprobrium associated with it. Moreover, in the fourteenth century Italy became the principal place of refuge for the Jews expelled from France and the German countries, who had traditionally specialized in lending at interest (cf. family names such as Luzzato [Lausitz], Ottolenghi [Oettlingen], Morpurgo [Marburg], Treves [Trier], Provenzzali, and Tedesco). In their concern for the needs of their citizens, during the fourteenth century the Italian cities adopted the custom of assigning the administration of the lending offices to Jews and thus regulating the clandestine Christian excesses of usury. According to A. Milano, the two principal centers of origin of the lenders were probably Germany for northern Italy and Rome for central Italy. For protection against ecclesiastical anathema, papal consent had been requested and obtained in advance on the following grounds: "for the purpose of preventing great harm to the population" (Nicholas V to the Duke d'Este, 1449); *ob imminentes necessitates pauperibus* (Innocent VIII to the magistrates of Siena, 1489). At the same time, the Holy See granted the Jewish lenders a concession in due form that served them as a standard and as protection (Jewish usurers of Lorraine also resorted to this) and collected fees from them. To the extent that the popes, whose treasury heretofore had been replenished by all of Christendom, had to depend increasingly on the revenues they derived from their own States, the sale of offices, and so on, the role of this resource increased in importance. If one could speak of "usury in the service of the Church" (G. Le Bras), these, correspondingly, were the papal usurers.

It is true that this Jewish usury was closely regulated. Its terms and conditions were stipulated in a document called the *condotta,* a charter or contract between the city or principality and the Jewish lender or lenders. The *condotta* fixed the days and hours when the office could be open, the type of security acceptable (it was forbidden to pledge religious articles, a soldier's arms, a student's books—generally a piece of clothing served as security[3]), and, especially, the rate of interest (generally between 15 and 30 per cent annually); it accorded the lender the right of residence, generally exempted him from wearing the rouelle, and made him a sort of municipal official—indispensable and unpopular. With the sole exception of lofty Genoa, in the fifteenth century there was not a single Italian city, large or small, that did not have at least one Jewish lending office.

The rate of interest and its fluctuations, that is, the return on the money, were naturally determined by local economic conditions; whatever they were, they seemed unbearable to the poor man who "to be able to buy today's bread had to give as security yesterday's coat and tomorrow's crops" (A. Milano). This usury was a plague on daily life. Indeed, at the beginning of the fifteenth century the mendicant orders, especially the Franciscans, in their longing for evangelical purity and with the interests of the poor at heart, undertook a campaign against lending at interest. They preached in cities and in the countryside, denouncing it as an anti-Christian plot, and despite prohibitions and even papal excommunications, clamored against "the Jewish usurers who slit the throats of the poor and feed on their substance." This crusade, which led to some anti-Jewish excesses and expulsions, had no lasting consequences and could not have had any on such a firmly entrenched custom. Some more realistic Franciscans then decided to reform the institution instead of reforming the custom and, in the second half of the fifteenth century, undertook to socialize credit by founding pawn offices. The time was ripe for the idea: in 1447 Bonefoy de Chalons, a Jewish financier who had settled in Piedmont, proposed opening a similar "pawn office" to the municipal officals of Turin.

---

[3] Unredeemed articles were sold after being repaired and renewed if it was a matter of a piece of clothing. Thus Jewish specialization in mending and sewing that doubtless contributed to their concentration—which still exists—in the clothing industries.

According to current historiography, pawn offices were created to combat the Jewish usurers and put an end to them. This is not exactly the way it worked out, and the subject is not without lasting appeal, for it is basically a matter of the eternal problem of perfecting human society. The mendicant monks vituperated against the Jews just as today's Communists denounce the capitalists. And, just as today, to make the dream become a reality the monks had to compromise, resort to specialists in managing money and their techniques, and finally turn into lenders at interest and bankers themselves. The first pawn offices were created with public contributions in 1462, and their loans were entirely gratis; thus, they were soon in bad shape. Their backers then called upon the Jewish moneylenders—and their funds; the pawn offices did not achieve any stability until they charged the interest necessary to cover the expenses of management and risks of all sorts. Human nature being what it is, the majority of the pawn offices, in their concern with the profit on their capital and its growth, then turned into commercial banks. Thence the fierce campaigns of the Dominicans, old rivals of the Franciscans, against these Christian lending institutions, campaigns that did not end until Leo X, and later the Council of Trent, approved the principle of collecting interest. Thereafter, pawnshops spread to all the Italian cities, as well as to the countries that had not expelled the Jews—in the wake of the Jews, one might say: there were some in Germany, none in Spain, England, and France (in Paris the first pawnshop was founded in 1777). Even in Italy, pawnshops and the Jewish lending offices coexisted for more than two centuries, the one collecting a lower interest and the other giving a client more courteous and more discreet service and many other advantages. Attilio Milano's comparison of the two with the service of public clinics and private hospitals is accurate and illustrative, and the two sectors maintained close relations in every respect.

But in the long run the socialized sector ended up by completely supplanting the private sector. In Rome, after some initial difficulties in the seventeenth century, the pawnshop became a powerful deposit bank with several branches, lending to the kings on their jewels, to the monastic orders on their lands, and to the papal sovereigns themselves. Around 1675 there were more than one hundred thousand transactions a year, more than the number of inhabitants (which says a great deal about the social role of lending on security). This did not mean that the Jewish *banchi*—some fifty of them—had lost their clientele, for they belonged to the more fortunate classes who regarded the pawnshop as beneath them; however, their operations were diminishing in size. Under these conditions, under Pope Innocent XI (1676–89) the closing of the *banchi*, which were lending at 12 per cent, became the order of the day. The Apostolic Chamber was understandably concerned not to take a hasty step to the detriment of the financial equilibrium of the Papal States, but, in the words of an anonymous polemicist, it should not "take the ghetto for its Peru"; in fact, the ghetto was at that time in a most miserable state, as we shall see below. Nor was the moral aspect of the question overlooked; the government of the Holy See convened a special congregation, the *Congregatio de Usuris*, to examine it. Some defenders of the lending offices came forward and advanced various arguments in their favor, among which was that of the *vergogna*, which went as follows: "Rome is a city of strangers where there are lay and ecclesiastical persons of every rank and condition who are ashamed to go to the pawn offices; thus the usurers of the ghetto are necessary." But the majority were in favor of closing "this abomination like the profaned sanctuary of which Daniel speaks, and Rome, which is a sanctuary because it is a sacerdotal city governed by the Vicar of Christ, preserves the abomination!" in the words of one of the theologians consulted. According to another, the time of the Jewish lenders was over, and just as a person who puts on a coat in January has no reason to leave it on in July, it was time to put an end to the traditional arguments in favor of the Jewish usurers, and the verse of Ecclesiastes, "To everything there is a season, and a time to every purpose under the heaven," was cited in support. More remarkable to our modern eyes was the advice to authorize the Jews to enter useful professions so as to let them close the *banchi* without completely ruining the ghetto.

But this advice was not followed. In 1684 Innocent XI closed the lending offices without giving the Jews in return the right to exercise any professions other than the traditional ones of dealers in secondhand goods and clothing. This led to the total decline of the Roman ghetto over the following centuries. In the other Italian cities the last Jewish lending offices disappeared during the eighteenth century.

Under the Renaissance popes the relaxation of Roman customs benefited the Jews. "Nowhere in Europe was the network of anti-Jewish regulations, elaborated by the Lateran Councils and enunciated in successive papal bulls, less carefully studied or more systematically neglected: nowhere was the Jewish community more free in body and in mind" (Cecil Roth). Rome became a place of refuge for the expelled Spanish Jews as well as for many marranos. Ibn Verga tells how the Jews of Rome offered Pope Alexander VI one thousand ducats not to let these undesirable foreigners enter, and how the pope turned around and fined them two thousand ducats to punish them for their lack of hospitality. His successors surrounded themselves with Jewish doctors and humanists and admitted them to their households as "friends and table companions" (*In nostrum familiarem, continuum commensalem recipimus,* said the diploma Clement VII gave Isaac Zarfati in 1530). Vasari reports that on Saturdays the Jews crossed the Tiber and went to meditate before the statue of Moses that Michelangelo had just erected.

If there was an area of Church government in which the Counter Reformation had important and immediate effects, it was that of the administration of the papal Jews. One of Ignacio de Loyola's first efforts in the course of a long stay in

Rome was to found a Jewish mission and a *Casa dei Catecumeni* (Home for Converted Jews), first undertaken with the aid of gifts from rich Christians. It was among the first neophytes that the classic indictments of the Talmud arose, at the very time when the intransigent Cardinal Caraffa, the future Pope Paul IV, was made the head of the revived Roman Inquisition. In 1553 the autos-da-fé of Jewish books began. In 1554 the Jews who had remained faithful to the Law of Moses were made to pay for the upkeep of the Home for Converted Jews, which already contained more than a hundred residents. In 1555, at the time of his elevation to the throne of Saint Peter, Pope Paul IV proclaimed in his bull *Cum nimis absurdum* that it was absurd to permit the Jews to inhabit the best parts of the city, to employ Christian domestics, and generally to abuse Christian charity; and he immediately enacted harsh regulations concerning them. In the first place, they were to be confined behind the walls of an unhealthy and narrow ghetto on the banks of the Tiber, and they were to refrain from all commerce with the exception of dealing in old clothing and secondhand goods. Essentially, these regulations were only a repetition of the canonical legislation of recent centuries, but the inflexible Paul IV, unlike all his predecessors, was going to apply them to the letter. All the Jews had to move to their "seraglio," and the pope had more than twenty Portuguese marranos burned in the city of Ancona. "Seeing that he was only looking for an occasion to annihilate them, many resigned themselves to abjuring; Israel was then like a stag at bay. . . ." (From *Vale of Tears*, a Jewish chronicle, c. 1575, by Joseph Ha-Cohen.) On the death of the octogenarian Paul IV, another contemporary exclaimed: "May God give us another pope kindly disposed to Israel and may He bind our wounds." But no matter who was pope, henceforth the fate of the Jews of Rome was sealed. Pius V expelled them from all the cities of the Papal States with the exception of Rome and Ancona; Gregory XIII introduced the *predica coativa,* a compulsory weekly sermon at which inattentive listeners were punished by flogging. And even Sixtus V, toward the end of the sixteenth century, who was favorable to them and surrounded himself with Jewish advisers, did not do much to change this new regimen.

A remarkable aspect of this regimen was the effort it made to convert the Jews. Beyond the *predica coativa*, whose exasperating effect is easy to imagine, more realistic measures were taken: a bonus of one hundred crowns was given to new converts; high prelates or the pope himself acted as godparents; a protective network was set up around the neophytes, who were forbidden to go into the ghetto or to associate with Jews. It must be added that the Roman Inquisition showed evidence of some respect for the mysteries of free will and managed to return to the ghetto the children whom relatives or other well-intentioned persons wanted to have baptized. It also managed to burn some relapsed converts and even a monk who had decided to embrace Judaism, but this was extremely rare. All in all, an average of fifteen Jews were baptized each year, and the ghetto numbered nearly three thousand inhabitants. Such a proportion, it is tempting to say, was wise and even providential, not threatening the existence of the ghetto-as-witness, but illustrating the mysterious attraction of the grace and solicitude of the pontiffs. A certain number of Jews from the countryside, Italian or foreign, also came to Rome to be converted and some remained there; eventually, these converts formed a quarter of their own, in the neighborhood of the ghetto. In 1724 a witness, who doubtless was exaggerating, put their number at five thousand, "living in five or six alleys but without a wall around them." Many great Roman families and numerous illustrious prelates are descended from this preserve, "sweetly scented roses which grew among the thorns of the race," according to the once-hallowed expression.

For more than three centuries the Jews of Rome vegetated behind the walls of their ghetto. Until 1684 some fifty privileged families were allowed to continue as lenders, but

Innocent XI revoked their concessions. This source of revenue, then, was stopped, and the Jewish congregation, the
"School" of the Jews, became so burdened with debts that it
was finally declared bankrupt. As an insolvent debtor, it was
then administered directly by its principal creditor, the
Apostolic Chamber, whose finances, for that matter, were
almost as muddled. The poverty of the ghetto caused many
worries for the papal government. One of the theologians
consulted on the subject of closing the lending offices was of
the mind that the Jews should be authorized to work at
other occupations. "Let them devote themselves to other arts
and trades as is done in Florence and elsewhere and which
here are forbidden by human laws, which are voluntary
laws, while the divine law on the prohibition of usury is a
necessary law. . . ." But while they inclined before the
"divine law," neither Innocent XI nor his successors wished
to repeal the "human laws." Dealing in used clothing and
secondhand goods, the only occupation permitted the
ghetto, became its essential economic base. The Jewish
secondhand dealers went through the streets of the Eternal
City from morning to night, shouting their cries (*Aeo!*). In
the ghetto the proverbially dexterous tailors and seam-
stresses reconditioned the clothing, repaired the tickings,
and, for better or worse, restored this strange merchandise
and put it into circulation again.

Dr. Ramazzini, who in 1700 wrote a remarkable treatise
on professional maladies, *De morbis artificum*, dedicated a
chapter of his book to the ills of the ghetto. "It is wrong,"
wrote this precursor, "for a stench to be regarded as natural
and endemic to the Jews; that which the lower classes
spread among them is due to the closeness of their homes
and to poverty. . . . Their wives and their daughters earn
their living with the needle; they do not know how to spin,
how to card, how to make fabrics or any art of Minerva
other than sewing. In this they are so practiced and so expert
that they mend clothing of wool, silk, and other materials so
skillfully that no trace of it appears; this is termed in Rome

rinacchiare. Such work compels them to apply their eyes closely. All the Jewish women, moreover, keep at their sewing throughout the day and far into the night, using a small lamp and thin wick. Hence they incur all the ailments consequent upon a sedentary life and in addition suffer in the end from serious shortsightedness; and by the time they are forty they are blind in one eye or else very weak of vision. . . . As for the men, they sit all day long in their booths stitching clothes, or stand looking for customers to whom they can sell old rags. Hence they are mostly cathetic, melancholy, and surly, and there are few even of the more wealthy who do not suffer from the itch. . . ."

Collecting and renovating the discards from the Roman wardrobe, then, was the principal livelihood of the ghetto that housed 3 or 4 per cent of the city's population; this means that the richest city in the world had a ghetto that was the poorest in the world. It did have certain other sources of revenue, such as providing beds for papal soldiers and furnishing palaces for foreign gentlemen who were there temporarily, as well as supplying contraband for those who were more daring. Moreover, the rentals had been fixed since the end of the sixteenth century, and it was impossible for Christian proprietors to evict the Jewish tenants; thus there was a dizzying increase in "under-the-table" deals. Those who held leases to the decrepit houses were the beneficiaries and they became the veritable plutocrats of the ghetto.

For the foreigners who were passing through, the ghetto became one of the not-to-be-missed tourist attractions of the Eternal City. Montaigne was there in 1581 and attended a circumcision, "the most ancient religious ceremony there is among men," and heard a compulsory sermon given by a "renegade rabbi" (see his *Journal de Voyage*); but as a prudent man and the son of a marrano to boot, he was sparing with his commentaries. At the end of the seventeenth century François Deseine described the ghetto in these strong terms: "They call the Jewish quarter *Il ghetto*. It is surrounded by walls and enclosed with gates so that at night this perfidious nation is cut off from communication with the Christians, and as they cannot live elsewhere nor extend their quarter and because there are very many of them—these scoundrels multiply quickly—several families live in the same room, which results in a perpetual unbearable stench throughout the quarter. . . ." A hundred years later the Chevalier Dupaty noted the same misery, but as a good son of the Enlightenment, he came to quite different conclusions: "As one can well imagine, the Jews in Rome live in the greatest misery; their misery involves conversion on the one side and death on the other. What a strange thing! The Jews are persecuted to embrace Christianity to increase it; and if the persecution were to succeed, Christianity would be destroyed. The faith of the Christian requires the unbelief of the Jew. People ask: when will the Jews then convert to Christianity? I ask, when will the Christians convert to tolerance?" But the general conclusions of the curious French who visited the ghetto can perhaps be summarized in the laconic judgment of President de Brosses: "The Jewish quarter is a big pile of rubbish."

Doubtless such impressions were reinforced by the willful intent of the Church government to stress the misery and the abasement of the Jews. If at all times the homage the Catholics had to pay the Vicar of Christ was magnified by a grandiose setting, that homage demanded of the Jews had its own cachet. Urban VIII (1623–44) forbade them to kiss his foot, letting them kiss only the place where it had rested instead. Clement IX in 1668 granted them a blessing when he put an end to the foot races of the Jews during Carnival, so dear to Roman hearts, and replaced them with an annual tribute to be paid to the keeper of the Eternal City, who would put his foot on the neck of the prostrate spokesman of the Jews and dismiss him, exclaiming "Go!" (*Andate!*). The humble addresses of the Jews of the ghetto to the sovereign of the Holy See were far more obsequious than anything the stylists of the other European courts could invent.

All of this display, which could not fail to capture the imagination of the Christians, was far less surprising to the rare Jewish visitors to the Eternal City, particularly the Germans, who were steeled against the spectacle of humiliations by centuries of familiarity. One of them, Abraham Levy of Horn, left a description of the ghetto in 1724 that is quite different from those that precede. According to him three quarters of the Jews of Rome were tailors and one quarter had other occupations such as furnishing the palaces of the foreign princes: "Because of their excellent work, they are favorably regarded by numerous cardinals." This observer does not go to any lengths on the misery of the Jews. He vaunts the beauty and even the wealth of their synagogue. The German Jew certainly did not see things from the same perspective as the French. He added, "I have forgotten to relate one single thing: the liberty which the Jews here enjoy which is on the whole fairly good. The only problem is, the Christians are intent on taking away their faith and sometimes they force them and bind them with such diabolical bonds that the Jews are trapped. First of all, the pope gives one hundred crowns to each person who converts, even if he is just a child. If he is someone who has already done a great deal of harm, and deserves punishment ten times over, from the moment he abandons the Jewish faith he is free. But they also try to trap them in many other ways." And this is what our man is particularly concerned with, and what he dedicates the second half of his long recital to: "the diabolical bonds," the pressures of all types, and he furnishes many examples, touching on the plain and open violence with which recruits were enlisted by the Home for Converted Jews, concluding, "I think when I see this that the prophesy of Moses is fulfilled: 'Your sons and your daughters will be delivered to another people and you will see it before your eyes.' For that often happens in

Rome: fathers or mothers, sometimes fathers and mothers[4] are parted from their children by violence."

Other countries, particularly Austria, followed the example of the Holy See in introducing the custom of compulsory sermons. But generally speaking, the papacy no longer had the same influence on the fate of foreign Jews as in the Middle Ages; besides, the only large Catholic regions that still tolerated Jews by this time were Italy, Austria, and Poland. Let us point out the great memoir about the legend of ritual murder prepared at the request of Polish Jews by Cardinal Ganganalli, the future Pope Clement XXIV (1769–74); this monument of theological and rabbinical scholarship, which once again demonstrated that the legend was unfounded, did not prevent the trials for ritual murder from continuing in Poland and elsewhere; but if the papacy had not taken this position, such trials would doubtless have been even more numerous and more cruel.

During the eighteenth century the fortunes of the papal Jews did not change. In 1798 French troops entered Rome: General Saint-Cyr immediately abolished the wearing of the rouelle, which delighted the Jews. But then he wanted the ghetto tailors to work for him every day, including Saturday,

---

[4] This unusual turn of phrase is explained by the fact that when only one of the parents decided to convert he could have his children baptized —in effect, torn away from the other parent. Simultaneous separation from both parents was much more rare, but not unknown. In such an instance, and with the help of the nuances of canon law, all sorts of situations could arise.

Shortly after Abraham Levy's voyage to Rome, Stella Bondi, a ghetto Jewess, informed the Home for Converted Jews of her intention of being baptized and offered her five children, three of whom had attained "the age of reason." When the woman did not go through with her resolve, the Roman Inquisition set these three free, and they were allowed to return to the ghetto with their mother; on the other hand, it ordered that the other two, girls who were under seven years of age, be baptized.

To illustrate the tale of Abraham Levy, let us recall the phrase that was current among the young men of the ghetto: "By God! I will slit your throat and then I will become a Christian!" Baptism, in effect, was considered as a means to escape the consequences of one's criminal pursuits.

which they found less enchanting, a reminder of how complicated it is to be a Jew. These things were settled, civil rights were accorded the Jews, and the ghetto did not have bad memories of the French occupation. Nor does it seem to have been inordinately distressed by the return of Pius VII, who was benevolent toward it. But his successor, Leo XII, reinstated all the practices of the past centuries, with the single exception of the rouelle, and the Jews of Rome once more had to begin paying for the board of their apostates while the Rothschilds of London, who had become the official bankers to the Papal States, took care of the indigents of the ghetto; this is how devious the ways of finance can be when a Jewish banker lends to a pope. If the Papal State was the most archaic in Europe, the ghetto was the most archaic peculiarity of that state. Italy began to seethe under the influence of new ideas, and the era of the *risorgimento* was at hand, but the ghetto played no part in it. Manin and other Jewish companions of Garibaldi came from Venice or the Piedmont, and it was with reason that the pope could praise the sagacity of his loyal Roman subjects. How to pronounce the demivowel *shva* constituted the principal intellectual concern of the ghetto from 1826 to 1845, giving rise to fierce polemics and even brawls. It was a Catholic priest, Abbot Ambrosoli (whose name deserves to be better remembered), who launched the first appeal for the enfranchisement of the Jews in Rome at the beginning of 1848: "I am perhaps the first," he exclaimed from the pulpit of St. Mary of Trastevere, "who, in a consecrated place before the tribunal of Christ, raises a cause which until now has only been pleaded at the bar of civil reason. . . . Whose fault is it that these people, deprived of civil rights, kept apart from all uplifting activity, have chosen the only path which might allow them some consideration, that of money? Whose fault is it if, excluded from honest occupations, they stoop to usurious operations and have not always been able to clear themselves of the accusation of greed and dishonesty? Isn't it our fault?"

✓ In April, 1848, on the order of Pius IX, the walls of the ghetto were torn down. In November the Roman revolution broke out, and the pope took the road to exile; when he returned, he refrained from any new reforms. Until the end of his long pontificate, the Jews, "those sole living ruins of Rome" in the words of the medievalist Gregorius, had to live in their sordid quarter, limit themselves to their ancient trades, and pay for the support of the apostates. In 1858 forced baptisms of Jewish children became an international scandal with the Edgar Mortara affair.[5] In Bologna a child of six years, whom the Catholic servant of the family had had baptized in secret, was taken from his parents by the police of the Inquisition and consecrated to the priesthood. All the Jewish communities of Europe were aroused; newspapers all over the world reported the incident; the great powers made representations to Rome. The only Jews who deplored this outcry were the Roman Jews. Their delegates were received by Pius IX with these words: "So this is how you thank me for the benefits I have given you. I could do you a great deal of harm and could lock you up again in your quarter. But my bounty is so great and my pity for your state so strong that I pardon you!" The Jewish spokesman burst into tears, swore that the ghetto had had nothing to do with the campaigns in the press, and reminded him of the ghetto's loyalty

[5] The Mortara affair was not the only one of its kind. In 1864 Fortunato Cohen, aged ten years, was baptized in similar circumstances. In *Rome Contemporaine*, Edmond About ironically described another case: "Mr. Padova, an Israelite businessman of Cento, had a wife and two children. A Catholic clerk seduced Mrs. Padova. He was surprised and pursued by her husband, and he fled to Bologna. Mrs. Padova followed him and took her children along. The husband rushed to Bologna and demanded at least the children. The authorities answered that the children, as well as their mother, had been baptized and that there was a chasm between his family and him. Nevertheless, they recognized his right to pay a pension, on which they all lived, including Mrs. Padova's lover. A few months later Mr. Padova was able to attend the marriage of his legitimate wife to the clerk who had seduced her. Officiating was His Eminence the Cardinal Opprizoni, archbishop of Bologna."

during the revolutionary period of 1848–9. The Holy Father calmed down: "Could I reject the child who wanted to become a Christian?" he exclaimed. "Besides, if the Mortaras had not had a Christian servant all of this would not have happened." (It was, as usual, the fault of the Jew!) At the end of the audience, the Jewish spokesman declared: "If you only knew, Your Holiness, how we deplore these poisoned polemics in which we well recognize the gratification of political passions!" Pius IX was satisfied and allowed the delegates to kiss his hand. He had already given orders to the police to make sure that there were no more Christian domestics in Jewish families. He had also had the Mortara child paraded through the Roman ghetto accompanied by a priest (552).

The condition of the ghetto on the eve of its abolition can be assessed from a request the community addressed to the papal sovereign at the beginning of 1870 to obtain an enlargement of the quarter and the repeal of the prohibitions that continued to weigh on its inhabitants: "There is very little air and light and in certain of our roads the sun penetrates only rarely or never." As to the people who lived on these roads, ". . . they are porters, ragpickers, match sellers, errand boys, buyers of old shoes, water carriers, and never anything else." After describing the misery of the ghetto, the signers of the petition "in the habit of blessing your name with beating heart and tears in eyes" exclaimed: "Hear us Holy Father, and let the Children of Israel once again know the effects of the generosity already attached to your noble name!"

A few months later Victor Emmanuel's troops entered Rome, and the Papal States disappeared from the map. The ghetto endured another fifteen years until the sanitation authorities of the city moved the inhabitants and demolished their hovels. Today, the tourist can visit the vestiges of it, and by the banks of the Tiber go through picturesque business streets where Jewish shops still predominate and wonder at the spectacle, which is unknown elsewhere in Europe, of little Jewish beggars along the approaches to the synagogue.

For the period from 1788 to 1887 there are precise statistics on the population of the ghetto. In the course of these hundred years there were 13,771 births and 9,994 deaths, and the population grew from 3,076 to 5,429 between the two censuses of 1809 and 1882. In the nineteenth century no other Italian community had such increase: the ghetto, epitome of Jewish misery, had much greater vitality than the other ancient centers, Venice and Leghorn, Florence and Trieste.[6] It goes without saying that local conditions must be taken into account, the growth or the decline of the city as a whole, and Jewish migratory movements. Moreover, in all the countries of the world, poor Jewish communities have always been more prolific than rich Jewish communities, just as before our very eyes the underdeveloped countries are growing much faster than the developed countries. We shall avoid making simplistic judgments about such a complicated subject. Suffice it to say that in Italy, just as in the other countries of the West, the autochthonous, emancipated, and middle-class Jews tended toward Malthusianism and began to decline in number at the very time in the antiquated Christian theocracy of Rome they were growing and multiplying in servitude. From which each can draw his own conclusions.

[6] For all of Italy, the Jewish population increased by 45 per cent from 1840–50 to 1938. For Rome alone, it increased 137 per cent. City by city, here are the figures:

	Around 1845	*1938*
Ancona	1,800	830
Ferrara	1,500	600
Florence	1,500	2,800
Leghorn	4,800	1,750
Milan	?	8,000
Rome	3,700	13,700
Turin	1,500	3,700
Trieste	4,000	5,000
Venice	2,500	2,000

appendix b

The Moors and
Their Expulsion

"Moriscos" was the name given to the last remaining Spaniards who stayed faithful to the law of Mohammed after the whole peninsula came under Christian domination. In the days of the glorious caliphate of Cordova, Islam was the dominant religion of Spain, but by the sixteenth century the Moriscos comprised only about 10 per cent of the country's population. From generation to generation the attraction of Christianity, which increased as the *Reconquista* progressed, impelled many Moslems to convert in the tolerant Spain of the Three Religions. The policies of the Catholic monarchs, however, lent Islam itself a different, but equally powerful attraction—the attraction that the faithful feel for their persecuted beliefs—and breathed new life into it in the Iberian Peninsula. Thus, the Spanish authors of the time tell us that after a century of struggles, the Moriscos had grown in number and were beginning to make inroads on Christianity. They were then declared unassimilable and were forced to follow the Spanish Jews into exile. This was the other face of the Spanish unification of the faith.

At the time of its conquest in 1492, the population of the kingdom of Granada accounted for around 5 per cent of the population of the peninsula; an almost equal number of *mudejares,* or conquered Moors, lived peacefully in the rest of Spain, especially in the kingdom of Valencia, where the nobles gained most of their profits from these skillful farmers. On the eve of their entry into Granada, Ferdinand and Isabella had solemnly proclaimed, in a fifty-five-point capitulation countersigned and confirmed by the flower of Spanish nobility, that the Moslems would be assured the free exercise of their religion and respect for their ancient customs. Point 38 of this capitulation extended this guarantee to the Jews of Granada, only to be broken four months later when these Jews were included in the general expulsion of the summer of 1492. For several years the other points were more or less respected; it is told that Inquisitor General Torquemada was the first to oppose forced baptisms.[1] The archbishop of Granada, Hernando de Talavera, attempted to win Moslem hearts by kindness, and sometimes he succeeded; it is known that he was popular among the Moriscos. But evangelization of this type was not fast enough for the impetuous Cardinal Cisneros, favorite of the Catholic monarchs, who came to Granada in 1499 to apply missionary procedures that were more in accordance with the customs of those exalted years. He seized Mohammed el-Zegri, the most influential Moslem preacher of the city, and put him in irons until he accepted Christianity. Other excesses of this type followed; el-Zegri himself had to put the torch to a pyre on which were heaped all the manuscripts of the Koran and Arabic books that could be found in Granada. Finally, a Morisco rebellion broke out and was put down in blood; it was followed by negotiations in which the sultan of Egypt took part; he threatened reprisals on the Christians living in his country. This was the beginning of both a tradition of resistance and a tradition of appeal to foreign aid, not a negligible consideration for the Spanish monarchs who were ceaselessly at war with the Turks, and sometimes it acted as a restraint. Finally, the Moriscos submitted and, except for those who could emigrate, allowed themselves to be bap-

[1] According to the Dominican Jaime Bleda, "the very wise doctor [Tomás de Torquemada] felt it was the lesser evil to let the Moors remain pure infidels than to make apostates of them because they had to remain in the power of their relatives and be exposed to the manifest danger of reverting to error." (*Cronica de los moros de España*, Valencia, 1618.) Bleda was a fierce opponent of the Moriscos.

tized collectively on condition that the Inquisition not be established in Granada for forty years. But how could they trust this promise? They had seen the solemn capitulation of 1492 trampled upon and now harbored fierce resentment against Christian treachery. To Isabella the Catholic, however, after this masquerade the Moriscos of Granada were Christians, just the same as her other Catholic subjects, and her devout heart was impatient to lead those of Castile to the true faith. To give them some incentive for this, on February 20, 1502, she decreed their expulsion, with the provision that the edict would be rescinded once they in their turn accepted baptism. The grounds for this edict are worth considering. The edict said that it was a great scandal for the queen to tolerate Moslems in her kingdom after the Moriscos of Granada had all been converted. The Moriscos of Castile were then accused of attempting to lead the new converts back into error, and here we recognize the same argument used against the Jews at the time of their expulsion ten years before. It was finally adduced that it was better to prevent than to punish and that it was just to punish the small for the crimes of the great (553).

Thus, ten years after the fall of Granada, Castile was nominally Christian. Adapting themselves to the situation that had been forced upon them, the Moriscos followed the example of the Jews and practiced their religion in secret, especially as the Inquisition generally left them in peace, either because they were less wealthy or because they had been promised immunity. A curious document tells us how they squared this with their conscience and initiated themselves into the art of mental reserve (*la taqiyya*). It contains the advice of a wise mufti of Algeria who wrote from Oran encouraging them to remain steadfast and to deceive their oppressors. "Know," he wrote to them, "that their *idols* are nothing but gilded wood and constructions of stone: they will do nothing for you; they are useless. Royalty belongs to God. He has not engendered any son; he has no wife." Then, going into details, this pastor stated: "If they force you to say a word of denial, if it is possible, do the contrary with secret words. If not, say what they want you to say and may your hearts be all the more steadfast in the religion of Islam, rejecting and denying with your hearts all that they make you say. . . . If they tell you that Jesus died on the cross (how they lie!) bear in mind that this was to give him more perfection and honor and that the Almighty lifted him to the heights of heaven to glorify him and to take him away from such perverse people."[2] The text of this advice is in Spanish, written in Arabic characters, a valuable indication of the cultural state of the Moriscos. Its conclusion informs us where probably lay their political hopes: "As for me, I will pray to the Almighty that He may turn the course of destiny in favor of Islam until you can worship God openly, without blame, without fear, thanks to the alliance of the Turks" (554).

These were the extremes to which the Moors of Castile were reduced ten years after the fall of Granada. Those of Aragon were better protected. In 1510 their lords wrenched a compromise from Ferdinand the Catholic at the Cortes of Monzon stipulating that "the Moors of the kingdom of Valencia will neither be expelled nor forced to accept baptism," which Charles V confirmed by solemn oath on his arrival in Spain in 1518. This state of affairs provoked a furor among the lower clergy and the common people, and all calamities were attributed to the presence of the Moriscos— a flood in 1517, as well as the sighting of a comet and the appearance of a horrible lion (555). In 1520 agitation against the "Flemish" emperor and the nobles who were his advisers focused on the Moriscos. The revolt that followed was touched off by a massacre perpetrated in Valencia on the pretext that they had killed a Christian child. During the summer of 1520 civil war broke out in Valencia and

---

[2] Cf. the Koran, Sura IV, 156: "And for their saying: 'We killed the Messiah, Jesus, son of Mary, the messenger of Allah,' though they did not kill him and did not crucify him, but he was counterfeited for them. . . .'"

Aragon, with the Christian *germanías* (brotherhoods) fighting against the landed nobility and their Moriscos. Whenever the rebels gained the upper hand, they offered their opponents a choice between baptism and death. In Gandia the entire population was baptized "in a ditch with the aid of brooms and braided switches." In the village of Polop the Moriscos, who had taken refuge in a castle, surrendered after being promised their lives. After the sacrament was administered, however, they were massacred to cries of: "Send their souls to heaven and their crowns to our pockets!" In all, the total number of converts was put at sixteen thousand; thousands of others fled to North Africa (556).

Once order was re-established, Charles V convened a junta to study the validity of these baptisms. He had already taken the precaution of asking the pope to release him from his oath of 1518, doubtless to be more free to judge. The theologians, by a majority of 21 to 1, decided that considering the fact that the Moriscos had not exclaimed *Nolo* (I do not wish) at the crucial moment and that they were neither drunk nor mad, they had acquiesced in full knowledge of what they were doing and should bear the consequences. Moreover, the bishop of Segorbe observed, if there was any coercion, it had been purged by those Moriscos who had attended Mass (compare this ferocious theology with the much more subtle one of 1391 and succeeding years).

Commissioners were then sent into the provinces to better Christianize the New Christians and to turn their mosques into churches. After this, Charles V again ordered them to become Christians, although in his eyes they already were; but by the time they reached this point, the emperor and his theologians were not to be balked by a contradiction. "Desiring to procure the salvation of your souls and to lead you from the error and delusion in which you live, we beg, exhort, and order you all to become Christians and to receive the water of holy baptism. If you do so, we command that you be accorded all the liberties and franchises to which you as Christians will have right according to the laws of the kingdom. If you do not do so, we will be forced to resort to other means." Two months later an edict established a new line of conduct for the unfortunate Moors of Valencia, setting out the Christian rites they had to follow and the Moslem customs they had to avoid, and ordered them to wear on their hats a crescent of blue cloth, the old badge of the infidels. Then the cup was full, and the Moriscos revolted, massacred their priests, and profaned their churches. The papal legate preached a crusade. As to the emperor, after first appealing to his German troops, he resorted to a very typical device. A sanction dated December, 1526, definitively abolished Islam in all of Spain, with all of its external manifestations, such as the distinctive clothing, the use of Arabic, and even the baths; but "such being his good pleasure," Charles V suspended the effective date for forty years. It should be added that the Moriscos presented the emperor, who was always short of funds, with a gift of eighty thousand ducats, and according to Menendez y Pelayo "he was defeated by Morisco gold."

It should also be mentioned that the lords continued to campaign actively in their favor. In 1540 Admiral Sancho de Cardona, one of the greatest lords of Aragon, was arrested by the Inquisition because he was not content to erect a mosque for his Moriscos but loudly denounced the churchmen who were oppressing them and even proposed writing to the Council of Trent to focus attention on their deplorable situation. Even more serious, he wanted to appeal to the Grand Turk to make him threaten reprisals. An abettor of heresy and guilty of dealings with the enemy, this great lord was given a relatively light punishment: a fine of two thousand ducats, penance, and reclusion "until he be otherwise disposed." Equally great lords, such as Rodrigue de Beaumont, one of the family of high constables of Navarre, and Don Gaspar Sanz, were implicated in similar attempts, particularly for having aided Moorish families to escape to Barbary. It goes without saying that they generally accepted remuneration for services of this type (557).

Beginning at this time, we see the Spanish Moriscos adopting *sui generis* customs imposed by their fate and fulfilling the function of the Jews in inquisitorial Spain both with regard to economic life and the collective Christian conscience. A certain style of life evolved: the Moriscos displayed an industriousness and a frugality that assured them of prosperity, and their money was used to protect them against the chicanery of the *alguaciles* (police officers) and the priests, it served to buy off the lords and the kings, and it became their chief political argument. They grew cautious, secretive, fiercely cohesive among themselves and, in the words of their great historian Caro Baroja, constituted a huge semisecret association: "The *alfaqui*, the doctor of the law, had to disguise his profession and proceed with caution. The head of the family had to hide his substance so that he would not be too noticeable; the rich man had to seem poor; the Moslem fanatic on certain occasions had to feign sentiments of Christian piety" (558). This association was nourished by the memory of the broken pledge of the capitulation of 1492 and the evils that succeeded it; it was agitated by Messianic hopes, which are the hopes of revenge; it was titillated by *jofores* (prophecies) announcing that with the aid of the Grand Turk the glorious empire of yesterday would be re-established. But while the persecutions and the humiliations revived the faith of the Moriscos and made the old customs more precious to them, at the same time their faith was evolving toward certain aspects of Christianity, giving birth to a sort of syncretic religion.[3] A number of the Moriscos did end by becoming good Christians, but this did

---

[3] ". . . Learned Moriscos . . . combined the laws of Christ and of Mohammed to create a special theology, which was propagated by works such as *El Atafria* by Ibn Chalab, translated into Castillian as 'The Disputation of the Moslems and the Christians,' which argued that the Jew Paul had corrupted the primitive evangelical doctrine, and the '*Hadith* of the Birth of Christ' which related how, in the place of the Savior, the Jews killed a person resembling him." (P. Boronat, *Los moriscos españoles*, Valencia, 1901, Vol. 1, p. 383.)

not mean they would be exempt from expulsion, as we shall see below.

If the analogies are obvious, the dissimilarities between the style of the Moriscos and that of the Jews are no less striking. In the first place, armed resistance became their *ultima ratio,* and a most efficient one! Moreover, they could count on foreign aid, for although the Grand Turk generally contented himself with verbal promises, the Barbary corsairs constantly came to their assistance or evacuated them to Africa, meanwhile pillaging the coasts of Spain (from this point of view, the Moriscos constituted an acute political problem for Madrid). As they had never had foreign allies of this type, the Jews had to fall back on their sublime internal homeland, the Talmud, and it was Talmudic culture that lent Iberian Judaism a unity and a vitality far beyond that of Islam. The Inquisition, for its part, did not treat the Jews and the Moriscos the same way, for individual trials of Moriscos were relatively rare. To the Inquisition, each Jew was a formidable opponent because he was literate, and tempting because he was considered to be rich. As far as the Moriscos were concerned, the Inquisition contented itself with occasional religious raids, checking on the customs of a hamlet or village of converts whom the priests had catechized poorly and brutally. Under these conditions, one can say that the promise of Charles V to exempt the Moriscos from the Inquisition for forty years was upheld for the most part.

The attitude of his successor, Philip II, was in keeping with his reputation as a scrupulous and devout sovereign. He respected the delay and waited until the end of the year 1566 to convene a junta that proposed a new sanction, published on January 1, 1567. This ordinance regulated the lives of the Moorish "New Christians" in detail. Their baths had to be demolished,[4] their clothing and the veils of their wives

---

[4] ". . . The apologists for the expulsion of the Moors and other authors as well treat the baths as something horrible, and the Granada historian

were forbidden, the doors of their houses had to be left open three days a week, and in three years they had to forget the Arabic language and use only Castilian. At the same time, catechization was redoubled. As to the character that this catechization might assume, a curious letter the Spanish ambassador to France wrote in 1569 sheds some light on this. After deploring the dissolute customs of the clergy and the exactions of an administration that acted as though it were in a conquered land, this ambassador, Francès de Alava, described a Mass he had attended in Granada in which the priest, at the moment of the consecration of the Host and the chalice, had hurled filthy abuse at his flock, ". . . something so contrary to the service of God that I trembled with all my flesh . . ." concluded this gentleman (559). Another document of the same era, the lamentation of an unknown Moor, describes the catechization thus:

> When the bell tolls, we must gather to adore the image foul;
> In the church the preacher rises, harsh-voiced as a screaming owl;
> He the wine and pork invoketh, and the Mass is wrought with wine;
> Falsely humble, he proclaimeth that this is the Law divine. . . .
> All our names are set in writing, young and old are summoned all;
> Every four months the official makes on all suspect his call.
> Each of us must show his permit, or must pay his silver o'er,
> As with inkhorn, pen and paper, on he goes from door to door.
> Dead or living, each must pay it; young and old, or rich or poor;
> God help him who cannot do it, pains untold he must endure! . . .
>
> In their hideous gaols they throw him, every hour fresh terrors weave,
> From his ancient faith to tear him, as they cry to him "Believe!"

Bermudez de Pedraza says: 'They washed themselves even in December!' as though it were a species of madness." (J. Caro Baroja, *Los Moriscos del reino de Granada*, Madrid, 1957, p. 128.)

And the poor wretch, weeping, wanders on from hopeless
    thought to thought,
Like a swimmer in mid-ocean, by the blinding tempest caught.
Long they keep him wasting, rotting, in the dungeon foul and
    black,
Then they torture him until his limbs are broken on the rack,
Then within the Plaza Hatabin the crowds assemble fast,
Like unto the day of Judgment they erect a scaffold vast.
If one is to be released, they clothe him in a yellow vest,
While with hideous painted devils to the flames they give the
    rest.
Thus are we encompassed round as with a fiercely burning
    fire,
Wrongs past bearing are heaped on us, higher yet and ever
    higher (560).

This lamentation fell into the hands of the Spaniards following the interception of an appeal for aid the Moriscos of
Granada had sent to North Africa. After temporizing for two
years, they lost faith in the eloquence of their supplications
and of their gifts and finally rebelled, fortified by promises
of support from Algiers and Constantinople. Aben Humeya,
a descendant of the old line of the Umayyads, was elected
king and leader of the rebellion. The civil war that ensued
lasted nearly two years, foreshadowing the Andalusian
revolutions and guerrilla battles. It was marked by incessant
massacres, rapes, and profanations, and the two camps
rivaled each other in cruelty: "All hands were red with
blood." Algiers sent only two cannons and a few hundred
volunteers, while Sultan Selim II, who had meanwhile
signed a peace treaty with Spain, preferred to use his fleet
for the conquest of Cyprus, much to the despair of the
Moriscos. "If we lose, Your Highness will be asked for a
reckoning and on the day of resurrection the judgment sentence will be borne for eternity . . ." they wrote to him
(561). Finally, the revolt was stamped out by Don Juan of
Austria, half brother of Philip II. Madrid then decreed a
general deportation of the Moriscos of Granada; in 1570

they had to leave their homes to be scattered across the whole kingdom of Castile with the train of suffering and misery that always accompanies operations of this type.

During all of this time the Moriscos of Valencia had not budged, relying on the proven methods of diplomacy and corruption. This patience was finally rewarded: at the end of 1571 a *concordia* promulgated by the emperor commanded that pity and clemency be shown toward them and that they be exempt from inquisitorial confiscations—including their *alfaquis,* circumcisers, and relapsed prisoners—in return for an annual subsidy of fifty thousand sueldos (2,500 ducats) per annum to the Inquisition.

Cosme Abenamir, the man who, with the support of the Valencian lords, brought this negotiation to a conclusion, reminds one in many ways (as one gets to know him through the records of the Inquisition) of the great Jews of the Spanish courts of yesterday. He and his two brothers, Don Fernando and Don Juan, had inherited an immense fortune in gold and silver from their father (an accounting of this money took two whole days, a witness stated). Don Cosme had been baptized at birth and knew the Pater Noster and the Ave Maria, but he did not know the Credo, the Salve, and the other Catholic prayers. His mother had instructed him in Islam when he was a child of eleven or twelve, and he had always believed in it "until I was seized by the Holy Office," he himself admitted. According to the accusation, he was "the principal pillar of Islam in the kingdom of Valencia and the principal adviser for all the Moriscos," who kissed his hand and his cloak and called him Amet or Ibrahim. This great caid had three black slaves attached to his household "who would have suffered a thousand deaths rather than say one word that could harm their master," as well as a servant woman, an Old Christian, Angela Aleman, who participated in the Moslem rites of the family and in time became completely Islamized. In addition, he was not afraid to sustain the superiority of the law of Mohammed over that of Jesus before his Old Christian friends. It was the general opinion of the Moriscos that "the Duke of Segorbe, the admiral, and the other lords and barons consent and desire that we be Moslems." Fortified by such support, Don Cosme made frequent trips to Madrid and made friends with the inquisitor Miranda, "His Majesty's commissioner for the Moriscos of this kingdom," who granted him and his brothers the right to bear arms and the valuable position as familiars of the Holy Office. Under these conditions it was in vain that the Inquisition of Valencia tried to arrest him in 1567. With the intervention of the *Suprema* of Madrid, which assured him of "His Majesty's pardon," he was set free on security of two thousand ducats without his case ever having come to trial (562).

Let us add that ten years later his splendor had dimmed greatly, either because his inheritance had been swallowed up by the Inquisition or because he had made some bad business deals. In 1578 he was, in his own words, a *pobre caballero;* his security was only five hundred ducats, his case was examined regularly, and he even seems to have been tortured. "I have been pardoned, I have paid seven thousand ducats, and today I no longer have enough to pay for the lies of the witnesses," he exclaimed at the time. The outcome of this second arrest is unknown, the records being incomplete. We shall conclude with the reflection of H. C. Lea on this subject: "Probably either the brothers had succeeded in raising a sum sufficient to satisfy the *Suprema*, or they were recognized as too poor to be worth further prosecution."

Throughout this case we catch a glimpse of the amazing role played by the Valencian lords who had become the zealous champions of the law of Mohammed in the name both of the paternal affection they bore their Moriscos and of the exploitation such a state of affairs made possible. Foreign observers did not fail to comment on such a curious situation. "The Moriscos are the favorites of all the lords of this country because it is from them that they derive almost all their profits," noted the Venetian ambassador Serrano (563). The Spanish prelates were more cautious. In response to a request for an opinion on the causes of the obstinacy of the Moriscos, one of them, the bishop of Orihuela, prudently put forward the example of the Swede: ". . . in the land of Lapland which is situated in the kingdom of Sweden and is under the jurisdiction of the archbishop of Upsala, there are an infinite number of pagans whose conversion to our holy faith is prevented by their lords, who fear losing their tributes and their income; possibly this same cause should be taken into consideration regarding the conversion of these people [the Moriscos]." Under these conditions nothing, or almost nothing, was done to make good Christians out of them; the first catechism printed for them did not see light of day until 1595 (by which time their expulsion had already been accepted in principle); the same year a petition from the Moriscos of Valencia complained that their instruction was confided to "idiotic persons, simpleton clerics, illiterates, foreigners, and Frenchmen who were much too young"; as to their churches, "The way they are today," wrote Father Crysnelo, "they are more apt to make a person lose an unsteady faith than to awaken faith where it does not exist" (564).

Let us return to the Moriscos who were expelled from Granada in 1570. The several consequences of this expulsion have been summarized perfectly by Caro Baroja, the Spanish ethnologist, who writes: "The uprooted Grenadine Morisco had adopted, on the one hand, the equivocal behavior taken by members of communities subjected to similar operations. He sought the basis of his support in the very uprooting itself. He adopted trades that involved great mobility and little real estate. Among these, the most frequent, according to the writers of the time, were muleteer and carrier. Being a muleteer, in addition to providing a good income, allowed him to carry news and to a certain extent to engage in espionage.

"On the other hand, in his traditional role as a skilled craftsman, journeyman, or peasant, hard-working, without any great needs, the Morisco once again presented a problem for Christian society. On the one side, it exploited him, and on the other it complained that he was causing a serious problem among the lower classes. . . . It poses a problem which seems very modern: the competition *en la mano de obra* between a group accustomed to a very low standard of living and another group with a generally higher level. Yesterday, as today, those who suffer the effects of competition eliminate their rivals without a second thought.

"In such cases the moral rules which are generally considered valid, the accepted norms of behavior, undergo specious interpretations within the society so that something which in the abstract is considered as good, and which is thought excellent among members of one's own group, is frowned upon in an enemy or competitive social group. . . . Industriousness is attributed to parsimony, frugality is avarice, and fecundity is due to lechery" (565).

Again, it should be recalled that in the Spain of that time hard work was far from a cardinal virtue. These were the conditions under which Spain was to complain unanimously of the "Morisco invasion." In 1588 the Sevillian Alonzo Gutierrez addressed the following complaints to Madrid: "These people multiply greatly, which is not true of the Old Christians, who go to Italy, Flanders, or the Indies. These Moriscos possess great wealth, although in general they do not show it because they are stingy and do not know how to spend a real once it is in their hands. Here in Seville and in Andalusia they buy and sell the foodstuffs, and a large part of the fabric trade, which is very profitable, is in their hands. They made a profession of rope-making, esparto, and other things which produce great revenue, and this wealth of theirs is suspect and very odious."

From Valencia, the bishop of Segorbe, Martin de Salvatierra, sent even more alarming information: "The number of these people has multiplied and doubled, they are entrenched in the best provinces of Spain where as domestic enemies they know all the faults and all the defects, dedicating themselves to the lower and mechanical occupations. It is into their hands that the principal wealth of the country is going. They deprive the Old Christians of their livelihood, force them to cultivate the land or go to the Indies or to war; we have seen that in various parts of Castile the Moriscos from Granada have become so wealthy that they farm revenues and taxes. . . . Some have more than one hundred thousand ducats. If we do not put an end to this, they will soon multiply to such an extent that they will surpass the Old Christians in numbers and in wealth, especially in gold and silver, which they hoard and do not spend, for they do not eat, drink, buy clothing, or wear shoes" (566).

Needless to say, in such cases the eye of the observer, blinded by passion, sees only what it wants to see. Besides the rich Moriscos there was a majority of miserable Moriscos, such as were described, for example, by the less-prejudiced eye of the Frenchman Barthélemy Joly, "working the rice paddies with water up to their knees. . . . If they had been Christians they would have been a pitiful sight to see" (567). But Jimenez de Reinoso, a Valencian inquisitor, also stated that "ordinarily experience tells us that one family of Old Christians needs as much to live on as two families of Moriscos" (568).

All the grievances that Christian Spain nurtured against the Moriscos were summarized by Cervantes with his habitual verve in "The Dialogue of the Dogs":

"The things I could tell you, Cipion, my friend, of this Moorish rabble if it were not that I am afraid I would not finish in two weeks! And if I were to go into details, I would not get through in two months. Nevertheless, I am going to tell you a little, and this will give you a general idea of what I saw and observed in these people. Only by exception does one find among so many of them one who truly believes in the holy Christian faith. Their one ambition is to come by and hoard minted money, and to acquire it they work and do not eat. Once a coin whose value is more than a farthing falls into their hands, they condemn it to life imprisonment and eternal darkness, and in this way, always hoarding and never spending, they come to accumulate the greatest amount of money to be found in Spain. They are its strongbox, its vault, its guardians, its custodians; they gather it all in, they hide it, they swallow it up. Just think how many of them there are—and every day they earn and put by a little or much, and remember that a slow fever can finish one off as well as a stroke. And as they multiply, the hoarders steadily increase and will go on increasing to infinity, as experience has shown. They don't know the meaning of chastity, nor do they ever take religious vows, either the men or the women. They all marry, and they all multiply, because frugality increases the powers of generation. They are not destroyed by war nor occupations that wear them out; they rob us without risk, and with the fruits of our patrimony, which they sell back to us, they wax rich. They have no servants, for they are their own; they spend nothing on the education of their children, because their only science is how to rob us. Of the twelve sons of Jacob who I have heard said went into Egypt, when Moses brought them out of that captivity they numbered six hundred thousand men, not counting the children and women. From this it can be inferred how the women of these will multiply, who are incomparably more."

The grievances against the Moors were then both of an economic order ("they rob us without risk," "they wax rich") and a religious order ("only by exception does one find among so many of them one who truly believes in the holy Christian faith"). Let us say a few words about these latter.

In the words of the exterminating angel of the Moriscos, the blessed Juan de Ribera, archbishop of Valencia, who campaigned for their expulsion from 1569 to 1609, a Morisco was congenitally incapable of being a good Christian. This pessimism also flowed from other pens, for example, that of the Franciscan Pedro Arias: "This evil caste has as its trunk Ishmael, brother of Isaac the patriarch. Just as that Ishmael abhorred and persecuted Isaac, today the Moors abhor the Christians . . ."–from which Brother Arias concluded that "the persecution will be eternal and endless" (569).

In his long memoir, Bishop Salvatierra of Segorbe discussed some very curious considerations on this subject. He noted, among other things, that the dispersion of the Moriscos of Granada had only aggravated things, turning them from farmers into city people, making their surveillance more difficult; it is a fact that persecuted religions gain an advantage by hiding in the cities. But especially he perceived the principal root of the evil in the close relationship between the law of Mohammed and that of Moses:

"It is proved and concluded that this abominable Moorish people is blind and rebellious in its infidelity and in its malice as were and are the Jews, for the sect of Mohammed participates in and is similar to the Law of Moses insofar as circumcision is concerned. God allows them to persevere in their rebellion as disciples and adoptive sons of the synagogue and of the Law of Moses. . . . It should be believed that God punishes them, letting them live in this rebellion until the end of the world just like the Jews; we see how easily the idolaters of the Indies receive the law of Jesus Christ because they do not make use of circumcision, of the Law of Moses, or of other ceremonies."

And the bishop summarized the faults and crimes of the Moriscos as follows:

"They retain and keep the Law of Moses with incorrigible and abominable obstinacy, living and persevering in the law of Mohammed; they are spies of the Turk, disturbers of the public peace, assassins and bandits, practicing infinite usuries and illicit trade" (570).

Thus, for the bishop of Segorbe, as for the great majority of Spaniards of his time, the unfortunate Moriscos had ended by becoming a sort of successor to the Jews, from whom they had in fact inherited various functions in Spanish society. But the parallel should not be pushed too far. In particular, the Moriscos did not have the leisure nor the genius to acquire the imposing special dimension of Judaism, which consisted in endlessly searching for the meaning of defeat and persecution to the point of in a sense identifying with them and of thus accumulating a prodigious historical memory. There were no Moriscos who wrote their own history, and their tribulations would have been forgotten, just like those of so many other peoples who no longer exist, if numerous Spaniards had not become interested in them from the sixteenth to the twentieth century. What we know of them we owe first of all to their persecutors. It was the bishop of Segorbe, again, who tells us that old or young the Moriscos were all circumcised; when he questioned the fathers on this subject, they told him that the sons "had been born that way naturally." To the same measure as they clung to circumcision, they feared baptismal water and tried to spare their newborn children its effects. Archbishop Juan de Ribera tells us that in the villages for months at a time the Moriscos presented the same infant for several consecutive baptisms to spare the others the evil; if by any chance the priest was surprised at the size of the infant, he was told that "the child was very large when he was born" (571). Naïve ruses of this type also recall certain Judeo-marrano practices.

᷾ Like a percentage of the Jews of Spain, a percentage of the Moriscos became good Christians in the course of the sixteenth century and blended completely into the Spanish people. Perhaps this was even true for the majority. In fact, the most reliable estimates for 1492 show a million Moriscos, while for 1609–14, the years of the expulsion, these estimates show three hundred thousand. Where, then, did the others go in the space of a century? A certain percentage must have emigrated, but we must also bear in mind the high birth rate of the Moriscos, that "multiplication" which so disturbed the Old Christians.

Let us observe once again that we cannot believe everything the witnesses of the time say. The fevered eye of the Spaniard saw Moriscos everywhere, all the more because the comings and goings of these muleteers and these peddlers were very visible (another similarity with the case of the Jews). On the other hand, those who became completely assimilated were not visible for that very reason. This truism bears repeating, for the old historians do not mention it, and the modern ones, such as Braudel or Lapeyre, sometimes tend to follow their example.

Besides the completely hispanicized Moriscos, there were some who became fervent Christians without blending into the mass of the Spanish people; there were even some of them among the ranks of the expelled, as we shall see below. Let us add, finally, that there were some Spaniards, both clerics and lay people, who managed to free themselves from the prejudices of the times and to plead the unpopular cause of the Moriscos.

One thing is certain. Among the various grievances raised against the Moriscos there was one that was not unfounded: that they were trying to put an end to their oppression by furthering the designs of the enemies of Spain and putting themselves at their disposal. Even before Henry IV mounted the throne of France, certain of them had had dealings with the little king of Navarre. We have already mentioned their appeals for aid to the Turks. Others did not burden themselves with such vast projects and formed into bands of outlaws who lent strong support to the Barbary corsairs. The Moriscos, then, posed a real political problem, even if the extent of this problem was vastly exaggerated by permanently inflamed imaginations and chronic spy fever.

Under these conditions the decision to rid Spain of them was taken early; in the summer of 1582, it seems, a junta met in Madrid and decided in principle to expel them, beginning with those of Valencia (572). Again the opposition of the lords had to be surmounted and a favorable occasion found, when Spain would not be at war and the fleet would be available to protect the coasts if a rebellion should break out. This led to a delay of more than a quarter of a century during which an infinity of plans for the "solution of the Morisco question" saw light of day. These projects often emanated from high prelates and statesmen and are interesting on several scores: they demonstrate how, in the course of a century, Spanish mentality progressed along totalitarian lines, and they offer more than one similarity with the Hitlerian procedures and thought processes, all the while being encumbered by theological motives that are sometimes disconcerting to modern eyes.

Once the principle of a "definitive solution" had been accepted, the problem was how to make the Moriscos disappear. According to an opinion of the time, as it was reported by a lawyer for the Inquisition of Valladolid, what was necessary was simply to burn them all. None other than the cardinal of Toledo put this forward in 1582 as one of the possible solutions. "The second way which seems convenient to me," wrote Archbishop Ribera, "is that His Majesty order vast executions of justice against them, naming officials of the Holy Office to concern themselves only with them. From the way in which they persevere in their heresy, we know their guilt to be so notorious that they could all be executed [*relajados*] without any other proofs. . . ." Dr. Fidalgo, the former prior of the order of Calatrava, "a great theologian in the service of God," proposed to put them all, men, women, and children, without exception, on boats without oars, tiller, or sails and send them to Africa (573).

Dr. Gutierrez of Seville demanded that the men be castrated "as they do to the slaves in the Indies on the least provocation; I do not give this as opinion but as a recommendation." Bishop Salvatierra made the same suggestion, extending it to the women (574). We thus enter on the path of solutions of slow extermination, of "deferred genocide" in modern terms. The Toledan Gomez de Avila proposed "to send them to different parts of the world, the men to one part and the women to another, thanks to which the cursed descendants of Hagar would be definitively extinguished for lack of communication between them." Certain of these propositions, in the words of their authors, had only charitable motives. It is thus that the bishop Juan Bautista Perez ("a shining light of Spanish history and a great ornament of the church," wrote Menendez y Pelayo) spoke out against exiling the Moriscos to Barbary, where these avowed apostates would be forced to reconvert and would end by definitely losing their souls; he proposed instead to "send them to Guinea where the pagans live, or to the northern islands where they would have no occasion to be Moors." *Una ysla despoblada* was also one of the possible solutions envisaged by the cardinal of Granada (575).

They could also, in the opinion of Cardinal de Guerrava, a member of the Council of State, "be declared rebels, common enemies of God and of His Majesty, to be used in the galleys, the mines, and elsewhere," as far as the men were concerned (the women and children and the old people to be "distributed" throughout Spain). This was, he explained, doing an act of Christian charity, a pious work agreeable to God; one could not, in fact, *sin escrupulo grande,* expel them to Barbary where they would again deny the faith they had professed after their baptism (576).

Finally, let us cite the above-mentioned inquisitor of Valladolid, Don Gonzalez de Celorigo, whose more rationalist and more modern scheme was to "register" the Moriscos and scatter them among the Old Christians: "Let them live separated from each other and let us list them by dioceses to know how many of them there are in each diocese; let them be registered as baptized Christians who should live and die in our holy faith. Those who do not consent to this should be free to leave the kingdom and be obliged to do so. They should be forbidden the use of the Arabic language and should not teach it to their children, under pain of death. They should also be forbidden to be muleteers and all other types of trade, no matter how humble and low they may be" (577).

It is important to point out that there was a minority of

ecclesiastics who saved Christian honor by speaking out against such extremes. Father Sobrino of Valencia denied that all the Moors were notorious heretics, and putting his finger on the root of the evil, he described their frightful exploitation by those same lords "who love a Morisco better than ten Old Christians. . . . What a misfortune that the concern of such vile interests opposes the common good, for if the Moriscos would convert, this state and its land would know security." Bishop Figueroa recalled "the heroic and meritorious work of the kings of the past" and counseled "confirming and perfecting the New Christians in the Christian religion by means of indoctrination and moderate coercion without arming troops or spilling blood." Moreover, in the course of the thirty years during which the fate of the Moriscos remained in suspense, seminaries were created for them and various improvements made in their catechization (578).

It was doubtless in the circles of Moriscos who were thus Christianized and instructed that a curious project, destined to deflect the threats that hung over their heads, germinated—a project culminating in the celebrated affair of the *plomos* (lead plates) of Sacromonte. Between 1588 and 1597 some twenty lead boxes and lead plates were discovered near Granada containing purported relics, such as one of Saint Stephen's bones and the cloth with which the Holy Virgin had dried her tears, as well as writings of Saint John and Saint James. These writings prophesied that the Arabs would become the Chosen People, "the most beautiful of men elected by God to save His law to the end of time," and tried to define the person of Christ in a manner satisfactory both to the New Testament and the Koran. They also confirmed the Immaculate Conception and gave astonishing details about Saint James's apostleship in Spain, both vital themes for the Spanish clergy of the time. Unfortunately for the Morisco authors of the hoax, the glorification of the Arabs and of the Koran passed unnoticed and did not produce the desired results, which were to amend the teachings of the Spanish Church on this point and thus to achieve a sort of fusion, both national and religious, between Moriscos and Old Christians. This did not mean that the myths did not at first enjoy a triumphal period of acceptance. A committee of eighteen theologians met in Madrid and recognized their authenticity; artillery salvos, pilgrimages, and veneration followed; there was even a question of including them in the New Testament. Rome was more skeptical and in 1641 condemned them strongly as "human fictions fabricated to ruin the Catholic faith, containing errors condemned by the Church, vices of Mohammedanism, and traces of the Koran." However, until the end of the eighteenth century, numerous Spanish churchmen battled in favor of them (the polemics on the subject of the *plomos* did not end until 1777, when writings of this nature were put on the Index) (579).

Ceaselessly discussed in the councils of state, ceaselessly demanded by public opinion, the final solution of the Moorish question was finally decided in 1608, during the reign of Philip III, by the all-powerful minister Lerma. The international situation was favorable: Spain had signed a peace treaty with England and a truce with the Low Countries that made the fleet and the armies available; moreover, Turkey's hands were tied by a war with the Persians. The only thing left was to overcome the opposition of the Valencian lords; to compensate them, Lerma proposed the very simple expedient of distributing the property of the Moriscos to them, which, incidentally, also served his own interests as a large landowner in the kingdom of Valencia. Under these conditions, the great lords yielded without too much difficulty (580).

The operation was carefully prepared. There were numerous problems to solve. Because the Moriscos were expelled as heretics, what was to be done with their children, who could not be accused of anything, as they had not attained the age of reason, and whose souls it was important to save? Tearing them from their parents and keeping them in Spain was the only correct solution according to good theology, but what if the parents opposed this? When consulted on this point, the theologians of Archbishop Ribera wondered if the *best means was to let the children leave or to kill the fathers,* and answered that *without any doubt one has the right to kill the fathers and the mothers if they represent an obstacle to the right of the baptized children to be raised in the Christian religion.* But as the hour of expulsion approached, it became evident that a blood bath would hardly make things easier. Besides, in the case of the Moriscos of Valencia, who were the first to go, it was decided to consider the departure of the children as a lesser evil, and they were allowed to leave. The Moriscos of Castile, who were less dangerous because they lived scattered among the Old Christians, were treated differently: the children could leave only if they accepted deportation to Christian lands, Italy or France. Thus, morality was safe (581).

. The expulsion, that "boldest and most barbarous plan of all times," according to Cardinal Richelieu, lasted five years (1609–14). To deport the Moriscos of Valencia, great preparations were made in the autumn of 1609; the fleet and the armies were assembled, all in the utmost secrecy, to nip in the bud any attempt at rebellion and to keep Spanish prestige from becoming tarnished ("to see that their voices do not reach Constantinople and, moreover, to keep these people from staging an uprising in the Sierras of Spain," as the Council of State declared). In fact, most of the Moriscos were evacuated without difficulty, and only a few survivors took to the hills in November of 1609 when the first news of the deplorable fate of the deportees filtered back. The expulsion of the Moriscos of Aragon and Castile, on the other hand, became a simple police operation and did not cause any trouble. The majority of the Moriscos were evacuated by sea to Oran, the Spanish beachhead in North Africa, and from there dispersed through the main neighboring Moslem principalities. Some were shipwrecked en route and drowned; others were massacred by Arab bandits; almost all were robbed. Other convoys of Moriscos were routed over-land to France, where Henry IV had ordered that "they be received with humanity in his lands and states," the first example, it seems, of France's tradition of asylum. Some settled in the southwest of France, others continued their journey to the Moslem lands. On the whole, their fate was much better. According to the most recent and careful esti-mate, that of Henri Lapeyre, the total number of Moriscos expelled was 275,000, of whom nearly fifty thousand had the privilege of going to France (582).

᾽ If you disregard the special case of the young children, the general norms for the expulsion were those of totali-tarian racism: a Morisco was deported because of what he was, not because of what he did or thought. There was not even any exception for mixed marriages, and these couples were also deported. In Valencia, Archbishop Ribera showed himself to be inflexible. It was in vain that a priest begged for a postponement for his two brothers-in-law, impeccable Christians, he assured, one of whom had two sons, "one destined for the priesthood, the other of tender age, still far from knowing what a Moor is, as when he heard that word he asked his mother, with the innocence of a child: '*Que cosa era Moro y si eran hombres y de que color . . .* [What is a Moor? Are they men? What color are they?].'" It was in vain that Bishop Sobrino praised the virtue of Sister Maria Vicente, who years before the expulsion had left her hus-band and her parents for the love of Christ: "A woman of twenty-four, beautiful and wise, who came to the patriarch [Ribera] and has always since persevered in the exercises of the spiritual life, living in the seminary like a holy Pelagian. And another young lady of the same seminary . . . dressed in gold and silver by her parents whom she left for the love

of Jesus. These and others like them were put on the boats
. . . and God is distressed at being deprived of such brides"
(583).

There were even fewer exceptions in collective cases. In
Castile and in Andalusia there were compact groups of
Moriscos, especially of the *mudejar* line, who to all appearances had been living very Christian lives for generations.
But the list of *cristianos nuevos* of Moorish stock maintained
by the Inquisition served as the criterion, and informers did
the rest. In Granada the local governor pointed to the case of
"honorable men who live in terror that some enemy or other
might say that they are Moriscos." The authorities in Madrid
hesitated for some time about the Moriscos of the region of
Murcia, who numbered several thousand. In the beginning
of 1612 the king dispatched a special investigator there,
Brother Juan de Pereda. He stated that "no one dresses in
the Moorish style, the majority drink wine and eat pork.
Almost all the witnesses affirmed warmly that as far as
Christianity is concerned, these *mudejares* are very different
[from the other Moriscos], and those who speak of them
most warmly are their confessors. In all the positive acts of
Christianity they do as the Old Christians, without any distinction. . . ." The investigator then described the moving
prayers and processions of the Moriscos of Murcia, begging
God and man that they be spared exile: "Vigils in the
churches, processions day and night with a great array of
banners and penitential robes, young girls in white tunics,
barefooted, hair disheveled, faces veiled, carrying heavy
crosses. . . ." Nevertheless, in April, 1614, the Moriscos of
Murcia were also deported. It seems that the only large
group to be spared, thanks to the efficacious protection of
their bishop, was that of Tortosa, some four hundred families (584).

Operations of this type have their own internal logic and
through the ages give rise to the same incidents or the same
expedients. In the case of the Moriscos, there were last-

minute attempts to escape their fate by taking refuge in convents and by hastily contracting marriages with Old Christians in the vain hope of thus evading deportation. There were cargoes of humans wandering over the seas and being repulsed from all shores, unable to disembark anywhere, and in despair, clandestine returns and condemnations to the galleys. There were many such returns as, among other things, the famous episode of the Morisco Ricote in *Don Quixote* testifies. When such vagabonds protested their Christianity, they were told to go and profess it in Italy or in France (585). A special note on the case of the Moriscos is furnished by the dilemmas in which the theologians became embroiled, and we see Archbishop Ribera boldly advocating the most horrifying act there was in the eyes of Spanish theology, a second baptism of the children left in Spain, because it was impossible to know (see page 345) if the first baptism had actually taken place (586).

The expulsion gave rise to general rejoicing, and Spain cheerfully ignored the sufferings and devastations it had caused, the impoverishment of the country, and the disappearance of dozens of villages from the face of the earth. "There will be a great deal of inconvenience," wrote the secretary of the king on the eve of the expulsion, "but joyous poverty, because so many blasphemies will have come to an end, will be very great wealth." Numerous processions of thanksgiving took place, there were commemorative feasts, and great numbers of hymns and songs of praise were composed (587).

There is no better indication of the completely clear conscience of Spanish public opinion than the interest it displayed in the pious tales of the martyrdom of the Moriscos deported to Africa who refused to deny the Christian faith. The titles of these accounts are eloquent: "Genuine account of Moriscos who denied the Catholic faith in the city of Allarache, Barbary, and of the martyrdom of the five natives of Cordova who refused to deny it" (Saragossa, 1610); "Letter that Antonio Osana, a Morisco expelled from Spain, a native of Madrid, sent to a friend" (Seville, 1618); "Martyrdom that the Moors of Tetuán inflicted on Francesca Trijo, Moor, native of Avila, one of those who were driven out at the time of the general expulsion" (Madrid, 1623). The contents were no less eloquent: "They raised a scaffolding for her [Francesca Trijo]. The Christian amazon climbed the rungs with the patience of Job, the courage of Saint Stephen; she served as an example for many renegades who perhaps renounced only out of fear. . . . She told us [continued the narrator, a Christian captive who was later freed]: 'I ask if any of you passes through my city of Avila that you recall how I am dying confessing the Holy Catholic faith' " (588).

None of these authors gives any evidence of being surprised or sorry that such admirable Spaniards were driven out of their country. At the very most, such facts contributed to the Maurophile tendency in Spanish literature that started in this era. Even after the disappearance of the Inquisition this attitude persisted among the Catholic historians, who engaged in polemics with those of anticlerical Spain on the subject of the expulsion of the Moriscos. In the twentieth century, at most we see a Boronat, who judged the expulsion salutary and good, shed "a tear of compassion in memory of those [the deportees] who, being Christians, were innocent . . ."; he reserves his pity for the lords who were deprived of their serfs "whose example seemed to revive in the memorable era of the expulsion the chivalrous and sublime loyalty of the legendary heroes of our Middle Ages" (589).

Here again Cervantes is a mirror of his time. We have already mentioned the episode of the Morisco Ricote who secretly returned to Spain. In a little-known *novella*, *The Troubles of Persiles and Sigismunda* (the last French translation dates from 1738), the author of *Don Quixote* goes even further. He makes the Moriscos Jarife and Rafaela curse their own race: "I was born a Morisco," exclaims Jarife, "and would to God I could deny it, but I am not less a

good Christian because God accords His grace as He will."
He also betrays his brothers and begs the king to rid the
country of "my impious race which pollutes Spain by its
profanations and which heaps evil on it by its stealing and
rape . . . [and] to load the galleys with the useless weight
of our Hagarian breed." One might think this theme possessed a particular attraction for Cervantes. But in the
investigation of these tragically paradoxical situations, which,
one should not forget, reflect the brutal tensions of a Spain
that was prey to the demons of *limpieza de sangre* and
hidalgueria, we find he was surpassed by Lope de Vega. The
latter, in *La Desdicha por la honra* (Misfortune for Honor),
presents the proud Felisardo, a descendant of the Abencer-
rajes, who does not know his origin and who reaches high
positions in Catholic Spain. When Felisardo learns that he is
of Moorish stock, his honor as a Christian Spaniard impels
him to follow the Moriscos into exile, despite all the supplications of his friends and protectors, the demands of that
honor being boundless (590).

We still should say a few words about the fate of the
expelled Moriscos. In France, where Lake Mouriscot near
Biarritz perpetuates their memory, they were assimilated
very quickly. Paradoxically, like everything else in their history, in North Africa they retained many more Hispanic
vestiges. Even today, certain families in Tetuán and Tunis
know that they are descended from the Morisco line, and
some of them still retain the keys to their former homes in
Spain. In Tunisia they founded the Haumat al-Andalous
quarter in the capital, as well as the cities of Tébourba,
Testour, El Ariana, and Kalalat al-Andalous. These indefati-
gable workers planted orchards and gardens, built roads,
and created such industries as fez making. They relearned
Arabic and forgot Spanish, but their familiar parlance re-
tains a few words of Spanish origin, such as *corran* (corral),
barguil (orchard), and *olla* (stew pot). As late as the beginning of the twentieth century, plays by Lope de Vega were
given in Testour in a language the actors as well as the

public hardly understood. We see then that the last Moriscos continued to cultivate the memory of their ungrateful homeland, although their fidelity cannot be compared to that of the Spanish Jews. We have said enough about this in different parts of this work for the reader to understand why this is so (591).

NOTES

1 Before Islam

(1) Josephus Flavius, *Antiquitates Judaicae*, XI, 5, 2, p. 133.

(2) See Salo W. Baron's detailed note in *A Social and Religious History of the Jews*, 2nd ed., New York, 1952, Vol. 1, pp. 370–72.

(3) Josephus Flavius, *Antiquitates Judaicae*, XVIII, 9, 4, p. 339.

(4) Arthur Christensen, *L'Iran sous les Sassanides*, Paris, 1936, p. 115.

(5) Cf. I. Scheftelowicz, *Die altpersische Religion und das Judentum*, Giessen, 1920, as well as A. Marmorstein, "Iranische und jüdische Religion," in *Zeitschrift für die neutestamentische Wissenschaft*, Giessen, 1927, p. 231.

(6) S. Baron, *The Jewish Community*, Philadelphia, 1942, Vol. 1, p. 154.

(7) *Talmud, Kiddushin*, 71 a and 71 b; *Menahoth*, 85 b. Cf. A. Neubauer, *La Géographie du Talmud*, Paris, 1868, pp. 321–23.

(8) Excerpt from the *Tanhuma Midrashim*, section *Noah*. Cf. S. Dubnow, *Weltgeschichte des jüdischen Volkes*, Berlin, 1926, Vol. 3, p. 471.

(9) Cf. S. Baron, *A Social and Religious History of the Jews*, New York, 1952, Vol. 2, pp. 204–9 ("Babylonian Supremacy").

(10) "When the Berbers were in Palestine, they had as king Djalout, who was killed by Dawoud. They then emigrated toward the west, and went all the way to Loubia and Merakia. . . ." (Ibn Khaldun, *Histoire des Berbers*, Algiers, 1852, trans. by Slane, Vol. 3, p. 301.)

(11) Procopius, *De Bello Vandalico*, 2, 10. Cf. E. F. Gautier, *Le Passé de l'Afrique du Nord*, Paris, 1942, p. 141.

(12) Cf. M. Simon, "Judaïsme berbère en Afrique ancienne," *Revue d'Histoire et de Philosophie religieuses*, 1946–1947, p. 20; S. Gsell, *Histoire ancienne de l'Afrique du Nord*, Paris, 1913, Vol. 4, p. 179.

(13) S. Gsell, *op. cit.*

(14) Monceaux, "Les Colonies juives dans l'Afrique romaine," *Revue des Études Juives* [cited below as R.E.J.], 1902, Vol. 44, p. 6.

(15) H. Lietzmann, *Histoire de l'Église ancienne*, Paris, 1937, Vol. 2, p. 21.

(16) Cf. A. Neubauer, *Géographie du Talmud*, Paris, 1868, pp. 372, 402.

(17) In particular this is the thesis developed by G. Rosen (*Juden und Phönizier*, Tübingen, 1929). According to M. Simon (*op. cit*, p. 27) it has been received quite favorably by historians.

(18) See, for example, A. Beaunier, "Premier Établissement des Israélites à Tombouctou" in *Bulletin de la Société de Géographie*, Paris, April–May, 1870; M. Delafosse, *Les Noires de l'Afrique*, Paris, 1922, p. 35. The linguistic arguments have been developed at length by J. J. Williams, *Hebrewisms of West Africa*, New York, 1930.

(19) *Histoire de l'Afrique et de l'Espagne intitulée Al-Bayano 'l-Mogrib*, Algiers, 1901, trans. by E. Fagnan, p. 25.

(20) G. Vajda, *Introduction à la pensée juive du moyen âge*, Paris, 1947, p. 66.

(21) N. Slouschz, *Judéo-Hellènes et Judéo-Berbères*, Paris, 1909, p. 251.

(22) Lieutenant Colonel de Lartigue, *Monographie de l'Aurès*, Constantinople, 1904, p. 328.

(23) *Ibid.*, p. 315.

(24) G.-H. Bosquet, *Les Berbères* (Collection "Que sais-je?"), Paris, 1957, p. 39.

(25) I have taken this construction from an article by D. V. de L. Milosz, "Les Origines Ibériques du peuple juif," *Nouvelles littéraires*, July 9 and August 10, 1932.

(26) F.-M. Marina, "Discurso historico-critico sobre la primera venida de los judios a España," in *Memorias de la Real Academia de la Historia*, Madrid, 1799, III, 317–469.

(27) Montesquieu, *L'Esprit des lois*, XXVIII, 1.

(28) *Monumenta Germaniae Historia* [hereafter referred to as *M.G.H.*], "Leges Visigothorum," XII, 3, 20. Also see S. Katz, *The Jews in the Visigothic and Frankish Kingdoms of Spain and Gaul*, Cambridge (Mass.), 1937, pp. 58 ff.

(29) See the discussion of this question in the work by Katz cited above, pp. 112 ff.

2 The Prophet

(30) Cf. the arguments advanced by R. Blachère (*Le Problème de Mahomet*, Paris, 1952, p. 32) as well as von Grunebaum (*Medieval Islam*, Chicago, 1946, p. 98, note 88).

(31) On this subject see thesis by P. Casanova (*Mohammed et la fin du monde*, Paris, 1911): Mohammed did not think that he would die and leave successors; he believed that the end of the world was at hand, and that he would be there. This belief in the proximity of the end of the world is clearly Christian, and Mohammed claimed that he was the last prophet announced by Jesus Christ, to complete and perfect his doctrine. This was that of the first Moslems as well as Mohammed himself . . ." (p. 12). Still (p. 4): ". . . Mohammed's real doctrine has been falsified, or at least disguised with the greatest of care. Simple reasons have led Abu Bekr first, and then Othman later, to reshape the sacred text from beginning to end. . . ."

(32) On this point, R. Blachère's peremptory statement ("The Jewish communities . . . remained active and influential; they gave the impression of practicing their religion strictly, but did not make any converts," *op. cit.*, p. 25) is not supported by any argument. See Marcel Simon in *Verus Israël*, Paris, 1948, p. 354 for the opposite argument, and especially the long discussion of Jewish proselytism in Arabia by Charles C. Torrey (*The Jewish Foundation of Islam*, New York, 1933, Chapter 1, "The Jews in Arabia").

(33) To what point were the anti-Jewish themes in the Koran influenced by the classical Christian concepts? On this subject, as on so many others, the opinions of the Orientalists diverge radically. Thus, Sir A. K. Gibb writes: "From attempts at persuasion, the Koran turns to denunciation and threats, in all (strangely enough) reproducing many themes of the old anti-Jewish polemic of the early Christian writers." (*Mohammedanism, an Historical Survey*, New York, 1955, p. 42.) On the other hand, C. Torrey writes: "Of the polemical thesis [against the Jews, for example] characteristic of that religion [Christianity] even in its crudest forms he [Mohammed] has not an inkling" (*op. cit.*, p. 61).

(34) On this point the specialists are reaching a consensus. Cf. for example, Grimme, *Mohammed*, I, p. 123; Caetani, *Studi di Storia orientale*, III, 236, 257; Blachère, *Le Problème de Mahomet*, pp. 86, 118, etc.

(35) E. Renan, *Essai de morale et de critique*, Paris, 1929, p. 58.

3 The Caliphs

(36) Cf. for example the study by G.-H. Bousquet, "Observations sur la nature et les causes de la conquête arabe," *Studia islamica*, 1956, Vol. 6, pp. 37–53.

(37) "De Haeresibus Liber," Migne, *Patrologie grecque*, Vol. 94, p. 763.

(38) *Inferno*, XXVIII, 31–6.

(39) Cf. A. d'Ancona, "La leggende di Maometto in Occidente," *Giornale storico de la litteratura italiana*, Turin, 1889, Vol. 13, p. 250.

(40) Cf. de Goeje, *Mémoire sur la conquête de la Syrie*, Leyden, 1900, p. 124.

(41) *Kitab Futuh Al-Buldan of Al-Balhaduri*, trans. by P. Hitti, New York, 1916, p. 188.

(42) Cf. *The Origins of Islam in its Christian Environment*, by R. Bell, London, 1926, p. 173 (according to the *Kitab Futuh Al-Buldan of Al-Balhaduri*).

(43) Cf. de Goeje, *op. cit.*, p. 152.

(44) "This story . . . is completely untrue," writes S. D. Goitein (*Jews and Arabs*, New York, 1955, p. 110).

(45) Cf. R. Blachère, *Le Problème de Mahomet*, pp. 30–31, note 1.

(46) Masudi, *Les Prairies d'or*, trans. by Barbier de Meynard, Vol. 1, p. 146.

(47) F. Macler, "Un document arménien sur l'assassinat de Mahomet par une Juive," *Mélanges Hartwig Derenbourg*, Paris, 1909, pp. 287 ff.

(48) "'Fetwa' relatif à la condition des 'dhimmis'," trans. by M. Belin, *Journal asiatique*, 1851, pp. 428–29.

(49) Cf. von Kremer, *Culturgeschichte des Orients*, Vienna, 1875, Vol. 1, p. 136.

(50) Cf. H. Lammens, "Le Khalife Walid et le partage de la mosquée des Omayades de Damas," *Études sur le siècle des Omayades*, Beirut, 1930, pp. 269–302.

(51) Lammens, "Un poet royal à la cour des Omayades," *op. cit.*, p. 235.

(52) According to de Goeje, *op. cit.*, p. 139.

(53) Mawerdi, *Les Statuts gouvernementaux*, trans. by E. Fagnan, Algiers, 1915, p. 298.

(54) Cf. "Apology of Al-Kindy," William Muir ed., *Journal of the Royal Asiatic Society*, Vol. 14, 1882, p. xii.

(55) S. D. Goitein, *Jews and Arabs*, pp. 98 ff.

(56) Yakubi, *Les Pays*, trans. by Gaston Wiet, Cairo, 1937, p. 1.

(57) Cf. I. Goldziher, *Vorlesungen über den Islam*, Heidelberg, 1925, pp. 36 ff.

(58) Subki, *Tabaqat al Chafi'iyya*, I, 268 (quoted by Goldziher, *op. cit.*).

(59) Cf. I. Goldziher, "Abu'l-Ala als Freidenker," *Z.D.M.G.*, 1875, Vol. 29, p. 640.

(60) Quoted by Adam Mez, *Renaissance of Islam*, London, 1937, p. 340.

(61) Ibn Qutaiba (d. 889), *Ta'wil Muhalataf Al-Hadith*, Cairo, 1925, p. 71.

(62) *Kitab Al-Hayawan* by Al-Jahiz. Cf. J.-M. Abd-el-Jalil, *Brève Histoire de la littérature arabe*, Paris, 1943, p. 278.

(63) A. Mez, *op. cit.*, p. 161.

(64) Goldziher, "Renseignements de source musulmane sur la dignité de Resch-Galuta," *R.E.J.*, 1884, Vol. 8, p. 124.

(65) Cf. "Apology of Al-Kindy," cited above.

(66) Cf. especially A. Mez, *op. cit.*, Chap. 4, "Christians and Jews."

(67) Quoted by L. Massignon, *Essai sur les origines du lexique technique de la mystique musulmane*, Paris, 1923, p. 54.

4   Islam and the Infidels

(68) Cf. A. S. Tritton, *The Caliphs and Their Non-Muslim Subjects*, Oxford, 1930, p. 136.

(69) *Response to the Christians* by Jahiz. Cf. J. Finkel, "A Risala of al-Jahiz," *Journal of the American Oriental Society*, 1927, Vol. 47, pp. 311–34.

(70) Alvaro de Cordova, *Indiculus Luminosus,* Migne, *Patrologie latine,* Vol. 121, pp. 554–55.

(71) Quoted in A. Mez, *Renaissance of Islam,* p. 33, note 1.

(72) Numerous examples are cited in the above work by Mez.

(73) Al-Moqadassi, *Descriptio imperii Moslemici,* de Goeje ed., Leyden, 1906, p. 183.

(74) Unpublished manuscript by Abu'l Mehasin (fifteenth century?) quoted by E. Fagnan, "Arabo-Judaica," *Mélanges Hartwig Derenbourg,* Paris, 1909, p. 116.

(75) " 'Fetwa' relatif à la condition des 'dhimmis'," trans. by M. Belin, *Journal asiatique,* 1851, p. 458.

(76) Manuscript by Abu'l Mehasin cited above, p. 117.

(77) *The Book of Religion and Empire,* by Ali Tabari, Mingana ed., Manchester, 1922.

(78) *Jesus in the Holy Quran* (reply to Dr. Zwemer, F.R.G.S.), by M. Din Chowdhury, B. A. s. l. n. d.

(79) Cf. A. S. Tritton, *op. cit.,* pp. 134 ff. and S. D. Goitein, *Jews and Arabs,* pp. 98 ff. as well as the article "Monophysistes," *Dictionnaire de Théologie catholique,* Vol. 10, p. 2,251.

(80) *The Chronography of Bar Hebraeus,* Budge ed., 1932, p. 475.

(81) *Chronicon anonymum pseudo-Dionysiam . . . ,* Chabot ed., Vol. 2, p. 147.

(82) Cf. *La Berbérie orientale sous les Hafsides,* by R. Brunschvig, Paris, 1940, p. 430.

(83) "The government of the Mameluks gave the coup de grace to Christianity in Egypt," writes M. G. Wiet (article "Kibt," in *Encyclopédie de l'Islam,* Vol. 2, p. 1,054). Great persecutions took place in 1279, 1283, 1301, 1321, 1354, 1419, 1422. See also Richard Gottheil, "Dhimmis and Moslems in Egypt," *Studies . . . in Memory of W. R. Harper,* New York, p. 367.

(84) Cf. the article "Église nestorienne," by Cardinal Tisserant in the *Dictionnaire de Théologie catholique,* Vol. 11, p. 187.

(85) J. Weulersse, *Paysans de Syrie et du Proche-Orient,* Paris, 1946, p. 89.

(86) Cf. L. E. Browne, B. D., *The Eclipse of Christianity in Asia,* Cambridge, 1933.

(87) Cf. the above-mentioned article by Cardinal Tisserant in the *Dictionnaire de Théologie catholique.*

(88) Cf. my study "Le Vizir Saad-ad-Daula, in *Évidences,* Paris, March, 1956.

(89) On this subject see the classic work (which is already more than a century old) of H. Geiger (*Was hat Mohammed aus dem Judentum entnommen*). See also D. Siderski, *Les Origines de legendes musulmanes,* Paris, 1933.

(90) Cf. the thesis by I. Wolfensohn, *Kaab al-Ahbar und seine Stellung im Hadit und in der islamischen Legendenliteratur,* Frankfurt, 1933.

(91) Cf. M. Steinschneider, "Polemische und apologetische Litteratur . . . zwischen Muslimen, Christen und Juden," *Abhandlungen für die Kunde des Morgenlandes*, Leipzig, 1877, p. 259.

(92) See the study of this apocalypse by M. Graetz in his *Geschichte der Juden*, Vol. 5, Appendix, note 16 [English: *History of the Jews*, Vol. 3, pp. 88–9].

(93) Quoted in S. Dubnow, *Weltgeschichte des jüdischen Volkes*, Berlin, 1926, Vol. 3, p. 451.

(94) *The Itinerary of Benjamin of Tudela*, trans. by Marcus Nathan Adler, New York, p. 40.

(95) *Ibid.*, pp. 44–5.

(96) S. D. Goitein, "Congregation versus Community . . ." *Jewish Quarterly Review*, January, 1954, Vol. 44, p. 304.

(97) B. Lewis, "La Légende sur l'origine juive des Califes fatimides" [in Hebrew], *Melilah*, Manchester, 1950, III–IV, p. 185.

(98) S. Dubnow, *op. cit.*, Vol. 3, p. 532.

(99) *Ibid.*, p. 533.

(100) Cf. G. Vajda, *Introduction à la pensée juive du moyen âge*, p. 42.

(101) Cf. M. Steinschneider, "An Introduction to the Arabic Literature," *J.Q.R.*, Vol. 13, p. 308.

(102) Cf. L. M. Simmons, "The letter of consolation of Maimum ben Joseph," *J.Q.R.*, 1889–1890, Vol. 2, p. 65.

(103) *Commentaire à Ibn Tofeil*, 1349, f° 130 b. Cf. M. Steinschneider, "Polemische und apologetische Litteratur in arabischer Sprache," *Abhandlungen für die Kunde des Morgenlandes*, 1877, Vol. 6, p. 366.

(104) Cf. G. Vajda, "Un chapitre de l'histoire du conflit entre la Kabbale et la philosophie," *Archives d'histoire doctrinale et littéraire du moyen âge*, Paris, 1956, p. 135.

(105) Al-Scheybani, in his *Droit de guerre musulman*. Quoted by I. Goldziher, "Usages juifs d'après la littérature des Musulmans," *R.E.J.*, 1894, Vol. 28, p. 91.

(106) Cf. S. D. Goitein, *Jews and Arabs*, p. 97.

(107) The following is based on the study by W. Fischel, "Joseph b. Phineas and Aaron b. Amram" in *Jews in the Economic and Political Life of Medieval Islam*, London, 1957, as well as on the article by L. Massignon, "L'Influence de l'Islam au moyen âge sur la fondation et l'essor des banques juives" (in *Bulletin des Études orientales*, 1931, Vol. 1). The Arab sources are the chronicles *Kitab al-Wuzara*, by Hilal as-Sabi, and *Nichdar al-Muhadara*, by At-Tanuhi.

(108) W. Fischel, *op. cit.* from the *Kitab al-Wuzara*, by Hilal as-Sabi, Leyden, 1904, pp. 306–7.

(109) Al-Miskawaih, *Kitab Tajarib al-Umam*, Oxford, 1920, quoted in W. Fischel, *op. cit.*, p. 32.

(110) The following is according to W. Fischel, *op. cit.*, pp. 68 ff., "The Banu Sahl of Tustar."

(111) All the following is principally based on the research of S. D. Goitein, notably *Jews and Arabs,* cited above.

(112) "The Cairo Geniza as a source for the history of Muslim civilization," by S. D. Goitein, *Studia islamica,* Paris, 1955, Vol. 3, p. 80.

(113) *Shebet Yehudah* of Ibn Verga, Sec. 43. Cf. M. Keyserling, "Une persécution des Juifs à Fez," *R.E.J.,* 1889, Vol. 39, p. 315.

(114) Ghazi ibn al-Waziti, "An answer to the 'dhimmis'," R. Gottheil ed., *Journal of the American Oriental Society,* 1921, Vol. 41, Part 4, p. 451.

(115) Fr. Gabrieli, *Storia e civilta musulmana,* Naples, 1947, p. 266; G. E. von Grunebaum, *Medieval Islam,* Chicago, 1946, p. 181.

(116) Cf. B. Heller, "Youscha al-akbar et les Juifs de Kheybar dans le roman d'Antar," *R.E.J.,* 1927, Vol. 84, pp. 113–35.

(117) A. S. Tritton, "Islam and the Protected Religions," *Journal of the Royal Asiatic Society,* April, 1931, p. 329.

(118) *Al-Mostatraf.* Collection of morsels chosen from here and there in all the branches of knowledge reputed to be attractive, by Ahmad al-Absihi, trans. by G. Rat, Paris, 1889.

(119) Abu Abd el-Rahman, cf. *Description de l'Afrique septentrionale d'El-Bekri,* trans. by Slane, Paris, 1859, p. 158; Abu'l-Ala el Ma'arri, cf. *Studies in Islamic Poetry,* R. A. Nicholson, Cambridge, 1921, p. 175; Ibn Hazm, cf. J. Goldziher, "Proben muhammedanischer Polemik gegen den Talmud," *Jeschurun,* Bamberg, 1873, Vol. 9, p. 44.

(120) Abu Yusuf Ya'kub, *Le Livre de l'impôt foncier (Kitab al-Kharadj),* trans. by E. Fagnan, Paris, 1921, p. 194.

B O O K   T W O | Spain

5 Moslem Spain

(121) Cf. Sanchez-Albornoz, "L'Espagne et Islam," *Revue historique,* 1932, Vol. 169, p. 5.

(122) On Ziriyab and his influence, see E. Lévi-Provençal, *Histoire de l'Espagne musulmane,* Cairo, 1944, Vol. 1, pp. 188–90.

(123) *Vie du bienheureux Jean de Gorze,* by John, Abbot of St. Arnulphe (cf. Lévi-Provençal, *op. cit.,* p. 383).

(124) Lévi-Provençal, *La Civilisation arabe en Espagne,* Paris, 1948, p. 114.

(125) Cf. R. Menendez-Pidal, *Origines del español*, Sec. 87–8.

(126) Cf. Lévi-Provençal, *op. cit.*, pp. 158–68.

(127) Salo W. Baron attributes this largely to the "fulminations of the churchmen against [the Jews]." See the discussion of the subject in his *Social and Religious History of the Jews*, Philadelphia, 1957, Vol. 3, p. 196.

(128) *Ibid.*, p. 148.

(129) According to Lévi-Provençal, *op. cit.*, pp. 324–32, this anecdote may be considered as authentic.

(130) *Judeum quendam cui nomen Hasdeu, quo nemimem unquam prudentiorem se vidisse aut audisse nostri testati sunt. . . .* (Cf. Lévi-Provençal, *Histoire de l'Espagne musulmane*, Paris, 1953, Vol. 3, p. 230.)

(131) According to the Arab chronicler Ibn Sa'id, Hasdai was able to make the Spanish Jews independent from Babylonia thanks to "the kind intervention" of the caliph, who helped him to obtain the work of the Babylonian Jews. (Cf. the text of Ibn Sa'id published by J. Finkel, *J.Q.R.*, 1927, Vol. 18, No. 1, p. 51.)

(132) The following is based principally on the two recent studies of Ibn Nagrela by J. Schirmann (*Jewish Social Studies*, 1951, Vol. 13, No. 2, pp. 99–128) and by S. M. Stern (in Hebrew, in *Zion*, 1950, Vol. 15, pp. 135–45).

(133) Cf. E. Garcia-Gomez, "Polemica religiosa entre Ibn Hazm e Ibn al-Nagrila," in *Al-Andalus*, 1936, Vol. 4, pp. 1–28.

(134) Dozy, *Histoire des Musulmans d'Espagne*, Leyden, 1932, Vol. 3, pp. 20–21.

(135) H. Pérès, *La Poésie musulmane en arabe classique au XIe siècle*, Paris, 1937, p. 268.

(136) S. Munk, *Notice sur Aboulwalid*, p. 105; in Graetz, Vol. 6, p. 59 [English: Graetz, Vol. 3, p. 279].

(137) Cf. S. Dubnow, *op. cit.*, Vol. 4, pp. 241–42.

(138) *Divan*, by Samuel Ha-Naguid, D. S. Sassoon ed., No. 403, Oxford, 1934.

(139) R. Dozy, in *Recherches sur l'histoire et la littérature de l'Espagne*, Leyden, 1860, Vol. 1, p. 299.

(140) Maimonides, *Responsa*, No. 134.

(141) S. D. Goitein, "The Cairo Geniza as a source for the history of Muslim civilization," *Studia Islamica*, 1957, Vol. 3, p. 77.

(142) Aronius, *Regesten*, Nos. 83, 103. On the conversion of Deacon Bodon, see my previous volume, *From the Time of Christ to the Court Jews*, p. 34.

(143) See the text of Ibn Sa'id quoted above, *J.Q.R.*, Vol. 18, No. 1, p. 48; see also Sa'id al-Andalousi, *Livre des catégories des nations*, R. Blachère ed., Paris, 1935.

(144) *"Unicus omnium philosophantium nobilissimus."* "I believe that Avicebron was Christian," wrote William of Auvergne, "because history

teaches us that in a fairly recent time the whole Arab Empire was subordinate to the Christian religion. . . ." Cf. J. Guttmann, "Guillaume d'Auvergne et la littérature juive," in *R.E.J.*, 1889, Vol. 36, p. 248.

(145) Cf. J. Millas Vallicrosa, *Selomo ibn Gabirol como poeta y filosofo*, Madrid, 1945, p. 88.

(146) Graetz, Vol. 6, p. 41, note 1.

(147) George Sarton, in his *Introduction to the History of Science* (Washington, 1931), dated the beginning of the period of European predominance in the history of exact thought with Abraham ibn Ezra.

(148) G. Vajda, *Introduction à la pensée juive du moyen âge*, p. 86.

(149) Cf. I. Goldziher, "Proben muhammedanischer Polemik gegen den Talmud," in Jeschurun, *Zeitschrift für die Wissenschaft des Judentums*, Breslau, 1871, Vol. 8, p. 78.

(150) The following is mainly from M. Diez Macho, *Mose ibn Esra como poeta y preceptista*, Madrid, 1953.

(151) Abraham ibn David, *Sefer ha-Kabbala*, Neubauer ed., p. 176.

(152) According to tradition, Judah Halevi was born in Toledo. The research of H. Schirmann has shown that he was born in Tudela, the confusion being due to the resemblance in the names and to the long periods the poet spent in Toledo.

(153) Cf. R. Menendez-Pidal, "Cantos Romanicos Andalusies," *Boletin de la R. Academia Española*, 1951, Vol. 31, pp. 187–270.

(154) "Contemporary thought, the whole pragmatic movement, may find its visions foreshadowed in Halevi's discussions. . . ." (H. Wolfsohn, "Maimonides and Halevi," *J.Q.R.* (N.S.), 1912, Vol. 2, pp. 297–327.)

(155) According to I. Baer, the great historian of Spanish Judaism, several passages of *The Kuzari* were borrowed from *The City of God*. (Cf. his *History of the Jews in Christian Spain*, Tel Aviv, 1945, pp. 53, 313, note 58.)

(156) See the remarks on this subject by H. J. Zimmels in his study *Ashkenazim and Sephardim*, London, 1958, in the chapter "Difference in Weltanschaung," pp. 233 ff.

(157) Cf. *Jewish Encyclopedia*, "Almohades," Vol. 1, p. 432.

(158) *Dabei war er wie ausdrücklich bezeugt wird, Vorsteher der jüdischen Gemeinde von Sevilla.* . . . (Graetz, Vol. 8, p. 98.) Millas Vallicrosa describes him as an *impenitente cantor de efebos, al gusto arabo*. (*Poesia sagrada hebraico-española*, p. 118, note 3.)

(159) A. Halkin, "L'Histoire des apostasies a l'époque des Almohades" [in Hebrew], in *Joshua Starr Memorial Volume*, Philadelphia, 1955, pp. 101–10.

(160) G. Levi della Vida, "Il regno di Granata nel 1465–1466 nei ricordi di un viaggiatore egiziano," *Al-Andalus*, 1933, Vol. 1, p. 309.

(161) I. Baer, *Die Juden im christlichen Spanien*, Vol. 2, No. 367.

6 La Reconquista

(162) The following descriptions on the status of the Jews in Christian Spain of the Middle Ages are in large part based on the research of Itzhak Baer, notably, the two collections of texts published by him (*Die Juden im christlichen Spanien*, Vol. 1, *Aragon*, Berlin, 1929; Vol. 2, *Castille*, Berlin, 1936) as well as his history (in Hebrew) of the Jews of Christian Spain (Tel Aviv, 1945). These works will be designated as follows: Baer, I, Baer, II, and Baer, *Toldot.* . . . Note: The Hebrew work *Toldot* . . . has been translated into English as *A History of the Jews in Christian Spain*, Philadelphia, 1961. Where I have been able to find the references, I have given them in brackets as [*History* . . . , Vol.–, p.–].

(163) J. Beraud-Villars, *Les Tourareg au pays du Cid*, Paris, 1946, p. 302.

(164) On the borrowings from the legend of Saint James in the legend of Mohammed, see the interesting reasoning, on this point as on so many others, of Americo Castro, *La Realidad historica de España*, Mexico, 1954, "La creencia en el apostol Santiago," pp. 136–62.

(165) Cf. the thorough study by C. Erdmann, "Der Kreuzzugsgedanke in Portugal," *Historische Zeitschrift*, 1930, pp. 25–53, as well as A. Waas, *Geschichte der Kreuzzüge*, Freiburg, 1956, pp. 106–8.

(166) Cf. Sanchez-Albornoz, in *España, un enigma historico*, Vol. 11, p. 43.

(167) A. Castro, *op. cit.*, p. 364.

(168) Baer, *Toldot* . . . , pp. 38, 40 [*History* . . . , Vol. 1, pp. 46 ff.].

(169) By King Ramon Berenguer IV; text of his charter in Baer, I, No. 28.

(170) See the detailed analysis of this charter by M. Vallecillo Avila, "Los judios de Castilla en la alta Edad Media," in *Cuadernos de historia de España*, 1950, Vol. 14, pp. 72–81.

(171) Cf. S. Baron, *A Social and Religious History of the Jews*, Vol. 3, p. 34.

(172) Cf. Baer, *Toldot* . . . , p. 56 [*History* . . . , Vol. 1, p. 64] as well as C. Dubler, *Über das Wirtschaftsleben auf der iberischen Halbinsel vom XI zum XIII Jahrhundert*, Geneva, 1943, pp. 10, 67, 83. For the later period, see *Toldot* . . . , p. 453.

(173) Cf. Sanchez-Albornoz, "L'Espagne et l'Islam," *Revue historique*, 1932, Vol. 169, p. 10.

(174) Legend mentioned in most of the works of medieval Jewish history. (Cf. S. Baron, *op. cit.*, p. 36.)

(175) Rabbi Eleazar bar Joel ha-Levi, quoted by Baer, *Toldot* . . . , p. 315, note 26.

(176) This is the opinion of I. Baer (cf. *Toldot* . . . , pp. 44–5).

(177) Baer, II, pp. 58–9.

(178) This anecdote was told by Rabbi H. Ehrenpreis, *Voyage d'un Juif en Espagne*, Paris, 1930, p. 29.

(179) Baer, II, No. 12. [Also *History* . . . , Vol. 1, p. 50.]

(180) *Ibid.*, No. 20. [Also *History* . . . , Vol. 1, p. 52.]

(181) See the remarkable unpublished thesis by Louis Schoffman, *Studies in the Relations between the Church and the Jews in Spain during the Reconquest*, Dropsie College, 1941, chapter on "Business Relations between the Church and the Jews," in which numerous examples are cited.

(182) M. Vallecillo Avila, *op. cit.*, p. 38.

(183) *Ibid.*, pp. 38, 42.

(184) Cf. the conciliar decisions cited in L. Schoffman's thesis, particularly the two councils of Gerona, 1068 and 1078.

(185) Baer, *Toldot* . . . , p. 38.

(186) Text in S. Dubnow, *op. cit.*, Vol. 4, p. 131.

(187) Baer, *Toldot* . . . , p. 64 [*History* . . . , Vol. 1, p. 51].

7 The Golden Age

(188) *Épître de Guillaume de Rubruquis à Louis IX, roi de France*, ed. of 1830, p. 329.

(189) *Enciclopedia Universal Ilustrada*, 1927, "Traje," Vol. 63, p. 628.

(190) Baer, *Toldot* . . . , p. 124, and L. Schoffman, *op. cit.*, section on "Dress of the Jews."

(191) . . . *los cristianos y los judios . . . andan vestidos los unos asi como los otros*, the code of *Las Siete Partidas* (see below) says with regard to the wearing of a distinctive badge. (Cf. Baer, II, p. 48.)

(192) Baer, II, p. 24.

(193) Article 4 of the Council of Valladolid of 1228, quoted by L. Schoffman in his thesis cited above.

(194) R. Menendez-Pidal, "Cantos Romanicos Andalusies," *Boletin de la R. Academia Española*, 1951, Vol. 31, pp. 187 ff.

(195) Chronicle of Alvar Garcia de Santa Maria, quoted by Vendrell de Millas, *Sefarad*, 1957, Vol. 17, No. 2, p. 383.

(196) Jewish ballad quoted by R. Menendez-Pidal: . . . *Y me salen a encontrar tres leyes a maravilla—los cristianos con sus cruces—los mores a la morisca—los judios con sus leyes.* . . . (*Poesia juglaresca y juglares*, Madrid, 1924, p. 410.)

(197) According to the *Cronica general*, Alfonso VI attributed the defeat of his army at Zalaca (1086) to the debilitating custom of baths and had them destroyed. (Cf. A. Castro, *op. cit.*, p. 117, note 5.)

(198) "Los banos publicos en los fueros municipales españoles," *Cuadernos de historia de España*, 1945, Vol. 3, pp. 15 ff.

(199) *Las Siete Partidas*, VII, 24, 8 (Baer, II, p. 47).

(200) Baer, II, pp. 114, 267, 330.

(201) See the *Responsa* of Isaac Barfat and Ascher ben Yechiel, quoted by L. Schoffman in his thesis, p. 163, note 4.

(202) *Las Siete Partidas,* VII, 24, 8 (Baer, II, p. 47). See also the decision of the Council of Zamora of 1313 (Baer, II, p. 120).

(203) The text of this synodal decision is quoted by L. Schoffman (in the Appendix).

(204) *. . . que judios . . . nin sean comadres nin compadres de los cristianos nin los cristianos e cristianas dellos. . . .* Article 4 of the statute of Valladolid of 1412 (Baer, II, p. 266).

(205) In 1344 the statement of the expenses of burial for Dona Mayor Ponce in the convent of the Carmelites of Toledo states: *"A las judias endicheras, 15 maravedis. . . ."* (Baer, II, p. 162.) In 1347 the municipal officials of Seville tried to prohibit this custom. (Baer, II, p. 160.)

(206) When the Inquisition tried to prosecute one of the listeners, he objected because, among other things, *"Bien saben vuestras mercedes que de solo oyr predicacion de rabi y en su synoga precisamente no se concluye heregia. . . ."* He was acquitted. (Baer, II, pp. 520, 524.)

(207) Decisions of the Council of Valladolid of 1322, Article 22 (quoted from L. Schoffman).

(208) Baer, I, p. 198, Sec. 13.

(209) Baer, II, p. 315 (from the *Urkundliche Beitrage,* by M. Stern, I, p. 48).

(210) A. Castro pointed to the prohibition by Henry IV of Castile of a similar procession in 1405 (*op. cit.,* p. 99, note 111).

(211) A. Castro, *op. cit.,* Appendix 3 ("Deismo en la Castilla del siglo XIV"), pp. 652–54.

(212) *Las Siete Partidas,* VII, 24, 1, 2, 4 (Baer, II, pp. 45–7). On the subject of the Jews' participation in the redaction of the codes, cf. Baer, II, p. 39.

(213) *El fuero real,* IV, 2, 1 (Baer, II, p. 40).

(214) *Libro de los fueros de Castilla* (Baer, II, pp. 34–9).

(215) Baer, I, p. 194.

(216) *Ibid.,* p. 646, Sec. 7.

(217) *Ibid.,* p. 152.

(218) Text quoted by L. Schoffman (Appendix).

(219) Cortes of Seville of 1252 (Baer, II, p. 49).

(220) A. A. Neuman, *The Jews in Spain,* Philadelphia, 1944, Vol. 2, pp. 191, 323, note 67.

(221) L. Schoffman (Appendix).

(222) *Las Siete Partidas,* VII, 24, 6.

(223) Baer, I, p. 2.

(224) Cf. A. Pacios Lopes, *La Disputa de Tortosa,* Madrid, 1957, in which (pp. 25 ff.) the author puts forward this exclusive role of the Jewish converts.

(225) A. A. Neuman, *op. cit.,* Vol. 2, p. 195.

(226) Baer, I, p. 204.

(227) *Ibid.,* p. 262. The letter is dated October 19, 1329.

(228) *Libro de los estados*, I, c. 93, in *Bibl. Aut. Esp.*, 151, pp. 337 ff. (Cf. Baer, *Toldot* . . . , pp. 84–5 [*History* . . . , Vol. 1, p. 121].)

(229) Cf. Baer, II, pp. 139–40. The great historian is referring to the research of Mercedes Gaibrois de Ballesteros, who published in the *Boletin de la Academia de Historia* in 1931 the testament of the infante Juan Manuel and who discovered *"in schönem Verständnis der Möglichkeiten mittelalterlicher Humanität,"* writes Baer, the sense of the allusive passage in *De las maneras del amor.*

(230) The role of the Jews of Alfonso X's entourage in the adoption and development of Castilian has recently been shown by A. Castro, *op. cit.*, pp. 451–68 ("Alfonso el Sabio y los judios").

(231) Quoted by A. Castro, *op. cit.*

(232) The above is in large part from the essay by R. Menendez-Pidal, "España y la introduccion de la ciencia arabe en Occidente," in *España, eslabon entre la cristianidad y Islam*, Madrid, 1956.

(233) Cf. the study by J.-C. Artau in *Homenaje a Millas Vallicrosa*, Barcelona, 1954, Vol. 1.

(234) J. Millas Vallicrosa, *El "Liber predicationis contra Judeos" de Ramón Lull*, Madrid, 1957, p. 21.

(235) Baer, *Toldot* . . . , p. 124 [*History* . . . , Vol. 1, p. 182].

(236) *Ibid.*, pp. 56–8. See also the documents published by him. The charter granted by Sancho II of Navarre in 1170 to the Jews of Tudela (Baer, I, p. 923) is a good example. [*History* . . . , Vol. 1, pp. 78 ff.]

(237) Cf. *Historia social y economica de España*, published in Barcelona in 1957 under the direction of J. Vicens Vives (Vol. 2). Cespedes del Castillo estimated the number of Jews in Spain at the end of the thirteenth century at more than 260,000 (pp. 45 ff., pp. 407 ff.).

(238) A. A. Neuman, *op. cit.*, Vol. 1, p. 187.

(239) Baer, *Toldot* . . . , pp. 137 ff. [*History* . . . , Vol. 1, pp. 189–212].

(240) In *España, un enigma historico*, Sanchez-Albornoz gives some names of these *tratadistas* of the eighteenth century. (Vol. 1, p. 669.)

(241) Baer, in *Toldot* . . . , pp. 122 ff. [*History* . . . , Vol. 1, pp. 178 ff.], dedicates an important section to the economic role of the Jews in Castile and Aragon in the thirteenth century.

(242) The finding was made by Baer, *Toldot* . . . , p. 133 [*History* . . . , Vol. 1, p. 196].

(243) A. Castro, *op. cit.*, p. 521.

(244) A. A. Neuman, *op. cit.*, Vol. 1, pp. 102 ff.; Baer, *Toldot* . . . , p. 66 [*History* . . . , Vol. 1, pp. 91 ff.].

(245) Cf. H. J. Zimmels, *Ashkenazim and Sephardim*, London, 1958, p. 157. The author of the treatise in question was the rabbi of Toledo Menachem ben Zerach (d. 1385); he had given it the expressive title *Zeda-la-Derech* ("Provisions for the Road" or "Snack"). See also Graetz, Vol. 8, pp. 30–2 [English: Graetz, Vol. 4, pp. 144–45].

(246) Baer, I, p. 9.

(247) H. J. Zimmels, *op. cit.*, p. 23.

(248) See the *excursus* of I. Baer, *Zum Urkundenwesen und Privatrecht der Juden in Spanien.* (Baer, I, Appendix 2, p. 1,052.)

(249) Letter of Moses Arragel to the grand master of the order of Calatrava, quoted by A. Castro, *op. cit.*, p. 466.

(250) The book *Shebet Yehudah*, by Solomon ibn Verga, trans. by Wiener, Hanover, 1856, p. 76.

(251) A slanderer had stated that an honorable family was descended from a slave. The celebrated Ibn Adret decided that this was worse than murder, "for a murderer only kills two or three souls, while this person has defamed thirty or forty souls, and the voice of the blood of the whole family cries from the earth. . . ." (End of the thirteenth century; cf. A. A. Neuman, *op. cit.*, Vol. 2, p. 7.)

(252) In this episode, the "knight of the forest," Don Silves, meets three furious duelists, a Christian, a Jew, and a Moor. (Cf. E. Hecht, "Duell eines Juden," *M.G.W.J.*, 1861, p. 275.)

(253) Cf. Fr. Diez, *Leben und Werke der Troubadours*, 1882. Bertrand de Born flourished 1180–95.

(254) Baer, I, p. 264.

(255) On Joseph Pichon of Seville, cf. Baer, II, 218–19; his assassination is described in all the classical works of Jewish history.

(256) Baer, *Toldot* . . . , pp. 161, 342, note 44 [*History* . . . , Vol. 1, pp. 239, 432, note 44].

(257) Baer, I, p. 711. In publishing the royal diploma authorizing Crescas to marry for a second time, this historian comments: "*Fälle von Bigamie bei den Juden in Spanien sind seit langem bekannt, und solche Ermächtigungen wie die obige sind . . . fast alltäglich und formelhaft.*"

(258) H. J. Zimmels, *op. cit.*, pp. 254–57.

(259) The censure of Yehiel ben Asher at the beginning of the fourteenth century echoes that of Moses de Coucy at the beginning of the thirteenth. (Cf. Zimmels, *op. cit.*, p. 255 and Neuman, *op. cit.*, Vol. 2, p. 11.)

(260) Quoted by Baer, *Toldot* . . . , pp. 160–61 [*History* . . . , Vol. 1, pp. 238–39].

(261) Graetz, Vol. 7, p. 254.

(262) Quoted by S. Dubnow, Vol. 5, p. 135.

(263) Quoted by Jacob Gordin in the article "Crescas," *Encyclopedia Judaica*, Vol. 5, p. 699.

(264) Baer, I, p. 763.

(265) Treatise "Ra'aya Mehemna" (later incorporated in the *Zohar*) quoted by Baer, *Toldot* . . . , p. 243 [*History* . . . , Vol. 1, p. 244].

(266) Baer, II, p. 545.

(267) As Sanchez-Albornoz says in listing the numerous high Spanish prelates killed on the battlefield. (*España, un enigma historico*, Vol. 1, pp. 321–22.)

(268) Sanchez-Albornoz, *op. cit.*, Vol. 1, p. 328.

(269) A. Castro, *op. cit.*, p. 488, where the term employed is *reconquista interior;* the term *subreconquista* is used in the first edition of the work (Buenos Aires, 1948, p. 527).

(270) Baer, I, pp. 755–56. The document in question is an appeal from the *aljama* of Saragossa to the other *aljamas* of Aragon asking them to participate in the expense. Baer thinks that it related to Petrus de Fonte Luporium, Grand Inquisitor of Aragon around 1405–12.

(271) L. Schoffman, thesis cited above, p. 30, and Baer, II, pp. 28, 54, 56, 103, 187, 220.

(272) Cf. L. Schoffman, thesis cited above, pp. 75–80.

(273) Baer, II, pp. 110–13.

(274) Cf. the unpublished thesis by Seymour Resnick, *The Jew as Portrayed in Early Spanish Literature,* New York, 1951, pp. 1–29.

(275) Baer, II, p. 45.

(276) *Ibid.,* p. 115, No. 125 ("Fuero de Sepulveda").

8 The Decline

(277) Cf. J. Millas Vallicrosa and L. Battle-Prats, "Un alboroto contre calle de Gerona en el ano 1331," in *Sefarad,* 1952, Vol. 2, pp. 297–336.

(278) Baer, II, Nos. 113, 138, 142, 145.

(279) *Histoire de messire Bertrand du Guesclin . . . nouvellement mise en lumière par Mᵉ. Claude Mesnard,* Paris, 1618, p. 155.

(280) Baer, II, pp. 196–98.

(281) *Ibid.,* p. 198, note.

(282) *Ibid.,* No. 217.

(283) Seymour Resnick, thesis cited above, p. 201.

(284) Cf. H. Graetz's opinions on Shemtob Ardutiel, alias Santos or Santob de Carrion: Vol. 7, pp. 345, 408–10. [English: Vol. 4, pp. 87, 114–15.] A. Castro calls Santob de Carrion "the great entry way of Spanish lyricism."

(285) Baer, II, No. 227.

(286) *Ibid.,* No. 243.

(287) *Shebet Yehudah,* by Solomon ibn Verga, trans. by Wiener, pp. 30–1. On this subject A. A. Neuman observes: "That the views expressed through the symbolic characters are fundamentally Ibn Verga's own views is clearly demonstrated in the latter part of the work when, dropping literary artifices, the author gives openly vent to his feelings. . . ." (A. A. Neuman, *Landmarks and Goals,* Philadelphia, 1953, p. 100.)

(288) On Abner of Burgos (Alfonso Burgensis) cf. Baer, *Toldot . . . ,* pp. 213 ff. [*History . . .* Vol. 1, pp. 327 ff.].

(289) Baer, II, No. 209 ("Aufzeichnungen des Samuel Carça über die Leiden der Juden während des Kastlischen Bürgerkrieges").

(290) *Ibid.*, No. 228.

(291) Quoted by S. Dubnow, Vol. 5, p. 248.

(292) On the importance of Seville, see *Historia economica y social de España* . . . , Vives, Vol. 2, p. 293. On the privileged situation of the Jews of Seville, see Baer, *Toldot* . . . , pp. 202–3 [*History* . . . , Vol. 1, pp. 311 ff.].

(293) On the Archdeacon Martínez and his agitation, see the documents published by Baer, II, pp. 202 ff., from which the above quotations were excerpted.

(294) In describing the spread of the disturbances, I have used, in addition to the documents published by Baer, the original descriptions of Hasdai Crescas and Chancellor Lopez de Ayala. As far as Aragon is concerned, the dossier put together by Baer (I, documents 407 to 450) is remarkably rich and eloquent.

(295) Baer, I, Nos. 417 and 432; also [*History* . . . , Vol. 2, p. 108].

(296) Baer, *Toldot* . . . , p. 366 [*History* . . . , Vol. 2, p. 97].

(297) *Ibid.*, p. 373 [*History* . . . , Vol. 2, p. 109].

(298) *Ibid.*, p. 374 [*History* . . . , Vol. 2, p. 110].

(299) Sanchez-Albornoz, *España, un enigma historico*, Vol. 2, p. 240.

(300) Baer, I, No. 415.

(301) Cf. Graetz, Vol. 7, pp. 90–2 [English: Graetz, Vol. 4, 186–87]; see also [*History* . . . , Vol. 2, p. 143].

(302) There is no treatise of Jewish history which does not accord a place to Solomon Halevi of Burgos as the prototype of the renegade; only I. Baer has given a more subtle interpretation. (Cf. *Toldot* . . . , pp. 391–96.) According to the Spanish historians his life was exemplary and his conversion miraculous. See in particular Cantera Burgos, *La Conversion del celebre talmudista Salomon Levi*, Santander, 1933, and L. Serrano O.S.B., *Los Conversos D. Pablo de Santa Maria y D. Alfonso de Cartagena*, Madrid, 1942.

(303) Cf. Fr. Cantera Burgos, *Alvar Garcia de Santa Maria*, Madrid, 1952, p. 280.

(304) Around 1465 Baron Leon de Rosmithal, who went to stand before the grave of Paulus de Sancta Maria, related that he had died in the odor of sanctity among the Spaniards and that his family descended from the family of the Mother of God. (Cf. "Viaje del noble bohemio Leon de Rosmithal," *Viajes por españa*, Fabie ed., Madrid, 1879, p. 55.)

(305) Cf. the work cited above by Professor Cantera Burgos, who attempted to trace the family tree of the Santa Maria family. According to Professor Sobregues Vidal, the Santa Marías were the same type as the great Castilian capitalists. (*Historia social y economica de España*, Barcelona, 1957, Vol. 2, p. 190.)

(306) According to the chronicler Garibay, "the great prelate Don Pablo de Santa Maria advised King Henry, with good reason, not to admit any Jew or any *converso* into the service of his royal household or into his council, or into the administration of the royal treasury."

(Quoted by Graetz, Vol. 8, p. 89 [English: referred to but not quoted in Graetz, Vol. 4, p. 185].)

(307) Baer, II, No. 254. Doubtless, the king had in mind the obligatory sermons that the *conversos* forced their former coreligionists to attend and that gave rise to new excesses.

(308) Baer, *Toldot* . . . , p. 373 [*History* . . . , Vol. 2, p. 109].

(309) H.-S. de Sopranis, "Contribucion a la historia ᴜᴄ la juderia de Jerez de la Frontera," in *Sefarad,* 1951, Vol. 11, No. 2, pp. 349 ff.

(310) Fr. Pedro Sanahuja, *Lerida en sus luchas por la fe (Judios, moros, conversos),* Lerida, 1946.

(311) Cf. E. Lambert, "Les Synagogues de Tolède," in *R.E.J.* 1927, Vol. 74, pp. 74 ff.

(312) Baer, II, No. 251.

(313) *Ibid.,* No. 258.

(314) Baer, I, p. 711.

(315) Cf. "Reflexions sur quelques doctrines de Spinoza et de Hasdaï Crescas," by A. Goldenson, *Mélanges de philosophie et de littérature juives,* Paris, 1957, pp. 95–152.

(316) Cf. the résumé of a sermon by Saint Vincent Ferrer in Valencia which J. Millas Vallicrosa gives. (*En torno a la predicacion judaica de San Vicente Ferrer,* Madrid, 1958.)

(317) Baer, I, p. 814.

(318) Cf. Fr. Vendrell de Millas, "La actividad proselita de San Vicente Ferrer," in *Sefarad,* 1953, Vol. 13, No. 1, p. 94.

(319) Baer, II, No. 275. (In a note, the great scholar demonstrates the determining role of Saint Vincent Ferrer in the publication of the statute of Valladolid.)

(320) Cf. A. Pacios Lopez, *La Disputa de Tortosa,* Madrid, 1957, Vol. 1, p. 48, note 28.

(321) A. Pacios Lopez, *op. cit.,* Vol. 1, p. 46.

(322) Seventy-fourth session of July 7, 1414. Cf. Pacios Lopez, *op. cit.,* Vol. 2, *Actas,* p. 567.

(323) This, in Fagès, *Histoire de saint Vincent Ferrer,* Paris, 1901, p. 44: "The fourteen rabbis abjured, except for Master Ferrer and Master Albo. . . . in the end, the force of truth was right for the largest number."

(324) Baer, II, No. 282.

(325) Ibn Verga, *Shebet Yehudah,* Sec. 49.

9 The Impasse—Marranism

(326) *Historia social y economica de España,* cited above, Vol. 2, p. 412.

(327) In 1430 in Castile "the Jews controlled about two-thirds of the indirect taxes and customs within the country. . . ." On the other hand, in general, "the Jews had no part in the administration of the

currency or of direct taxes or the judiciary, fields in which the *conversos* prevailed." (Cf. Baer, *Toldot* . . ., pp. 454–55) [*History* . . ., Vol. 2, pp. 250–51].)

(328) Cf. Baer, *Toldot* . . ., p. 459, quoting the preacher R. Isaac Arama [*History* . . ., Vol. 2, p. 359].

(329) Nicolas V to the Bishop of Tarragona, September 20, 1453. (Cf. M. Stern, *Urkundliche Beiträge über die Stellung der Päpste zu den Juden*, Kiel, 1893, No. 56, p. 63.)

(330) Baer, II, No. 392, pp. 437–44.

(331) *Ibid.*, No. 407, p. 480.

(332) Cf. N. Lopez Martinez, *Los judaizantes castellanos y la Inquisicion en tiempo de Isabel la Catolica*, Burgos, 1954, p. 118, and Baer, II, Nos. 405 and 407.

(333) Cf. Baer, II, No. 399 (trial of the *converso* Juan de Pineda, who had represented the order of Santiago at the papal court).

(334) Baer, II, No. 397, p. 463.

(335) Cf. Mario Esposito, "Una manifestazione d'incredulita religiosa nel medioevo" in *Archivo Storico Italiano*, 1931, Vol. 89, p. 44 ("Diego Gomez e la setta di Medina del Campo").

(336) Fernan Perez de Guzman, *Generaciones y semblanzas*, Buenos Aires, 1947, p. 59.

(337) Cf. Baer, II, No. 116, referring to *Cronicas generales de España*, R. Menendez-Pidal ed., 1918, p. 159.

(338) De Palencia, *Cronica de Enrique IV*, Paz ed., Vol. 3, p. 123.

(339) Cf. Resnick, thesis cited above.

(340) S. Mitrani-Samaran, "Le Sac de Cordoue et le testament d'Antonio Montoro," *R.E.J.*, 1907, Vol. 54, p. 236. See also [*History* . . ., Vol. 2, p. 311].

(341) S. Mitrani-Samaran, "Le Débat entre Anton de Moros et Gonzalo Dávila," *R.E.J.*, 1906, Vol. 52, p. 151.

(342) M. Kayserling, "Un chansonnier marrane, Antoine de Montoro," in *R.E.J.*, 1901, Vol. 43, p. 263.

(343) S. Resnick, thesis cited above, p. 139 ("*Coplas del conde de Paredes a Juan Poeta en una perdonança de Valencia*").

(344) N. Lopez Martinez, *Los judaizantes castellanos y la Inquisicion*, Burgos, 1954, p. 57.

(345) Bernáldez, "Historia de los Reyes Catolicos," *Bibl. Aut. Esp.*, Vol. 70, p. 599.

(346) Cf. the lecture by S. de Madariaga published under the title *Spain and the Jews*, London, 1946: "Bernaldez, a simple, kindly though anti-Jewish priest, accuses the Jews, among other horrible crimes, of cooking their meat in oil, but considering that today, four and one half centuries after the expulsion, the whole of Spain does so, it would appear that at least in cooking—no negligible index—Spain is gone Jewish."

(347) Baer, *Toldot* . . ., p. 477 [*History* . . ., Vol. 2, pp. 288–89].

(348) Baer, II, No. 410, p. 500 (memoir of the "fiscal procurer" Petrus Perez).

(349) *Ibid.*, No. 302, p. 317.

10 The Inquisition

(350) Machiavelli, *The Prince and the Discourses*, New York, Modern Library, 1940–50, pp. 81–2. On the subject of Ferdinand of Aragon's Jewish descent on his mother's side, see A. Castro, *op. cit.*, p. 586.

(351) Ep. XCIII, No. 10. (Cf. E. Vacandard, *L'Inquisition*, Paris, 1907, p. 19.)

(352) J. de Maistre, *Lettres à un gentilhomme russe sur l'Inquisition espagnole*, Lyons, 1837, p. 38.

(353) Ludwig Pastor, *Geschichte der Päpste*, Freiburg, 1925, Vol. 2, p. 624.

(354) Lucien Wolf, *Jews in the Canary Islands*, London, 1906, p. 108. The examples above are also taken from this collection of documents regarding the Inquisition in the Canary Islands.

(355) S. Dubnow, Vol. 5, p. 39.

(356) Ibn Verga, *Shebet Yehudah*, Sec. 64.

(357) *Ibid.*, Sec. 62.

(358) Bernáldez, *Histoire des Rois Catholiques*, Chap. 44.

(359) From S. Dubnow, Vol. 5, p. 392, note 1.

(360) Baer, *Toldot . . .*, p. 499 [*History . . .*, Vol. 2, p. 327]. A. Dominguez Ortiz quotes a document from 1515 that mentions six thousand "reconciled" prisoners and six hundred burned. (*La Clase social de "los conversos" en Castilla*, Madrid, 1957, p. 62.)

(361) H. C. Lea, "Brianda de Bardaxi," in *Chapters from the Religious History of Spain*, Philadelphia, 1890, pp. 469–79.

(362) Baer, *Toldot . . .*, pp. 509–10 [*History . . .*, Vol. 2, p. 343].

(363) Baer, II, pp. 449–67. (Cf. the Llorente collection in the Bibl. Nat. de Paris.)

(364) J. Vicens Vives, *Ferran II: la ciutat de Barcelona*, Barcelona, 1936, p. 376.

(365) Baer, *Toldot . . .*, p. 526.

(366) Contemporary manuscript in Hebrew quoted by A. A. Neuman, *op. cit.*, Vol. 1, p. 58.

(367) Baer, II, p. 451; also [*History . . .*, Vol. 2, p. 374].

(368) Baer, II, p. 458; also [*History . . .*, Vol. 2, pp. 498–99].

(369) Baer, II, p. 501; also [*History . . .*, Vol. 2, pp. 386–89].

(370) According to the records of the trial of La Guardia, published 1887 by Father F. Fita, trans. by E. de Molenes. (*Torquemada et l'Inquisition*, Paris, 1897, p. 17.)

(371) de Molenes, *op. cit.*, p. 86.

(372) For example, quite recently, N. Lopez Martinez, professor of theology in the seminary of Burgos, in his doctoral thesis *Los judaizantes castellanos y la Inquisicion*, Burgos, 1954.

(373) Baer, II, pp. 404–8.

(374) Colmenares, *Historia de Segovia*, Segovia, 1637, Chap. 25.

(375) Abraham ben Ardutiel, quoted by Baer, *Toldot . . .*, p. 581, note 109.

(376) Cf. Baer, *Toldot . . .*, p. 555 [*History . . .*, Vol. 2, p. 436]; also [Graetz, Vol. 4, p. 376].

(377) Numerous attempts have been made to estimate the number of exiles of 1492; none is very satisfactory. Cf. Baer, *Toldot . . .*, p. 582, note 110 [*History . . .*, Vol. 2, p. 510, note 13]; cf. also the old article by J. Loeb, "Le Nombre des Juifs de Castille et d'Espagne au Moyen Age," *R.E.J.*, 1887, Vol. 14, pp. 161–83).

(378) As late as the twentieth century, treasures hidden on the eve of the expulsion were discovered in dredging. (Cf. H. Sancho, "La Juderia del Puerto de Santa Maria," *Sefarad*, 1953, Vol. 13, p. 322.)

(379) Bernáldez, *Histoire des Rois Catholiques*, Seville, 1870, Vol. 1, pp. 339, 341. See also H. C. Lea, *A History of the Inquisition of Spain*, Vol. 1, p. 139.

(380) On this matter see the reflections of Baer, *Toldot . . .*, p. 556.

(381) Juan del Encina, "Egologa Quarta." (Cf. Menendez y Pelayo, *Antologia de poetos liricos castillanos*, 1912, Vol. 7, p. 47.)

(381a) B. Seneraga, *De Rebus Gennensibus Commentaria*, XXIV, 8, 24, 25.

(382) Graetz, Vol. 8, p. 392 [English: Graetz, Vol. 4, p. 376]. (Cf. A. Herculano, *History of the Origin and Establishment of the Inquisition in Portugal*, Stanford, 1926, p. 254.)

11 Spain's Fateful Hour

(383) J. Vicens Vives, *Aproximacion a la historia de España*, Vol. 3, p. 12.

(384) This manuscript, which was published in 1924 by Menendez y Pelayo, is quoted by A. Dominguez Ortiz in his work, to which we will refer many times, *La Clase social de "los conversos" en Castilla en la edad moderna*, Madrid, 1957, p. 86.

(385) Quoted by Ernst Schäfer, *Beiträge zur Geschichte des spanischen Protestantismus und der Inquisition im sechszehnten Jahrhundert*, Gütersloh, 1902, Vol. 2, p. 363.

(386) On this subject, see E. Schäfer, *op. cit.*, Vol. 1, pp. 86–91, 163–66. It should be noted that this is a Protestant historian.

(387) This document was reproduced *in extenso* by Henry Charles Lea in his classic *A History of the Inquisition in Spain*, Vol. 3, pp. 24–6. (German translation: *Geschichte der spanischen Inquisition*, Leipzig, 1912, Vol. 2, pp. 173–76.) [Note: all future references will be to the New York edition, 1922.]

(388) The former secretary of the Inquisition, Juan Antonio Llorente, went over to the French in 1808 and was put in charge of the archives of the Inquisition at a time when they were nearly completely intact. In 1817 he published his *Histoire critique de l'Inquisition d'Espagne* in Paris, which continues to be an irreplaceable source thanks to the wealth of its documentation.

(389) E. Schäfer, *op. cit.*, pp. 24–7.

(390) This is the figure given by Dominguez Ortiz, *op. cit.*, p. 196.

(391) de Molenes, *op. cit.*, p. 66.

(392) "Voyage de Barthélemy Joly en Espagne (1603–1604)," Barrau-Dihigo ed., *Revue hispanique*, 1909, Vol. 20, p. 120.

(393) According to Marcel Bataillon, "Honneur et Inquisition; Michel Servet pursuivi par l'Inquisition espagnole," *Bulletin hispanique*, 1925, Vol. 27, pp. 15–17.

(394) According to E. Schäfer, *op. cit.*, Vol. 1, p. 68.

(395) *Ibid.*, pp. 125 ff.

(396) Here is how the Inquisition justified the traveling exposition of the *sambenitos*, in the case of a grandfather of Luis de Léon: ". . . let them begin by placing the *sambenitos* in other cities of this district before Belmonte [the city where the family of the condemned lived] so that it seems that it is a general and equal measure, and that no one may say that he is being done wrong and that it is unjust. . . ." (Adolphe Coster, "Luis de Léon," *Revue hispanique*, 1921, Vol. 53, p. 35, note 2.)

(397) E. Schäfer, *op. cit.*, Vol. 1, p. 20, note 2.

(398) Dominguez Ortiz, *op. cit.*, p. 152, note 41.

(399) *Ibid.*, p. 180, note 56.

(400) *Ibid.*, p. 83, note 3.

(401) Cf. Dominguez Ortiz, quoting a memo dated 1633 from Juan Bautista de Villadiego, secretary of the Inquisition of Llerena ("El proceso inquisitorial de Juan Nuñez de Saravia," *Hispania*, 1955, Vol. 15, p. 577).

(402) According to H. C. Lea, *op. cit.*, Vol. 1, pp. 116 ff.

(403) Cf. the study by A. Coster on Luis de Léon cited above.

(404) Cf. Marcel Bataillon, *Erasme et l'Espagne*, Paris, 1937, p. 528.

(405) E. Schäfer, *op. cit.*, Vol. 1, p. 433.

(406) A. Coster, *op. cit.*, p. 429.

(407) See the unpublished thesis, which has been particularly useful to us, by Albert A. Sicroff, *Les Statuts de pureté de sang en Espagne aux XVIe et XVIIe siècles*, Paris, 1955, pp. 477–78.

(408) Arturo Farinelli, *Marrano (storia di un vituperio)*, Geneva, 1925.

(409) Account of Vicenzo Querini, in C. von Höfler, *Depeschen der venezianischen Botschaft*, Vienna, 1884.

(410) A first-rate résumé of the popular state of mind, and the reasons why the Spaniards were suspected of Judaizing by the Italians, was made by Benedetto Croce in *La Spagna nella vita italiana durante la Rinascenza*, pp. 214–16.

(411) Fernand Braudel, *La Méditerranée et le monde méditerranéen à l'époque de Philippe II*, p. 761, citing the account of the Venetian ambassador Bernardo Navagero.

(412) "Relation de voyage en Espagne de Camille Borghèse," in *L'Espagne aux XVIᵉ et XVIIᵉ siècles*, Morel-Fatio ed., Heilbronn, 1878, p. 183.

(413) Quoted by Farinelli, *op. cit.*, p. 54, note 1.

(414) Farinelli, p. 54.

(415) Bonaventure des Périers, *Discours non plus mélancoliques*, Chap. 9.

(416) Rabelais, *Oeuvres completes*, La Pléiade ed., p. 50; see also pp. 415, 923.

(417) Épîtres," Allen ed., quoted by M. Bataillon, *Erasme et l'Espagne*, p. 83.

(418) *Colloquia latina*, Bindseil ed., Vol. 1, p. 377.

(419) Cf. Edward Glaser, "Referencias antisemitas en la literatura peninsular de la Edad de Oro," in *Nueva Revista de filologia hispanica*, 1954, Vol. 8, p. 41, note 5.

(420) Quoted by Farinelli, *op. cit.*

(421) *Quinquagenas*, Vol. 1, p. 280, quoted by Farinelli, p. 67. Fernandez de Oviedo was a glorious captain, and the first historian of the West Indies.

(422) Thesis cited above by Sicroff, p. 357.

(423) Dominguez Ortiz, *op. cit.*, Appendix 3c, p. 231.

(424) In the juridical treatises of the time, relating to those who were incapacitated, it is sometimes a matter of *conversos* of Jewish stock only, and sometimes *conversos* of Jewish or Moorish stock; there were also treatises which indicated expressly that Jewish blood constituted an absolute impediment to access to honors and dignities, while Moorish blood is not entirely incompatible with them. (Cf. Dominguez Ortiz, *op. cit.*, Appendix 3, "Opiniones de Teologos y juristas sobre los statutos.")

(425) Dominguez Ortiz, *op. cit.*, pp. 55–6.

(426) *Ibid.*, p. 60.

(427) *Ibid.*, pp. 58–9.

(428) *Ibid.*, pp. 61–73.

(429) *Apologia in duas partes divisa pro iis qui a patriarcharum Abrahae videlicet, Isaac et Jacob, reliquis sati, de Christe Jesu et fide catholica pie ac sancte sentiunt.* . . . (Cf. Dominguez Ortiz, *op. cit.*, pp. 43–4.)

(430) *Ibid.*, p. 43.

(431) Sicroff, unpublished thesis cited above, p. 258.

(432) On the resistance of the Jesuits against the statutes and their capitulation, see Sicroff, pp. 504–5 and Dominguez Ortiz, pp. 70–3.

(433) On the theories of Escobar del Corro, see Sicroff, pp. 420–47.

(434) Dominguez Ortiz, pp. 205–8. Fernand Braudel (*La Méditerranée . . . à l'époque de Philippe II*, p. 620) believes that the attribution of *el Tizón* to Cardinal Mendoza y Bobadilla is false. According to

tradition, the wise cardinal, upset by the affront to his nephew, who was refused admission into a military order, had tried to take revenge by publishing this collection of genealogies.

(435) Dominguez Ortiz, *op. cit.*, p. 58.

(436) Marcel Bataillon, "Les Nouveaux Chrétiens de Segovie en 1510," *Bulletin hispanique,* 1956, Vol. 58, pp. 207 ff.

(437) Dominguez Ortiz, *op. cit.*, Appendix 3c, p. 229.

(438) M. Bataillon has written on this subject, in discussing a story by Lope de Vega, *La Desdicha por la "honra":* "[It] presents us with the exterior fatality of honor incarnated in the prejudice of the purity of blood. . . . Although those who treat of Spanish honor speak little of it, this manifestation of *honra* is much more typically Spanish than the matrimonial vengeances of Calderon; and it is perhaps because of that that no dramatist has dared to treat this subject seriously, to write tragedies of *limpieza de sangre*, as there have been tragedies of conjugal honor. However, the taboo which seems to have weighed on such a burning topic did not apply to the comic genre. . . . Not only in Cervantes, but also in Lope de Vega, in Quinones de Benavente. . . . It is clear that only comedy and the *entremés* could poke fun at the excesses and the deviations of the Old Christian mind. . . ." (M. Bataillon, "La Desdicha por la 'honra,'" in *Nueva Revista de Filologia Hispanica*, 1947, Vol. 1, p. 28.)

(439) Dominguez Ortiz, *op. cit.*, p. 141, speaks of "a twentieth of the population of the country."

(440) *Ibid.*, p. 189.

(441) "Traité composé par un religieux de l'ordre des frères mineurs," attributed to Brother Francisco de Uceda, quoted by Dominguez Ortiz (pp. 226–29) and by Sicroff (pp. 266 ff.).

(442) Dialogue of Sabino and Juliano, in *Los Nombres de Nuestro Señor*, the masterpiece of Luis de Léon. The allusion was only understood by the Inquisition in 1609, well after the death of Luis de Léon. (Cf. M. Bataillon, *Erasme et l'Espagne*, p. 810.)

(443) *Historia de los heterodoxos españoles*, Madrid, 1880, Vol. 1, p. 632.

(444) *La Sociedad española en el siglo XVIII*, Madrid, 1955, p. 49.

(445) Mme. d'Aulnoy, *Relation du voyage d'Espagne*, Paris, 1699, Vol. 3, p. 129. [Translated into English as *Travels into Spain*, London, 1706.]

(446) "Voyage de Barthélemy Joly en Espagne (1603–1604)" Barrau-Dihigo ed., *Revue hispanique*, 1909, Vol. 20, p. 162.

(447) *Don Quixote*, Part 1, Bk. 3, Ch. 6.

(448) *Discurso politico-economico* by Capmany, quoted by Dominguez Ortiz, *op. cit.*, p. 150.

12 The Marranos of Portugal

(449) Cf. Cecil Roth, *A History of the Marranos*, Philadelphia, 1947, Chapter 7, pp. 168–94, as well as his study, "The Religion of the Marranos," *J.Q.R.*, 1931, pp. 3–31.

(450) Cf. Dominguez Ortiz, *El proceso inquisitorial de Juan Nuñez de Saravia*, article quoted (p. 574): "The rich Marrano Nuñez de Saravia had sent for a circumcisor from Amsterdam for his father, who was on his deathbed in Bordeaux, and the circumcisor then went to Bayonne to circumcise other Marranos."

(451) Thus, in a petition of the "Portuguese" to King Philip IV in 1630, speaking of the marranos living abroad: *Y todos viven cristianamente.* (*R.E.J.*, 1904, Vol. 49, p. 64.)

(452) C. Roth, *A History of the Marranos*, p. 241.

(453) "Les Mémoires de Josselmann de Rosheim," trans. by S. Schwarzfuchs, *F.S.J.U.* quarterly magazine, Paris, October, 1954, p. 23.

(454) Quoted by H. J. Zimmels (*Die Marranen in der rabbinische Litteratur*, Berlin, 1932, p. 20), after a treatise of Rabbi Yabez published in Amsterdam in 1781.

(455) C. Roth, *op. cit.*, pp. 148, 153.

(456) *Exemplar Humanae Vitae*, by Uriel da Costa, trans. by H. E. Duff and Pierre Kaan, Paris, 1926.

(457) A. Herculano, *History of the Origin and Establishment of the Inquisition in Portugal*, trans. from Portuguese, Stanford, 1926, p. 453.

(458) A. Herculano, *op. cit.*, p. 460, note 23.

(459) Cardinal Crescentiis "would be satisfied with a small pension or, on occasion, a few precious stones. . . ." Msgr. Ardinghello, the secretary of the pope, "would be happy to have a few pairs of perfumed gloves and a stone worth fifty cruzados." As to the pope, ". . . he must be given something, as well as Durante, Bernaldez, de la Cruz and Julio, the chamberlains and favorites of the pope. And Cardinal Tiotino, too, according to the nature of the business. . . ." (A. Herculano, *op. cit.*, p. 515, note 56, quoting the accounts of the Portuguese envoys.)

(460) A. Herculano, *op. cit.*, p. 449.

(461) *Ibid.*, p. 564.

(462) *Ibid.*, p. 318.

(463) *Ibid.*, p. 535.

(464) Antonio José Saraiva, *A inquisição portuguesa*, Colecçao "Saber," Lisbon.

(465) H. Girard, *Le Commerce français à Séville au temps des Habsbourg*, Bordeaux, 1932, pp. 39–40.

(466) C. Roth, *op. cit.*, p. 347.

(467) *Ibid.*, p. 400, note 5.

13 The Marrano Dispersion

(468) It seems that no Jewish historian has paused to study this influx of marranos into France at the time of the expulsion of the Moriscos. However, they, in their "Report to Henry IV," after having listed the "houses" the king could count on in Spain, referred to "other nations there are in Spain, which are of the religion of Christ and others of the religion of Moses [which] would stand on the side of France, and these are numerous. . . ." (*Mémoires du duc de la Force*, Paris, 1843, Vol. 1, p. 345.) According to Francisque Michel (*Histoire des races maudites de la France et de l'Espagne*, Paris, 1847) "in 1610 there reached and entered France, in several waves, by land and by sea, more than 150,000 Moriscos. . . . A great multitude of Jews had joined them . . . who, not having the resources to go to Africa, had settled in France under the guise of Christians, particularly in Auvergne" (pp. 71, 94). However, according to the recent research of Henri Lapeyre, only fifty thousand Moriscos had entered France.

Even if the figures are not correct, the fact itself that a contingent of Portuguese marranos went to French territory at the time of the Morisco exodus cannot be doubted. Under the tolerant reign of Henry IV, the atmosphere was propitious for this.

Ambassador Philippe Canaye, after having informed the king in 1601 of the financial transactions between the "marranos of Portugal" and the court of Spain, added: "An important Jew who took part in these dealings told me that if Your Majesty would allow his nation to live in France, France would gain from it and would people the kingdom with more than fifty thousand educated and industrious persons. . . ." (*Lettres et Ambassade de Messire Philippe Champagne*, Paris, 1635, p. 62.)

More thorough research could perhaps shed some light on this immigration into France of marranos camouflaged as Moriscos. According to Henri Baraude, Alphonse Lopez, the agent of the Duc de Richelieu and a Portuguese Jew born in Aragon, was the ambassador of the Moriscos under Henry IV and "their defender in their frightful exodus through France." According to the same author, "during the whole XVIIIth century, there was a constant infiltration of Jews under the name of Moriscos, often confused with them. . . ." (H. Baraude, *Lopez* . . . , Paris, 1933, pp. 11, 33.)

According to Leon Brunschwicg, "in the early years of the XVIIth century, Portuguese in quite large numbers came to settle in Nantes, not without creating protest . . . Henry IV took the refugees under his protection, and intended to keep them in Nantes despite all opposition. . . ." (L. Brunschwicg, *Les Juifs de Nantes et du pays nantais*, Nantes, 1890, pp. 12 ff.)

We know that Spinoza's family, among others, were numbered among these "Portuguese."

(469) Cf. S. Dubnow, Vol. 5, p. 479, and Graetz [English: Vol. 4, pp. 268–74, 356] as well as Appendix 7 ("Glücklicher Zustand der Juden in der Türkei; Mose Kapsali").

The appeal of Sultan Mohammed II has also been mentioned by the Italian chronicler Angiolello (around 1468). (Cf. G. Walter, *La Ruine de Byzance*, Paris, 1958, Appendix, p. 343, note 3.)

(470) *Le Voyage de Monsieur d'Aramon, ambassadeur du Roy au Levant*, Paris, 1887, p. 31; Nicolas de Nicolay, *Les Navigations, Pérégrinations et Voyages faits en la Turquie*, Antwerp, 1576, p. 245.

(471) Jos. Nehama, *Histoire des Israélites de Salonique*, Vol. 5 (1593–1669), Paris, 1959, p. 20.

(472) Cf. the article "Marranos" in the *Enciclopedia Judaica Castellana* (Vol. 7, pp. 289 ff.), which cites some names of converts to Islam.

(473) Quoted by H. Monin, "Les Juifs de Paris à la fin de l'Ancien Régime," *R.E.J.*, 1891, Vol. 23, p. 90.

(474) Cf. the article by Dominguez Ortiz cited above, "El proceso inquisitorial de Juan Nuñez de Saravia," *Hispania*, 1955, Vol. 15, p. 377.

(475) Cf. Fernand Braudel, *La Méditerranée et le monde méditerranéen à l'époque de Philippe II*, quoting a report by Fr. de Vera to Philip II, in 1601. (Paris, 1949, p. 707.)

(476) Cf. Canovas de Castillo, *Estudios del reinado de Felipe IV*, quoting Robillard de Beaurepaire: ". . . It is sad to find that these prisoners do not merit any attention except on the part of the circumcised bourgeoisie of Jerusalem, that is, the Israelites who live in Rouen. . . ." (Madrid, 1888, Vol. 2, p. 485.)

(477) Graetz, Vol. 8, p. 399, quoting J. Aboab, *Nomologia*: ". . . These miserable people had no better consolation than to be sold as slaves to Jews, where they would know natural pity."

(478) The French agent in Leghorn, da Silva, to the Count of Maurepas, March 19, 1736. (Arch. Nat., A.E., BI, 725, F° 400.)

(479) Cf. I. Revah, "Spinoza et les hérétiques de la communauté judéo-portugaise d'Amsterdam," *Revue de l'histoire des Religions*, 1958, Vol. 154, pp. 173–218.

(480) Cf. Cecil Roth, *op. cit.*, who, on pages 303–8, produces several examples of this "most remarkable phenomenon."

(481) According to the "Avisos" of Barrionnevo, cited in *Historia social y economica de España*, Vol. 3, p. 320. It seems that it was a matter of a plan for the readmission into Spain of a group of Jews, a plan which never came to anything. The Cansinos were royal interpreters or dragomans, a post handed down from father to son, in the Spanish possession of Oran. (Cf. Graetz, Vol. 10, Appendix 2.)

In 1674, after the expulsion of the Jews of Oran, this same Cansino, or perhaps his son, tried to wreak vengeance on the court of

Spain and, with the French consul in Leghorn as intermediary, offered his services to Louis XIV. See the interesting report of Consul Catalendy dated May 18, 1674, Arch. Nat., A.E., BI, 695.

(482) Thus Graetz, Vol. 10, p. 128 [English: Graetz, Vol. 4, p. 63], writing about the penances imposed on da Costa, said: "The Amsterdam rabbis and the communal council, consisting of Marranos, adopted as a model the gloomy form of the tribunal of the Inquisition."

(483) H. J. Zimmels, *Ashkenazim and Sephardim*, p. 283 (cited above).

(484) *Ibid.*, p. 62.

(485) "Relation de J.-B. Labat," published by A. t'Serstevens in *La Comédie ecclésiastique*, Paris, 1927, pp. 120 ff.

(486) *Coryat's crudities*, London, 1611. Quoted by C. Roth, *Transactions of the Jewish Historical Society of England*, 1924–1927, Vol. 11, p. 218.

(487) Unpublished manuscript by João Pinto Delgado, quoted by J. Revah in the introduction to *Poema de la reina Ester*, Lisbon, 1954, p. xx.

(488) The following is based principally on *The House of Nasi (I: Dona Gracia; II: The Duke of Naxos)* by Cecil Roth, a sure and elegant diptych, as are all the works of this excellent English historian, but too apologetic in places, and also on the puerile *Le Duc de Naxos*, by J. Resnick (Paris, 1936). While carrying the apologetic tendency to the extreme, Resnick sometimes seems to catch a better glimpse of certain aspects of the character of his hero than Roth does.

(489) The French ambassador de Pétremol to Charles IX, August 11, 1564. (Cf. Charrière, *Négociations de la France dans le Levant*, Vol. 2, pp. 735 ff.)

(490) See the text to the treaty of October 18, 1569, and the discussion of the different versions, in Resnick, *op. cit.*, pp. 167–80.

(491) The French ambassador Grandchamp to Charles IX, October 3, 1569. (Cf. Charrière, *op. cit.*, Vol. 3, pp. 80 ff.)

(492) Father F. Strada, *Histoire de la guerre de Flandre*, trans. by Du Ryer, Paris, 1644, pp. 272 ff.

(493) Cf. J.-A. Goris, *Étude sur les colonies marchandes méridionales à Anvers*, Louvain, 1925, Chapter 6: "Le rôle politico-religieux des colonies méridionales," and J.-H. Prins, "Guillaume d'Orange et les Juifs" [in Hebrew], *Zion*, Jerusalem, 1950, Vol. 15, pp. 93–105.

(494) From documents published by A. Arce under the title "Espionaje y ultima aventura de José Nasi (1569–1574)," *Sefarad*, 1953, Vol. 12, No. 2, pp. 257 ff.

(495) de Pétremol to Charles IX. (Cf. Charrière, *op. cit.*, Vol. 2, pp. 735 ff.)

(496) The following is based principally on the chapter on the Sabbatian heresy by G.-G. Scholem in his masterly work, *Major Trends in Jewish Mysticism*, New York, 1954, as well as on the research of Graetz, which will remain irreplaceable on this point as on so many others. As far as the Dönmeh of Salonica are concerned, see the recent study by M. Ben Zvi, in *Les Tribus dispersées*, Paris, 1959.

(497) G.-G. Scholem, *op. cit.*, p. 314.

(498) Graetz, Vol. 10, pp. 207–10 [English: Graetz, Vol. 5, p. 139]; H. Kellenbenz, *Sephardim an der unteren Elbe*, Wiesbaden, 1958, pp. 51, 83.

(499) Cf. the documents published by A. Danon, "Une secte judéo-musulmane en Turquie," *R.E.J.*, 1897, Vol. 35, pp. 264 ff.

(500) Cf. Herbert J. Bloom, *The Economic Activities of the Jews of Amsterdam in the Seventeenth and Eighteenth Centuries*, Williamsport, Pa., 1937, particularly pp. 111, 208.

(501) "Épître invective" by Orobio de Castro, quoted by J. Revah in his study *Spinoza et Juan de Prado*, Paris, 1959, p. 25. Revah has shown that this was applied by Castro to a friend of Juan de Prado, and not to Prado himself as Carl Gebhardt thought.

(502) Wilhelm Windelband, *Die Geschichte der neueren Philosophie*, Leipzig, 1919, Vol. 1, p. 239.

(503) In a letter to his friend Louis Meyer, Spinoza referred to Crescas as follows: ". . . The more recent Peripatetics, as I at least think, misunderstood the argument of the Ancients by which they strove to prove the existence of God. For, as I find it in the works of a certain Jew, named Rab Chasdai, it reads as follows."

(504) Robert Misrahi in the Pléiade edition of the *Oeuvres complètes* of Spinoza, p. 1,447, note 21.

(505) Here is the passage in question in which Nietzsche summarized his point of view on the Jews: "Every nation, every individual, has unpleasant and even dangerous qualities—it is cruel to require that the Jew should be an exception. Those qualities may even be dangerous and frightful in a special degree in his case; and perhaps the young Stock Exchange Jew is in general the most repulsive invention of the human species. Nevertheless, in a general summing up, I should like to know how much must be excused in a nation which, not without blame on the part of all of us, has had the most mournful history of all nations, and to which we owe the most loving of men (Christ), the most upright of sages (Spinoza), the mightiest book, and the most effective moral law in the world?"

(506) Alain (E. Chartier), *Spinoza*, Paris, 1959, Preface, p. vii.

(507) "Spinoza über Staat und Religion, Judentum und Christentum," in *Hermann Cohens jüdische Schriften*, Berlin, 1924, Vol. 3, p. 333. (Cf. also the account of H. Cohen of the *Biographie de Spinoza* by J. Freudenthal.)

(508) Carl Gebhardt, in his introduction to the writings of Uriel da Costa, *Die Schriften des Uriel da Costa*, Amsterdam-Heidelberg, 1922, pp. xxiii, xl.

Conclusion   Modern Spain

(509) Cf. *Historia social y economica de España*, Vol. 3, p. 252.
(510) *Ibid.*, p. 162.
(511) The statistical data on this are taken from the work cited in Note 509, Vol. 3.
(512) de Laborde, *Itinéraire descriptif de l'Espagne*, Paris, 1808, Introduction, p. xliv; Aulnoy, *Relation du voyage d'Espagne*, Paris, 1699, Vol. 3, p. 220; J. B. Labat, *La Comédie ecclésiastique*, A. t'Serstevens ed., Paris, 1927, p. 81.
(513) *Historia social y economica de España*, Vol. 3, p. 304.
(514) *Ibid.*, p. 260. In the seventeenth century the number of foreigners living in Spain was put at 150,000.
(515) *Ibid.*, pp. 35, 102.
(516) F. Braudel, *La Méditerranée et le monde méditerranéen à l'époque de Philippe II*, p. 589.
(517) Henri Lapeyre, *Géographie de l'Espagne morisque*, Paris, 1959, pp. 1, 49, 149.
(518) Hannah Arendt, *The Origins of Totalitarianism*, New York, 1951, pp. 194–97.
(519) *Historia social y economica de España*, Vol. 4, pp. 90, 118.
(520) Dominguez Ortiz, *op. cit.*, pp. 240, 246.
(521) The letters of Don Fernando de Vera were published in the *Memorial Historico Español*, Madrid, 1864, Vol. 18, pp. xi–xxix.
(522) *Ibid.*, p. 18, note 15.
(523) *Ibid.*, p. 209.
(524) Cf. *Enciclopedia Universal Ilustrada*, Vol. 30, p. 533, which also gives the meaning: *El inmoral y obsceno.*
(525) Sicroff, *op. cit.*, p. 469. In 1681 the Grand Inquisitor Vallardes protested against the use of wet nurses of New Christian stock in certain aristocratic homes, for "they corrupt their children by their milk." (Lea, *Spanische Inquisition*, Vol. 2, pp. 357–58.) Which recalls the following memorandum, taken from the archives of the Ministry of Justice of the Third Reich:
"After the birth of her child, a pure-blooded Jewess sold her mother's milk to a pediatrician, hiding the fact that she was Jewish. Babies of German blood were nourished on this milk in a maternity hospital. The accused woman will be tried for fraud. The purchasers of the milk have been wronged, for the milk of a Jewish woman cannot be considered nourishment for German children. The accused woman's impudent attitude is another insult. The investigation of the affair, however, has been suspended in order not to disturb the parents, who are unaware of these facts. I shall discuss with the Minister of Health the hygienic and racial aspects of the question."

(Cf. L. Poliakov, *Bréviare de la haine*, Paris, 1951, p. 69, translated into English as *Harvest of Hate*, New York, 1954, p. 59.)

(526) Sicroff, *op. cit.*, p. 3; Dominguez Ortiz, *op. cit.*, pp. 232, 235.

(527) Ortiz, *op. cit.*, p. 198.

(528) Marcel Bataillon, "La desdicha por la 'honra': genesis y sentido de una novela de Lope de Vega," in *Nueva Revista de Filologia Hispanica*, 1947, p. 28.

(529) Dominguez Ortiz, *op. cit.*, pp. 56, 129; *Historia social . . .*, Vol. 4, p. 116.

(530) Royal order of January 31, 1835 (Dominguez Ortiz, *op. cit.*, p. 137); law of May 16, 1865.

(531) Dominguez Ortiz, *op. cit.*, pp. 131–36; B. Braustein, *The Chuetas of Mallorca*, New York, 1936; R. Graves, "A Dead Branch on the Tree of Israel, the Xuetas of Majorca," *Commentary*, February, 1957.

(532) Here is an example of such a conversion to Judaism, as told by a press service in May, 1960:

"A Spanish nobleman, who claimed to descend from Marranos converted to Christianity by the Inquisition in the fifteenth century, has returned to Judaism and been recognized as a Jew by the rabbinical tribunal of Rehovot in Israel.

"Miss Isabel Monios, fifty-five, of the island of Mallorca, has gone back to her former family name of Yamin Oz.

"She is the daughter of a former general in Franco's army, and she says that a large part of the general staff of the Spanish army consists of descendants of Marranos. . . .

"Miss Monios says that a few years ago she had decided to return to Judaism, for her father had asked his whole family to reconvert as soon as it became possible.

"She declared: 'I intend to return to Mallorca to build a synagogue there and to bring from Israel professors of religion, to lead the Marranos back to Judaism.' " (Bulletin of the Jewish Telegraphic Agency, London, May 27, 1960.)

(533) *Historia social . . .*, Vol. 3, p. 504.

(534) Cf. A. Castro, *El pensamiento de Cervantes*, Madrid, 1924, pp. 292 ff., especially pp. 304–5. The anti-Semitic profession of faith by Sancho Panza is in Part 2, Chap. 8 of *Don Quixote*.

(535) Cf. J. A. Van Praag, "Los Protocolos de los sabios de Sion y la Isla de los Monopantos de Quevedo," *Bulletin hispanique*, 1949, Vol. 51, pp. 169–73. It is this Hispanicist who identified Quevedo's pamphlet as the missing link between the legends of the Middle Ages and the *Protocols*. For the translation of the texts of Quevedo, I have followed *The Comical Works of Don Francisco de Quevedo*, London, 1742.

(536) Sicroff, pp. 308–13.

(537) This text is quoted by Dominguez Ortiz in his work *La Sociedad española en el siglo XVIII*, Madrid, 1955, p. 229, note 25.

(538) Casanova, *Mémoires*, Vol. 11, p. 49.

(539) "The Christians," wrote this ambassador, "because of the advice given by a minister to make these people [the Moriscos] leave . . . accuse them of Judaism; according to them, he did not give advice in conformity with their religion by making this large number of inhabitants leave after they had been considered as Christians." (*Voyage en Espagne d'un ambassadeur marocain,* trans. by H. Sauvaire, Paris, 1884, p. 115.)

(540) *Cartas eruditas y curiosas . . . por el muy ilustre Senor D. Fr. Benito Geronymo Feyjoo y Montenegro,* Madrid, 1774, Vol. 3, Letter VIII, pp. 85 ff., 115.

(541) Cf. Jean Sarrailh, *L'Espagne éclairée de la seconde moitié du XVIIIᵉ siècle,* Paris, 1954, p. 493.

(542) Dominguez Ortiz, pp. 127–28, as well as *La sociedad española en el siglo XVIII* by the same author, p. 233.

(543) Desdevises du Dezert, "Notes sur l'Inquisition espagnole au XVIIIᵉ siècle," *Revue hispanique,* 1899, Vol. 6, p. 489; H. C. Lea, *Geschichte der Spanischen Inquisition,* Vol. 2, p. 365.

(544) Du Peyron, *Nouveau voyage en Espagne,* Paris, 1782, Vol. 3, pp. 181, 186, and Voltaire, *Essai sur les moeurs et l'esprit des nations,* Vol. 2, p. 351; Abbé de Vayrac, *État présent de l'Espagne, où l'on voit une géographie du pays,* Paris, 1718, Vol. 1, p. 47; "Voyage du Père François de Tours en Espagne," Barrau-Dihigo ed., *Revue hispanique,* 1921, Vol. 53, p. 37.

(545) H. C. Lea, *Geschichte der Spanischen Inquisition,* Vol. 2, pp. 360 ff.; and E. Clarke, *État présent de l'Espagne et de la nation espagnole, lettres écrites à Madrid pendant les années 1760 et 1761,* Paris, 1770, Vol. 1, pp. 111, 139; Desdevises du Dezert, "Notes sur l'Inquisition espagnole," study cited above, p. 470.

(546) *Un voyage d'affaire en Europe,* memoirs of Jean-Everard Zetner, Reuss ed., Strasbourg, 1907, p. 43.

(547) H. C. Lea, *Chapters from the Religious History of Spain,* Philadelphia, 1890, pp. 204–5.

(548) Jean Sarrailh, *L'Espagne éclairée de la seconde moitié du XVIIIᵉ siècle,* pp. 240, 302, 382. Among other things of which the Inquisition accused Olavide was that he taught that the earth revolves around the sun. (Cf. Diderot's pamphlet, *Don Pablo Olavide, précis historique.*)

(549) H. C. Lea, *Chapters from the Religious History of Spain,* pp. 73, 167 ff.; also *Enciclopedia Universal Ilustrada,* Vol. 64, article "Tribunal" (*La Inquisicion española*): ". . . in general the Inquisition was respected and loved in all of Spain; thus the patriotic juntas re-established it wherever they could, as in Cataluña, Galicia, Cuenca, and Murcia. . . ." P. 372.

Appendices

(550) The following is from the selection of papal bulls and conciliar decrees collected and annotated by Solomon Grayzel, *The Church and the Jews in the XIIIth Century,* Philadelphia, 1933.

(551) What follows is based principally on the numerous works published during the past thirty years by the excellent scholar Attilio Milano, either as monographs or as articles in *La Rassegna mensile di Israel,* plus research by the author done between 1955 and 1957 at the Archivio di Stato in Rome in preparing a doctoral thesis.

(552) The text of Abbot Ambrosoli's sermon was published by A. Berliner in *Geschichte der Juden in Rom,* Frankfurt, 1893, Vol. 3, pp. 205–8. The account of Pius IX's interview with the Jewish delegates and the other details on the Mortara affair are on pp. 153–58.

(553) Cf. the analysis of the edict of February 20, 1502, by A. de Circourt, *Histoire des Mores mudéjares et des Morisques,* Paris, 1846, Vol. 2, pp. 103 ff.

(554) J. Cantineau, "Lettre du Moufti d'Oran aux Musulmans d'Andalousie," *Journal asiatique,* Vol. 210, January–March, 1927.

(555) P. Boronat y Barrachina, *Los Moriscos españoles y su expulsion,* Valencia, 1901, Vol. 1, p. 130.

(556) A. de Circourt, *op. cit.,* Vol. 2, pp. 168 ff.

(557) See the works by A. de Circourt and Boronat cited above; the latter published in the *Coleccion diplomatica* annexed to Vol. 1 the trials of Sancho de Cardona and Rodrigue de Beaumont, pp. 443 ff., 473 ff.

(558) J. Caro Baroja, *Los Moriscos del reino de Granada,* Madrid, 1957, p. 102.

(559) Quoted by F. Braudel, *La Méditerranée et le monde méditerranéen à l'époque de Philippe II,* p. 580.

(560) H. C. Lea, *The Moriscos of Spain: Their Conversion and Expulsion,* London, 1901.

(561) A. de Circourt, *op. cit.,* Vol. 3, p. 235.

(562) The trial of Cosme Abenamir was published by Boronat, Vol. 1, pp. 542–69. See also Lea, *Spanische Inquisition,* Vol. 2, p. 401 [English: Vol. 3, pp. 362–64].

(563) F. Braudel, *op. cit.,* p. 578.

(564) Boronat, Vol. 1, Nos. 29 (Sec. 45) and 30; Vol. 2, p. 498.

(565) Caro Baroja, *op. cit.,* pp. 217–19.

(566) Boronat, Vol. 1, pp. 626, 635.

(567) "Voyage de Barthélemy Joly en Espagne (1603–1604)," *Revue hispanique,* 1909, Vol. 20, p. 70.

(568) Boronat, Vol. 1, p. 596.

(569) *Ibid.,* Vol. 2, p. 591.

(570) *Ibid.,* Vol. 1, No. 27 of the *Coleccion,* pp. 627–28, 630.

(571) *Ibid.,* Vol. 1, p. 620 ("naturalmente asi nascieron"); Vol. 2, p. 254 ("nacido muy grande").

(572) *Ibid.,* p. 300.

(573) *Ibid.,* Vol. 1, pp. 366, 604; Vol. 2, p. 24.

(574) *Ibid.,* Vol. 1, pp. 634, 637.

(575) *Ibid.,* Vol. 2, p. 62; Vol. 1, pp. 365, 606.

(576) *Ibid.,* Vol. 2, p. 22.

(577) *Ibid.,* Vol. 1, p. 367.

(578) *Ibid.,* Vol. 2, pp. 13–20, 137, 147, 149.

(579) H. C. Lea, *Chapters from the Religious History of Spain,* pp. 108–18; M. Menendez y Pelayo, *Historia de los heterodoxos españoles,* Madrid, 1928, Vol. 2, pp. 343–48.

(580) Boronat, Vol. 2, pp. 115–19, 178.

(581) *Ibid.,* p. 530; Henri Lapeyre, *Géographie de l'Espagne morisque,* Paris, 1959, pp. 153 ff.

(582) Lapeyre, *op. cit.,* pp. 1, 66, and all of Chap. 1.

(583) Boronat, Vol. 2, pp. 244, 538.

(584) Lapeyre, pp. 181, 191 ff., 196–207, 273.

(585) *Ibid.,* pp. 185, 278.

(586) Boronat, Vol. 2, p. 252.

(587) *Ibid.,* pp. 235, 264 ff.

(588) de Circourt, *op. cit.,* Vol. 3, Appendix 9, p. 300.

(589) Boronot, Vol. 2, pp. 197, 363. Such misplaced compassion is typical of a mind accustomed to dividing people into men of "pure blood" and men of "impure blood," in other words, between men who are worth a great deal and men who are worth little. In a much more extreme way, the Nazi sensibility, the sensibility of racism pushed to its extreme, was concerned about the tensions and trials to which the killers of the S.S. and the death camps were submitted, for whom it reserved all its commiseration, to the exclusion of the victims, the Jewish "sub-men." (Cf. Poliakov, *Bréviare de la haine,* Paris, 1951 [*Harvest of Hate,* New York, 1954].)

(590) "La Desdicha por la 'honra': genesis y sentido de una novela de Lope de Vega," *Nueva Revista de Filologia Hispanica,* Vol. 1, 1947, pp. 13 ff.

(591) Caro Baroja, *Los Moriscos del reino de Granada,* pp. 254–57; Fernando Valderrama, *Les "Moriscos" de Tunisie,* Informations UNESCO, No. 341, October 5, 1959.

Index

Aaron ben Amram, 49, 69–70
Abbasids (caliphs), 37–39, 53, 70, 89
Abd al-Malik, Caliph, 35
Abd al-Mumin, 54
Abd-ar-Rahman (ruler of Arab Spain), 89, 91
Abd-ar-Rahman II, 89
Abd-ar-Rahman III, Caliph, 89, 91
Abendauth (Abraham ibn David), 127
Abner of Burgos, 154
Abraham, 10, 12, 13, 20, 26, 41, 59, 64
Abu Bakr, Caliph, 29, 33
Abu Ishak, 95
Abu Kathir, 42
Abulafia, Abraham, 128, 138
Abu'l-Ala, 43, 49, 81
Abu'l-Aswad, 4
Abu'l Fadl, Hasdai, 96, 97
Abu Nasr, 70–71
Abu Sa'ad, 70, 71
Abu Yusuf, *see* Hasdai ibn Shaprut
Adiabene, 6
Adoniram, tomb reputedly in Spain, 16
Akhtal, 35
Akiba, Rabbi, 12
Al Abbasi, Caliph, 62
Alcantara, Spanish military order of, 109, 223
Alexander II, Pope, 114
Alexander VI, Pope, 202, 219
al-Faruk invented by Hasdai ibn Shaprut, 91
Alfonso VI of Castile, 101, 113, 115, 125
Alfonso VII of Castile, 117

Alfonso VIII of Castile, 125
Alfonso X of Castile ("the Wise"), 126, 128, 144, 145
Alfonso XI of Castile, 121
Alfonso IX of León, 115
Algerian Jews, 15
Ali (Mohammed's son-in-law), 37
Alitienz, Abraham, Rabbi, 195
Al-Jahiz, 43
Al-Kindy, 44
al-Makdisi, 91
al-Mamun, 38
Almohades (caliphs), 75, 104–05, 110, 112
Almoravides (caliphs), 75, 101, 110, 117
Al-Mostatraf, 79
al-Muktadir (king of Saragossa), 96
Alphonsine (astronomical) Tables, 128
Alvaro, Bishop, 48–49
Amadis de Gaula, 134
American Indians, Spanish racial attitudes on, 289, 290
Amoraim, 8
Amorites and Berbers, 11
Amram, Gaon of Babylonia, 107
Anilaeus, 6
Apocrypha, importance to Portuguese Jews, 234, 235
Arabia, 7th-century conditions, 20–21
Arabic language, 38, 58, 63, 90, 99, 100, 132, 133
Arabic (Indo-Arabic) numeral system introduced in Europe, 128
Arabs, common origin with Jews, 58
Christian tribes, 20, 22
Jewish tribes, 20, 21, 22

Aramaic language, 9, 12
Arbues, Pedro de (Maestre de Epila), 192
Arghun, Khan, 56
Arians and Arianism, 17, 30, 88
Arias Montano Institute, 85
Armenians, 68
Arragel, Moses, Rabbi, 133
Ashkenazim, 3, 99
Asinaeus, 6
Assumpção, Diego da, 236
atheism among Spanish Jews, *see* Judaism, freethinkers
Augustine, Saint, 54, 183
autos-da-fé, 188, 205, 212, 214, 289, 295, 296
Averroism, 135, 136
Avicebron, *see* Ibn Gabirol
Avicenna (*Treatise of the Soul*), 127
Ayala, Lopez de (*Rimado de Palacios*), 152, 158, 159
az-Zahir, 70–71

Baal worship, 12
Babylonian Jews, 4–11
Babylonian Talmud, 3, 7, 8, 10, 95
badges for Spanish Jews, 116, 117, 149, 152
Baghdad, Caliphate of, *see* Abbasids
Bahaira the monk, legend of, 32–33
Bajazet, sultan of Turkey, 246
Baltanas, Domingo, 225
Bardaxi, Brianda de, 192
Bar Hebraeus, 53, 54
Bedouins, 20
Benedict XIII, Pope, 167, 169
Benjamin of Tudela, 61, 62
Beranese (tribe), 15
Berbers, 11, 13, 14, 75, 110
Berceo, Gonzalo de, deacon, 143
Bernáldez, 200
Bible, censored by Inquisition, 215, 298
   criticism by Moslems, 42
   used by Portuguese Jews, 234
Black Death, Jews blamed for, 147, 148
Bodo, deacon, 96
Book of Religion and Empire, The, 51
Bostonai, 60
Botr (tribe), 15

bourgeoisie, in Spain and Portugal, 129–32, 143, 193, 204, 231–32, 238–42, 246, 248, 268
   under Islam, 39–40, 52–53, 68–74
Bugalho, Gil Vaz, 236
burning of heretics, 188, 190, 192, 197, 205, 208, 209, 236, 239, 240, 247

cabalists and cabalism, 138, 261, 263, 266
Caballería, Alfonso de la, 192, 195
Caballería, Pedro de la, 175, 192
caballero, origin of, 231, 284
Calatrava, Spanish military order of, 109
Calvinism, 232, 257
Cantigas, by Alfonso the Wise, 144
capitalism and commercial development,
   in Europe, 193, 204, 231–32, 233, 237–38, 268
   under Islam, 39–40, 52–53, 68–74
Çarça, Samuel, Rabbi, 155
Carmona, Arredondo (*Senatus Consulta Hispaniae*), 293
Carolingians, 106
Carthage founded by Semites, 11–12
censorship by Inquisition, 215–16, 298–300
Cervantes, 230, 231, 279, 281, 286, 287, 290
Charlemagne, 56, 202
Charles the Bald of France, 106
Charles V of Spain, 223, 224, 236, 254, 255
Charles VI of Spain, 295
Christian principalities in Moslem Spain, 88, 91, 107, 110
Christian view of Islam, 29–30
Christiani, Pablo, 142
Christianity, compared with communism, 184
   decline in Islamic world, 57, 75
   Great Schism, 159, 167, 170
   influence on Islam, 24–28, 32–33
chuetas, 289
churches, use as mosques, 35
Cid, from Moslem *Sidi*, 89
Cid Campeador, El, 108, 143
Cidellus, *see* Ferrizuel, Joseph

Circumcision, Islamic view, 25, 60, 65
renounced by Portuguese Jews, 234
Cisneros, Cardinal, 214
Clement V, Pope, 143
Clement VII, Pope, 157, 159, 237
clothing prescribed for Spanish Jews, 116–18
College of Santa Maria de Jesus, 223
Communism compared with Christianity, 184
concubinage among Spanish Jews, 135
Constance, Council of, 169
conversions to Islam, 37, 38, 46, 48, 49, 51, 60, 65, 67, 90
conversions, Christian to Jewish, 125, 193–95
conversions, Jewish to Christian, 18, 122–25, 154–69, 177–82, 199–201
Copts, 54
Corro, Escobar del, 226
Costa, Uriel da, 236, 250, 278
Counter Reformation, 255
Crescas, Hasdai, 135, 137, 164–65, 273
Crucifixion, Islamic denial of, 25
issue of Jewish culpability for, 16, 178, 286, 292
Crusades and Crusaders, 27, 49, 50, 54, 57, 77, 78, 109
crypto-Judaism, 212, 217, 218, 234, 236, 245

Dagobert, king of France, 32
Daniel, 62
Dante (*Divine Comedy*), 30, 88
Dávila, Gonzalo, 179
decalvatio, 18
de-Christianization ceremonies for *conversos*, 175, 195–97
Delgado, João Pinto, 252–53
Denys of Tell-Mahre, 54
dhimmis ("protected" ones), 11, 34–37, 41, 44–46, 52, 74, 80, 88
Djavidbey, Mohammed, 267
Docetists, 30
Donmeh sect, 244, 265–67
Du Guesclin, Bertrand, 150
"Dutch Jerusalem" (Amsterdam), 250, 268, 269

Ecija, Yuçaf de, 126
Edict of Expulsion, 195, 198
Edict of Grace, 186, 211
Edom, 61
Elvira, Council of, 17
Encina, Juan del, 200
Erasmus, 220
Erwig, king of Spain, 18
Escalona, derived from Biblical Escalon, 16
Espina, Alfonso de, 180–81
Esther, regarded as saint by Portuguese Jews, 234
Etz Chaim rabbinical school of Amsterdam, 269
exilarchs, 5, 8, 44, 60, 61
Eymerich (Inquisitorial manual), 186
Ezekiel, 62
Ezra, 24, 36

Falashas, 13
Fatimids (caliphs), 62, 75
fellahs under Islam, 52, 53, 55
Fendelawa (tribe), 15
Ferdinand of Aragon, 173, 183, 186, 192, 198, 246
Ferdinand III of Castile, 111
Fernando de Antequera, king of Aragon, 117
Ferrer, Vincent, Saint, 165–70
Feyjoo, Benito, 293–94
Flemish Protestants supported by Marranos, 257
Floridablanca, 288, 293
Fourth Lateran Council, 116
Franciscans, restrictions against *conversos*, 223
Franco, Yuce, trial of, 196–97
Frank, Jacob, and Frankist cult, 266–67
Fulani, 13

Gabriel, Archangel, 21
Garcia, Benito, trial of, 197
Gargantua, 220
Gazeta de Amsterdam, 268
Genghis Khan, 56
Geniza of Old Cairo Synagogue, 71–74, 96
geonim of Babylonia, 92
Ghazali, 81, 103
ghettos in Spain, 153, 166

ghetto vecchio, 25
ghiyar worn by Jews and Christians, 36
Gnosticism, 40, 266, 274
Goedsche, Hermann (*Nach Sedan*), 292
Goliath, 11
Gonsalvo, Domenico, canon, 127
Gourara (Jewish state), 15
Greek influences on Islam, 34, 40
Greek, language of Umayyads, 34
"Greek science," *see* Hellenism and Greek rationalism
Gregory VII, Pope, 113
Guerra, Don Joseph, 271
Guibert of Nogent, 29
Guicciardini, 201, 204
Guzmán, Fernán Pérez de, 176–77

Habbus, king of Granada, 93
hadith, 23, 34, 40, 41, 46, 60
Hadrumetum tablets, 12
Hagar, 59
Haggadah, 7, 60
Hakim, Caliph, 49, 52, 75
Halevi, Judah, 75, 96, 100–04
Halevi, Solomon, 134, 160–62
Halorki, Joshua (Jeronimo de Santa Fe), 160, 161, 167–69, 194
Harun al-Rashid, 38
Hasdai, ibn Shaprut (Abu Yusuf), 91–93, 96
Hassan, 14
Hayawaith of Balkh, 62, 63, 274
Hebrew language, 12, 63, 99, 100
Hellenism and Greek rationalism, 9, 62, 63, 136, 137, 138
Henry II of Trastamara (king of Castile), 149, 150
Henry III of Castile, 134, 163
Henry IV of Castile, 182
Heraclius, Emperor, 32
Hermosilla, Diego de, 220–21
Hilkata Gibbarwa, 95
Hillel, Rabbi, 5
Hindu influence on Islam, 38, 40
Hisham, Caliph, 89
Hispano-Morisco culture, impact on Christian Europe, 88
Honorius III, Pope, 117
Hrosvitha, 90
Hulagu, 56

humanism attacked by Inquisition, 214–215

Ibanez, Vicente Blasco (*Los Muertos Mandan*), 289
Ibn Adhari, 14
Ibn Adret, Solomon, Rabbi, 136
Ibn Alfaxa, 94
Ibn al-Furat, 70
Ibn al Jonayd Ibrahim, 45
Ibn Aqnin, 104, 105
Ibn as-Zaqaq, 94
Ibn Butlan, 44
Ibn Ezra, Abraham, 96, 98, 273
Ibn Ezra, Moses, 99, 100
Ibn Ferrizuel, Joseph (Cidellus), 101, 125
Ibn Ferrizuel, Solomon, 101
Ibn Gabirol, Rabbi (Avicebron), 95, 97, 98
Ibn Habit, 43
Ibn Haiyan, 87
Ibn Hassan, Yequtiel, 96, 97
Ibn Hazm, 42, 81, 89, 93, 95, 97, 99, 107
Ibn Ishaq, 32
Ibn Khaldun, 11, 30, 105
Ibn Negrela, Samuel and Joseph, 93–96
Ibn Sahl, Abraham, 104
Ibn Sa'id, 97
Ibn Saktar, Isaac, *see* Yishaki
Ibn Salam, Abdallah, 60
Ibn Sina, Sa'id, 91
Ibn Tibbon, Judah, 133
Ibn Verga, 75, 133, 154, 169, 170, 171, 172, 190, 191
Ibn Yahuda, Moses ibn Samuel, 105
Ibn Zarzal, Abraham, 105
Immaculate Conception, cult borrowed by Islam, 25
Index librorum prohibitorum, 298
Innocent IV, Pope, 124, 141
Inquisition, abolished, 300
    archives, 209–11
    autos-da-fé, 188, 205, 212, 214, 289, 295, 296
    executions, total number, 209
    investigative procedures, 186–90, 209–13
    origins, 183–84
    prisons, 206

sambenitos, 186, 189, 205, 211, 212, 217
tortures, 189, 207, 208
Institute of Oriental Languages founded, 128
Isaac, 41
Isaac ben Said, 128
Isaac of Fez (Isaac ben Jacob Alfasi), 99
Isabella of Castile, 173, 178, 183, 186, 198, 199
Isawites (sect), 66
Ishmael and Ishmaelites, 20, 41, 59, 60, 61
Ismael bar Joseph, Rabbi, 10
Israel ben Salih, 70
Israeli, Isaac, 15
"Israiliyah," 60
Izates, king of Adiabene, 6

Jacobites, 30
Jahiz, 47–48, 49, 52
Jahiz Hayawan, 79
James I of Aragon, 124
James, Saint, Spanish order of, 109, 223
Jehoiachin, king of Judah, 5, 10
Jerawa (tribe), 15
Jerome, Saint, Order of, restrictions against *conversos*, 223
Jesuits, initial tolerance of *conversos*, 226
Jesus, Islamic view of, 23, 24, 25, 32, 36, 52, 59
Jew of Malta, by Marlowe, 260
Jewish "betrayal" of Spain to Arabs, 18, 87
Jewish-Christian relations under Islam, 51–52
Jewish ministers in caliphates, 62
Jewish population in modern Spain, 295
Jewish social classes in Spain, 132, 138, 170, 171
Jewish women, high status in North African colonies, 74
low status in Parthian Empire, 8
perpetuated crypto-Judaism in Spain, 236
"Jewish world conspiracy" myth, 181
Jews and Arabs, common origin, 59

Jews expelled from Spain, *see* Spanish Jews, expulsion from Spain
Jews in Moslem literature, 76–80, 81–82
jizya (tax), 37
Johanan ben Zakkai, 10
Johannes of Göritz, 90, 92
John of Damascus, Saint, 30, 34
John II of Portugal, 201
John III of Portugal, 238
Jopes (Joppe), derived from Jaffa, 16
Joseph, king of the Khazars, 92
Joseph ben Phineas, 49, 69–70
Joseph ben Schalom, 65
Josephus, 6
Joshua, 11
Juan I of Aragon, 158
Juan I of Castile, 157
Juan II of Castile, 130, 182
Juan Manuel, 126
Judah ben Asher, 159
Judah ben Ezekiel, Rabbi, 9
Judaism, freethinkers, 62–63, 135–36, 172, 176, 178, 269–75
influences on Islam, 24–26, 60
spread to Far East, 55
survival under Islam, 75
and Zoroastrianism, 6, 7
Judaizers, 173, 175, 186, 194–96, 206, 214, 215, 218, 219, 288
Judean War, 12, 13
Judeo-Moslem sects, 61, 66–67

Kaab l'Ahbar, 60
Kaaba, 20
Kahina, 14, 15
Kainuka (tribe), 20
Kapanjis (sect), 265–66
Karaite (sect), 67–68
Keturah, 59
Khadijah, 21, 23
Khalid, 31
kharaj (land tax), 34, 81
"Kings of the Three Religions," 111
Kistanios, 247
Kitab al-Kharadj (Book of the Land Tax), 81
Kuraiza (tribe), 20
Kuzari, The (J. Halevi), 102–03

Ladino (language), 86, 249, 265
Lainez, Diego de, 226

Las Navas, victory of, 109
Leibnitz, 271
Léon, Luis de, 216, 217, 230
Lepanto, battle of, 260
Levi ben Shemtov, Rabbi, 195
libros verdes (green books), 285
Libya Jewish colony, 12
limpieza, 224, 226, 228, 230, 282, 284, 285, 287, 288
  see also "purity of the blood" statutes
linajudos, 284, 285
Liutprand, bishop, 91
Llorente (inquisitor), 209
Louis the Pious, king of France, 96
Loyola, Ignacio de, 226
Lucas of Tuy, 18
Lucero, 214
Lull, Raymond (*Dialogue of the Three Sages*), 128
Luna, Beatrice de, 254
Luther and Lutheranism, 214–16, 220

Machiavelli, 183, 201, 204
Magians, 47, 52
Mahuza, 6
Maimonides, 63, 64, 65, 75, 96, 104, 196, 273
Maimunism, 135, 136
Maistre, Joseph de, 184
Mamelukes, 54, 56
Manichaeans and Manichaeism, 52, 63
Mansur family, 34, 35
Manuel I of Portugal, 201
Maqueda, derived from Makeda, 16
March, Juan, 289
marrano, origin of word, 218
  word applied to all Spaniards, 219–21
marrano dispersion, to France, 245, 248, 249
  to Italy, 248, 249, 251, 252, 255
  to Low Countries, 248, 250, 251, 254, 268
  to North Africa, 247, 250
  to Palestine, 261
  to Salonica, 246, 247
  to Turkey, 245–46, 248, 255–60
Martin, king of Aragon, 137
Martin V, Pope, 167, 170

Martin, Raymond (*Dagger of Faith*), 129
Martinez, Ferrant, 156, 157, 159
Mary, queen of Hungary, 255
Masudi, 33, 41, 42
Mauretanian Jewish colony, 12
Mauroy, Henri, 225
Mawerdi, 37
Meadows of Gold, by Masudi, 41
Mebo ha-Talmud, 95
Mecca temple, built by Abraham and Ishmael, 59
Medyna (tribe), 15
mellahs of North Africa, 11
Mendes family, 254, 255
  see also Nasi family
Menendez y Pelayo, 202, 230
Merovingians, Moslems repulsed in Gaul, 86, 88
Merwan, Caliph, 37
messianic movements, 213, 237, 260–63
metuentes, 22
Mickiewicz, Adam, 267
midrashim, story themes borrowed by Moslems, 77
milla system in Islam, 35, 46
Miquez, João (Juan Micas), 254, 255, 259
  see also Nasi family
Mishnah, oral transmission of, 23, 41
Moawia, 34
Mohammed, biography of, 19–23
Mohammed II, sultan of Turkey, 245
Molcho, Salomon, 237
Mongols and Mongolia, 53, 55, 56
Monophysites (sect), 30, 54
monotheism, 6, 12, 20, 22, 35, 39
Mont, Dalmacio de, canon, 148
Montoro, Antonio de, 178–79, 182
Moriscos, 170, 214, 232, 245, 281, 290
Moroccan Jews, 15, 35
Moros, Anton de, 179
Mosaic law adapted to Islam, 24, 25
Moses, 7, 24, 59, 98
Moses ben Nachman, Rabbi, 142
Moses of Narbonne, 65
mosques, use of churches, 35
Mozarabes and Mozarabic rites, 90, 110, 139, 140
Muktadir, Caliph, 69
Mundir II of Saragossa, 96

Mushkhanites, 66
Mutanabbi, 43
Mutawakkil, Caliph, 49

Nadir (tribe), 20
Najran (tribe), 20
Nakib Al-Alawhin, 53
Nasara (Christians), 27
nasi, 92, 95
Nasi family (formerly Mendes family), 255–61
Nasrani (sect), 76
Nathan ha-Babli, 61
Nathan of Gaza, 261, 262
Nestorian Christians, 20, 30, 31, 55, 56
Nicholas V, Pope, 120, 173, 181
Nietzsche, 6, 277
North African Jewish colonies, 11–15, 72, 90
    refuge for Iberian Jews, 173, 247
Numidia Jewish colony, 12

occupational patterns, of Armenians under Ottomans, 68
    of Christians under Islam, 48, 49
    of Jews under Islam, 48, 49, 68
    of Jews in Portugal, 233
    of Jews in Spain, 129, 231, 232
Olavide, Pablo, 299
Oldenbourg, Heinrich, 262
Ole!, transliteration of Allah, 89
Olivares, 293, 294
Ortiz, Dominguez, 229, 230
Othman, Caliph, 19
Ottoman Empire, treatment of Jews, 247

Palencia, Council of, 153
Palestine as a battleground, 31
Parthian Empire, Jews in, 5–8
Paul, Saint, visits to Spain, 16
Paul IV, Pope, 219, 258
Paz, Duarte da, 239
Pedro the Cruel, king of Castile, 149, 150, 152
Pekid-ha-Soharim ("representative of the merchants"), 69
Penaforte, Ramon, 142
Persecutions of Jews and Christians by Moslems, 49–54, 64–65, 74–76, 90

Pinto, Isaac de, 251
Polanco, Juan de, 226
Procopius, 11
Persian influences on Islam, 34, 38
Peter the Cruel, king of Castile, 105
Philip II of Spain, 224, 257
Philip III of Spain, 281
Phoenicians in Africa, 11, 12, 13
Pichon, Joseph, 134
Poema del Cid, 143
Poeta, Juan, 179–80
Polanca, Juan de, 226
Poland, spread of Karaite sect, 68
polygamy among Spanish Jews, 135
Polyglot Bible, 214
Pombal, Marquis of, 242
Prado, Juan de, 270, 271
Protestant attacked by Inquisition, 214–16
    aided by Jews, 257
Protocols of the Sages of Zion, 292
Proverbios Morales, 152–53
"public" Jews of Spanish Inquisition, 171, 172, 180, 181, 194, 202
    in Portugal, 202
"Purity of the Blood" statutes, 190, 221, 222, 226, 228, 230, 283, 288, 292

qaysaria (markets of Baghdad), 40
quemadero, for burning of heretics, 205, 209
Querido, Jacob, 264
Quevedo, Francisco de (The Island of Monopanti), 290–92

Rab, 9, 60
Ramadan substituted for Yom Kippur by Mohammed, 22
Reccared, Visigoth king of Spain, 17
Reconquista, 88, 107–12, 140
Reformation attacked by Spanish Inquisition, 214–16
Religious tolerance of Islam, 25–37, 41, 42, 45, 94
Renan on Mohammed, 24
Reubeni, David, 237
ritual murder myth in Spain, 144, 145, 196, 266, 294
Roderic of Toledo, 18
Ruzbah, 70

Saadia, Gaon, 42, 63
Sabbath observance required by
  Spanish law, 122, 123
  evidence of nonobservance de-
  manded of ex-Jews, 18
Sabbatians, 261–68
Sabians, 52, 76
Sabi'in (baptizers), 27
Safed, 261
Sahl ben Nazir, 70
Sa'id of Toledo, 107
sambenitos (garments of shame),
  186, 189, 205, 211, 212, 217
Samuel, 9
Samuel of Medina, 246
Samuel the Moroccan, 125
Sancta Maria, Alfonso, 177
Sancta Maria, Paulus, 165, 177, 225,
  227–28
  see also Halevi, Solomon
Santaella, 223
Santa Fe, Jeronimo de, *see* Halorki,
  Joshua
Santiago de Compostela (shrine),
  108, 140
Santos, Rabbi (*Proverbios Morales*),
  152
Santotis, 216
Sargon II, 4
Satire Menippee, 219
Saxons Christianized by coercion,
  56, 202
Scandinavia, trade with Arabs, 68
science, role of Spanish Jews in dis-
  semination through Europe,
  127, 128
Seder 'Olam, 6
Sefarad identified with Spain, 133
Sefardi, Moses (Pedro Alfonso), 125
Selim II, sultan of Turkey, 259–60
Seneor, Abraham, Rabbi, 199
Sephardim, 3, 85, 249, 268
Servetus, 210
Sextus IV, Pope, 190
Shepherds' Crusade, 147
Shi'ite sect of Islam, 37, 75
Shylock, origin of character, 260
Siete Partidas, Las (Castilian Gen-
  eral Code), 118, 119, 122, 124,
  145
Siliceo, Juan Martinez, archbishop,
  224–25, 227

Simon ben Yochai, Rabbi, 61
slave trade, in Islamic world, 40, 70,
  73
  Jews sold as slaves, 201
  slave raids, 70, 91
social relations between Spanish
  Christians and Jews, 118–20
Socinian sect, 275
Solomon bar Simeon, 54
South African Boers, racism of, 282
Spain, evolution of modern characteristics, 279–283
  clergy, 280
  degradation of work, 280, 281,
  283
  depopulation of countryside, 279
  industrial development retarded,
  204, 232
  influence of Moslem past, 88–89
  predominance of "nobility," 279
Spanish Jews, antiquity of, 16–17
  expulsion from Spain, 85, 117,
  118, 120, 130, 131, 145, 183,
  186, 195, 198–200, 204, 213,
  245
  population figures, 129–30
  pre-eminence, 133, 134
  see also Sephardim
Spanish language, borrowings from
  Arabic, 89
Spanish population, 14th and 15th
  centuries, 129–30, 170
  considered Jewish by Europeans,
  218–20
  depopulation of Spain, 279, 283
  social and economic classes, 279–
  80
Spinoza, 98, 165, 250, 262, 268–
  78, 299
sufism, 43, 45
Sulaiman ibn Yahya, *see* Ibn Gabirol
suq al Sagha (money market), 40
Sura, Academy of, 60
synagogues turned into churches,
  163, 164

Tabari, Ali, 51
Taghlib (tribe), 20
Talavera, Hernando de, 214, 225
Talmud, oral transmission of, 23, 41
Tarik, general, 87
Tauregs, 110
"Tax of Thirty Deniers," 141

Tertullian, 54
Thomas, Saint, 55
Thousand and One Nights, 40, 76, 77
Tiberias as Jewish homeland, 259, 261
Titus, 13
Tizón de la nobleza española, 227, 285
Tobit, considered saint by Portuguese Jews, 234
Toledo, derived from Toledoth, 16
Torquemada, 18, 189–91, 197, 214
Torrejoncillos, friar (*Centinela contra Judíos*), 292–93
Tortosa, Council of, 141
Tortosa, Disputation of, 167, 168
tortures applied by Inquisition, 189, 207, 208
translation activities in medieval Spain, 127, 128, 133
Trent, Council of, 216
Tunisian Jews, 15
Turkey as refuge for marranos, 245, 246, 247

Umar, Caliph, 29, 32, 34, 36, 46, 60, 81
Umayyads (caliphs), 31, 34, 35, 37, 53, 89

Valladolid, Council of, 117, 124
Valladolid, statute of, 167
Vega, Lope de, 197, 287

Vespasian, 13
Villanova, Vidal de, canon, 48
Villeneuve, Arnaud de, 128
Visigoth kings of Spain, 17, 87, 88, 109
Vives, Luis, 215, 230
Voltaire, 250–51, 293, 296, 299

William of Auvergne, 98

Yahudi (Jews), 22, 76
Yakub, 70
Yakubi, 40
Yehiel ben Asher, Rabbi, 133
Yizhaki, 98
Yom Kippur supplanted by Ramadan in Islam, 22
Yudghanites (sect), 66

Zalaqa, battle of, 112
Zamora, Council of, 149
Zarathustra, 6
Zealots, 13
Zend-Avesta, 6
zero, concept introduced in Europe, 128
Zevallos, Geronimo de, 283–84
Zevi, Sabbatai, 261–67
Zionism, Joseph Nasi as precursor, 260
   Tiberias as Jewish homeland, 259
Ziriyab, 89
Zohar, 138
Zoroastrianism, 6, 7, 40, 63